THE CHRISTIAN WRITERS
MARKET GUIDE
2025

THE CHRISTIAN WRITERS
MARKET GUIDE

2025

Your Comprehensive Resource for Getting Published

STEVE LAUBE

CWI CHRISTIAN WRITERS INSTITUTE

TABLE OF CONTENTS

FOREWORD

RESEARCH SAYS YOU'RE LIKELY TO SKIP THIS SECTION. BUT DON'T. I promise not to merely tell you all about this book, which you can deduce from the "Table of Contents." Nor will I rhapsodize about Steve Laube (great as he is). In short, I want to avoid all the predictable Foreword folderol that might make you abandon it.

You bought this guide, so you could . . .

➢ avoid rejection slips
➢ do your homework, and study the markets
➢ find an agent
➢ find a publishing house
➢ remain a lifelong learner
➢ express your faith-based worldview in your writing.

So let's stipulate that you understand what this book is all about and what it's for, and I'll launch you into it with a bit of training.

I have been emphasizing to my online students the importance of a good elevator pitch. If that's a new term to you, it's simply a label for what you would say to literary agents or editors if you found yourself with them on an elevator.

What would you say if you introduced yourself as a writer and they asked what you were working on? You have only until they reach their floor. Your goal is to get them to ask you to send your manuscript.

Two of the most common mistakes I see are: (1) assuming you have time to include character names and plot points for a novel or a list of chapter titles for a nonfiction book and (2) teasing the prospect by posing questions, the way you would try to lure readers with back-cover or advertising copy.

In truth, you shouldn't assume you'll have even sixty seconds. Your elevator pitch must be streamlined to a sentence or two. For my first novel, mine was simply, "I'm writing about a judge who tries a man for a murder the judge committed." That was either going to intrigue a buyer or it wasn't.

I didn't use character names, didn't even tell the judge's gender (which happened to be female) or what happens. The entire premise is obvious: How long could a person stand such an assault on her conscience?

As for avoiding a sales-copy approach, remember that ultimately you're pitching the professional to become your publishing partner. Don't leave that person in the dark. Give answers, not questions.

A bad example: "My nonfiction book is about a man challenged to build a ship in a bottle and make it look professional, though he is not creative or handy. Could he do it? Or will he give up in frustration?"

Rather: "My nonfiction book shows that any adult with two healthy hands can produce a professional-looking ship in a bottle, even if he or she isn't creative or handy."

That pitch tells the potential partner the premise, and it also can serve as a reminder to the writer to stay on point through the entire writing process.

A bad fiction example: "A mysterious threat causes a young prince to abandon the love of his life and confront a danger so great it could mean life or death for him."

That sounds more like a movie blurb. The agent or editor doesn't know when this novel is set, what the threat is, what or whom is the love of his life, what the even greater danger is, or whether he succeeds or dies.

Rather: "A medieval prince discovers his fiancée is part of a plot to kill his father, so he can become king and she, queen. He leads the fight against her and an army as big as the king's own and, in the process, discovers a new love."

So, cut your elevator pitch to the bone. Be sure it tells more than it asks. And also use it as a mission statement to keep you on point as you finish your book.

In the event you don't find yourself on an elevator with an agent or an editor, find one in this guide and pitch electronically. That proposal can be as long as it needs to be.

If *The Christian Writers Market Guide* plays a part in your selling a piece of your work this year, be sure to let Steve Laube and his team know.

Godspeed.

— Jerry B. Jenkins
www.JerryJenkins.com

INTRODUCTION

WRITING IS A SERIOUS BUSINESS. It is also a serious calling. The privilege of having your words influence other people's thinking or inspiring their spirit is a gift from God. A number of publication opportunities for great writing from great authors exist. Traditional methods for publication remain, but the diversity of online opportunities are seemingly endless. In addition, independent-publication options have made it easier to see your byline on a book, on a blog post, or in an online magazine.

Since many Christian bookstores have closed, it may seem like the Christian publishing industry is shrinking; but it is not. It is simply changing. Therefore, you must research more effectively to find the best place for your work. The problem with online search engines is the immense number of results you receive. Then the results depend on that site's search-engine optimization and those who have paid to have their sites show at the top. *The Christian Writers Market Guide* has curated the information for you. Now you can find what is targeted specifically for the Christian market and your areas of interest.

One of the biggest mistakes a writer can make is to ignore the guidelines of an agent, an editor, or a publishing house. In the past, some publications dropped their listings in this guide because writers failed to follow the instructions in it. Editors are looking for writers who understand their periodicals or publishing houses and their unique approaches to the marketplace. This book will help you be such a writer. With a little time and effort, you can meet an editor's expectations, distinguish yourself as a professional, and sell what you write.

If you can, I recommend you attend a writers conference, whether in person or online. (We have many listed inside.) It is good to meet new people and become familiar with the best teachers in the industry. If you cannot get to a conference, consider exploring the courses available online at *ChristianWritersInstitute.com*. There are almost 50 to choose from, and you can enjoy them at any time on any device.

If this is the first time you've used this guide, read the "How to Use This Book" section. If you run into an unfamiliar term, look it up in the "Publishing Lingo" section in back and learn the terminology.

Please be aware that the information in this guide is provided by the companies or individuals through online questionnaires and email inquiries, as well as their websites and writers guidelines. The companies or individuals do not pay to be listed in this guide. The entries are not endorsed by me or The Christian Writers Institute. We make every attempt to verify the accuracy of the information provided. The entries are for information only. Any transaction(s) between a user of the information and the individuals or companies listed is strictly between those parties.

May God bless your writing journey. We are on a mission to change the world, word by word. To that end, strive for excellence and make your work compelling and insightful. Great writing is still in demand. But it must be targeted, crafted, critiqued, edited, polished, and proofread until it shines.

My thanks go to Lin Johnson whose invaluable work makes this all possible. She keeps tabs throughout the year on market changes, so every listing is accurate to the best of our information at the time of publication. (Our online version of this guide, *ChristianWritersMarketGuide.com*, is updated regularly during the year.) As the editor-administrator of the online and print editions, she is the genius behind the details. In addition, I would also like to acknowledge my wife, Lisa. Her love, support, and encouragement have been incalculable. We make a great team!

Steve Laube
President Emeritus
The Christian Writers Institute
and
President
The Steve Laube Agency
24 W. Camelback Rd. A-635
Phoenix, AZ 85013
www.christianwritersinstitute.com
www.stevelaube.com

To update a listing or to be added to the next edition or online, go to *christianwritersmarketguide.com*. Click on the Get Listed tab, and fill out the form.

For direct-sales questions, email the publisher:
admin@christianwritersinstitute.com.

For books and courses on the writing craft, visit The Christian Writers Institute:
www.christianwritersinstitute.com.

HOW TO USE THIS BOOK

THE CHRISTIAN WRITERS MARKET GUIDE 2025 IS DESIGNED to make it easier for you to sell your writing. It will serve you well if you use it as a springboard to become thoroughly familiar with the markets best suited to your writing style and areas of interest and expertise.

As you look through this guide, you may run into words in the listings that you are not familiar with. If so, check "Publishing Lingo" at the back of the book.

GETTING ACQUAINTED WITH THIS BOOK

Start by getting acquainted with the setup of this guide.

Book Publishers

Part 1 lists traditional book publishers and anthology series with information about what they are looking for. Notice that many houses accept manuscripts only from agents or through meeting with their editors at a writers conference. If you need a literary agent, check the agent listings in chapter 17.

Independent Book Publishing

Since independent book publishing is a viable option today, Part 2 provides resources to help you. Chapter 3 lists independent book publishers, many of which provide all the services you need as packages or à la carte options. If you decide to publish on your own, chapters 4 and 5 list design, production, and distribution services. You'll also want to hire a professional editor and proofreader, so see chapter 20 for help in this area.

Periodical Publishers

Part 3 lists periodical—magazine, journal, newspaper, and newsletter—publishers. Chapter 6 will help you find markets by topics (e.g., marriage, evangelism) and types (e.g., how-to, poetry, personal experience). Although these lists are not comprehensive, they provide a shortcut for finding appropriate markets for your ideas.

Cross-referencing may be helpful. For example, if you have an idea for a how-to article on parenting, look at the lists in both the how-to and parenting categories. Also, don't overlook writing on the same topic for different periodicals, such as money management for a general adult magazine, a teen magazine, a women's newsletter, and a magazine for pastors. Each would require a different slant, but you would get more mileage from one idea.

Specialty Markets

In Part 4, you'll find nonbook, nonperiodical markets like devotionals and drama. Here you can explore types of writing you may not have thought about but can provide a steady writing income.

Support for Writers

As a writer, you'll need support to keep going. Part 5 provides information for various kinds of support.

One of the best ways to get published today is to meet editors at writers conferences. Check out chapter 18 for a conference or seminar near you or perhaps in a location you'd like to visit. Before deciding which conference to attend, check the websites for who is on faculty, what houses are represented, and what classes are offered that can help you grow your craft and writing business. You may also want to factor in the size of the conference. Don't be afraid to stretch outside your comfort zone.

For ongoing support and feedback on your manuscripts, join a writers group. Chapter 19 lists groups by state and internationally. If you can't find one near you, consider starting one or join an online group.

Since editors and literary agents are looking for polished manuscripts, you may want to hire a professional editor. See chapter 20 for people who offer a variety of editorial services, including coaching.

Whether you publish your book with a royalty house or go the independent route, you'll need to do most, if not all, of the promotion. If you want to hire a specialist with contacts, check out chapter 21, "Publicity and Marketing Services." And if you need accounting or legal help, check out chapter 22.

One way to promote your message and your books is through speaking. If you need help in this area—and most writers do—see chapter 23, "Speaking Services." There you will find organizations and conferences that train speakers and/or connect them with groups looking for speakers.

Since writers who stagnate don't get published, check out chapter 24 for education resources to help you improve your writing style, write different types of manuscripts, and learn the business of writing and publishing. You'll find a variety of free and paid resources, including podcasts and classes.

Entering a writing contest can boost your sales, supplement your writing income, lead to publication, and sometimes give you valuable feedback on your writing. Check out chapter 25 for a list of contests and awards by genre. Many of them are not Christian oriented, but you can enter manuscripts with a Christian worldview.

USING THIS BOOK

Once you get acquainted with this guide, start using it. After you identify potential markets for your ideas and/or manuscripts, read their writers guidelines. If these are available on the website, the URL is included. Otherwise, email or send (with a SASE) for a copy. Also study at least one sample copy of a periodical (information to obtain one is given in most listings) or the book publisher's website to see if your idea truly fits there. Never send a manuscript without doing this market study.

Above all, keep in mind that this guide is only a starting point for your research and change is the one constant in the publishing industry. It is impossible for any market guide to be 100 percent accurate since editors move around, publications and publishing houses close, and new ones open. But this guide is an essential tool for getting published in the Christian market and making an impact on God's Kingdom with your words.

PART 1

TRADITIONAL BOOK PUBLISHERS

1

TRADITIONAL BOOK PUBLISHERS

Before submitting your query letter or book proposal, it's critical that you read and follow a publisher's guidelines exactly. In many cases, the guidelines are available on the website and a direct link is given in the listing. If you do not have a literary agent—and even if you do—check out a publisher thoroughly before signing a contract.

Note: Not all the imprints listed in entries below are in this book, and some may be in separate entries here or in other sections.

1517 MEDIA
Augsburg Fortress, Beaming Books, Broadleaf Books, Fortress Press

ABINGDON PRESS
810 12th Ave. S, Nashville, TN 37203 | 615-749-6000
www.abingdonpress.com
Constance Stella, senior acquisitions editor
  Denomination: United Methodist
  Parent company: United Methodist Publishing House
  Mission statement: to provide the best, most effective religious publications available
  Submissions: Publishes 120 titles per year; receives 2,000 submissions annually. First-time authors: fewer than 5%. Submit

proposal with sample chapters through the website. Bible: CEB.

Genres and topics: Christian living/spirituality, leadership, theology, academic

Royalty: minimum 7.5%

Guidelines: *www.abingdonpress.com/submissions*

Tip: "We're focusing on material to help pastors and other leaders do their jobs, and focusing more squarely on Methodist and other mainline leaders, churches, readers."

ABUNDANCE BOOKS

417 Forest St. #445, Kalamazoo, MI 49048 | 616-648-1795

books@abundance-books.com | *abundance-books.com*

Jenn Dafoe-Turner, acquisitions editor

Mission statement: to publish books that inspire people to live life full and free

Submissions: Publishes three to five titles per year; receives 20 submissions annually. First-time authors: 75%. Length: 90–300 pages. Submit proposal with sample chapters via email or the website. Conference contact a plus. Responds in two to four weeks. Bible: ESV, NLT, NKJV, NASB.

Genres and topics: African-American, Asian, Christian living/spirituality, Hispanic, self-help, Bible studies, children, devotionals; fiction: mystery, romance

Royalty: 7–15%, no advance

Types of books: audiobook, ebook, hardcover, offset paperback, POD

Guidelines: *abundance-books.com/guidelines*

Tip: "All proposals should include a marketing plan that includes current audience reach."

AMBASSADOR INTERNATIONAL

411 University Ridge, Ste. B14, Greenville, SC 29601 | 864-751-4844

publisher@emeraldhouse.com | *www.ambassador-international.com*

Katie Cruice Smith, senior editor

Mission statement: to magnify Jesus while promoting His gospel through the written word

Submissions: Publishes 50 titles per year; receives 750 submissions annually. First-time authors: 50%. Length: minimum 144 pages. Submit proposal with sample chapters via email, mail, or website. Responds in one month. Bible: KJV, NIV, ESV, NKJV, NASB.

Genres and topics: biography, business, Christian living/spirituality, finances, theology, Bible studies, children, devotionals; fiction: teen/YA

Royalty: 15–20%, 25% for ebooks; no advance

Types of books: ebook, hardcover, paperback

Guidelines: *ambassador-international.com/get-published/submission-guidelines*

Tip: "We're most open to a book which has a clearly defined market and the author's total commitment to the project. We do well with first-time authors. We have full international coverage. Many of our titles sell globally."

AMERICAN CATHOLIC PRESS

16565 S. State St., South Holland, IL 60473-2025 | 708-331-5485

acp@acpress.org | *www.americancatholicpress.org*

Rev. Michael Gilligan, executive director

Denomination: Catholic

Submissions: Publishes four titles per year; receives 10 submissions annually. Query first by mail; no simultaneous submissions. Responds in two months. Bible: NAS.

Genres and topics: liturgy

Royalty: flat fee of $25–100

First print run: 3,000

Tip: "We publish only materials on the Roman Catholic liturgy. No poetry or fiction."

AMG PUBLISHERS

6815 Shallowford Rd., Chattanooga, TN 37421 | 423-894-6060

sales@amgpublishers.com | *www.amgpublishers.com*

Amanda Jenkins, acquisitions and sales manager

Parent company: AMG International

Mission statement: to meet people's deepest needs, spiritual and physical, while inspiring hope, restoring lives, and transforming communities in Jesus' name

Submissions: Publishes 10 titles per year; receives 300 submissions annually. First-time authors: 50%. Length: minimum 150 pages. Agent not required. Email proposal with sample chapters, or submit on *ChristianBookProposals.com*. Responds in six months. Bible: NASB, ESV, NIV, KJV, CSB.

Genres and topics: Bible characters, Bible study, Christian living/ spirituality, self-help, spiritual growth, women's issues, Bible

5

studies, devotionals

Royalty: starts at 14%, sometimes gives advance

Types of books: ebook, offset paperback, POD

Imprints: AMG (reference, Bible studies, Bibles, devotionals), Living Ink (YA fiction), God and Country Press (military/history devotionals)

Guidelines: *amgpublishers.com/index.php/author-guidelines*

Tip: "Looking for good, biblical content that does not offer a personal or denominational slant."

ANCIENT FAITH PUBLISHING

PO Box 3027, Munster, IN 46321 | 561-306-4615

www.ancientfaith.com/ancient-faith-publishing

Donna Ryan, director of publishing; dryan@ancientfaith.com

Marci Rae Johnson, managing editor; marcij@ancientfaith.com

Denomination: Orthodox Christian

Parent company: Ancient Faith Ministries, Inc.

Mission statement: to carry out the Great Commission of Jesus Christ through accessible and excellently crafted publications and creative media that educate, edify, and evangelize, leading to a living experience of God through His Holy Orthodox Church

Submissions: Publishes 15-18 titles per year; receives 30 submissions annually. First-time authors: 50%. Length: 60,000 words, 250-300 pages. Email proposal with complete manuscript. No agents. Responds in six to eight weeks. Bible: RSV, ESV, NKJV.

Genres and topics: African-American, Asian, Christian living/ spirituality, church year, Hispanic, prayer, worship, children, YA

Royalty: 6-12%, no advance

First print run: 1,500-5,000

Types of books: audiobook, ebook, offset paperback, POD

Imprint: Ancient Faith Kids (children)

Guidelines: *www.ancientfaith.com/documents/4/AFP-Submission-Guidelines-2024.pdf*

Tip: "We publish books by, and for, Orthodox Christians. Most of our readers are Orthodox (or working to become so) and are primarily interested in Orthodox materials; our experience has shown that this is the niche market in which we operate most effectively."

ANEKO PRESS

PO Box 652, Abbotsford, WI 54405 | 715-223-3013
jeremiah@lspbooks.com | *www.anekopress.com*
Jeremiah Zeiset, president

Parent company: Life Sentence Publishing, Inc.
Mission statement: to publish books for ministry
Submissions: Publishes 20 titles per year; receives 50 submissions annually. First-time authors: 20%. Length: 30,000–100,000 words. Submit proposal with complete manuscript through the website. Responds in two weeks. Bible: KJV, ESV, NKJV. Niche is publishing ministry-related books.
Genres and topics: Christian living/spirituality
Royalty: 30%, no advance
First print run: 1,000–5,000
Types of books: audiobook, ebook, hardcover, offset paperback
Guidelines: *anekopress.com/write-for-us*
Tip: "The majority of our authors are in ministry as missionaries or other similar ministries."

ANGLICAN HOUSE PUBLISHERS

info@anglicanhousepublishers.org | *anglicanhousepublishers.org*
Rev. Ben Jefferies, liturgical book developer

Denomination: Catholic
Mission statement: to publish bible-centered Anglican authors and satisfy the liturgical publishing needs of the church and to promote spiritual formation and showcase the Anglican Way of being a Christian
Submissions: Email proposal with sample chapters. Responds in three months minimum.
Genres and topics: denomination, discipleship, ministry
Types of books: ebook, paperback
Guidelines: *anglicanhousepublishers.org/submissions*

ASHBERRY LANE

13607 Bedford Rd. NE, Cumberland, MD 21502 | 866-245-2211
r.white@whitefire-publishing.com | *AshberryLane.com*
Roseanna White, senior fiction editor

Parent company: WhiteFire Publishing
Mission statement: to publish heartfelt stories of faith
Submissions: Publishes 5–10 titles per year; receives 50 submissions

annually. First-time authors: 10%. Length: 60,000–110,000 words. Email proposal with sample chapters. Responds in three months.

Genres and topics: fiction: historical romance, romance, romantic suspense

Royalty: 50% for ebooks, 10% of retail for print; sometimes offers advance of $500–2,000

Types of books: POD

Guidelines: *ashberrylane.com/submissions*

Tip: "Please be familiar with our titles and mission."

ASPIRE PRESS

PO Box 3473, Peabody, MA 01961 | 800-358-3111

LynnettePennings@tyndale.com | *www.hendricksonrose.com/lp/hr-aspire-press*

Lynnette Pennings, managing editor

Parent company: Hendrickson Publishing Group/Tyndale House Ministries

Mission statement: to provide counseling for Christian living

Submissions: Only agent, *ChristianBookProposals.com,* or conference contact. Need credentials in helping others.

Genres and topics: Christian living/spirituality, counseling

Tip: Publishes books that are "compassionate in their approach and rich with Scripture," giving "godly insight and counsel for those personally struggling and for believers who have a heart to minister and encourage others."

AUGSBURG FORTRESS

PO Box 1209, Minneapolis, MN 55440–1209 | 800-328-4648

afsubmissions@1517.media | *www.augsburgfortress.org*

Suzanne Burke, publisher, congregational resources

Denomination: Evangelical Lutheran Church in America

Parent company: 1517 Media

Mission statement: to develop engaging resources for Lutheran congregations

Submissions: Email proposal with sample chapters or a query. Responds in 60 days, only if fits publishing needs.

Genres and topics: Bible study, Christian living/spirituality, leadership, worship

Guidelines: *ms.augsburgfortress.org/downloads/Submission%20 Guidelines.pdf*

AVE MARIA PRESS

PO Box 428, Notre Dame, IN 46556 | 800-282-1865, ext. 1
submissions@mail.avemariapress.com | *www.avemariapress.com*
Josh Noem, editorial director

> **Denomination:** Catholic
> **Mission statement:** to serve the spiritual and educational needs of individuals, groups, and the Church as a whole
> **Submissions:** Publishes 40 titles per year; receives 350 submissions annually. First-time authors: 30%. Length: 20,000-60,000 words. Email or mail proposal with sample chapters. Responds in three to four weeks. Bible: RSV2CE, NABRE.
> **Genres and topics:** Advent, African-American, Christian living/spirituality, death and dying, evangelism, faith formation, family, grief, healing, Hispanic, marriage, ministry, parenting, prayer, theology, curriculum, ministry resources, small-group study guides
> **Royalty:** 10%, advance of at least $1,000
> **Types of books:** ebook, hardcover, offset paperback
> **Guidelines:** *www.avemariapress.com/manuscript-submissions*
> **Tip:** "Our most successful books identify and address a specific felt-need for a potential reader. We are eager to work with authors who have robust platforms and direct connections to their potential readers."

B&H KIDS

200 Powell Pl., Ste. 100, Brentwood, TN 37027-7707 | 615-251-2000
www.bhpublishinggroup.com/categories/kids
Michelle Freeman, publisher; michelle.freeman@lifeway.com
Anna Sargeant, associate publisher; anna.sargeant@lifeway.com

> **Denomination:** Southern Baptist
> **Parent company:** B&H Publishing/Lifeway Christian Resources
> **Mission statement:** to help kids develop a lifelong relationship with Jesus and to empower parents and church leaders to guide the spiritual growth of the next generation
> **Submissions:** Any book for children or teens with a Christian message. Themes include but are not limited to adventure, attributes of God, Bible-story retellings, biblical virtues, church, community, diversity and inclusion, family, relationships, friendships, prayer, emotions, and theology. Publishes 18-24 titles per year; receives hundreds of submissions annually. First-time authors: 10-20%. Length: depends on age group. Agent only. Responds in one to three months. Bible: CSB.

Genres and topics: Bible stories, board books, devotionals, first-chapter, middle grade, picture books, teen/YA

Royalty: 18–22%, gives advance

Types of books: audiobook, board books, ebook, hardcover, offset paperback, picture books

Guidelines: available via email

Tip: "We are a conservative Christian publishing house that publishes Protestant authors. Note that illustrations for children's books are not necessary or suggested."

B&H PUBLISHING GROUP

200 Powell Pl., Ste. 100, Brentwood, TN 37027-7707 | 615-251-2000

www.bhpublishinggroup.com

Matthew Hawkins, senior acquisitions editor

Logan Pyron, acquisitions, academic

Ashley Gorman, acquisitions and development editor, women's

Denomination: Southern Baptist

Parent company: LifeWay Christian Resources

Mission statement: to provide Bible-centered content that impacts hearts and minds, inspiring people in their lifelong relationship with Jesus Christ, because every word matters

Submissions: Publishes 90 titles per year; receives thousands of submissions annually. First-time authors: 10%. Agent only. Responds in two to three months. Bible: CSB.

Genres and topics: Bible study, Christian living/spirituality, church growth, evangelism, leadership, marriage, parenting, theology, women, worship, academic, Bible reference/commentaries, children

Royalty: gives advance

Types of books: ebook, hardcover, offset paperback

Imprints: B&H Publishing (trade books), B&H Kids (children), B&H academic (textbooks), Holman Bibles

Guidelines: not available

Tip: "Be informed that the market in general is very crowded with the book you might want to write. Do the research before submitting."

BAAL HAMON PUBLISHERS

244 Fifth Ave., Ste. T279, New York, NY 10001 | 646-233-4017

submissions@baalhamon.com | *www.baalhamonpublishers.com*

Temitope Oyetomi, managing and acquisitions editor

Parent company: Joy and Truth Christian Ministry

Mission statement: to be a global leader in publishing, distinguished by superlative production and distribution and an unwavering commitment to truth and integrity

Submissions: Publishes 30 titles per year; receives 90 submissions annually. First-time authors: 60%. Length: 50,000–70,000 words. Agent not required. Email proposal with sample chapters. Responds in one to two weeks. Bible: ESV.

Genres and topics: African-American, Christian living/spirituality, counseling, health, marriage, parenting, self-help, biography, devotionals; fiction: most genres except fantasy, science fiction, and apocalyptic

Royalty: 60%, sometimes gives advance

First print run: hardcover, 1,000; paperback, 3,000

Types of books: ebook, hardcover, offset paperback, POD

Guidelines: *www.baalhamonpublishers.com/guidelines.html*

Tip: "Include a good analysis of similar books in the market and why yours will be better than most."

BAKER ACADEMIC

6030 E. Fulton Rd., Ada, MI 49301 | 616-676-9185
submissions@bakeracademic.com | *bakeracademic.com*
Robert Hosack, senior acquisitions editor
Anna Moseley Gissing, senior acquisitions editor
Brandy Scritchfield, acquisition editor

Parent company: Baker Publishing Group

Mission statement: to publish books that are notable for their inherent quality and deemed essential reading by students and scholars

Submissions: Publishes 50 titles per year. First-time authors: 10%. Agent preferred or conference contact. Or email proposal with sample chapters, submit through *ChristianBookProposals.com* or Writers Edge.

Genres and topics: Bible, Christian education, counseling, evangelism, leadership, ministry, missions, preaching, religion, spiritual formation, theology, worship, academic, professional

Royalty: gives advance

Types of books: ebook, hardcover, offset paperback

Guidelines: *bakeracademic.com/pages/submit-a-proposal*

Tip: "Baker Academic welcomes book proposals from prospective authors holding relevant academic credentials (which usually means a PhD or similar degree in the field of the proposed book and a teaching position at a recognized institution of higher learning)."

BAKER BOOKS

6030 E. Fulton Rd., Ada, MI 49301 | 616-676-9185
bakerpublishinggroup.com/bakerbooks
Brian Vos, editorial director
Eddie LaRow, acquisitions editor

> **Parent company:** Baker Publishing Group
> **Mission statement:** to build up the body of Christ through books that are relevant, intelligent, and engaging
> **Submissions:** Only agent, *ChristianBookProposals.com*, or conference contact.
> **Genres and topics:** apologetics, Christian living/spirituality, culture, discipleship, leadership, marriage, ministry, parenting, theology
> **Types of books:** ebook, hardcover, offset paperback
> **Guidelines:** *bakerpublishinggroup.com/contact/submission-policy*

BAKER PUBLISHING GROUP

Baker Academic, Baker Books, Bethany House, Brazos Press, Chosen, Revell

BANNER OF TRUTH

PO Box 621, Carlisle, PA 17013 | 717-249-5747
info@banneroftruth.co.uk | *banneroftruth.org*
Ian Thompson

> **Genres and topics:** biography, Christian living/spirituality, church life, history, ministry, theology, children, commentaries, devotionals
> **Types of books:** ebook, hardcover, offset paperback
> **Guidelines:** *banneroftruth.org/us/about/contact-us/submit-a-manuscript*
> **Tip:** "What makes a Banner book? It must be a book worthy of publication irrespective of its likely commercial success; it must pass theological and doctrinal scrutiny; it must promote practical Christian living; it most likely has enduring application and will be as relevant in 100 years as it is today; it must be well written and carefully edited; it must be well produced."

BARBOUR PUBLISHING, INC.

PO Box 719, Uhrichsville, OH 44683 | 740-922-6045
submissions@barbourbooks.com | *www.barbourbooks.com*
Annie Tipton, senior acquisitions editor, nonfiction
Paul Muckley, senior acquisitions editor, Bible and reference
Rebecca Germany, senior editor and acquisitions, fiction

Mission statement: to inspire the world with the life-changing message of the Bible

Submissions: Agent only.

Genres and topics: Christian classics, Christian living/spirituality, activities and puzzles, Bible reference/commentaries, Bible stories, children, devotionals, journals, planners; fiction: Amish, contemporary, historical, romance, suspense/thriller

Types of books: offset paperback

Imprints: Barbour Books (nonfiction), Barbour Fiction (novels), Barbour Reference, DayMaker (planners), Barbour Young Adult (nonfiction, devotionals), Barbour Kidz (children), Barbour Español (Spanish speaking), Barbour Bibles

Guidelines: *www.barbourbooks.com/frequently-asked-questions*

BEAMING BOOKS

510 Marquette Ave., Minneapolis, MN 55403 | 800-960-9705
www.beamingbooks.com
Naomi Krueger, senior acquisitions editor

Denomination: Evangelical Lutheran Church in America

Parent company: 1517 Media

Submissions: Publishes 24 titles per year; receives 250 submissions annually. Board books for ages birth-3, picture books for ages 3-8, activity books for ages 3-8, early-reader and first-chapter books for ages 5-9, nonfiction books for ages 5-9 and 8-12, fiction for ages 8-12, activity books for families, devotionals for children ages 0-12 and families. First-time authors: 50%. Length: 500 words for picture books. Agent only. Responds in three months. Bible: NIV, CEB.

Genres and topics: activities and puzzles, children, devotionals

Royalty: gives advance

Guidelines: *www.beamingbooks.com/info/submissions*

Tip: "Look at what we've published before. Read a few of our books."

BETHANY HOUSE PUBLISHERS

7808 Creekridge Cir., Ste. 250, Bloomington, MN 55439 | 952-829-2500
bakerpublishinggroup.com/bethanyhouse
Andy McGuire, editorial director
David Long, nonfiction acquisitions editor
Jeff Braun, nonfiction acquisitions editor
Jennifer Dukes Lee, nonfiction acquisitions editor
Jessica Sharpe, senior fiction acquisitions editor
Rochelle Gloege, fiction acquisitions editor

Parent company: Baker Publishing Group

Mission statement: to publish high-quality writings that represent historical Christianity and serve the diverse interests and concerns of evangelical readers

Submissions: Publishes 75–85 titles per year. Only agent or conference contact. Bible: NIV.

Genres and topics: Christian living/spirituality, family, prayer, relationships, theology, devotionals; fiction: Amish, biblical, contemporary, fantasy, historical, Regency, romance, romantic suspense

Royalty: varies, gives advance

Types of books: ebook, hardcover, offset paperback

Guidelines: *bakerpublishinggroup.com/contact/submission-policy*

Tip: "The best opportunities for new authors come via literary agencies, conferences, writing communities, and author referrals. Get connected."

BOLD VISION BOOKS

PO Box 2011, Friendswood, TX 77549-2011 | 281-797-3920
boldvisionbooks@gmail.com | *www.boldvisionbooks.com*
Larry Leech, editor in chief
Kaley Rhea, fiction acquisition editor

Mission statement: to publish compelling, creative, and beautiful books to change the world and further the message of Christ through the written word

Submissions: Publishes 25 titles per year; receives 250 submissions annually. First-time authors: 85%. Length: 50,000–60,000 words. Nonfiction: only agent or conference contact. No agent required for fiction. Email proposal with sample chapters. Responds in six months. Bible: any but no more than five per book.

Genres and topics: Christian living/spirituality, crafts, women, writing, devotionals, journals, YA; fiction: contemporary, historical, romantic comedy, suspense, teen/YA

Royalty: 25%, sometimes offers advance of $1,000–5,000

First print run: 1,000

Types of books: ebook, hardcover, offset paperback, POD

Imprints: Stone Oak Publishing (indie), Nuts 'n Bolts (writing, teaching, speaking, management, crafts), Optasia Books (pastors)

Guidelines: *www.boldvisionbooks.com/bold-vision-books-publishing*

Tip: "Give us a fresh approach to a time–honored concept. Build your platform through ministry, not numbers."

BRAZOS PRESS

6030 E. Fulton Rd., Ada, MI 49301 | 616–676–9185

submissions@brazospress.com | *bakerpublishinggroup.com/brazospress*

Katelyn Beaty, editorial director and acquisitions

Robert Hosack, senior acquisitions editor

Parent company: Baker Publishing Group

Mission statement: to draw upon the riches of the Christian story to deepen our understanding of God's world and inspire faithful reflection and engagement

Submissions: Authors typically hold advanced degrees and have established publishing platforms.

Genres and topics: nonfiction

Guidelines: *bakerpublishinggroup.com/brazospress/submitting-a-proposal*

Tip: "We welcome book proposals from scholars, church leaders, activists, artists, and writers who have something to say and can write with both skill and passion, demonstrating that serious writing can also be lively and compelling."

BRIMSTONE FICTION

1440 W. Taylor St., Ste. 449, Chicago, IL 60607 | 224–339–4159

rowena.brimstonefiction@gmail.com | *www.brimstonefiction.com*

Rowena Kuo, CEO and executive editor

Submissions: Publishes 8–12 titles per year; receives 60 submissions annually. First-time authors: 60%. Length: 60,000–100,000 words. Agent preferred, conference contact a plus. Email proposal with sample chapters or complete manuscript. Responds in six to eight weeks. Bible: NIV.

Genres and topics: fiction: adventure, fantasy, historical, romantic suspense, science fiction, speculative, teen/YA, time travel, women's

Royalty: 30% of profits, no advance

Types of books: ebook, POD

Guidelines: *brimstonefiction.com/submission-guidelines*

Tip: "We welcome new and multipublished authors and/or authors with or without agents. If you have a good story, come and meet us at writers conferences or through our website."

BROADLEAF BOOKS

PO Box 1209, Minneapolis, MN 55440-1209 | 800-328-4648

submissions@broadleafbooks.com | *www.broadleafbooks.com*

Valerie Weaver-Zercher, senior acquisitions editor

Lisa Kloskin, acquisitions editor

Denomination: Evangelical Lutheran Church in America

Parent company: 1517 Media

Mission statement: to inspire transformation in readers and their communities to foster a more open, just, and compassionate world

Genres and topics: Christian living/spirituality, culture, social justice

Guidelines: available on website

Tip: "Please note that we receive a large volume of proposals. You will receive a response only if we see your proposal as a potential fit for our program."

BROADSTREET PUBLISHING GROUP

8646 Eagle Creek Cir., Ste. 210, Savage, MN 55378 | 855-935-2000

proposals@broadstreetpublishing.com | *www.broadstreetpublishing.com*

Tim Payne, editorial director

Submissions: Publishes 100+ titles per year. Agent preferred. Email proposal with sample chapters.

Genres and topics: Bible promises, biography, Christian living/spirituality, biography, children, coloring books, devotionals, fiction, journals

Imprints: Belle City Gifts (journals and planners), Broadstreet Kids (children)

Guidelines: *broadstreetpublishing.com/contact*

CALLA PRESS PUBLISHING

1495 Timbercreek Dr., Stephenville, TX 76401 | 972-971-8745

callapresspublishing@gmail.com | *www.callapresspublishing.com*

Samantha Cabrera, founder, publisher

Madison Aichele, executive director; madison.callapresspublishing@gmail.com

Denomination: Christian Reformed

Mission statement: to spread the gospel truth through pure, lovely, and noble books

Submissions: Publishes 10 titles per year; receives 200 submissions annually. First-time authors: 75%. Length: 50,000 words. Agent not required but preferred. Submit at *ChristianBookProposals. com*, or email query or proposal with complete manuscript or sample chapters. Conference contact a plus. Responds in five to eight months. Bible: ESV, NLT. Currently requires fully illustrated children's picture books. Periodically closes to submissions, so check the website to see if it is open.

Genres and topics: Christian living/spirituality, children, devotionals, fiction, teen/YA

Royalty: 20%, no advance

First print run: 300–500

Types of books: ebook, hardcover, offset paperback, POD

Guidelines: *www.callapresspublishing.com/book-submissions*

Tip: "The work must be polished grammatically, be biblically sound, and preferably be in the active voice."

CASCADE BOOKS

199 W. 8th Ave., Ste. 3, Eugene, OR 97401 | 541-344-152
proposal@wipfandstock.com | *wipfandstock.com/search-results-grid/
?imprint=cascade-books*

Parent company: Wipf and Stock

Submissions: Email proposal with sample chapters. Responds in one to two months.

Genres and topics: religion, theology

Types of books: ebook, POD

Guidelines: *wipfandstock.com/submitting-a-proposal*

CASCADIA PUBLISHING HOUSE

126 Klingerman Rd., Telford, PA 18969
editor@CascadiaPublishingHouse.com | *CascadiaPublishingHouse.com*
Michael A. King, publisher and editor

Submissions: Looking for creative, thought-provoking, Anabaptist-related material.

Genres and topics: nonfiction

Imprint: DreamSeeker Books

Guidelines: *www.cascadiapublishinghouse.com/submit.htm*

Tip: "All Cascadia books receive rigorous evaluation and some form of peer or consultant review."

CASTLE QUAY BOOKS

89 Gilson St., Little Britain, ON, Canada K0M 2C0 | 416-573-3249
larrywillard@rogers.com | *castlequaybooks.com*
Marina Hofman, director of professional services

Parent company: Castle Quay Communications, Inc.

Mission statement: to advance the Canadian and American Christian writing community, with the purpose of developing and publishing inspirational, balanced, moral, quality titles by both established and new authors, promoting quality messages that will inform, challenge, inspire, and uplift all readers

Submissions: Publishes 10-12 titles per year; receives 35-40 submissions annually. First-time authors: 20%. Length: 180 pages/40,000-50,000 words. Agent not required. Submit through *ChristianBookProposals.com*; or email query first, then proposal with sample chapters. Responds in four to six weeks. Bible: ESV, NASB.

Genres and topics: African-American, art, Asian, biography, business, Christian living/spirituality, culture, family, finances, Hispanic, history, leadership, politics, self-help, social issues, social justice, teaching, theology, women, women in leadership, children, gift, memoir, teen/YA

Royalty: 12-16%, sometimes gives advance

First print run: 1,000-3,000 paperback, 1,000 hardcover

Types of books: audiobook, ebook, hardcover, offset paperback, POD

Guidelines: *castlequaybooks.com/pages/submitting-a-manuscript*

Tip: "Children's books must have an illustrator."

CATHOLIC BOOK PUBLISHING CORP.

77 W. End Rd., Totowa, NJ 07572 | 973-890-2400
info@catholicbookpublishing.com | *www.catholicbookpublishing.com*
Anthony Buono, editor

Denomination: Catholic

Submissions: Mail query first. No simultaneous submissions. Responds in two to three months.

Genres and topics: Christian living/spirituality, liturgy, prayer

Royalty: negotiable, no advance
Imprint: Resurrection Press (popular nonfiction)
Guidelines: *catholicbookpublishing.com/page/faq#manuscript*

CELEBRATE LIT PUBLISHERS

35459 Stockton St., Beaumont, CA 92223 | 909-520-8603
Celebratelit@celebratelit.com | *www.celebratelitpublishing.com*
Denise Barela, acquisitions editor
Sandra Barela, president

Denomination: Reformed
Mission statement: to encourage you and change your life
Submissions: Publishes 20-30 titles per year; receives 100
  submissions annually. First-time authors: 80%. Length: 70,000
  words. Agent not required. Email proposal with complete
  manuscript. Responds in eight weeks. Bible: ESV.
Genres and topics: African-American, Asian, Bible study, Hispanic,
  first-chapter, journals; fiction: all except science fiction
Royalty: 70%, no advance
Guidelines: *www.celebratelitpublishing.com/submit-a-manuscript*
Tip: "Include a solid marketing plan."

CF4K

Geanies House, Fearn, Tain, Ross-shire IV20 1TW, Scotland, UK |
01862-871011
Catherine.Mackenzie@christianfocus.com | *www.christianfocus.com/*
  products/category/309/childrens-books
Catherine MacKenzie, children's editor

Parent company: Christian Focus Publications
Mission statement: to help children find out about God and get
  them enthusiastic about reading the Bible, now and later in their
  lives
Submissions: Email or mail proposal with sample chapters.
  Responds in three to six months.
Genres and topics: Christian living/spirituality, Bible stories,
  biography, crafts, devotionals, game books, puzzles and activities
Types of books: hardcover, paperback
Guidelines: *www.christianfocus.com/about/childrens-guidelines*
Tip: "Read our website please. Don't send us stuff we don't publish."

CHALICE PRESS

11939 Manchester Rd. #110, Des Pares, MO 63131

submissions@chalicepress.com | *chalicepress.com*

Denomination: Disciples of Christ

Parent company: Christian Board of Publication

Submissions: Publishes 12 titles per year; receives hundreds submissions annually. Email query first.

Genres and topics: contemporary issues, leadership, social justice, spiritual maturity, church resources; fiction: contemporary, historical after 1800

Guidelines: *chalicepress.com/pages/write-for-us*

Tip: "Every Chalice contract begins with an 'Affirmation of Diversity': The Christian Board of Publication and its imprints affirm the faith and gifts of persons regardless of race, color, religion, gender, national origin, age, disability, sexual orientation, or gender expression and will not publish material that opposes this affirmation."

CHARISMA HOUSE

600 Rinehart Rd., Lake Mary, FL 32746 | 407-333-0600

Debbie.Marrie@CharismaMedia.com | *www.charismahouse.com*

Debbie Marrie, VP of acquisitions and content development

Denomination: Charismatic/Pentecostal

Parent company: Charisma Media/Plus Communications, Inc.

Mission statement: to inspire people to encounter the power of the Holy Spirit

Submissions: Publishes 50-60 titles per year; receives 150-200 submissions annually. First-time authors: fewer than 10%. Length: 50,000-60,000 words/224-256 pages. Agent preferred, or email proposal with sample chapters. Responds in one month. Bible: MEV.

Genres and topics: African-American, Christian living/spirituality, end-times prophecy, fitness, health, Hispanic, spiritual warfare

Royalty: 16-25%, sometimes gives advance

Types of books: audiobook, ebook, hardcover, offset paperback, POD

Imprints: Siloam (natural health remedies), FrontLine (current events, end-times prophecy)

Guidelines: available via email

Tip: "Three key areas we evaluate are the concept, the writing quality, and the author's platform."

CHOSEN

6030 E. Fulton Rd., Ada, MI 49301 | 616-676-9185
bakerpublishinggroup.com/chosen
Kim Bangs, editorial director

Denomination: Charismatic

Parent company: Baker Publishing Group

Mission statement: to publish authors who recognize the gifts and active ministry of the Holy Spirit with messages that transform lives and equip Christians to advance the Kingdom of God

Submissions: Publishes 30 titles per year; receives 75 submissions annually. First-time authors: 75%. Length: 224-240 pages. Agent not required. Conference contact, proposal with sample chapters. Bible: any.

Genres and topics: Charismatic

Royalty: varies, sometimes gives advance

Types of books: audiobook, ebook, hardcover, offset paperback

Guidelines: not available

CHRISM PRESS

13607 Bedford Rd. NE, Cumberland, MD 21502 | 301-876-4876
submissions@chrismpress.com | *www.chrismpress.com*
Karen Ullo, editor
Rhonda Ortiz, editor
Marisa Stokely, editor
William Gonch, editor

Parent company: WhiteFire Publishing

Mission statement: to publish stories informed by Catholic and Orthodox Christianity that may not be able to find a home in either mainstream secular or Christian (evangelical) presses

Submissions: Publishes 6-12 titles per year; receives 50 submissions annually. First-time authors: 25%. Length: 60,000-120,000 words. Email query first. Responds in three months.

Genres and topics: fiction: all, teen/YA

Royalty: 50% for ebooks, 10% for print; sometimes gives advance

Types of books: audiobook, ebook, POD

Guidelines: *www.chrismpress.com/submissions*

Tip: "We are acquiring adult and young-adult fiction that reflects a Catholic or Orthodox Christian worldview and appeals to Catholic and/or Orthodox readers. Please read our submissions guidelines and FAQ."

CHRISTIAN FOCUS PUBLICATIONS

Geanies House, Fearn, Tain, Ross-shire IV20 1TW, Scotland, UK | 01862–871011

submissions@christianfocus.com | *www.christianfocus.com*

Willie MacKenzie, director of publishing

Catherine Mackenzie, children's editor; Catherine.Mackenzie@christianfocus.com

> **Genres and topics:** Christian living/spirituality, theology, academic, biography, children, commentaries
>
> **Types of books:** hardcover, paperback
>
> **Imprints:** Christian Focus (popular adult titles), CF4K (children), Mentor (serious readers), Christian Heritage (classic writings from the past)
>
> **Guidelines:** *www.christianfocus.com/about/adult-guidelines;* children's: *www.christianfocus.com/about/childrens-guidelines*
>
> **Tip:** "Read our website please. Don't send us stuff we don't publish."

CHURCH PUBLISHING INCORPORATED

19 E. 34th St., New York, NY 10016 | 800–242–1918

astuart@cpg.org | *www.churchpublishing.org*

Airié Stuart, publisher

Phil Marino

> **Denomination:** Episcopal
>
> **Genres and topics:** Bible study, biography, Christian living/spirituality, finances, leadership, prayer, retirement, social justice, theology, worship, academic
>
> **Types of books:** audiobook, ebook, hardcover, paperback
>
> **Guidelines:** *www.churchpublishing.org/manuscriptsubmission*
>
> **Tip:** "CPI's core publishing program is structured around *The Book of Common Prayer; The Hymnal 1982;* and the specialized books and resources used in the liturgy, faith formation, governance, life, and mission of the Episcopal Church."

CKN CHRISTIAN PUBLISHING

submissions@cknchristianpublishing.com | *cknchristianpublishing.com*

Patience Bramlett, acquisitions and managing production editor

> **Parent company:** Wolfpack Publishing
>
> **Mission statement:** to publish books that will help readers to rise and develop their understanding of God's Word and to apply it more abundantly to their lives

Submissions: Agent only. Responds in three months.

Genres and topics: fiction only: Amish, historical, mystery, romance, science fiction, westerns

Royalty: up to 35%

Types of books: ebook, POD

Guidelines: *cknchristianpublishing.com/Christian-manuscript-submissions*

Tip: "We are dedicated to bringing readers wholesome novels that ensure there's something for everyone to read. No sexually explicit scenes, graphically violent descriptions, or streams of profanity."

CLADACH PUBLISHING

PO Box 336144, Greeley, CO 80633 | 970-371-9530

cathyl@cladach.com | *www.cladach.com*

Catherine Lawton, publisher and editor

Submissions: Publishes three or four titles per year; receives 50 submissions annually. First-time authors: 50%. Length: 120-300 pages. Agent not required. Author referral or conference contact. Responds in three months. Bible: NIV, NRSV.

Genres and topics: Christian living/spirituality, healing, memoir/personal narrative, nature, relationships, devotionals, poetry; fiction: frontier, literary

Royalty: 10-20%, gives advance of $100

Types of books: audiobook, ebook, offset paperback, POD

Imprint: AGATES (poetry)

Guidelines: *cladach.com/authors*

Tip: "We seek creative, marketable book ideas from Christian authors who are credible, in community, and who share our vision to publish books that show God at work in this world and that inspire readers to get involved."

CLC PUBLICATIONS

PO Box 1449, Fort Washington, PA 19034 | 215-542-1242

submissions@clcpublications.com | *www.clcpublications.com*

David Fessenden, editorial coordinator

Parent company: CLC Ministries International

Mission statement: to make evangelical Christian literature available to all nations so that people may come to faith and maturity in the Lord Jesus Christ

Submissions: Publishes 6-12 titles per year; receives 60 submissions annually. First-time authors: 30%. Length: 20,000-80,000 words.

Agent preferred. Email proposal with sample chapters. Responds in six to eight weeks. Bible: ESV.

Genres and topics: Christian living/spirituality

Royalty: 12–16%, sometimes gives advance

Types of books: audiobook, ebook, offset paperback

Guidelines: *www.clcpublications.com/about/prospective-authors-submissions*

Tip: "Try to be both succinct and complete in your submission."

COLLEGE PRESS PUBLISHING

1307 W. 20th St., Joplin, MO 64804 | 417-623-6280

collpressjoplin@gmail.com | *www.collegepress.com*

Denomination: Church of Christ

Submissions: Email or mail query or proposal with sample chapters. Responds in two to three months.

Genres and topics: apologetics, biography, Christian living/spirituality, academic, Bible reference/commentaries, Bible studies

Guidelines: *www.collegepress.com/pages/for-authors*

CONVERGENT BOOKS

1745 Broadway, New York, NY 10019 | 212-366-2724

dreed@penguinrandomhouse.com | *www.randomhousebooks.com/imprint/convergent-books*

Derek Reed, editorial director

Mathew Burdette, editor and acquisitions

Parent company: The Crown Publishing Group/Penguin Random House

Mission statement: to seek out diverse viewpoints and honest conversations that shed light on the defining challenges facing people of faith today; to help readers ask important questions, find paths forward in disagreement, and shape the way faith is expressed in the modern world

Submissions: Publishes 12–16 titles per year; receives 100–150 submissions annually. First-time authors: 10%. Length: 204–300 pages/45,000–65,000 words. Agent only. Responds in a few weeks to two months. Bible: NIV, ESV.

Genres and topics: African-American, Asian, Christian living/spirituality, deconstruction/reconstruction of faith, friendship, Hispanic, marriage, memoir/personal narrative, parenting, self-help, social issues, social justice, wellness, essays, poetry

Royalty: 10–15%, gives advance of $10,000 to high six figures
Types of books: audiobook, ebook, hardcover, offset paperback
Guidelines: not available
Tip: "Have a good agent and a good platform."

CREATIVE COMMUNICATIONS FOR THE PARISH

1564 Fencorp Dr., Fenton, MO 63026 | 800-325-9414
submissions@creativecommunications.com | *catholic.creativecommunications.com*

Denomination: Catholic
Parent company: Bayard, Inc.
Mission statement: to communicate the gospel of Jesus to the whole
body of Christ through new and innovative worship and devotional
materials which can be used and distributed by churches and schools
to encourage faith and evangelize
Submissions: Email or mail complete manuscript or proposal with
sample chapters. Responds in 10 weeks.
Genres and topics: Christian living/spirituality, ministry, prayer,
sacraments, worship, children, devotionals, ministry resources,
puzzles and activities, teen/YA
Types of books: paperback
Guidelines: *catholic.creativecommunications.com/Pages/Item/7341/*
Submissions.aspx

CROSSLINK PUBLISHING

1601 Mt. Rushmore Rd., Ste. 3288, Rapid City, SD 57701 | 888-697-4851
publisher@crosslink.org | *www.crosslinkpublishing.com*
Rick Bates, managing editor

Parent company: CrossLink Ministries
Submissions: Publishes 35 titles per year; receives 500 submissions
annually. First-time authors: 85%. Length: 12,000–60,000 words.
Submit on the website. Responds in one week.
Genres and topics: Christian living/spirituality, Bible studies, children,
devotionals, fiction, nonfiction
Royalty: 10% for print, 20% for ebooks; no advance
First print run: 2,000
Imprint: New Harbor Press
Guidelines: *www.crosslinkpublishing.com/submit-a-manuscript*
Tip: "We are particularly interested in providing books that help
Christians succeed in their daily walk (inspirational, devotional, small
groups, etc.)."

CROSSRIVER MEDIA GROUP

4810 Gene Field Rd. #2, St. Joseph, MO 64506 | 816-752-2171

deb@crossrivermedia.com | www.crossrivermedia.com

Debra L. Butterfield, editorial director

Mission statement: to publish high-quality books and materials that help women build a battle-ready faith

Submissions: Publishes four to eight titles per year; receives 60-75 submissions annually. First-time authors: 30-40%. Length: 50,000-80,000 words. Email proposal with sample chapters, or submit it through the website. Conference contact a plus. Responds in 12-16 weeks. Bible: any except NIV.

Genres and topics: Bible study, Christian living/spirituality, family, inspirational, marriage; fiction: biblical, contemporary, historical, mystery, romance

Royalty: 8-12%, no advance

Types of books: ebook, hardcover, POD

Guidelines: *www.crossrivermedia.com/guidelines*

Tip: "Read our website and follow the proposal guidelines."

CROSSWAY

1300 Crescent St., Wheaton, IL 60187 | 630-682-4300

submissions@crossway.org | www.crossway.org

Todd Augustine, senior acquisitions editor

Samuel James, associate acquisitions editor

Champ Thornton, children's book acquisitions

Parent company: Good News Publishers

Mission statement: to publish books that combine the truth of God's Word with a passion to live it out, with unique and compelling Christian content

Submissions: Publishes 150 titles per year; receives 500 submissions annually. First-time authors: 1%. Length: minimum 25,000 words. Agent not required. Email or mail query first. Responds in six weeks if proposal is requested. Bible: ESV.

Genres and topics: Bible study, Christian living/spirituality, contemporary issues, spiritual growth, worldview, academic, Bible reference/commentaries, devotionals

Royalty: varies, gives advance

First print run: varies

Types of books: audiobook, ebook, hardcover, offset paperback

Guidelines: *www.crossway.org/submissions*

Tip: "A well-written query letter is essential. If a proposal is requested, be sure it is well written."

CSS PUBLISHING COMPANY, INC.

5450 N. Dixie Hwy., Lima, OH 45807-9559 | 419-227-1818
editor@csspub.com | *www.csspub.com*
David Runk, publisher

> **Mission statement:** to help Protestant pastors and lay leaders share the Good News of Jesus Christ
>
> **Submissions:** Publishes 20 titles per year; receives 50 submissions annually. First-time authors: 10%. Length: 80-240 pages, depending on subject matter. Email or mail proposal with sample chapters or a query. Responds in six months. Bible: NRSV, NIV, RSV, ESV, TLB.
>
> **Genres and topics:** Christian education, ministry, preaching, stewardship, worship, Bible studies, church resources, drama, ministry resources, sermons
>
> **Royalty:** 7-10%, flat fee of $350-500 for sermon books, no advance
>
> **Types of books:** ebook, POD
>
> **Guidelines:** *store.csspub.com/page.php?Custom%20Pages=10*
>
> **Tip:** "Use solid biblical research."

D6 FAMILY MINISTRY

114 Bush Rd., Nashville, TN 37217 | 615-361-1221
books@d6family.com | *D6family.com*
Dr. Danny Conn, director of books and strategic projects

> **Denomination:** Free Will Baptist
>
> **Parent company:** National Association of Free Will Baptists
>
> **Mission statement:** to build believers through church and home
>
> **Submissions:** Publishes 8-12 titles per year; receives 40 submissions annually. First-time authors: 20%. Length: 30,000-80,000 words. Agent not required. Email proposal with sample chapters. Responds in three months. Bible: any.
>
> **Genres and topics:** discipleship, family, Free Will Baptist history, marriage, theology, academic
>
> **Royalty:** 16-20%, sometimes gives advance of $500
>
> **Types of books:** audiobook, ebook, offset paperback
>
> **Imprints:** D6 Family (family ministry, generational discipleship, and Christian living), Randall House (theology, Free Will Baptist history, and Bible study), Randall House Academic (academic texts)
>
> **Guidelines:** *rhpweb.s3.amazonaws.com/Book-Proposal-Guide.pdf*

Tip: "The majority of our audience is conservative evangelical Christian."

DAVID C COOK

4050 Lee Vance Dr., Colorado Springs, CO 80918 | 719-536-0100

www.davidccook.org

Michael Covington, VP of publishing and acquisitions, pastors, leaders, and women's

Susan McPherson, acquisitions, women in leadership

Luke McKinnon, acquisitions editor, apologetics and worldview

Mission statement: to equip the Church with Christ-centered resources for making and teaching disciples

Submissions: Publishes 40 titles per year; receives 1,200 submissions annually. First-time authors: 10%. Length: 45,000–50,000 words. Only agent or conference contact. Responds in one month.

Genres and topics: Christian living/spirituality, discipleship, family, leadership, marriage, men, parenting, women, Bible reference/commentaries, Bible studies, church resources, devotionals, teen/YA

Royalty: 12–22%, gives advance

Types of books: ebook, hardcover, offset paperback, POD

Imprint: Esther Press (women)

Guidelines: *davidccook.org/submissions-and-writer-guidelines*

Tip: "We look for significant platform, excellent writing, and relevant content."

DOVE CHRISTIAN PUBLISHERS

PO Box 611, Bladensburg, MD 20710 | 240-342-3293

editorial@dovechristianpublishers.com | *www.dovechristianpublishers.com*

Raenita Wiggins, acquisitions editor

Parent company: Kingdom Christian Enterprises

Mission statement: to entertain, edify, equip, and encourage people through products that glorify and honor Jesus Christ and His Kingdom and to provide new and emerging Christian authors with a forum for their creative and Kingdom-building voices

Submissions: Publishes 10 titles per year; receives 300 submissions annually. First-time authors: 95%. Length: 100–220 pages. Submit proposal with sample chapters through the website. Responds in four to six weeks or not interested. Bible: NIV.

Genres and topics: Christian living/spirituality, church life, discipleship, ministry, prayer, Bible studies, children, devotionals;

fiction: fantasy, historical, humor, mystery, romance, science
fiction, suspense/thriller

Royalty: 10–25%, no advance

Types of books: ebook, hardcover, POD

Guidelines: *www.dovechristianpublishers.com/publish-with-us*

Tip: "Author should establish a platform and familiarize themselves
with book marketing and promotion prior to submission."

EERDMANS BOOKS FOR YOUNG READERS

4035 Park East Ct. SE, Grand Rapids, MI 49546 | 800-253-7521

kmerz@eerdmans.com | *www.eerdmans.com/youngreaders*

Kathleen Merz, editorial director

Courtney Zonnefeld, assistant editor

Parent company: Wm. B. Eerdmans Publishing Co.

Mission statement: to engage young minds with books—books that
are honest, wise, and hopeful; books that delight us with their
storyline, characters, or good humor; books that inform, inspire,
and entertain

Submissions: Publishes 12–18 titles per year; receives 1,500
submissions annually. First-time authors: 5–10%. Length: picture
books, 1,000 words; middle-grade books, 15,000–30,000 words.
Mail proposal with complete manuscript or sample chapters.
Responds in four months only if interested.

Genres and topics: African-American, animals, history, multicultural,
nature, social issues, middle grade, picture books, teen/YA

Royalty: gives advances

Types of books: audiobook, ebook, hardcover

Guidelines: *www.eerdmans.com/submissions*

Tip: "We are always looking for well-written picture books and novels
for young readers. Make sure that your submission is a unique,
well-crafted story; and take a look at our current list of titles to get
a sense of whether yours would be a good fit for us."

EERDMANS, WM. B. PUBLISHING CO.

4035 Park East Ct. SE, Grand Rapids, MI 49546 | 800-253-7521

submissions@eerdmans.com | *www.eerdmans.com*

Trevor Thompson, senior acquisitions editor

Andrew Knapp, acquisitions editor

Lisa Ann Cockrel, acquisitions editor

Submissions: Publishes 100 titles per year. Email proposal with complete manuscript or sample chapters. Responds in two months.

Genres and topics: biography, Christian living/spirituality, contemporary issues, ethics, history, ministry, theology, academic, Bible reference/commentaries

Royalty: sometimes gives advance

Imprint: Eerdmans Books for Young Readers (children and teens)

Guidelines: *www.eerdmans.com/Pages/Item/2068/Submission-Guidelines.aspx*

Tip: "Review submission guidelines carefully and check recent catalogs for suitability. Target readerships range from academic to semipopular. We are publishing a growing number of books in Christian life, spirituality, and ministry."

ELK LAKE PUBLISHING, INC.

35 Dogwood Dr., Plymouth, MA 02360-3166 | 508-746-1734

ElkLakePublishingInc.com

Deb Haggerty, publisher and editor in chief; Deb@ElkLakePublishingInc.com

Jane Daly, acquisitions editor; Jane.Daly.ELPI@gmail.com

PeggySue Wells, acquisitions editor; PeggySue.Wells.ELPI@gmail.com

Deb DeArmond, acquisitions editor; deborahdearmond@gmail.com

Les Stobbe, acquisitions editor; lhstobbe123@gmail.com

Mission statement: to captivate our readers and carry them to places of escape, encouragement, education, and entertainment—to broaden their horizons and urge them to new heights. More than anything else, we want to point people to Jesus Christ

Submissions: Publishes 75-100 titles per year; receives 250 submissions annually. First-time authors: 90%. Length: 45,000-110,000 words. Agent not required; conference contact a plus. Submit through *ChristianBookProposals.com,* or email proposal with sample chapters. Responds in less than a month. Bible: NASB, ESV.

Genres and topics: Christian living/spirituality, fiction, middle grade, YA

Royalty: 40%, no advance

Types of books: audiobook, ebook, POD

Guidelines: *elklakepublishinginc.com*

Tip: "Be professional, know your audience, know what you will do to sell your book."

EMANATE BOOKS

PO Box 141000, Nashville, TN 37214-1000 | 615-889-9000

www.thomasnelson.com/emanatebooks

Janene MacIvor, senior editor

Parent company: Thomas Nelson Publishers/HarperCollins Christian Publishing

Mission statement: to reflect the work of the Holy Spirit, feed His church, and help a new generation hear from God and grow in their spiritual journey

Genres and topics: Charismatic, Christian classics

Types of books: audiobook, ebook, hardcover, offset paperback

ENCLAVE PUBLISHING

24 W. Camelback Rd. A-635, Phoenix, AZ 85013

acquisitions@enclavepublishing.com | *www.enclavepublishing.com*

Steve Laube, publisher and acquisitions editor

Parent company: Oasis Family Media

Mission statement: to publish out-of-this-world stories that are informed by a coherent theology

Submissions: Publishes 12–18 titles per year; receives 200 submissions annually. First-time authors: 20–30%. Length: 80,000–140,000 words. Author referral, conference contact, or proposal with sample chapters through the website. Responds in 60–90 days.

Genres and topics: fiction: allegory, fantasy, science fiction, speculative, supernatural

Royalty: industry standard, no advance

First print run: 2,000–5,000

Types of books: audiobook, ebook, hardcover, offset paperback

Imprint: Enclave Escape (YA)

Guidelines: *www.enclavepublishing.com/guidelines*

Tip: "Keep word count above 80,000 words and below 140,000. Too often we are sent books that are either far too short or extremely long."

END GAME PRESS

PO Box 206, Nesbit, MS 38651 | 901-590-6584

submissions@endgamepress.com | *www.endgamepress.com*

Hope Bolinger, managing and acquisitions editor

Michelle Medlock Adams, executive editor, Wren & Bear Books

Edwina Perkins, executive editor and acquisitions, Harambee Press

Mission statement: to leverage all of its resources to make the greatest positive impact possible by holding a high standard for the books it publishes in both design and quality, while also making the experience a good one for each of the authors in the End Game

Press family

Submissions: Publishes 20 titles per year; receives 300 submissions annually. First-time authors: 25%. Length: depends on the genre. Agent only. Responds in two to three months. Bible: any.

Genres and topics: Christian living/spirituality, faith, marriage, parenting, prayer, fiction

Royalty: 20–25%, gives advance

Types of books: audiobook, ebook, hardcover, paperback

Imprints: Wren and Bear Books (children and YA), Harambee Press (ethnic/BIPOC), Generation Hope (chapter books, middle grade, and YA), Li'l Liberty (children with focus on Americana), Fusion (hybrid publishing)

Guidelines: *www.endgamepress.com/submissions*

Tip: Also publishes general-market books.

EXEGETICA PUBLISHING

PO Box 241, Fort Walton Beach, FL 32549 | 816–269–8505

editor@exegeticapublishing.com | *www.exegeticapublishing.com*

Mission statement: to encourage Christians and non-Christians alike to engage with the Bible, to understand the world around them, and to "taste and see that the Lord is good," as Psalm 34:8 exhorts

Submissions: Publishes 10 titles per year; receives 30 submissions annually. First-time authors: 10%. Length: 200–300 pages. Email proposal with sample chapters. Responds in two to four weeks. Bible: NASB, NKJV, ESV.

Genres and topics: Bible, Christian living/spirituality, theology, academic

Royalty: 10%, no advance

Types of books: ebook, offset paperback

Imprint: Grace Acres Press (trade nonfiction)

Guidelines: *exegeticapublishing.com/submit-a-proposal*

Tip: "Follow submission guidelines with solid biblical resources."

EXPANSE BOOKS

15 Lucky Ln., Morrilton, AR 72110 | 501–289–9319

scriveningspress@gmail.com | *expansebooks.pub*

Linda Fulkerson, owner and acquisitions editor

Erin R. Howard, managing editor; expansebooks@gmail.com

Parent company: Scrivenings Press, LLC

Mission statement: to spread God's word through our writing

Submissions: Publishes three titles per year; receives 100 submissions annually. First-time authors: 30%. Length: 60,000–90,000 words. Agent not required, conference contact a plus. Email proposal with sample chapters, or submit it through the website. Responds in four to six weeks. Bible: any.

Genres and topics: fiction: YA, dystopian, fairy tales, fantasy, magical realism, speculative, time travel

Royalty: 12% print, 50% ebook, 40% pages read in Kindle Unlimited; no advance

Types of books: ebook, hardcover, POD

Guidelines: *expansebooks.pub/submissions*

Tip: "We are a small publishing house, and we try to keep a family feel among our staff and authors. We encourage all our authors to encourage one another and to cross-promote books from other authors within our company."

FAITHWORDS

1 Franklin Park, 6100 Tower Cir., Ste. 210, Franklin, TN 37067 | 615-221-0996

www.faithwords.com

Beth Adams, editorial director

Sean McGowan, editor and acquisitions

India Hunter, associate editor and acquisitions

Parent company: Hachette Book Group

Genres and topics: African-American, apologetics, Bible study, Christian living/spirituality, culture, Hispanic, marriage, memoir/personal narrative, parenting, social issues, theology

Royalty: minimum 10%, gives advance

Types of books: ebook, hardcover, offset paperback

Tip: "Have a clear, well-written proposal and a solid platform."

FIRST STEPS PUBLISHING

PO Box 571, Gleneden Beach, OR 97388 | 541-961-7641

publish@firststepspublishing.com | *www.FirstStepsPublishing.com*

RJ McRoberts, submissions editor

Submissions: Publishes three to five titles per year; receives 30 submissions annually. First-time authors: 90%. Length: 50,000–80,000 words. Query first on the website form. Responds in 8-12 weeks, although reply is not guaranteed.

Genres and topics: fiction: fantasy, historical, mystery, science fiction, suspense/thriller

Royalty: 15–30%, no advance

Types of books: audiobook, ebook, hardcover, POD

Imprints: White Parrot Press (children), WestWind Press (middle grade and YA)

Guidelines: *www.firststepspublishing.com/get-published*

Tip: "Initial response is based on your query letter, so ensure that it is enticing and well-written. We only accept unpublished, professionally edited manuscripts. Overuse of gratuitous language will not be accepted."

FLYAWAY BOOKS

100 Witherspoon St., Louisville, KY 40202–1396

submissions@flyawaybooks.com | *www.flyawaybooks.com*

Jessica Miller Kelley, senior acquisitions editor

Denomination: Presbyterian

Parent company: Westminster John Knox Press/Presbyterian Publishing Corporation

Submissions: Email proposal with complete manuscript. Responds in six weeks or not interested.

Genres and topics: picture books

Types of books: hardcover, paperback, picture books

Guidelines: *www.flyawaybooks.com/submissions*

Tip: "Flyaway Books embraces diversity, inclusivity, compassion, care for each other, and care for our world. Many of our books explore social justice and other contemporary issues. Some retell familiar religious stories in new ways, while others carry universal themes appealing to those with any, or no, religious background."

FOCUS ON THE FAMILY

8605 Explorer Dr., Colorado Springs, CO 80995 | 719–531–5181

www.focusonthefamily.com

Larry Weeden, editor in chief

Submissions: Only agent, *ChristianBookProposals.com*, or Writers Edge. Books are published by Tyndale House Publishers.

Genres and topics: family, marriage, parenting, children

Types of books: ebook, hardcover, offset paperback

Tip: "We're looking for proposals that exhibit great content and good writing, hopefully combined with a strong author platform. And we're always looking for good children's books."

FORTRESS PRESS

PO Box 1209, Minneapolis, MN 55440-1209

www.fortresspress.com

Laura Gifford, editor-in-chief; giffordl@fortresspress.com

Yvonne D. Hawkins, acquisitions editor, ministry; hawkinsy@fortresspress.com

Bethany Dickerson, associate acquisitions editor, theology, culture, literature,
religious history, biblical studies; dickersonb@fortresspress.com

Denomination: Evangelical Lutheran Church in America

Parent company: 1517 Media

Genres and topics: Bible study, Christian living/spirituality, counseling, culture, ethics, history, leadership, ministry, philosophy, social justice, theology, academic, Bible reference/commentaries

Types of books: hardcover, offset paperback

Guidelines: *www.fortresspress.com/info/submissions*

FORWARD MOVEMENT

412 Sycamore St., Cincinnati, OH 45202-4110 | 800-543-1813

sgunn@forwardmovement.org | *www.forwardmovement.org*

Scott Gunn, executive director

Richelle Thompson, managing editor

Denomination: Episcopal

Mission statement: to offer resources that strengthen and support discipleship and evangelism

Submissions: Email proposal with sample chapters. Responds in four to six weeks.

Genres and topics: Bible study, discipleship, evangelism, leadership, prayer

Types of books: ebook, offset paperback

Guidelines: *www.forwardmovement.org/Pages/About/Writers-Guidelines. aspx*

Tip: "While many of our resources are targeted for an Episcopal/ Anglican audience, we also offer some materials for a broader reach."

THE FOUNDRY PUBLISHING

PO Box 419527, Kansas City, MO 64141 | 800-877-0700

RMcFarland@thefoundrypublishing.com | *www.thefoundrypublishing.com*

René McFarland, submissions editor

Bonnie Perry, editorial director

Denomination: Nazarene, Wesleyan

Mission statement: to empower people with life-changing ways to engage in the mission of God

Submissions: Length: 45,000–60,000 words. Email proposal with sample chapters. Responds in eight weeks.

Genres and topics: Christian living/spirituality, ministry

Guidelines: *www.thefoundrypublishing.com/book-manuscript-submission-faqs.html*

Tip: "Because we are a denominational publisher of holiness literature, our books reflect an evangelical Wesleyan stance in accord with the Church of the Nazarene. We seek practical as well as serious treatments of issues of faith consistent with the Wesleyan tradition."

FRANCISCAN MEDIA

28 W. Liberty St., Cincinnati, OH 45202 | 513-241-5615

proposal@FranciscanMedia.org | *www.FranciscanMedia.org*

Christopher Heffron, editorial director

Denomination: Catholic

Submissions: Publishes 20–30 titles per year. Email proposal with sample chapters. Responds in six to eight weeks. Bible: NRSV. Seeks manuscripts that inform and inspire adult Catholics, other Christians, and all who are seeking to better understand and live their faith. Goal is to help people "Live in love. Grow in faith."

Genres and topics: Christian living/spirituality, spiritual growth, fiction

Royalty: 10–14%, gives advance of $1,000–3,000

Guidelines: *www.franciscanmedia.org/writers-guidelines*

Tip: "Special consideration will be given to book proposals that show how the book relates to one or more of the teachings of St. Francis or the Franciscan charism."

GENERATION HOPE

PO Box 206, Nesbit, MS 38651 | 901-590-6584

submissions@endgamepress.com | *www.endgamepress.com/generation-hope*

Hope Bolinger, imprint editor

Parent company: End Game Press

Mission statement: to grow young writers in their craft, encourage entrepreneurial pursuits, and publish their work to reach readers in their generation in a unique way

Submissions: First-time authors: 100%. Submit proposal with complete manuscript. Responds in two to three months. Bible: any.

Genres and topics: fiction: first-chapter, middle grade, teen/YA
Types of books: ebook, paperback
Guidelines: *www.endgamepress.com/submissions*
Tip: "We are looking for clean manuscripts that are safe for readers in the age group of the book, books that aren't afraid to tackle some harder issues, while still being filled with hope."

THE GOOD BOOK COMPANY

1805 Sardis Rd. N, Ste. 102, Charlotte, NC 28270 | 866-244-2165
submissions@thegoodbook.com | *www.thegoodbook.com*
Tim Thornborough, publishing director
Carl Laferton, senior editor

Mission statement: to promote, encourage, and equip people to serve our Lord and Master Jesus Christ
Submissions: Email or mail proposal with sample chapters.
Genres and topics: Bible study, Christian living/spirituality, evangelism, children, devotionals, teen/YA
Types of books: ebook, paperback
Guidelines: *www.thegoodbook.com/authors*
Tip: "Our aim with all our resources is to get people directly interacting with the Bible. So we expect our authors to facilitate that process, rather than just commenting on their own view of what the Bible says. A primary question we ask of any resource submitted to us is: Does it handle the Bible well (i.e., taking note of the context of each passage), and is it helping people understand its message?"

GOOD BOOKS

307 W. 36th St., 11th Floor, New York, NY 10018 | 212-643-6816
agehring@skyhorsepublishing.com | *skyhorsepublishing.com/good-books*
Abigail Gehring, editorial director

Parent company: Skyhorse Publishing
Submissions: Email proposal. Responds in four to six weeks if interested. Salem Books imprint is now subsumed under Good Books.
Genres and topics: Christian living/spirituality, cooking, crafts, health, justice
Types of books: ebook, hardcover, paperback
Guidelines: *skyhorsepublishing.com/good-books/submissions*
Tip: "Before submitting a proposal, we suggest you click around our site and take a look at the kinds of books we've published. This will help you gain an idea of what we're looking for."

GRACE ACRES PRESS

PO Box 22, Larkspur, CO 80118 | 303-681-9995
Anne@graceacrespress.com | *www.GraceAcresPress.com*
Anne R. Fenske, publisher

Parent company: Exegetica Publishing
Mission statement: to grow your faith one page at a time
Submissions: Publishes six titles per year; receives 20 submissions annually. First-time authors: 75%. Length: 100–300 pages. Email or mail query first. Responds in one month. Bible: NKJV, NIV.
Genres and topics: Bible study, biography, discipleship, evangelism, missions
Royalty: 10–15%, no advance
First print run: 500–2,000
Types of books: ebook, hardcover, offset paperback, POD
Guidelines: available via email
Tip: "Explain your contribution as a copartner in marketing your book."

GRACE PUBLISHING

PO Box 1233, Broken Arrow, OK 74013-1233 | 918-346-7960
editorial@grace-publishing.com | *www.grace-publishing.com*
Terri Kalfas, editor
Susan King, editor, Short and Sweet; shortandsweettoo@gmail.com

Parent company: The Jomaga Group
Mission statement: to develop and distribute biblically based resources that challenge, encourage, teach, equip, and entertain Christians young and old in their personal journeys
Submissions: Publishes four to six titles per year. First-time authors: varies. Length: 30,000–40,000 words. Agent not required, conference contact a plus. Email proposal; no simultaneous submissions. Responds in three months. Bible: any.
Genres and topics: Christian living/spirituality, anthologies, Bible studies, memoir
Royalty: varies, no advance
Types of books: POD
Guidelines: *grace-publishing.com/manuscript-submission*
Tip: "Write tight; know your subject; don't take Scripture verses out of context."

GUIDEPOSTS BOOKS

110 William St., Ste. 901, New York, NY 10038 | 212-251-8100
bookeditors@guideposts.org | *www.guideposts.org*
Carolyn Mandarano, senior managing editor
Jane Haertel, fiction editor; jhaertel@guideposts.org

Parent company: Guideposts, Inc.
Submissions: Publishes 20-30 titles per year. Agent only.
Genres and topics: Christian living/spirituality, memoir/personal narrative, devotionals; fiction: contemporary, women's
Tip: "For new Guideposts writers, devotionals require an audition by sending in three sample devotions. We select only a few new writers each year. Contributors write on a work-for-hire basis. Guideposts holds the copyright. For more information or to submit devotional auditions, please email Carolyn Mandarano, *cmandarano@guideposts.org.*"

HARAMBEE PRESS

PO Box 206, Nesbit, MS 38651 | 901-590-6584
submissions@endgamepress.com | *www.endgamepress.com/harambee-press*
Edwina Perkins, acquisitions editor

Parent company: End Game Press
Mission statement: to raise up the ethnic voice; and to give a place for BIPOC authors to communicate, through publication, with each other and the world
Submissions: Agent not required. Email proposal with sample chapters. Responds in two to three months. Bible: any.
Genres and topics: fiction, nonfiction
Types of books: ebook, paperback
Guidelines: *www.endgamepress.com/submissions*
Tip: "We are looking for writers who want to express the diversity of their culture and writers who have stories or life lessons, whether through fiction or nonfiction. Authors should carry a message of hope and redemption."

HARBOURLIGHT BOOKS

PO Box 1738, Aztec, NM 87410
customer@harbourlightbooks.com | *www.pelicanbookgroup.com*
Nicola Martinez, editor-in-chief

Parent company: Pelican Book Group

Mission statement: to publish quality books that reflect the salvation and love offered by Jesus Christ

Submissions: Length: 25,000–80,000 words. Submit proposal with sample chapters through the website. Responds in three to four months. Bible: NIV, NAB.

Genres and topics: fiction: adventure, crime, family saga, mystery, suspense, westerns, women's

Royalty: 40% on download, 7% on print; sometimes gives advance

Types of books: audiobook, ebook, hardcover, offset paperback, POD

Guidelines: *pelicanbookgroup.com/ec/index.php?main_page=page&id=55&zenid=06f25d411f1d61bfa008693b5b246c4*

HARPERCHRISTIAN RESOURCES

501 Nelson Pl., Nashville, TN 37214

harperchristianresources.com

Parent company: HarperCollins Christian Publishing

Mission statement: to equip people to understand the Scriptures, cultivate spiritual growth, and live an inspired faith with Bible study and video resources from today's most trusted voices

Genres and topics: Bible studies, ministry programs, small-group study guides

Types of books: offset paperback, video

HARPERCOLLINS CHRISTIAN PUBLISHING

HarperChristian Resources

Thomas Nelson: Emanate Books, Nelson Books, Thomas Nelson Fiction, Thomas Nelson Gift, Tommy Nelson, W Publishing Group

Zondervan: Zonderkidz, Zondervan Academic, Zondervan Books, Zondervan Gift, Zondervan Reflective

HARPERONE

353 Sacramento St. #500, San Francisco, CA 94111–3653 | 415–477–4400

Stephanie.Smith@harpercollins.com | *harperone.com*

Stephanie Smith, senior editor

Parent company: HarperCollins Publishing

Mission statement: to publish books for the world we want to live in

Submissions: Publishes 75 titles per year; receives 10,000 submissions annually. First-time authors: 5%. Length: 160–256 pages. Agent only. Responds in three months.

Genres and topics: Christian living/spirituality

Royalty: 7.5–15%, gives advance
Types of books: ebook, hardcover, offset paperback

HARVEST HOUSE PUBLISHERS

PO Box 41210, Eugene, OR 97404-0322 | 800-547-8979
harvesthousepublishers.com
Audrey Greeson, acquisitions editor, nonfiction
Ruth Samsel, senior acquisitions editor, gifts
Kyle Hatfield, senior acquisitions editor, children and family
Emma Saisslin, associate trade editor and acquisitions

Mission statement: to glorify God by providing high-quality books and products that affirm biblical values, help people grow spiritually strong, and proclaim Jesus Christ as the answer to every human need
Genres and topics: Christian living/spirituality, family, relationships, Bible reference/commentaries, Bible studies, children, fiction, gift
Types of books: board books, ebook, hardcover, paperback
Imprint: Harvest Kids (children)

HENDRICKSON PUBLISHERS

PO Box 3473, Peabody, MA 01961-3473 | 800-358-3111
roberthand@tyndale.com | *www.hendricksonrose.com*
Robert A. Hand, acquisitions editor
Patricia Anders, editorial director

Parent company: Tyndale House Ministries
Mission statement: to meet the publication needs of the religious studies academic community worldwide and to produce thoughtful books for thoughtful Christians
Submissions: Publishes 16 titles per year; receives 50–100 submissions annually. First-time authors: 40%. Length: trade, 75,000–100,000 words; academic, 100,000–200,000 words. Only agent, *ChristianBookProposals.com*, or conference contact. Responds in two to three months.
Genres and topics: archaeology, church history, culture, marriage, ministry, parenting, theology, academic, Bible reference/commentaries, biblical studies, language studies
Royalty: 12–14%, gives advance
First print run: varies
Types of books: audiobook, ebook, hardcover, offset paperback
Imprints: Hendrickson Publishers (trade books), Hendrickson

Academic (academic), Rose Publishing (Bible reference for everyone), RoseKidz (children), Aspire Press (counseling), Hendrickson Bibles (Bibles)

Guidelines: available via email

Tip: "Please be sure to look at our website to see what kind of books we publish."

INTERVARSITY PRESS

430 Plaza Dr., Westmont, IL 60559 | 630-734-4000

mail@ivpress.com | ivpress.com

Al Hsu, associate editorial director, trade, and acquisitions

Ted Olsen, associate publisher and editorial director, trade books

Jon Boyd, editorial director, IVP Academic

Elissa Schauer, executive editor and IVP Kids editor

> **Parent company:** InterVarsity Christian Fellowship
> **Mission statement:** to publish thoughtful Christian books that shape both the lives of readers and the cultures they inhabit, speaking boldly into important cultural moments, providing timeless tools for spiritual growth, and equipping Christians for a vibrant life of faith
> **Submissions:** Publishes 100 titles per year; receives 800 submissions annually. First-time authors: 20%. Length: 30,000-100,000 words. Only agent or conference contact. Responds in three months. Bible: NIV.
> **Genres and topics:** African-American, Asian, Bible study, Christian living/spirituality, church leadership, church life, counseling, culture, Hispanic, justice, ministry, psychology, spiritual formation, theology, academic, Bible reference/commentaries, Bible studies, children
> **Royalty:** 14-18%, sometimes gives advance
> **Types of books:** audiobook, ebook, hardcover, offset paperback, POD
> **Imprints:** IVP Academic (undergraduate and graduate students, professors, scholars), IVP Formatio (spiritual formation), IVP Bible Studies (study guides), IVP Praxis (church leadership), IVP Kids (children), IVP Español (Spanish)
> **Guidelines:** available via email
> **Tip:** "We accept submissions only from agents or from authors who have had direct contact with an editor."

INVITE RESOURCES

5700 W. Plano Pkwy., Ste. 1600, Plano, TX 75093 | 214-291-8094

lwagner@inviteresources.com | www.inviteresources.com

Lori Wagner, content editor

Denomination: Wesleyan/Arminian
Parent company: St. Andrew Methodist Church, Plano, Texas
Mission statement: to share the promise of Christ's New Creation
Submissions: Publishes 22–26 titles per year; receives 40 submissions annually. First-time authors: 30%. Length: 20,000–50,000 words. Agent not required. Email proposal with complete manuscript or sample chapters. Responds in two to four weeks. Bible: no preference.
Genres and topics: Bible study, Christian living/spirituality, theology, academic, devotionals
Royalty: 8–15%, no advance
Types of books: ebook, hardcover, offset paperback, POD
Imprints: Invite Press (trade books), Invite Academic (focus on the academy)
Guidelines: *www.inviteresources.com/editorial-standards*
Tip: "We are about accessible ideas, presented in an engaging and relatable fashion. This is not to say we want fluff; in fact, we desire books with academic rigor and theological reasoning, but without the difficult writing. We are not interested in boring books. We want our books to be approachable and helpful resources that speak to today's issues."

IRON STREAM MEDIA

100 Missionary Ridge, Birmingham, AL 35242 | 888-811-9934
submissions@ironstreammedia.com | *www.ironstreammedia.com*
Dr. John Herring, publisher

Submissions: Publishes 20–25 titles per year; receives 150 submissions annually. First-time authors: 30%. Length: 50,000–90,000 words. Only agent or conference contact. Responds in three months. Bible: NASB.
Genres and topics: Christian living/spirituality, family, leadership, memoir/personal narrative, parenting, relationships, women, Bible studies, devotionals; fiction: romance, romantic suspense, speculative, suspense, westerns
Royalty: escalating, gives advance
Types of books: audiobook, ebook, offset paperback, POD
Imprints: Iron Stream (nonfiction), Iron Stream Fiction (novels), Iron Stream Kids (board and picture books, Bible storybooks), Brookstone Publishing Group (independent publishing), Life Bible Study (digital Bible study curriculum direct to churches)
Guidelines: *ironstreammedia.com/resources/submission-process*

Tip: "Focus on hook, comps, and marketing sections in book proposal. Also, provide a great list of influencers."

JOURNEYFORTH

1430 Wade Hampton Blvd., Greenville, SC 29609 | 864-546-4600
journeyforth@bjupress.com | *journeyforth.com*
Charlotte Bradley, acquisitions editor

> **Parent company:** BJU Press
> **Mission statement:** to publish stories that will inspire young minds, shape character, instill a biblical worldview, and promote academic success by developing proficient readers and critical thinkers
> **Submissions:** Publishes one to four titles per year; receives 50-100 submissions annually. First-time authors: 45%. Length: ages 6-8, 8,000-10,000 words; ages 9-12, 30,000-40,000 words; ages 12 and up, 40,000-60,000 words. Agent not required. Email or mail proposal with sample chapters. Responds in six to eight months. Bible: KJV, NKJV, ESV, NASB.
> **Genres and topics:** Bible study, Christian living/spirituality, youth biography, Bible studies, first-chapter, middle grade, teen/YA; fiction: adventure, biblical, contemporary, fantasy, folktales, historical, mystery, westerns
> **Royalty:** 10-15%, sometimes gives advance
> **Types of books:** ebook, offset paperback
> **Guidelines:** *www.bjupresshomeschool.com/journeyforth-writers-guidelines*
> **Tip:** "We are particularly interested in acquiring contemporary fiction for all ages, chapter books for beginning readers, and YA fiction. Our market is not open to stories that include profanity or minced oaths, magic or witchcraft, time travel, and characters who engage in unscriptural activities without a biblical consequence. We are not currently accepting picture book, short story, poetry, curriculum, memoir, adult fiction, or adult nonfiction manuscripts."

JUDSON PRESS

1075 First Ave., King of Prussia, PA 19406 | 800-458-3766
acquisitions@judsonpress.com | *www.judsonpress.com*
Rachael Lawrence, senior editor

> **Denomination:** American Baptist
> **Parent company:** American Baptist Home Mission Societies
> **Mission statement:** to produce Christ-centered leadership resources for the transformation of individuals, congregations, communities,

and cultures

Submissions: Publishes 12 titles per year; receives 300 submissions annually. First-time authors: 25%. Length: 128–244 pages. Email or mail proposal with sample chapters or a query. Responds in three to six months. Bible: NRSV.

Genres and topics: African-American, Asian, Christian education, Christian living/spirituality, discipleship, Hispanic, history, ministry, church resources, devotionals, ministry resources

Royalty: 10–15%, sometimes gives advance

First print run: 2,500

Types of books: ebook, offset paperback, POD

Guidelines: *www.judsonpress.com/Pages/Info/For-Authors.aspx*

Tip: "Most open to practical books that are unique and compelling, for a clearly defined niche audience. Theologically and socially we are a moderate publisher. And we like to see a detailed marketing plan from an author committed to partnering with us."

KREGEL PUBLICATIONS

2450 Oak Industrial Dr. NE, Grand Rapids, MI 49505 | 616-451-4775
KPacquisitions@kregel.com | *www.kregel.com*
Rachel Kirsch, managing editor

Mission statement: to develop and distribute—with integrity and excellence—trusted, biblically based resources that lead individuals to know and serve Jesus Christ

Submissions: Only agent, *ChristianBookProposals.com*, Writers Edge, or conference contact.

Genres and topics: Bible study, biography, Christian living/spirituality, church life, contemporary issues, discipleship, family, marriage, ministry, parenting, theology, women, Bible reference/commentaries, Bible studies, children, devotionals, teen/YA; fiction: historical, romance, romantic suspense, teen/YA

Guidelines: *www.kregel.com/contact-us/submissions-policy*

LEAFWOOD PUBLISHERS

1694 Campus Ct., ACU Box 29138, Abilene, TX 79699 | 325-674-2720
jason.fikes@acu.edu | *www.leafwoodpublishers.com*
Jason Fikes, director

Denomination: Church of Christ

Parent company: Abilene Christian University

Mission statement: to inspire fresh and deeper conversations about faith and life one book at a time

Submissions: Publishes 20 titles per year; receives 200 submissions annually. First-time authors: 40%. Length: 50,000 words. Agent preferred. Submit to *ChristianBookProposals.com,* or send proposal with sample chapters through the website. Responds in at least six months. Bible: NIV.

Genres and topics: Bible studies, Christian living/spirituality, ministry, spiritual formation, spiritual growth, theology, women's interests

Royalty: negotiated based on experience, gives advance that also is negotiated based on experience

First print run: 1,500

Types of books: ebook, hardcover, offset paperback

Guidelines: *store.acupressbooks.com/pages/author-resources*

Tip: "We enhance diverse and innovative authors (neurotypicals and those who are more atypical, age, gender, race, Christian tradition). Our audience is university based (Christian higher education) and lay people. Fresh conversations require innovation, creativity, love, courage, humility, gentleness, hospitality, freedom, and grace. We talk a lot about being practical. Practical means 'Will this book inspire fresh and deep conversations about faith and life?'"

LEXHAM PRESS

1313 Commercial St., Bellingham, WA 98225

thains@lexhampress.com | *www.lexhampress.com*

Todd Hains, associate publisher, acquisitions and development

Parent company: FaithLife Corporation, makers of Logos Bible Software

Mission statement: to increase biblical literacy, thoughtful Christian reflection, and faithful action around the world by publishing a range of Bible study materials, scholarly works, and pastoral resources

Submissions: Submit proposal with sample chapters through the website. Responds in eight weeks or not interested. Publishes innovative resources for Logos Bible Software.

Genres and topics: Bible study, ministry, theology, academic, Bible reference/commentaries, children

Types of books: ebook, hardcover, paperback

Guidelines: *www.lexhampress.com/manuscript-submission*

LIGHTHOUSE PUBLISHING

754 Roxholly Walk, Buford, CA 30518 | 770-709-2268

info@lighthousechristianpublishing.com | *lighthousechristianpublishing.com*

Andy Overett, president

Parent company: Lighthouse eMedia and eMusic

Mission statement: to provide high-quality original works at the least possible prices

Submissions: Publishes 30 titles per year; receives 200 submissions annually. First-time authors: 80%. Length: fiction, 300–320 pages. Email proposal with complete manuscript. Responds in four to six weeks. Bible: NASB.

Genres and topics: all topics, fiction, nonfiction, African-American, Hispanic

Royalty: 50%, no advance

Types of books: audiobook, ebook, POD

Guidelines: *lighthouseebooks.com/custom.html*

Tip: Looking for unique stories.

LIGUORI PUBLICATIONS

1 Liguori Dr., Liguori, MO 63057–9999 | 800–325–9521

manuscript_submission@liguori.org | www.liguori.org

Denomination: Catholic

Mission statement: to be the leading provider of Roman Catholic publications for every stage of faith and life in an ever-changing world

Submissions: No simultaneous submissions. Submit proposal with sample chapters. Responds in 8–12 weeks.

Genres and topics: sacraments, saints, Bible studies, biography, devotionals

Guidelines: *www.liguori.org/submit-your-manuscript*

LITURGICAL PRESS

PO Box 7500, Collegeville, MN 56321–7500

submissions@litpress.org | www.litpress.org

Therese Ratliff, director

Denomination: Catholic

Mission statement: to cultivate and amplify texts and voices that deepen the faith and knowledge of a richly diverse Church

Submissions: Submit proposal with complete manuscript or sample chapters through the website. Responds in six weeks.

Genres and topics: Bible, liturgy, prayer, theology

Guidelines: *www.litpress.org/Authors/submit_manuscript*

LOVE INSPIRED

195 Broadway, 24th floor, New York, NY 10007 | 212-207-7900
www.LoveInspired.com
Tina James, executive editor, Love Inspired Suspense
Melissa Endlich, senior editor
Shana Asaro, editor

Parent company: Harlequin/HarperCollins Publishers
Mission statement: to uplift and inspire through stories
Submissions: Publishes 144 titles per year; receives 500–1,000 submissions annually. First-time authors: 15%. Length: 55,000 words. Agent not required. Submit complete manuscript through the website. Responds in three months. Bible: KJV.
Genres and topics: fiction: romance, romantic suspense
Royalty: on retail, gives advance
Types of books: mass-market paperback
Imprints: Love Inspired (contemporary romance), Love Inspired Suspense (contemporary romantic suspense)
Guidelines: *harlequin.submittable.com/submit*
Tip: "We're looking for compelling stories with engaging characters, a sustained conflict, and an emotionally satisfying romance."

LOYOLA PRESS

8770 W. Bryn Mawr Ave., Chicago, IL 60631-3515 | 773-281-1818
submissions@loyolapress.com | *www.loyolapress.com*
Gary Jansen, director and executive editor, acquisitions

Denomination: Catholic
Mission statement: to create books and multimedia products that facilitate transformative experiences of God so that people of all ages can lead holy and purposeful lives with and for others
Submissions: Publishes 20 titles per year; receives 500 submissions annually. Length: 25,000–75,000 words/150–300 pages. Email or mail query. Responds in four to six weeks. Bible: NRSV (Catholic Edition).
Genres and topics: Catholicism, Christian living/spirituality
Royalty: gives advance
Types of books: paperback
Guidelines: *www.loyolapress.com/general/submissions*
Tip: "Looking for books and authors that help make Catholic faith relevant and offer practical tools for the well-lived spiritual life."

MOODY PUBLISHERS

820 N. LaSalle Blvd., Chicago, IL 60610 | 800-678-8812
submissions@moody.edu | www.moodypublishers.com
Trillia Newbell, acquisitions director
John Hinkley, acquisitions editor, marriage, family, parenting, workplace, church
Catherine Strode Parks, acquisitions editor, issues, Christian life, middle grade

Parent company: Moody Bible Institute

Mission statement: to resource the church's work of discipling all people

Submissions: Publishes 50 titles per year; receives thousands of submissions annually. First-time authors: 20%. Length: depends on genre. Agent preferred, conference contact a plus. Email proposal with sample chapters. Responds in six to eight weeks.

Genres and topics: Christian living/spirituality, counseling, leadership, women, Bible studies, devotionals, middle grade

Royalty: gives advance

Types of books: audiobook, ebook, hardcover, offset paperback

Guidelines: *www.moodypublishers.com/About/faq/submitting-proposals*

Tip: "Please review our website to see the latest books to help determine what we are looking for."

MOUNTAIN BROOK FIRE

submissions@fire.mountainbrookink.com | fire.mountainbrookink.com
Alyssa Roat, managing editor

Parent company: Mountain Brook Ink

Mission statement: to publish quality worldbuilding, spellbinding plots, and high-stakes adventures with a whole lot of heart for middle grade, young adult, and adult audiences

Submissions: Length: middle grade, 50,000–65,000 words; YA, 75,000–100,000 words; adult, 80,000–120,000 words. Conference contact only. Responds in two months. Bible: KJV, NKJV, NIV.

Genres and topics: fiction: middle grade, YA, fantasy, science fiction, speculative, steampunk, superhero, supernatural

Royalty: 30–40%, gives advance of $25

Types of books: audiobook, ebook, POD

Guidelines: *fire.mountainbrookink.com/submission-guidelines*

Tip: "Manuscripts need not be explicitly 'Christian'; we are equally happy with general market. However, we're looking for fiction that is clean. Books having a Christian worldview without having a faith thread will work as well."

MOUNTAIN BROOK INK

submissions@mountainbrookink.com | *www.mountainbrookink.com*
Miralee Ferrell, publisher and lead acquisitions editor

Mission statement: to publish fiction you can believe in that embodies restoration and/or renewal

Submissions: Publishes 12 titles per year; receives 50+ submissions annually. First-time authors: 75%. Length: minimum 75,000 words. Email proposal with sample chapters or a query. Responds in two months. Bible: KJV, NKJV, NIV.

Genres and topics: fiction: biblical, contemporary, historical, mystery, romance, romantic suspense, suspense/thriller, women's

Royalty: 30–40%, gives advance of $25

Types of books: audiobook, ebook, POD

Imprint: Mountain Brook Fire (speculative fiction)

Guidelines: *mountainbrookink.com/submission-guidelines-for-inquiries*

Tip: "Send the best work you've done, preferably that's been edited so it shines."

MT ZION RIDGE PRESS

295 Gum Springs Rd. NW, Georgetown, TN 37336 | 423-458-4256
mtzionridgepress@gmail.com | *mtzionridgepress.com*
Tamera Lynn Kraft, managing editor

Mission statement: to publish Christian fiction off the beaten path and Christian nonfiction for those who want to go deeper in their faith

Submissions: Publishes 12–15 titles per year; receives 30 submissions annually. First-time authors: 70%. Length: 60,000–100,000 words. Agent not required, conference contact a plus. Email query first. Responds in two to three months. Bible: NIV, NKJV, ESV, NLT, KJV.

Genres and topics: Christian living/spirituality, Bible studies, children, devotionals; fiction: fantasy, historical, mystery, romance, romantic suspense, science fiction, speculative, suspense/thriller, teen/YA, westerns, women's

Royalty: 30%, no advance

Types of books: audiobook, ebook, offset paperback, POD

Guidelines: *www.mtzionridgepress.com/about*

Tip: "Submit stellar writing."

MY HEALTHY CHURCH

1445 N. Boonville Ave., Springfield, MO 65802 | 417-831-8000
newproducts@myhealthychurch.com | *www.myhealthychurch.com*

Denomination: Assemblies of God

Parent company: Gospel Publishing House

Mission statement: to equip believers and church leaders who seek a healthy, Spirit-empowered life

Submissions: Agent only. Responds in two to three months.

Genres and topics: Christian living/spirituality, church leadership, discipleship, leadership, ministry, academic, Bible studies, church resources

Types of books: ebook, hardcover, paperback

Guidelines: *myhealthychurch.com/store/startcat.cfm?cat=tWRITGUID*

Tip: "The content of all our books and resources must be compatible with the beliefs and purposes of the Assemblies of God."

NAVPRESS

3820 N. 30th St., Colorado Springs, CO 80904

inquiries@navpress.com | www.navpress.com

Deborah Gonzalez, acquisitions and developmental editor

Caitlyn Carlson, senior editor

Parent company: The Navigators

Mission statement: to support readers as they know Christ, make Him known, and help others do the same

Submissions: Publishes 20 titles per year; receives 1,000 submissions annually. First-time authors: 40%. Length: 40,000 words. Only agent or author referral. Responds in two months.

Genres and topics: Christian living/spirituality, discipleship, leadership, practical theology, prayer, spiritual growth, women, Bible studies

Royalty: 16–22%, gives advance

Guidelines: *www.navpress.com/faq*

Tip: "Proposals with strong discipleship elements are preferred. Authors should have a ministry platform that supports their discipleship elements. NavPress does not accept unsolicited manuscripts."

NELSON BOOKS

PO Box 141000, Nashville, TN 37214-1000 | 615-889-9000

www.thomasnelson.com/nelsonbooks

Hanha Parham, acquisitions editor

Parent company: Thomas Nelson Publishers/HarperCollins Christian Publishing

Mission statement: to publish biblically informed books from a Christian perspective that enhance the spiritual and personal growth

of our readers
Submissions: Agent only.
Genres and topics: biography, business, Christian living/spirituality, leadership, spiritual growth, devotionals
Types of books: audiobook, ebook, hardcover, offset paperback
Guidelines: not available

NEW GROWTH PRESS

PO Box 4485, Greensboro, NC 27404 | 336-378-7775
submissions@newgrowthpress.com | *www.newgrowthpress.com*
Rush Witt, acquisitions editor and manager

Mission statement: to reach every church and home with gospel-centered resources that point to Jesus and help every person grow closer to Christ
Submissions: Email proposal with sample chapters. Responds in six weeks or not interested.
Genres and topics: Christian living/spirituality, counseling, family, parenting, relationships, Bible studies, children, devotionals, fiction, teen/YA
Types of books: audiobook, ebook, paperback
Guidelines: *newgrowthpress.com/manuscript-submissions*
Tip: "Manuscript submissions must follow the downloadable, standard New Growth Press template."

NEW LIFE PUBLISHING HOUSE

admin@newlifepublishinghouse.life | *newlifepublishinghouse.life*
Tassyane Assis, publisher

Mission statement: to do more than publish books, to help authors build their legacies
Submissions: First-time authors: 100%. Length: 30,000–50,000 words. Email or mail proposal with sample chapters, or use the website form. Conference contact a plus. No agents. Responds in two to four weeks. Offers writing coaching for new writers who do not know how to get started. Also publishes general-market books that add value to readers as long as they do not contradict the Bible in any way.
Genres and topics: Christian living/spirituality, family, finances, marriage, parenting, psychology, self-help, devotionals
Royalty: 70%, no advance
Types of books: audiobook, ebook, hardcover, offset paperback,

POD

Guidelines: available via email

Tip: "Writing a book and getting it published with the right people is more than about the money. It's about the legacy you are leaving behind."

NORTHWESTERN PUBLISHING HOUSE

N16W23379 Stone Ridge Dr., Waukesha, WI 53188–1108 | 800–662–6022

submissions@nph.wels.net | *online.nph.net*

John Braun

Denomination: Wisconsin Evangelical Lutheran Synod

Mission statement: to deliver biblically sound, Christ-centered resources within the Wisconsin Evangelical Lutheran Synod and beyond

Submissions: Email or mail proposal with sample chapters.

Genres and topics: family, history, theology, Bible reference/commentaries, devotionals

Types of books: hardcover, paperback

Guidelines: *online.nph.net/manuscript-submission*

Tip: "We are always looking for new and exciting Bible-based materials to publish!"

OLIVIA KIMBRELL PRESS

PO Box 4452, Winchester, KY 40392 | 859-577-1071

submissions@oliviakimbrellpress.com | *oliviakimbrellpress.com*

Gregg Bridgeman, editor-in-chief

Mission statement: to uplift fellow believers and encourage seekers in this fallen world

Submissions: Publishes 10–20 titles per year; receives 80–100 submissions annually. First-time authors: 10%. Length: 80,000 words maximum. Agent preferred, conference contact a plus. Email or mail proposal with sample chapters. No simultaneous submissions. Responds in two months. Bible: KJV, NKJV. Specializes in true-to-life, meaningful Christian fiction and nonfiction titles intended to uplift the heart and engage the mind. Primary focus on "Roman Road" small-group guides or reader's guides to accompany nonfiction and fiction and fiction stories of suspense, intrigue, or family sagas with an inspirational or romantic theme.

Genres and topics: Christian living/spirituality, health, marriage, devotionals, teen/YA; fiction: fantasy, romance, romantic suspense, science fiction, suspense/thriller

Royalty: 50%, sometimes gives advance of $300-2,000

Types of books: audiobook, ebook, hardcover, POD
Imprints: Sign of the Whale (biblical and speculative fiction), House of Bread (nutrition)
Guidelines: *oliviakimbrellpress.com*
Tip: "No westerns."

OUR DAILY BREAD PUBLISHING

3000 Kraft Ave. SE, Grand Rapids, MI 49507 | 616-974-2210
ourdailybreadpublishing.org
Dawn Anderson, executive editor and acquisitions
Katara Patton, executive editor, VOICES
Joel Armstrong, content editor and acquisitions
   Parent company: Our Daily Bread Ministries
   Mission statement: to feed the soul with the Word of God
   Submissions: Publishes 24–36 titles per year; receives 100 submissions annually. First-time authors: fewer than 10%. Length: approximately 192 pages. Prefers agent or conference contact. Responds in three months. Bible: NIV, NLT, ESV.
   Genres and topics: African-American, Asian, Bible study, Christian living/spirituality, contemporary issues, Hispanic, men, pop reference, prayer, social issues, women, Bible studies, children, devotionals
   Royalty: 12–18%, no advance
   First print run: 3,000–50,000
   Types of books: audiobook, board books, ebook, hardcover, offset paperback
   Imprint: VOICES Collection (primarily African-Americans)
   Guidelines: not available
   Tip: "We look for strong, Bible-based content with practical application for everyday living."

OUR SUNDAY VISITOR, INC.

200 Noll Plaza, Huntington, IN 46750-4303 | 260-356-8400
www.osv.com
Scott Richert, publisher
   Denomination: Catholic
   Mission statement: to help Catholics fulfill their calling to discipleship, strengthen their relationship with Christ, deepen their commitment to the Church, and contribute to its growth and vitality in the world
   Submissions: Publishes 30–40 titles per year; receives 500 submissions annually. First-time authors: 10%. No simultaneous submissions.

Query first through the website. Responds in 8-10 weeks. Actively seeking submissions for children: board books for infants and toddlers, picture books for younger readers (ages 3-6), short chapter books for middle-grade readers (ages 7-10), and works of interest to tweens and young teens.

Genres and topics: apologetics, biography, Christian living/spirituality, church life, culture, evangelism, family, history, marriage, ministry, parenting, prayer, children, devotionals, prayer guides

Royalty: 10-12%, gives advance of $1,500

Types of books: board books, ebook, hardcover, paperback, picture books

Imprint: OSV Kids (children and teens)

Guidelines: *osv.submittable.com/submit*

Tip: "All books published must relate to the Catholic Church; unique books aimed at our audience. Give as much background information as possible on author qualification, why the topic was chosen, and unique aspects of the project. Follow our guidelines. We are expanding our religious-education product line and programs."

P&R PUBLISHING

1102 Marble Hill Rd., PO Box 817, Phillipsburg, NJ 08865 | 908-454-0505

acquisitions@prpbooks.com | www.prpbooks.com

Joy Woo, acquisitions and development editor

David Almack, director of acquisitions

Melissa Craig, children's editor

Denomination: Reformed

Mission statement: to publish excellent books that promote biblical understanding and godly living as summarized in the Westminster Confession of Faith and Catechisms

Submissions: Publishes 35-40 titles per year; receives 300 submissions annually. First-time authors: 10%. Length: 150-200 pages. Agent not required. Email proposal with sample chapters. Responds in three months. Bible: ESV.

Genres and topics: Christian living/spirituality, counseling, family, marriage, theology, women, academic, children, church resources, devotionals, teen/YA

Royalty: 12-14%, gives advance

First print run: 3,000-5,000

Types of books: audiobook, ebook, hardcover, offset paperback

Guidelines: *www.prpbooks.com/manuscript-submissions*

Tip: "We are looking for content from a Reformed theological perspective."

PACIFIC PRESS

1350 N. Kings Rd., Nampa, ID 83687 | 208-465-2500
booksubmissions@pacificpress.com | www.pacificpress.com
Scott Cady, acquisitions editor

Denomination: Seventh-day Adventist

Parent company: Seventh-day Adventist Church

Mission statement: to provide readers with a wide variety of books that connect them with God and help them develop a relationship with Him; provide information about God, His character, and His ways; and encourage and uplift them in the struggles of life

Submissions: Publishes 35-40 titles per year; receives 500 submissions annually. First-time authors: 5%. Length: 40,000-90,000 words/128-320 pages. Email query first. Responds in one to three weeks.

Genres and topics: Bible study, biography, Christian living/spirituality, contemporary issues, health, history, marriage, memoir/personal narrative, parenting, prayer, theology, children; fiction: end-times, historical

Royalty: 12-16%, gives advance of $1,500

Types of books: ebook, hardcover, paperback, picture books

Guidelines: *www.pacificpress.com/authors___artists/books*

Tip: "Most open to spirituality, inspirational, and Christian living. Our website has the most up-to-date information, including samples of recent publications. For more information, see *www. adventistbookcenter.com*. Do not send full manuscript unless we request it after reviewing your proposal."

PARACLETE PRESS

PO Box 1568, Orleans, MA 02653-1568 | 508-255-4685
submissions@paracletepress.com | www.paracletepress.com
Robert Edmonson, editor
Michelle Rich, editor

Denomination: Catholic, Protestant

Submissions: Publishes 40 titles per year. Only agents or author with Paraclete relationship. Responds in one month.

Genres and topics: Advent/Christmas picture books, Christian living/spirituality, grief, Lent/Easter picture books, prayer, children; fiction: contemporary, fantasy, horror, science fiction

Imprint: Raven (fiction)
Guidelines: *www.paracletepress.com/pages/submission-guidelines*

PARAKLESIS PRESS

113 Winn Ct., Waleska, GA 30183 | 404-274-8615
submissions@paraklesispress.com | *ParaklesisPress.com*
Sally Apokedak, editor

Mission statement: to delight children with fun language; smart, humble, comical, relatable characters; charming illustrations; and exciting plots, all while also giving these young minds plenty of food for thought

Submissions: Publishes four titles per year; receives 75 submissions annually. First-time authors: 50%. Length: 32–400 pages. Email proposal with complete manuscript. Responds in three months. Bible: ESV.

Genres and topics: children: picture books, contemporary, fantasy, mystery

Royalty: 10–50%, gives advance

Types of books: POD hardcover and paperback

Guidelines: *paraklesispress.com/submit-to-us*

Tip: "Write something interesting and entertaining that doesn't need a ton of editing and that is not offensive to Christians and you'll have a good chance of getting published here."

PARSONS PUBLISHING HOUSE, LLC

PO Box 410063, Melbourne, FL 32941 | 850-867-3061
info@parsonspublishinghouse.com | *www.parsonspublishinghouse.com*
Diane Parsons, owner and senior editor

Mission statement: to allow authors' voices to be heard as they lift up the name of Jesus Christ

Submissions: Publishes four to six titles per year; receives 20 submissions annually. First-time authors: 35%. Length: 40,000 words. Email proposal. No agents. Responds in three to four weeks. Bible: NKJV, ESV.

Genres and topics: Christian living/spirituality, spiritual growth

Royalty: 10%, no advance

Types of books: ebook, hardcover, offset paperback, POD

Guidelines: available via email

Tip: "Use scriptural teachings that point to the good news of the Gospel of Christ (uplifting/positive)."

PAULINE BOOKS & MEDIA

50 Saint Paul's Ave., Boston, MA 02130-3491 | 617-522-8911
editorial@paulinemedia.com | pauline.org

Denomination: Catholic
Parent company: Daughters of St. Paul
Mission statement: to be a trusted provider of excellent Catholic content that nurtures families and individuals to integrate their faith with their everyday lives
Submissions: Publishes 25 titles per year; receives 300 submissions annually. First-time authors: 12%. Agent not required. Email proposal with complete manuscript or sample chapters. Responds in six to eight weeks. Bible: NRSV.
Genres and topics: Christian living/spirituality, evangelism, family, prayer, spiritual formation, theology, board books, devotionals, fiction, first-chapter, graphic novels, middle grade, picture books, teen/YA
Royalty: 5-10%, gives advance
First print run: varies
Types of books: ebook, hardcover, offset paperback
Guidelines: *pauline.org/publishing*

PAULIST PRESS

997 Macarthur Blvd., Mahwah, NJ 07430-9990
submissions@paulistpress.com | www.paulistpress.com
Paul McMahon, editorial director
Donna Crilly, senior academic editor

Denomination: Catholic
Mission statement: to publish quality materials that bring the good news of the Gospel to Catholics and people of other religious traditions; support dialogue and welcome good scholarship and religious wisdom from all sources across denominational boundaries; foster religious values and wholeness in society, especially through materials promoting healing, reconciliation, and personal growth
Submissions: Email or mail proposal with sample chapters. Responds in six to eight weeks.
Genres and topics: academic, children
Types of books: ebook, paperback
Guidelines: *www.paulistpress.com/Pages/Center/auth_res_0.aspx*

PELICAN BOOK GROUP

Harbourlight Books, Prism Book Group, Pure Amore, Watershed Books, White Rose Publishing

THE PILGRIM PRESS

1300 E. 9th St. #1100, Cleveland, OH 44114 | 216-736-3875
proposals@thepilgrimpress.com | *thepilgrimpress.com*
Kathryn Martin, acquisitions editor

Denomination: United Church of Christ
Parent company: United Church of Christ
Mission statement: to publish books that nurture spiritual growth, cultivate religious leadership, and provoke the soul for the sake of a just world
Submissions: Email proposal with sample chapters. Reviewed on a quarterly basis.
Genres and topics: Christian living/spirituality, leadership, prayer, preaching, theology, Bible studies, biography, memoir, ministry resources
Types of books: paperback
Guidelines: *thepilgrimpress.com/pages/acquisitions*
Tip: "We do not publish Christian fiction or anti-LGBTQ commentaries."

PRAYERSHOP PUBLISHING

11969 E. Davis Ave., Brazil, IN 47834 | 812-238-5504
jon@prayershop.org | *prayershop.org*
Jonathan Graf, publisher

Parent company: Church Prayer Leaders Network
Mission statement: to take readers deeper in their prayer relationship with Jesus Christ and help churches become houses of prayer by discipling and equipping individuals in the aspects of prayer
Submissions: Publishes four to six titles per year; receives 15 submissions annually. First-time authors: 15%. Length: maximum 35,000 words. Agent not required. Email proposal with sample chapters. Responds in six weeks. Bible: NIV.
Genres and topics: prayer, children, prayer guides, teen/YA
Royalty: 10-15%, no advance
First print run: 3,500
Types of books: ebook, offset paperback, POD
Guidelines: *www.prayerleader.com/prayershop-publishing/submissions*

Tip: "We love books that can be used for a 21-day, 30-day, or 40-day prayer initiative by a congregation. We look most seriously at authors who have an audience, whether online or through speaking, or authors who will buy a quantity of books from the first press run."

PRISM BOOK GROUP

PO Box 1738, Aztec, NM 87410

customer@prismbookgroup.com | www.prismbookgroup.com
Jacqueline Hopper, acquisitions editor; jhopper@prismbookgroup.com
Paula Mowery, acquisitions editor; pmowery@prismbookgroup.com

Parent company: Pelican Book Group
Mission statement: to publish quality books that reflect the salvation and love offered by Jesus Christ
Submissions: Length: 25,000–80,000 words. Query first, then submit proposal with sample chapters through the website. Responds in three to four months. Bible: NIV, NAB.
Genres and topics: fiction: contemporary, fantasy, historical, mystery, romance, romantic suspense, science fiction, suspense/thriller, teen/YA
Royalty: 40% download, 7% print; sometimes gives advance
Types of books: ebook, POD
Imprints: Prism Lux (Christian), Prism CW (clean and wholesome)
Guidelines: *pelicanbookgroup.com/ec/index.php?main_page=page&id=76*
Tip: "Our books offer clean and compelling reads for the discerning reader. We will not publish graphic language or content and look for well-written, emotionally charged stories, intense plots, and captivating characters."

PURE AMORE

PO Box 1738, Aztec, NM 87410
customer@pelicanbookgroup.com | pelicanbookgroup.com
Nicola Martinez, editor-in-chief

Parent company: Pelican Book Group
Mission statement: to publish quality books that reflect the salvation and love offered by Jesus Christ
Submissions: Length: 40,000–45,000 words. Submit proposal with sample chapters through the website. Responds in one to four months. Only contemporary Christian romance. Pure Amore romances are sweet in tone and conflict. These stories are the emotionally driven tales of youthful Christians between the ages

of 21 and 33 who are striving to live their faith in a world where Christ-centered choices may not fully be understood.

Genres and topics: fiction: romance

Royalty: 40% download, 7% print; sometimes gives advance

Types of books: ebook, POD

Guidelines: *pelicanbookgroup.com/ec/index.php?main_page=page&id=69*

Tip: "Pure Amore romances emphasize the beauty in chastity, so physical interactions, such as kissing or hugging, should focus on the characters' emotions, rather than heightened sexual desire; and scenes of physical intimacy should be integral to the plot and/or emotional development of the character or relationship."

RESOURCE PUBLICATIONS

199 W. 8th Ave., Ste. 3, Eugene, OR 97401 | 541-344-1528

proposal@wipfandstock.com | *wipfandstock.com/search-results/?imprint=resource-publications*

Parent company: Wipf and Stock

Submissions: Email proposal with sample chapters. Responds in one to two months.

Genres and topics: biography, fiction, poetry, sermons

Types of books: ebook, POD

Guidelines: *wipfandstock.com/submitting-a-proposal*

RESURRECTION PRESS

77 West End Rd., Totowa, NJ 07572 | 973-890-2400

info@catholicbookpublishing.com | *www.catholicbookpublishing.com*

Anthony Buono, editor

Denomination: Catholic

Parent company: Catholic Book Publishing Corp.

Submissions: Mail proposal with sample chapters. Responds in four to six weeks.

Genres and topics: Christian living/spirituality, healing, ministry, prayer

Royalty: negotiable, no advance

Guidelines: *catholicbookpublishing.com/pages/faq*

REVELL

6030 E. Fulton Rd., Ada, MI 49301 | 616-676-9185

bakerpublishinggroup.com/revell

Andrea Doering, editorial director
Kelsey Bowen, senior acquisitions editor
Grace Cho, senior acquisitions editor

Parent company: Baker Publishing Group
Mission statement: to publish practical books that will help bring the Christian faith to everyday life
Submissions: Only agent, *ChristianBookProposals.com*, or conference contact.
Genres and topics: apologetics, Bible study, biography, Christian living/spirituality, church life, culture, family, marriage, memoir/personal narrative, children, fiction, teen/YA
Types of books: ebook, hardcover, mass-market paperback, offset paperback

ROSE PUBLISHING

PO Box 3473, Peabody, MA 01961 | 800-358-3111
lpennings@tyndale.com | *www.hendricksonrose.com*
Lynette Pennings, managing editor

Parent company: Hendrickson Publishing Group/Tyndale House Ministries
Mission statement: to make the Bible and its teachings easy to understand
Genres and topics: Bible, Bible reference/commentaries, wall charts
Types of books: hardcover, paperback

ROSEKIDZ

PO Box 3473, Peabody, MA 01961 | 800-358-3111
kmcgraw@tyndale.com | *www.hendricksonrose.com*
Karen McGraw, senior acquisitions editor

Parent company: Hendrickson Publishing Group/Tyndale House Ministries
Mission statement: to help kids grow closer to God in a hands-on way
Submissions: Email manuscript.
Genres and topics: activities and puzzles, children, crafts, devotionals, fiction
Types of books: board books, hardcover, offset paperback, PDF download

SALEM BOOKS

122 C St. NW, Ste. 515, Washington, DC 20001
kathyrn.riggs@salembooks.com | *www.regnery.com/custom/salem-books*

Kathyrn Riggs, senior acquisitions editor

Parent company: Good Books/Skyhorse Publishing

Mission statement: to help people grow in their faith and find comfort, encouragement, practical advice, and timeless wisdom in compelling books by trusted authors

Submissions: Agent only. All new books will be published under the Good Books imprint of Skyhorse Publishing.

Genres and topics: apologetics, Christian living/spirituality, culture, end-times prophecy, family, leadership, memoir/personal narrative, men, spiritual formation, spiritual growth, women, women's issues, worldview, biography, devotionals

Types of books: ebook, paperback

Tip: Especially interested in books by female and minority authors.

SCRIVENINGS PRESS, LLC

15 Lucky Ln., Morrilton, AR 72110 | 501-289-9319

scriveningspress@gmail.com | *scriveningspress.com*

Linda Fulkerson, owner and publisher

Erin R. Howard (for speculative submissions only), expansebooks@gmail.com

Mission statement: to publish clean and/or Christian fiction

Submissions: Publishes 40 titles per year; receives 100 submissions annually. First-time authors: 20%. Length: 60,000–90,000 words. Agent not required. Conference contact, or email proposal with sample chapters. Responds in four to six weeks. Bible: any.

Genres and topics: devotionals, fiction, middle-grade fiction, nonfiction, YA fiction: any except horror

Royalty: no advance

Types of books: POD

Imprints: Scrivenings Press (general fiction), Expanse Books (speculative fiction), ScrivKids (upper middle grade), ScrivInspire (devotionals)

Guidelines: *scriveningspress.com/submissions*

Tip: "Polish your manuscript before submitting it. It's a good idea to read it out loud and correct any errors. Get feedback from beta readers. And read widely in your genre, as well as outside your genre, to keep up with trends in the Christian publishing industry."

SCRIVKIDS

15 Lucky Ln., Morrilton, AR 72110 | 501-289-9319

scriveningspress@gmail.com | *scrivkids.com*

Linda Fulkerson, owner and acquisitions editor

Parent company: Scrivenings Press, LLC

Mission statement: to spread God's word through our writing

Submissions: Publishes two or three titles per year; receives 100 submissions annually. First-time authors: 30%. Length: 30,000–50,000 words. Agent not required, conference contact a plus. Email proposal with sample chapters through the website. Responds in four to six weeks. Bible: any.

Genres and topics: fiction: middle grade

Royalty: 12% print, 50% ebook, 40% pages read in Kindle Unlimited; no advance

Types of books: ebook, hardcover, POD

Guidelines: *scriveningspress.com/submissions*

Tip: "We are a small publishing house, and we try to keep a family feel among our staff and authors. We encourage all our authors to encourage one another and to cross-promote books from other authors within our company."

SMYTH & HELWYS BOOKS

6316 Peake Rd., Macon, GA 31210-3960 | 478-757-0564

proposal@helwys.com | *www.helwys.com*

Leslie Andres, editor

Mission statement: to contribute to the life and ministry of the church and provide a bridge between the church and the academy

Submissions: Email or mail proposal with sample chapters. Responds in several weeks.

Genres and topics: Bible study, Christian living/spirituality, leadership, ministry

Types of books: ebook, hardcover, paperback

Guidelines: *www.helwys.com/submit-a-manuscript*

THOMAS NELSON FICTION

PO Box 141000, Nashville, TN 37214-1000 | 615-889-9000

www.thomasnelson.com/fiction

Becky Monds, editorial director

Laura Wheeler, acquisitions editor

Kimberly Carlton, acquisitions editor

Parent company: Thomas Nelson Publishers/HarperCollins Christian Publishing

Mission statement: to inspire the world by meeting the needs of people with content that promotes biblical principles and honors

Jesus Christ

Submissions: Agent only.

Genres and topics: fiction: Amish, contemporary, historical, humor, mystery, romance, suspense/thriller

Types of books: audiobook, ebook, offset paperback

Guidelines: not available

Tip: "What we are looking for: great writers who are passionate about their stories, a willingness to work hard and engage with readers— coupled with a true love of readers—a unique angle on or a unique connection to their story matter, a great attitude."

THOMAS NELSON GIFT

PO Box 141000, Nashville, TN 37214-1000 | 615-889-9000

www.thomasnelson.com/gift

Adria Haley, senior acquisitions editor

Jessica Lamb, acquisitions editor

Parent company: Thomas Nelson Publishers/HarperCollins Christian Publishing

Mission statement: to inspire the world by meeting the needs of people with content that promotes biblical principles and honors Jesus Christ

Submissions: Agent only.

Genres and topics: devotionals, gift

Types of books: ebook, hardcover, offset paperback

Guidelines: not available

Tip: "A gift book is designed to be shared. It's a beautiful keepsake that makes an ideal gift, a way to mark a special occasion or holiday, a message of the heart; and it usually satisfies a strong felt need. Gift books are as much an experience as a collection of words to be read."

THOMAS NELSON PUBLISHERS

Emanate Books, Grupo Nelson, Nelson Books, Thomas Nelson Fiction, Thomas Nelson Gift, Tommy Nelson, W Publishing

TOMMY NELSON

PO Box 141000, Nashville, TN 37214-1000 | 615-889-9000

www.tommynelson.com

Bri Gallagher, acquisitions editor

Parent company: Thomas Nelson Publishers/HarperCollins Christian Publishing

Mission statement: to expand children's imaginations and nurture their faith while pointing them to a personal relationship with God

Submissions: Only agent or conference contact.

Genres and topics: Bible storybooks, board books, devotionals, first-chapter, middle grade, picture books

Types of books: board books, hardcover, offset paperback, picture books

TORCHBEARER PRESS

PO Box 306190, Nashville, TN 37230 | 877-474-2693

Torchbearer@rhboyd.com | *rhboyd.com/pages/author-services*

David Groves, director of publications

Denomination: Baptist

Parent company: R.H. Boyd

Mission statement: to provide educational, inspirational, and culturally relevant content

Submissions: Agent not required. Email proposal with sample chapters.

Genres and topics: African-American, Bible study, biography, Christian living/spirituality, marriage, Bible studies, children, coloring books, ministry resources, puzzles and activities

Types of books: ebook, hardcover, paperback

Guidelines: *rhboyd.com/pages/author-services*

Tip: "We are a small publishing company that extends consideration to unknown and previously unpublished authors."

THE TRINITY FOUNDATION

PO Box 68, Unicoi, TN 37692 | 423-743-0199

tjtrinityfound@aol.com | *www.trinityfoundation.org*

Thomas W. Juodaitis, president

Mission statement: to promote the Christian religion

Submissions: Publishes two titles per year; receives 12 submissions annually. First-time authors: 10%. Length: 200 pages. Email or mail proposal. Responds in one month. Bible: KJV, NKJV.

Genres and topics: apologetics, philosophy, theology

Royalty: flat fee of $1,500 for theology and philosophy books, no advance

First print run: 500-1,000

Types of books: ebook, hardcover, offset paperback

Guidelines: available via email

Tip: "Familiarize yourself with the content on our website."

TULIP PUBLISHING

PO Box 3150, Lansvale, NSW 2166, Australia | +61 2 9055 2195
submissions@tulippublishing.com.au | *tulippublishing.com.au*
Brett Lee-Price, general manager

Denomination: Reformed
Mission statement: to equip the Church with resources that will help stretch and grow readers in their spiritual formulation, development, and knowledge
Submissions: Publishes four titles per year; receives 20 submissions annually. First-time authors: 40%. Length: 250–350 pages. Email proposal with sample chapters through the website. Responds in two to three months. Bible: ESV.
Genres and topics: Christian living/spirituality, theology
Royalty: 30–40%, no advance
First print run: 1,000
Types of books: ebook, hardcover, offset paperback
Guidelines: *tulippublishing.com.au/about/submissions*
Tip: "Be concise and succinct in your proposal; have your manuscript read and proofed by others, like family or friends, before submission."

TWENTY-THIRD PUBLICATIONS

977 Hartford Tpke., Waterford, CT 06385 | 800-321-0411
resources@twentythirdpublications.com

Denomination: Catholic
Parent company: Bayard, Inc.
Mission statement: to provide lifelong faith formation through wholistic catechesis at all stages of faith development
Submissions: Email proposal with sample chapters.
Genres and topics: Christian living/spirituality, Christmas, Easter, prayer, Bible studies, catechetical resources, children, church resources, devotionals, puzzles and activities, teen/YA
Types of books: paperback
Guidelines: *twentythirdpublications.com/pages/submissions*

TYNDALE HOUSE PUBLISHERS

351 Executive Dr., Carol Stream, IL 60188 | 630-668-8300
www.tyndale.com
Kara Leonino, acquisitions manager, nonfiction
Stephanie Broene, acquisitions director, fiction

Elizabeth Jackson, senior acquisitions editor, fiction

Jillian Schlossberg, senior acquisitions editor, nonfiction

Mission statement: to help readers discover the life-giving truths of God's Word

Submissions: Publishes 100+ titles per year. First-time authors: 5%. Length: fiction, 75,000–100,000. Only agent, author referral, or conference contact. Responds in three to six months. Bible: NLT.

Genres and topics: biography, Christian living/spirituality, counseling, family, finances, leadership, marriage, memoir/personal narrative, parenting, children, devotionals, teen/YA; fiction: biblical, contemporary, historical, mystery, romance, suspense/thriller

Types of books: audiobook, ebook, hardcover, offset paperback

Imprints: Tyndale Kids (children), Wander (YA), Tyndale Español (Spanish), Tyndale Refresh (health and wellness), Tyndale Elevate (Christian worldview topics and apologetics), Tyndale Momentum (nonfiction), Hendrickson Publishers (nonfiction), Rose Publishing (Bible study helps)

TYNDALE KIDS

351 Executive Dr., Carol Stream, IL 60188 | 630-668-8300

kidsandwandersubmissions@tyndale.com | *www.tyndale.com/kids*

Talia Messina, acquisitions editor

Parent company: Tyndale House Publishers

Mission statement: to bring kids and families closer to God through publishing books with excellent content, creative formats, and outstanding design

Submissions: Publishes 10–15 titles per year; receives 300–400 submissions annually. First-time authors: 5%. Length: varies according to the age group. Only agent or conference contact. Responds in two to three months. Bible: NLT.

Genres and topics: Bible stories, board books, devotionals, fiction, first-chapter, middle grade, nonfiction, picture books, teen/YA

Royalty: 10–24%; gives advance that varies according to platform, previous sales history, and uniqueness of proposal

Types of books: audiobook, ebook, hardcover, offset paperback, POD

Imprint: Wander (YA fiction and nonfiction)

Guidelines: not available

Tip: "Looking for a solid, well-written proposal; strong platform; excellent writing."

THE UPPER ROOM BOOKS

1908 Grand Ave., Nashville, TN 37212 | 800-972-0433
proposals@upperroom.org | *upperroombooks.com*
Michael S. Stephens, editorial director

Denomination: United Methodist
Parent company: The Upper Room
Mission statement: to encourage prayer and daily disciplines that help people create daily life with God
Submissions: Publishes 12 titles per year; receives 50 submissions annually. First-time authors: 50%. Length: 112-248 pages. Mail proposal with sample chapters. Responds only if interested. Bible: NRSV.
Genres and topics: Christian living/spirituality, culture, healing, leadership, Lent, relationships, spiritual formation, stewardship, church resources, devotionals, worship resources
Royalty: 10-15%, sometimes gives advance
Types of books: audiobook, ebook, hardcover, offset paperback, POD
Imprints: Fresh Air Books (spiritually curious people interested in the relevance of faith in our culture), Discipleship Resources (leadership and stewardship resources)
Guidelines: *upperroombooks.com/submissions*
Tip: "Upper Room Books encourage the use of inclusive language in reference to God and humanity."

W PUBLISHING

PO Box 141000, Nashville, TN 37214-1000 | 615-889-9000
www.thomasnelson.com/wpublishing
Kyle Olund, senior acquisitions editor
Lisa-Jo Baker, senior acquisitions editor

Parent company: Thomas Nelson Publishers/HarperCollins Christian Publishing
Submissions: Agent only.
Genres and topics: Christian living/spirituality, memoir/personal narrative
Types of books: audiobook, ebook, hardcover, offset paperback
Guidelines: not available
Tip: "W prides itself on the ability to provide authors a nurturing, faith-friendly, boutique style publishing experience."

WARNER PRESS

2902 Enterprise Dr., Anderson, IN 46013 | 765-644-7721

editors@warnerpress.org | *www.warnerpress.org*

Julie Campbell, product and acquisitions editor

Denomination: Church of God

Mission statement: to equip the church, to advance the Kingdom, and to give hope to future generations

Submissions: Publishes three to five titles per year; receives 50+ submissions annually. First-time authors: 50%. Email complete manuscript. Responds in six to eight weeks. Bible: KJV, NIV, ESV, NKJV.

Genres and topics: Bible studies, small-group resources, small-group study guides

Royalty: based on the author and type of book, sometimes gives advance

Types of books: ebook, offset paperback

Guidelines: *www.warnerpress.org/submission-guidelines*

Tip: "Do your research, and visit our website to view what we already produce."

WATERBROOK & MULTNOMAH

10807 New Allegiance Dr. #500, Colorado Springs, CO 80921 | 719-590-4999

info@waterbrookmultnomah.com | *www.waterbrookmultnomah.com*

Jamie Lapeyrolerie, acquisitions editor

Sara Rubio, executive editor, children's

Bunmi Ishola, children's editor and acquisitions

Drew Dixon, executive editor and acquisitions

Will Anderson, acquisitions editor

Parent company: The Crown Publishing Group/Penguin Random House

Submissions: Publishes 60 titles per year; receives 300 submissions annually. First-time authors: 15%. Length: 208-400 pages. Agent only. Responds in one to two months.

Genres and topics: Christian living/spirituality, home and lifestyle, memoir/personal narrative, relationships, spiritual growth, Bible studies, children, devotionals; fiction: Amish, historical, romantic suspense

Royalty: gives advance

Types of books: audiobook, ebook, hardcover, offset paperback, POD

Imprint: Ink & Willow (gifts)

Tip: "We recommend working with an agent whose clientele aligns with your strengths as a writer."

WATERSHED BOOKS
PO Box 1738, Aztec, NM 87410
customer@pelicanbookgroup.com | *www.pelicanbookgroup.com*
Nicola Martinez, editor-in-chief
- **Parent company:** Pelican Book Group
- **Mission statement:** to publish quality books that reflect the salvation and love offered by Jesus Christ
- **Submissions:** Length: 25,000–65,000 words. Submit proposal with sample chapters through the website. Responds in three to four months. Bible: NIV, NAB. Interested in series ideas.
- **Genres and topics:** fiction: teen/YA, adventure, coming-of-age, crime, mystery, romance, science fiction, supernatural, suspense, westerns
- **Royalty:** 40% on download, 7% on print; sometimes gives advance
- **Types of books:** POD
- **Guidelines:** *pelicanbookgroup.com/ec/index.php?main_page=page&id=60*
- **Tip:** "We want to see something other than dystopian."

WESTMINSTER JOHN KNOX PRESS
100 Witherspoon St., Louisville, KY 40202–1396
submissions@wjkbooks.com | *www.wjkbooks.com*
Jessica Miller Kelley, senior acquisitions editor
- **Denomination:** Presbyterian
- **Parent company:** Presbyterian Publishing Corporation
- **Submissions:** Publishes 60 titles per year. Email proposal with sample chapters. Responds in two to three months.
- **Genres and topics:** Bible study, culture, ethics, ministry, theology, worship, academic
- **Types of books:** hardcover, offset paperback
- **Imprints:** Flyaway Books (children), Geneva Press (Presbyterian Church USA)
- **Guidelines:** *www.wjkbooks.com/Pages/Item/1345/Author-Relations.aspx*

WHITAKER HOUSE
1030 Hunt Valley Cir., New Kensington, PA 15068 | 724-334-7000
www.whitakerhouse.com
Amy Bartlett, managing and acquisitions editor
- **Denomination:** Charismatic/Pentecostal
- **Parent company:** Whitaker Corporation
- **Mission statement:** to advance God's Kingdom by publishing biblically

focused authors who proclaim the power of the gospel and minister to the spiritual needs of people around the world

Submissions: Publishes 75–100 titles per year; receives 200 submissions annually. First-time authors: 30%. Length: 50,000–80,000 words. Only takes proposals if requested by house representative or from recognized source. Responds in one to six months. Bible: KJV.

Genres and topics: African-American, Asian, Charismatic, Christian living/spirituality, Hispanic, children, devotionals, fiction

Royalty: 15–18%, sometimes gives advance

Types of books: audiobook, board books, ebook, hardcover, offset paperback, POD

Imprint: Whitaker Playhouse (parents of young children)

Guidelines: *s3.amazonaws.com/whitaker-house-s3/wp-content/uploads/20190828134818/WhitakerHouse-Book-Submission-Guidelines.pdf*

Tip: "Follow the questions and suggestions on our submission guidelines."

WHITE ROSE PUBLISHING

PO Box 1738, Aztec, NM 87410
customer@pelicanbookgroup.com | *www.pelicanbookgroup.com*
Nicola Martinez, editor-in-chief

Parent company: Pelican Book Group

Mission statement: to publish quality books that reflect the salvation and love offered by Jesus Christ

Submissions: Length: short stories, 10,000–20,000 words; novelettes, 20,000–35,000 words; novellas, 35,000–60,000 words; novels, 60,000–80,000 words. Submit proposal with sample chapters through the website. Responds in three to four months. Bible: NIV, NAB.

Genres and topics: fiction: romance

Royalty: 40% on download, 7% on print; sometimes gives advance

Types of books: ebook, POD

Guidelines: *pelicanbookgroup.com/ec/index.php?main_page=page&id=58*

Tip: "The setting for White Rose books can be contemporary, historical or futuristic. They can be straight romances or include other factors, such as mystery, suspense, or supernatural elements, etc.; however, an element of faith must be present in all White Rose stories—without becoming overbearing or preachy. Please specify in your proposal if your story includes elements beyond simple romance."

WHITECROWN PUBLISHING

13607 Bedford Rd. NE, Cumberland, MD 21502 | 866-245-2211

marisa@whitecrownpublishing.com | *www.whitecrownpublishing.com*

Marisa Stokley, associate publisher

Janelle Leonard, managing editor; janelle@whitecrownpublishing.com

Parent company: WhiteFire Publishing Group

Mission statement: to meld faith and royal fiction in romantic tales that will appeal to teens and adults and encourage them to embrace being daughters of the King

Submissions: Publishes 6-12 titles per year; receives 100 submissions annually. First-time authors: 25%. Length: 60,000-110,000 words. Agent not required. Email proposal with sample chapters. Responds in three months. Bible: KJV for historicals.

Genres and topics: fiction: royal romance, royalty

Royalty: print, 10% on retail; ebooks, 50% on net; sometimes gives advance that depends on sales history

Types of books: audiobook, ebook, hardcover, offset paperback, POD

Guidelines: *whitecrownpublishing.com/submissions*

Tip: "We're looking for stories that include royalty as one of the primary elements, which appeal to lovers of 'princess stories' but also offer depth and faith."

WHITEFIRE PUBLISHING

13607 Bedford Rd. NE, Cumberland, MD 21502 | 866-245-2211

r.white@whitefire-publishing.com | *www.whitefire-publishing.com*

Roseanna White, managing editor

Mission statement: to publish books that shine the Light of God into the darkness and embrace the motto of "Where Spirit Meets the Page"

Submissions: Publishes 24 titles per year; receives 200 submissions annually. First-time authors: 20%. Length: 60,000-100,000 words. Email query first. Responds in three months. Bible: KJV for historicals.

Genres and topics: nonfiction: all topics; fiction: contemporary, general, historical, romance, suspense, women's

Royalty: 50% on ebooks, 10% on print; advance of $1,500-2,000

Types of books: audiobook, ebook, POD

Imprints: WhiteSpark (young readers), Ashberry Lane (romance), WhiteFire (nonfiction and fiction), Chrism Press (Catholic and Orthodox fiction)

Guidelines: *whitefire-publishing.com/submissions*
Tip: "Familiarize yourself with our titles and mission."

WHITESPARK PUBLISHING

13607 Bedford Rd. NE, Cumberland, MD 21502 | 866-245-2211
r.white@whitefire-publishing.com | *www.whitefire-publishing.com*
Roseanna White, managing editor

Parent company: WhiteFire Publishing
Mission statement: to engender a love of reading in kids with faith-based books
Submissions: Publishes 5-10 titles per year; receives 100 submissions annually. First-time authors: 10%. Email query first. Responds in three months.
Genres and topics: nonfiction: middle grade, picture books, YA
Royalty: 50% on ebooks, 10% on print; sometimes gives advance of $200-1,000
Types of books: audiobook, ebook, picture books, POD
Guidelines: *whitespark-publishing.com/submissions*
Tip: "Come with fresh ideas on how to reach the young readership."

WILD HEART BOOKS

14250 Hwy. 55 W, Blacksburg, SC 29702 | 704-363-0360
submissions@mistymbeller.com | *wildheartbooks.org*
Denise Weimer, acquisitions and editorial liaison

Parent company: Misty M. Beller Books, Inc.
Mission statement: to provide the kind of exciting historical stories readers love, complete with heroes to make them swoon, strong heroines, and inspirational messages to encourage their faith
Submissions: Publishes 30 titles per year; receives 50 submissions annually. First-time authors: 20%. Length: 55,000-80,000 words. Agent not required, conference contact a plus. Email proposal with complete manuscript or sample chapters. Responds in one week. Bible: KJV.
Genres and topics: fiction: historical romance
Royalty: 35-45%, no advance
Types of books: audiobook, ebook, hardcover, large print, POD
Guidelines: *www.wildheartbooks.org/submissions.html*
Tip: "We prefer series instead of standalones."

WILLIAM CAREY PUBLISHING

10 W. Dry Creek Cir., Littleton, CO 80120 | 720-372-7036
submissions@WCLBooks.com | *www.missionbooks.org*
Vivian Doub, publishing manager

> **Parent company:** Frontier Ventures
> **Mission statement:** to edify, equip, and empower disciples of Jesus
> to make disciples of Jesus and prompt breakthrough among
> unreached peoples
> **Submissions:** Email query first. Responds in three to six months.
> **Genres and topics:** biography, ethnography, missions, academic
> **Types of books:** ebook, paperback
> **Guidelines:** *missionbooks.org/pages/submission-guidelines*
> **Tip:** "We want our books to sound like the intelligent conversation you
> have with friends over dinner. You may site statistics and research
> (like you might reference an article in a reputable source), but
> you are sharing it in the context of a story that makes the research
> matter to real people doing Kingdom work."

WINGED PUBLICATIONS

PO Box 8047, Surprise, AZ 85374 | 623-910-4279
cynthiahickey@outlook.com | *www.wingedpublications.com*
Cynthia Hickey, CEO/president
Gina Welborn, acquisitions editor
Christina Rich, acquisitions editor
Patty Smith Hall, acquisitions editor

> **Submissions:** Publishes 50 titles per year. First-time authors: 25%.
> Length: minimum 20,000 words. Conference contact, or email
> proposal with sample chapters. Responds in two weeks. Bible: NIV.
> **Genres and topics:** self-help, devotionals; fiction: humor, dystopian,
> fantasy, historical romance, mystery, romance, romantic suspense,
> science fiction, suspense/thriller, teen/YA, women's
> **Royalty:** 60%, no advance
> **Types of books:** ebook, POD
> **Imprints:** Soaring Beyond (nonfiction), Aisling Books (fantasy,
> dystopian, science fiction), Jurnee Books (young adult, middle
> grade), Gordian Books (mystery, suspense, thriller), Forget Me Not
> Romances (contemporary and historical romances), Take Me Away
> Books (noninspirational)
> **Guidelines:** *wingedpublications.com/what-were-looking-for*
> **Tip:** "Send the cleanest proposal you can."

WIPF AND STOCK PUBLISHERS

199 W. 8th Ave., Ste. 3, Eugene, OR 97401–2960 | 541–344–1528

rodney@wipfandstock.com | *www.wipfandstock.com*

Rodney Clapp, editor

> **Submissions:** Publishes 500+ in all imprints per year. Email proposal with sample chapters. Responds in two months.
> **Genres and topics:** Bible, church history, ethics, history, ministry, philosophy, theology, academic
> **Types of books:** ebook, offset paperback
> **Imprints:** Resource Publications (leaders, pastors, educators), Cascade Books (academic)
> **Guidelines:** *wipfandstock.com/submitting-a-proposal*
> **Tip:** "It is your responsibility to submit a manuscript that has been fully copyedited by a professional copy editor."

WORDCRAFTS PRESS

912 E. Lincoln, Tullahoma, TN 37388 | 615–397–8376

wordcrafts.net

Mike Parker, publisher; mike@wordcrafts.net

Paula K. Parker, acquisitions editor; paula@wordcrafts.net

Kristen Ownby, acquisitions editor; kristen@wordcrafts.net

Shanda Perkins, acquisitions editor; shanda@wordcrafts.net

> **Parent company:** WordCrafts, LLC
> **Mission statement:** to tell stories that help us make sense of the world
> **Submissions:** Publishes 24–36 titles per year; receives 300 submissions annually. First-time authors: 50%. Length: fewer than 100,000 words. Agent not required. Conference contact or email query first through the website. Responds in four weeks.
> **Genres and topics:** Bible study, Christian living/spirituality, memoir/personal narrative; fiction: biblical, historical
> **Royalty:** 70% of income, no advance
> **Types of books:** audiobook, ebook, hardcover, POD
> **Guidelines:** *www.wordcrafts.net/how-to-submit*
> **Tip:** "Send us your best work."

WORTHY KIDS

6100 Tower Cir., Ste. 210, Franklin, TN 37067 | 615–221–0996

www.hachettebookgroup.com/imprint/worthykids

Peggy Schaefer, associate publisher and acquisitions

Parent company: Worthy Publishing/Hachette Book Group

Mission statement: to create books that are much more than just words and pictures—they're an opportunity for a moment of joy between a child and his or her loved one

Submissions: Publishes 30–35 titles per year; receives 200 submissions annually. First-time authors: fewer than 10%. Length: maximum 200 words for board books, 600 words for picture books. Agent only. Responds in one month. Bible: NLT.

Genres and topics: holidays, board books, first-chapter, middle grade, picture books

Royalty: varies, sometimes gives advance

First print run: 10,000

Types of books: audiobook, board books, ebook, hardcover, offset paperback, picture books

Guidelines: available via email

Tip: "Carefully study the types of books our house has published; and submit proposals that show an understanding of the marketplace, include recent competitive titles, and identify what sets your book apart."

WORTHY PUBLISHING

6100 Tower Cir., Ste. 210, Franklin, TN 37067 | 615-932-7600

www.worthypublishing.com

Beth Adams, editorial director

Sean McGowan, editor and acquisitions

Ryan Peterson, senior editor and acquisitions

India Hunter, associate editor and acquisitions

Parent company: Hachette Book Group

Mission statement: to publish books that combine faith, creativity, and culture while establishing the next generation of voices who believe that living faith can transform the world

Submissions: Publishes 36 titles per year. Agent only.

Genres and topics: biography, Christian living/spirituality, contemporary issues, culture, leadership, marriage, parenting, relationships, social justice, spiritual growth, devotionals, fiction, gift

Types of books: audiobook, ebook, hardcover, paperback

Imprints: Worthy Books (broad spectrum of genres), Worthy Kids (children), Ellie Claire (gifts)

YWAM PUBLISHING

PO Box 55787, Seattle, WA 98155 | 800-922-2143
books@ywampublishing.com | *www.ywampublishing.com*
Tom Bragg, publisher

Parent company: Youth With A Mission
Mission statement: to encourage Christians to make a difference in a needy world
Submissions: Email proposal with sample chapters. Responds only if interested.
Genres and topics: Christian living/spirituality, evangelism, family, leadership, missions, prayer, relationships, Bible studies, biography, devotionals
Types of books: audiobook, ebook, paperback
Guidelines: *www.ywampublishing.com/topic.aspx?name=submission*

ZONDERKIDZ

3900 Sparks Dr. SE, Grand Rapids, MI 49512 | 616-698-6900
ZonderkidzSubmissions@harpercollins.com | *www.zonderkidz.com*
Katherine Easter, senior acquisitions editor

Parent company: Zondervan/HarperCollins Christian Publishing
Mission statement: to inspire young lives through imaginative, innovative, and educational resources that represent a Christian worldview and build up God's children and teens
Submissions: Agent only.
Genres and topics: Bibles, children, teen/YA
Types of books: board books, ebook, hardcover, offset paperback, picture books
Guidelines: not available
Tip: "We are seeking fresh fiction and nonfiction for children ages 0-18. We look for engaging picture books and board books, timeless storybook Bibles, faith-centric fiction from established authors, and nonfiction from key voices in the Christian sphere."

ZONDERVAN

Editorial Vida, Zonderkidz, Zondervan Academic, Zondervan Books, Zondervan Gift, Zondervan Reflective

ZONDERVAN ACADEMIC

3900 Sparks Dr. SE, Grand Rapids, MI 49512 | 616-698-6900
submissions@zondervan.com | *www.zondervanacademic.com*

Katya Covrett, VP and publisher

Parent company: Zondervan/HarperCollins Christian Publishing
Mission statement: to reflect the breadth and diversity—both theological and global—within evangelical scholarship while maintaining our commitment to the heart of orthodox Christianity
Submissions: Email query. Responds in six weeks or not interested. Bible: NIV.
Genres and topics: academic, Bible reference/commentaries
Types of books: ebook, hardcover, offset paperback
Guidelines: *zondervanacademic.com/publishing-with-us*

ZONDERVAN BOOKS

PO Box 141000, Nashville, TN 37214 | 615-889-9000
www.zondervan.com
Paul Pastor, senior acquisitions editor
Andrea Palpant Dilley, senior acquisitions editor
Keren Baltzer, associate publisher and acquisitions

Parent company: HarperCollins Christian Publishing
Submissions: Publishes 120 titles per year. Agent only. Bible: NIV.
Genres and topics: biography, Christian living/spirituality, church life, contemporary issues, family, finances, marriage, ministry, Bible reference/commentaries
Types of books: audiobook, ebook, hardcover, offset paperback

ZONDERVAN REFLECTIVE

3900 Sparks Dr. SE, Grand Rapids, MI 49512 | 616-698-6900
submissions@zondervan.com | *www.zondervan.com/zondervanreflective*
Kyle Rohane, senior acquisitions editor

Parent company: Zondervan/HarperCollins Christian Publishing
Mission statement: to provide guidance and inspiration for effective leadership in business and ministry
Submissions: Email query. Responds in six weeks or not interested. Bible: NIV.
Genres and topics: contemporary issues, culture, leadership, ministry
Types of books: ebook, hardcover, offset paperback
Guidelines: *www.harpercollinschristian.com/authors/manuscript-information*
Tip: "The authors are expected to have demonstrable expertise on the subject being addressed."

2

BOOK ANTHOLOGY SERIES

CHICKEN SOUP FOR THE SOUL
PO Box 700, Cos Cob, CT 06807-0700
www.chickensoup.com
Amy Newmark, publisher and editor-in-chief
> **Parent company:** Chicken Soup for the Soul Publishing, LLC
> **Purpose statement:** to share happiness, inspiration, and hope
> **Submissions:** Send complete manuscript only through the website form. If no response by two months before the book's on-sale date, not interested. Accepts 101 per book per year. Accepts submissions from children and teens.
> **Types of manuscripts:** personal experience, poetry, theme-related
> **Topics/upcoming books:** *www.chickensoup.com/story-submissions/ possible-book-topics*
> **Length:** 1,200 words maximum
> **Rights:** nonexclusive
> **Payment:** $250 plus ten copies of the book, one month after publication
> **Guidelines:** *www.chickensoup.com/story-submissions/story-guidelines*
> **Tip:** "The most powerful stories are about people extending themselves, or performing an act of love, service or courage for another person."

DIVINE MOMENTS
PO Box 1233, Broken Arrow, OK 74013-1233 | 918-346-7960
terri@grace-publishing.com | *grace-publishing.com*
Terri Kalfas, compiler and editor
> **Parent company:** Grace Publishing/The Jomaga Group, LLC
> **Purpose statement:** to show the possibility of changing someone's life, heart, or mind
> **Submissions:** Email complete manuscript as attachment. Responds in

one to three months. Accepts 200 per year.

Types of manuscripts: fiction, personal experience, poetry, theme-related

Topics/upcoming books: *Divine Detours, Questionable Moments, Unexpected Kindness, Christmas 2025*

Length: 250–2,000 words

Rights: first, reprint with info on where and when previously published

Payment: copy of book; royalties are donated to Samaritan's Purse

Guidelines: *grace-publishing.com/manuscript-submission/divine-moments-guidelines*

Tip: "Submit work that is in line with the book theme."

JESUS CAN BOOK SERIES

1314 S. 1st St. #128, Milwaukee, WI 53204 | 414-999-0015

steph@christianwriterscollective.com | *christianwriterscollective.com*

Stephanie Reynolds, founder

Parent company: Christian Writers Collective, LLC

Purpose statement: to glorify God, evangelize the lost, and help fund the God-given dreams of its writers

Submissions: Email manuscript in body of message or use the website form. Responds in one to three weeks. Accepts various numbers per year. Bible: KJV. Accepts submissions from teens.

Types of manuscripts: personal experience, poetry, testimony, theme-related

Topics/upcoming books: *Jesus Can ... Show You The Truth,* deadline January 10; *Jesus Can ... Love You Through Your Pain,* deadline June 10

Length: 500–750 words

Rights: all, writers allowed to republish exactly with credit line

Payment: 1% of profit for up to two years after publication date, up to eight months after publication

Guidelines: *christianwriterscollective.com/share-your-story-1*

Tip: "We want every testimony/article in a Jesus Can book to speak to the heart of the reader because it is written from the heart. Therefore, as much as possible, write as if you were having a face-to-face conversation with the reader. Avoid the arrogant air of a professional writer and please do not preach! Humbly share your story of how Jesus saved you, and pray that He would use your testimony/story to help others come to a saving relationship with Him."

LIFE REPURPOSED

michelle@faithcreativitylife.com | www.faithcreativitylife.com
Michelle Rayburn, publisher and editor-in-chief

Parent company: Faith Creativity Life Books

Purpose statement: to help readers find hope in the trashy stuff of life

Submissions: Submit complete manuscript only through the website form. Responds in two weeks to two months. Accepts 60–100 manuscripts per year. Bible: NLT.

Types of manuscripts: devotion, fiction, humorous, personal experience, poetry, theme-related

Topics/upcoming books: resilience, gardening

Length: 300–1800 words

Rights: first, reprint with info on where and when previously published

Payment: copies of book

Guidelines: *www.faithcreativitylife.com*

Tip: "Pieces should be encouraging and uplifting, inspiring readers by showing how the writer found hope through their own struggle. They should be faith-based but not preachy. Writers should show vulnerability and authenticity as well as creativity. Humor is a plus!"

SHORT AND SWEET

1113 Brookside Dr., Franklin, TN 37069 | 615-202-6019
susan@susankingedits.com | grace-publishing.com
Susan King, compiler and editor

Parent company: Grace Publishing/The Jomaga Group, LLC

Purpose statement: to inspire and/or entertain through use of excellent style

Submissions: Email complete manuscript as attachment. Responds in four months after deadline. Accepts 100 manuscripts per year. Bible: NIV, KJV, NASB.

Types of manuscripts: fiction, personal experience, poetry, theme-related

Topics/upcoming books: *Growing Older with Grace (and a little humor)*

Length: 250–1,500 words

Rights: first

Payment: copy of book; royalties are donated to World Christian Broadcasting

Guidelines: *grace-publishing.com/manuscript-submission/short-sweet-anthology-guidelines*

Tip: "Read guidelines carefully and thoroughly and ask questions."

PART 2

INDEPENDENT BOOK PUBLISHING

3

INDEPENDENT BOOK PUBLISHERS

PUBLISHING A BOOK YOURSELF NO LONGER CARRIES THE STIGMA self-publishing has had in the past—if you do it right. Even some well-published writers are now hybrid authors, with independently published books alongside their royalty books. Others have built their readerships with traditional publishers, then moved to independent publishing where it is possible to make more money per sale.

Independent book publishers require the author to pay for part of the publishing costs or to buy a certain number of books. They call themselves by a variety of names, such as book packager, cooperative publisher, self-publisher, hybrid publisher, custom publisher, subsidy publisher, or simply someone who helps authors get their books printed. Services vary from including different levels of editing and proofreading to printing your manuscript as is.

Whenever you pay for any part of the production of your book, you are entering into a nontraditional relationship. Some independent publishers also offer a form of royalty publishing, so be sure you understand the contract you receive before signing it.

Some independent publishers will publish any book, as long as the author is willing to pay for it. Others are as selective about what they publish as a royalty publisher. Some independent publishers will do as much promotion as a royalty publisher—for a fee. Others do none at all.

If you are unsuccessful in placing your book with a royalty publisher but feel strongly about seeing it published, an independent publisher can make printing your book easier and often less expensive than doing it yourself. POD, as opposed to a print run of 1,000 books or more, could save you upfront money, although the price per copy is higher. Having your manuscript produced only as an ebook is also a less-expensive option.

Entries in this chapter are for information only, not an endorsement of publishers. For every complaint about a publisher, several other authors may sing the praises of it. Before you sign with any company, get more than one bid to determine whether the terms you are offered are competitive.

A legitimate independent publisher will provide a list of former clients as references. Also buy a couple of the publisher's previous books to check the quality of the work: covers, bindings, typesetting, etc. See if the books currently are available through any of the major online retailers.

Get answers before committing yourself. You may also want someone in the book-publishing industry to review your contract before you sign it. Some experts listed in the "Editorial Services" chapter review contracts.

If you decide not to use an independent publisher but do the work yourself, at least hire an editor, proofreader, cover designer, and interior typesetter-designer. The "Editorial Services" and "Design and Production Services" chapters will help you locate professionals with skills in these areas, as well as printing companies. Plus the "Distribution Services" and "Publicity and Marketing Services" chapters can help you solve one of the biggest problems of independent publishing: getting your books to readers.

AMPELOS PRESS

951 Anders Rd., Lansdale, PA 19446 | 267-436-2503
mbagnull@aol.com | *writehisanswer.com/ampelospress*
Marlene Bagnull, publisher
> **Types:** ebook, POD
> **Services:** copyediting, design, manuscript evaluation, proofreading, substantive editing
> **Production time:** six months
> **Books per year:** two
> **Tip:** "Especially interested in issues fiction and nonfiction, as well as books about missions and the needs of children. Author pays a one-time fee, maintains all rights, and receives 100% royalty from Amazon KDP."

BELIEVERS BOOK SERVICES

2329 Farragut Ave., Colorado Springs, CO 80907 | 719-641-7862
dave@believersbookservices.com | *believersbookservices.com*
Dave Sheets, owner
> **Types:** ebook, gift book, hardcover, paperback, picture book, POD
> **Services:** à la carte options, author websites, copyediting, design, distribution, manuscript evaluation, packages of services,

proofreading, substantive editing

Production time: three months

Books per year: 45–50

Tip: "Start thinking about strategy for publishing, marketing, and launching as soon as possible in the process. This strategy process will help produce a stronger book."

BK ROYSTON PUBLISHING

PO Box 4321, Jeffersonville, IN 47131 | 502-694-5385

bkroystonpublishing@gmail.com | *www.bkroystonpublishing.com*

Julia A. Royston, CEO

Types: audiobook, ebook, hardcover, offset paperback, picture book

Services: à la carte options, author websites, coaching, copyediting, design, manuscript evaluation, marketing, online bookstore, packages of services, promotional materials, proofreading

Production time: two to three months

Books per year: 50

Tip: "Prior to submission for review, please at least spell-check."

BOOKBABY

7905 N. Crescent Blvd., Pennsauken, NJ 08110 | 877-961-6878

info@bookbaby.com | *www.bookbaby.com*

Types: comic book, ebook, gift book, hardcover, offset paperback, picture book, POD

Services: copyediting, design, distribution, manuscript evaluation, online bookstore, proofreading, social-media ads, substantive editing

Production time: varies

Tip: "When you work with BookBaby, you'll have every resource you need, such as book-cover design, editing, ebook creation, audiobook creation, and marketing services, all in one place! Plus, we also have our own storefront, BookBaby Bookshop."

BRIDGE LOGOS, INC.

14260 W. Newberry Rd. #409, Newberry, FL 32669 | 800-444-4484

info@bridgelogos.com | *www.bridgelogos.com*

Peggy Hildebrand, acquisitions editor

Types: audiobook, ebook, hardcover, paperback

Services: copyediting, design, distribution, proofreading, substantive editing, royalty contracts

Production time: 12–18 months

Books per year: 40

Tip: Traditional house that requires new Bridge Logos authors and authors with no established marketing platform to purchase 1,000–3,000 books at a discount. "Looking for well-written, timely books that are aimed at the needs of people and that glorify God. Have a great message, a well-written manuscript, and a specific plan and willingness to market your book. Looking for previously published authors with an active ministry who are experts on their subject."

BROWN CHRISTIAN PRESS

16250 Knoll Trail Dr., Ste. 205, Dallas, TX 75248 | 972-381-0009

publishing@brownbooks.com | www.brownbooks.com/brown-christian-press

Types: audiobook, ebook, gift book, hardcover, paperback

Services: copyediting, design, distribution, ghostwriting, indexing, marketing, proofreading, substantive editing

Production time: six months

Tip: "We are a relationship publisher and work with our authors from beginning to end in the journey of publishing."

CALLED WRITERS CHRISTIAN PUBLISHING

1900 Rice Mine Rd. N. 401, Tuscaloosa, AL 35406 | 205-872-4509

shannon@calledwriters.com | CalledWriters.com

Shannon McKinney, relationship builder

Types: offset paperback, POD

Services: à la carte options, copyediting, design, manuscript evaluation, marketing, packages of services, proofreading, substantive editing, royalty contracts

Production time: six months

Books per year: two

Tip: "God will open the right doors for you at the right time. Don't give up."

CAPTIVATE PRESS

3001 Shelley Lynn Dr., Arnold, MO 63010 | 636-633-7846

captivatepress@gmail.com | captivatepress.site

Isabella Witt

Types: ebook, gift book, hardcover, offset paperback

Services: design, distribution, marketing, proofreading, substantive editing, royalty contracts

Production time: one year
Books per year: 20–30
Tip: "Make sure you submit your best work. There is a lot of competition, and we only choose the work that we like the best."

CHRISTIAN FAITH PUBLISHING

832 Park Ave., Meadville, PA 16335 | 800-955-3794
Chris@christianfaithpublishing.com | www.Christianfaithpublishing.com
Chris Rutherford, president

Types: ebook, hardcover, offset paperback, POD
Services: à la carte options, copyediting, design, distribution, indexing, manuscript evaluation, marketing, packages of services, promotional materials, royalty contracts
Production time: eight to ten months
Books per year: 1,200
Tip: "Be mindful of the fact that it is quite challenging to publish a book and have commercial success."

CLM PUBLISHING

PO Box 1217, Grand Cayman, Cayman Islands KY-11108 | 345-926-2507
production@clmpublishing.com | www.clmpublishing.com

Types: ebook, gift book, hardcover, offset paperback, picture book, POD
Services: copyediting, design, distribution, illustrations, indexing, manuscript evaluation, marketing, online bookstore, proofreading, substantive editing
Production time: three to six months
Books per year: eight
Tip: "Be willing to do some marketing."

CLOVERCROFT PUBLISHING GROUP

307 Verde Meadow Dr., Franklin, TN 37067 | 615-538-8557
shane@clovercroftpublishing.com | clovercroftpublishing.com
Shane Crabtree, COO

Types: audiobook, ebook, gift book, hardcover, offset paperback, picture book, POD
Services: à la carte options, author websites, coaching, copyediting, design, distribution, indexing, manuscript evaluation, marketing, online bookstore, packages of services, promotional materials, proofreading, substantive editing, royalty contracts, international rights
Production time: four to six months

Books per year: 25

Tip: "Start planning your marketing early!"

COLEMAN JONES PRESS

13155 Noel Rd., Ste. 910, Dallas, TX 75240 | 561-720-5772

colemanjonespress.us

Tracee and Ross Jones, owners

Types: audiobook, curriculum, ebook, hardcover, picture book, POD

Services: author websites, design, distribution, marketing, packages of services, promotional materials

Production time: three to six months

Tip: "Write for the sake of getting the gospel out, not for the money. When choosing a cover or illustrator, make sure your design looks like something that is in major retail stores."

COVENANT BOOKS

11661 Hwy. 707, Murrells Inlet, SC 29576 | 843-507-8373

info@covenantbooks.com | www.covenantbooks.com

Denice Hunter, president

Types: ebook, hardcover, offset paperback, POD

Services: à la carte options, copyediting, design, distribution, marketing, online bookstore, packages of services, royalty contracts

Production time: six months

Tip: "Publishing a book can be a fun and enlightening process. Take your time, and choose a publisher you feel comfortable with."

CREATIVE ENTERPRISES STUDIO

1507 Shirley Way, Ste. A, Bedford, TX 76022-6737 | 817-312-7393

AcreativeShop@aol.com | www.creativeenterprisesltd.com

Mary Hollingsworth, publisher

Types: audiobook, ebook, gift book, hardcover, offset paperback, picture book, POD

Services: author websites, book trailer, coaching, copyediting, design, ghostwriting, marketing, proofreading, substantive editing, warehousing

Production time: seven months, depending on type and length of book

Books per year: varies

Tip: "Contact us by email to set a phone conference to discuss your work before proceeding otherwise."

CREDO HOUSE PUBLISHERS

2200 Boyd Ct. NE, Grand Rapids, MI 49525-6714

publish@credocommunications.net | *www.credohousepublishers.com*

Timothy J. Beals, publisher

Types: offset paperback

Services: à la carte options, author websites, copyediting, design, distribution, indexing, manuscript evaluation, marketing, online bookstore, packages of services, promotional materials, proofreading, substantive editing

Production time: three months

Books per year: 30

Tip: "Come prepared. Be persistent. Get published."

DEEP RIVER BOOKS, LLC

PO Box 310, Sisters, OR 97759 | 541-549-1139

submit@deepriverbooks.com | *www.deepriverbooks.com*

Andy Carmichael, publisher

Types: audiobook, ebook, hardcover, offset paperback, POD

Services: copyediting, design, distribution, manuscript evaluation, marketing, online bookstore, packages of services, promotional materials, substantive editing, royalty contracts

Production time: 9–14 months

Books per year: 30–35

Tip: "Check our website on how we work with authors before you submit."

DEEPER REVELATION BOOKS

PO Box 4260, Cleveland, TN 37320-4260 | 423-478-2843

info@gmail.com | *deeperrevelationbooks.org*

Mike Shreve, CEO

Types: ebook, gift book, hardcover, offset paperback, POD

Services: à la carte options, author websites, copyediting, design, distribution, indexing, manuscript evaluation, marketing, online bookstore, promotional materials, proofreading, substantive editing

Production time: three to six months

Books per year: 25–30

Tip: "The root of the word *authority* is the word *author*. When you emerge as a reputable author on a specific subject, in the minds of the public, you are an authority in that area."

DESCENDANT PUBLISHING

PO Box 29, Byron Center, MI 49315 | 616-290-7829

contact@descendantpublishing.com | *www.descendantpublishing.com*

Troy Hooker, managing editor

Types: audiobook, curriculum, ebook, POD

Services: coaching, copyediting, design, distribution, marketing, online bookstore, packages of services, proofreading, royalty publishing

Tip: "We can walk you through the process one step at a time, helping you to bring your story to market at a fraction of the cost."

DESTINY IMAGE PUBLISHERS

167 Walnut Bottom Rd., Shippensburg, PA 17257 | 717-532-3040

manuscripts@norimediagroup.com | *norimediagroup.com/pages/publish-with-us*

Types: ebook, paperback

Services: copyediting, design, manuscript evaluation, marketing, proofreading, substantive editing

Production time: one year

Tip: Traditional publisher that requires prepurchase of 500–3,000 copies. "Focuses on Spirit-empowered themes: supernatural God encounters, healing/deliverance, prophecy and prophetic ministry, gifts of the Holy Spirit, prayer and intercession, the presence and glory of God, and dreams/dream interpretation."

EABOOKS PUBLISHING

5840 Red Bug Lake Rd., Winter Springs, FL 32708 | 407-712-3431

Cheri@eabookspublishing.com | *www.eabookspublishing.com*

Cheri Cowell, founder and publisher

Types: audiobook, ebook, gift book, hardcover, POD

Services: à la carte options, author websites, copyediting, design, distribution, indexing, manuscript evaluation, marketing, packages of services, promotional materials, proofreading, substantive editing, royalty contracts

Production time: six months

Books per year: 50

Tip: "Contact for a free consultation to see if we can partner with you to make your publishing dreams come true."

eBOOK CONVERSION AND LISTING SERVICES

PO Box 57, Glenwood, MD 21738 | 443-280-5077

sales@taegais.com | *ebooklistingservices.com*

Amy Deardon, CEO

> **Types:** audiobook, ebook, POD
> **Services:** à la carte options, design, distribution, marketing, packages
> of services, promotional materials
> **Production time:** one to three months
> **Books per year:** 20
> **Tip:** "We empower independent authors to become successful. Unlike
> most other independent publishers, we set you up so you are
> the publisher, rather than publishing through the independent
> company. You can create your own publishing company name and
> logo, and we help you with that. You remain fully in charge of all
> decisions, rights, and profits from start to forever. Once your book
> is published, you can buy as few or as many books as you want at
> the lowest printer's price (a 200-page book costs less than $3.50);
> and books are delivered in a week or two through Amazon. We
> also have additional packages that can list your book with the
> Library of Congress and help you rank higher on Amazon's search
> engines so readers can actually find your book and buy it. We
> provide you with ownership of your book and work with you to
> make that succeed."

ELECTRIC MOON PUBLISHING

13518 Heritage Dr., Bonner Springs, KS 66012 | 913-827-2225

info@emoonpublishing.com | *www.electricmoonpublishing.com*

Johnny Hyatt, managing partner

> **Types:** audiobook, ebook, gift book, hardcover, offset paperback,
> picture book, POD
> **Services:** à la carte options, author websites, book trailer, copyediting,
> design, distribution, indexing, manuscript evaluation, marketing,
> packages of services, promotional materials, proofreading,
> substantive editing, royalty contracts
> **Production time:** 8–10 months
> **Books per year:** 8–12
> **Tip:** "Feel free to ask questions of the services and publishing
> models offered. We are here to help and would enjoy an initial
> conversation with you."

EMBOLDEN MEDIA GROUP

PO Box 953607, Lake Mary, FL 32795-3607

info@emboldenmediagroup.com | *emboldenmediagroup.com/book-publishing*

Types: ebook, POD

Services: à la carte options, copyediting, design, distribution, manuscript evaluation, marketing, packages of services, proofreading, substantive editing

Tip: "Our Elite Publishing Package allows you to let your message get the polish it needs so that it reaches deep into the hearts of your readers by putting it through Embolden Media Group's complete book publishing editorial and production process. If you choose to partner with us in getting your book into the hands of readers who need it most, you will be taken through the full editorial and production process common in most traditional publishing houses—from start to finish. If you would rather skip or omit any step in the process, à la carte services are available. Your book must be fully written and complete before you embark on any of our Get Published Packages."

ENCOURAGE PUBLISHING

1116 Creekview Cir., New Albany, IN 47150 | 812-987-6148

leslie@encouragebooks.com | *encouragepublishing.com*

Leslie Turner, publisher

Types: audiobook, ebook, gift book, hardcover, offset paperback, picture book, POD

Services: copyediting, design, distribution, manuscript evaluation, marketing, online bookstore, packages of services, promotional materials, proofreading, substantive editing, royalty contracts

Production time: 14 months

Books per year: 5-10

Tip: "Mission statement required (see guidelines at *encouragepublishing. com/books*)."

FAIRWAY PRESS

5450 N. Dixie Hwy., Lima, OH 45807-9559 | 419-227-1818

david@csspub.com | *www.fairwaypress.com*

David Runk, president

Types: ebook, hardcover, offset paperback, POD

Services: à la carte options, copyediting, design, manuscript evaluation, proofreading

Production time: 6-12 months

Books per year: 10–15

Tip: "No derogatory racist content. Christian content preferred."

FAMILY&FRIENDS MICRO-PUBLISHING

200 E. 38th St., Marion, IN 46953 | 765-618-3269, text only

jim@jameswatkins.com | *www.jameswatkins.com/publishing*

James Watkins, owner

Types: offset paperback, picture book, POD

Services: à la carte options, coaching, design, manuscript evaluation, packages of services, substantive editing

Production time: two weeks

Books per year: 10

Tip: "Our service is specifically designed for authors who do not have a platform (well-trafficked website and socials, large email list, and busy speaking schedule), who won't reach a large audience. We offer a high-quality book and get it on Amazon for one-tenth the cost of most self/independent publishers."

FIESTA PUBLISHING

PO Box 44984, Phoenix, AZ 85064 | 602-795-5868

julie@fiestapublishing.com | *www.fiestapublishing.com*

Julie Castro, owner

Types: ebook, hardcover, offset paperback, POD

Services: à la carte options, copyediting, distribution, marketing, promotional materials, proofreading, substantive editing

Production time: four to six months

Books per year: five to seven

Tip: "Be willing to listen to an established publisher and act accordingly. There is a difference between a book and a great book! Look for publisher integrity and their purpose for having the publishing company."

FUSION HYBRID PUBLISHING

PO Box 206, Nesbit, MS 38651 | 901-590-6584

submissions@endgamepress.com | *www.endgamepress.com/fusion*

Alice H. Murray, acquisitions editor

Types: audiobook, ebook, gospel tract, hardcover, offset paperback, picture book, POD

Services: à la carte options, copyediting, design, distribution, indexing, manuscript evaluation, marketing, online bookstore, packages of services, promotional materials, proofreading, substantive editing

Production time: 6–12 months

Books per year: three to four

Tip: "Fusion is a great option for those who are excited to get to market faster than traditional houses and have a great audience already."

GOODWILL MEDIA SERVICES CORP.

105 Macclamrock Ct., Cary, NC 27518 | 347-247-2106

goodwillmediaservices.sofia@gmail.com | goodwillmediaservices.com

Sofia Delgado, author relations consultant

Types: audiobook, ebook, gift book, hardcover, offset paperback, picture book, POD

Services: à la carte options, author websites, coaching, copyediting, design, distribution, indexing, manuscript evaluation, marketing, online bookstore, packages of services, promotional materials, proofreading, substantive editing

Production time: three months

Books per year: 25+

Tip: "Don't settle for limitations. Break free from the constraints of traditional publishing and experience the freedom of self-publishing. With our support, you can chart your own course as a Christian author."

THE GRACE CHAPTER

244 Fifth Ave., Ste. T279, New York, NY 10001 | 646-233-4017

publishers@gracechapter.com | www.gracechapter.com

Temitope Oyetomi, director

Types: ebooks, hardcover, offset paperback, POD

Services: à la carte options, author websites, copyediting, design, distribution, indexing, manuscript evaluation, marketing, online bookstore, packages of services, proofreading, substantive editing, royalty contracts

Production time: three to eight weeks

Number of books published per year: 30

Tip: "We prefer you tell us your budget for what you need to do, and we'll see what services we can tailor to the budget. This way, you can achieve your goals no matter your budget."

HARRISON HOUSE

167 Walnut Bottom Rd., Shippensburg, PA 17257 | 717-532-3040

manuscripts@norimediagroup.com | *norimediagroup.com/pages/publish-with-us*

Types: ebook, paperback

Services: copyediting, design, manuscript evaluation, marketing, proofreading, substantive editing, royalty contracts

Production time: one year

Tip: Traditional publisher that requires prepurchase of 500–3,000 copies.

HONEYCOMB HOUSE PUBLISHING

315 3rd St., New Cumberland, PA 17070 | 215-767-9600

dave@fessendens.net | *www.davefessenden.com/honeycomb-house-publishing-llc*

David Fessenden, publisher

Types: POD

Services: à la carte options, author websites, copyediting, design, distribution, manuscript evaluation, marketing, packages of services, promotional materials, proofreading, substantive editing

Production time: three to six months

Books per year: one or two

Tip: "Prepare a book proposal even if you plan to self-publish/subsidy publish."

IMMORTALISE

PO Box 656, Noarlunga Centre, SA 5168 Australia

info@immortalise.com.au | *www.immortalise.com.au*

Ben Morton, editor

Types: ebook, hardcover, offset paperback, picture book

Services: à la carte options, copyediting, design, manuscript evaluation, online bookstore, proofreading, substantive editing

Production time: varies

Tip: "All our services are optional and there is no cost for enquiries. We will publish any book so long as the content is not likely to get anyone sued."

INSCRIPT BOOKS

PO Box 611, Bladensburg, MD 20710 | 240-342-3293

admin@dovechristianpublishers.com | *www.inscriptpublishing.com*

Allison Kelsey, editorial director

Types: ebook, hardcover, offset paperback, POD

Services: à la carte options, copyediting, design, distribution, manuscript evaluation, marketing, packages of services, proofreading, substantive editing, royalty contracts
Production time: six to eight weeks
Books per year: 12
Tip: "Full submission requirements, qualifications, and online forms are listed on our website. For consideration, please follow them carefully. We do not accept snail-mail submissions. We do not accept email submissions apart from the forms on our website."

LAKE DRIVE BOOKS

6757 Cascade Rd. SE #162, Grand Rapids, MI 49546 | 616-737-1480
info@lakedrivebooks.com | lakedrivebooks.com
David Morris, publisher

Types: audiobook, ebook, hardcover, offset paperback, POD
Services: distribution, marketing
Production time: one year
Books per year: eight
Tip: "See our website to understand our publishing and if you would be a fit. Submissions must be in book-proposal form. There's a template on the About section of the site."

LONDON LANE DESIGNS

35 London Ln., Sharpsburg, GA 30277 | 770-710-3137
londonlanedesigns@gmail.com | LondonLaneDesigns.com
Gloria Erickson, owner and lead designer

Types: ebook, hardcover, POD
Services: à la carte options, author websites, design
Production time: two to four weeks with fully edited manuscript
Books per year: varies
Tip: "Do your research. Some publishers are very expensive and will retain the rights to your book. Good independent publishers will publish your book, and you keep complete control over rights and design. London Lane Design will work with you to create the book of your dreams, and you will keep control."

MORGAN JAMES PUBLISHING

5 Penn Plaza, 23rd Floor, New York City, NY 10001 | 516-900-5711
terry@morganjamespublishing.com | www.morganjamespublishing.com
W. Terry Whalin, acquisitions editor

Types: audiobook, ebook, offset paperback, picture book, POD

Services: design, distribution, manuscript evaluation, marketing, online bookstore, proofreading, royalty contracts with 20–25% royalties and small advance

Production time: 10–12 weeks, bookstore distribution in 9–10 months

Books per year: 180–200, 25–30 in the faith division

Tip: "Beginning our 21st year in publishing. Over 6,000 titles and 25 million books in print. Top independent publisher—rated nine times from *Publishers Weekly* and distribution into 98% of the bookstores in North America, including over 180 online plus brick-and-mortar bookstores. Our books have been on the *New York Times* bestseller list over 28 times and over 100 times on the *Wall Street Journal* bestseller list.

"Free marketing and coaching training for authors and a private Facebook group with over 1,300 authors. Over the lifetime of the agreement, the author is required to purchase 2,000 copies at the print cost plus $3. Our author support team builds a free BookFunnel page for each author to give away a free ebook to build their email list. These free downloads drive print sales and count against the book purchase requirement.

"Email proposal with sample chapters or full manuscript. Only 30% of authors have literary agents."

NORDSKOG PUBLISHING

2716 Sailor Ave., Ventura, CA 93001 | 805-642-2070
www.nordskogpublishing.com
Michelle Shelfer, managing editor

Types: hardcover, paperback

Services: copyediting, design, marketing

Tip: "Looking for the best in sound theological and applied Christian-faith books, both nonfiction and fiction."

PRAIRIE FALLS BOOKS EDITING & DESIGN SERVICES

4810 Gene Field Rd. #2, St. Joseph, MO 64506 | 816-752-2171
deb@crossrivermedia.com | *prairiefallsbooks.com*
Debra L. Butterfield, managing editor

Types: ebook, hardcover, offset paperback, POD

Services: à la carte options, copyediting, design, packages of services, proofreading, substantive editing

Production time: one to two months

Books per year: 15-20

Tip: "Review our website first and then schedule a consultation."

REDEMPTION PRESS

1602 Cole St., Enumclaw, WA 98022 | 360-226-3488

acquisitions@redemption-press.com | *www.redemption-press.com*

Carol Tetzlaff, associate publisher

Types: audiobooks, ebooks, gift books, hardcover, offset paperback, picture books, POD

Services: à la carte options, author training, author websites, brick and mortar bookstore, coaching, copyediting, design, distribution, indexing, manuscript evaluation, marketing, online bookstore, promotional materials, proofreading, rewrites, substantive editing, theological review

Also offers: editing and marketing services outside a publishing contract

Production time: 6-18 months

Books per year: 100+

Tip: "Redemption Press is known for our commitment to sustaining the finest standards of editing and publishing in the Christian publishing industry. As an established collaborative custom publishing house, we offer both the individualized care of a small press and the comprehensive resources of a traditional house. At our core, we are dedicated to fulfilling our mission of amplifying the message of Christian authors with excellence.

"With our specialized services, we strive to maintain the utmost purity and integrity of your message while simultaneously ensuring its reach extends to the widest possible audience. We take great joy in delivering books that not only enrich and inspire readers but also demonstrate the care, passion, and commitment put into each step of the production process. You can place your trust in Redemption Press, the premier publisher specializing in transforming stories into powerful and inspiring messages of unwavering faith, boundless hope, and ultimate redemption."

RENOWN PUBLISHING

424 W. Bakerview Rd., Ste. 105, Bellingham, WA 98248 | 360-836-0672

caleb@renownpublishing.com | *renownpublishing.com*

Caleb Breakey

Types: audiobook, ebook, hardcover, offset paperback, POD
Services: legacy storytelling
Production time: 14–18 months
Books per year: 10–20
Tip: "Let story do the work."

SALVATION PUBLISHER AND MARKETING GROUP

PO Box 40860, Santa Barbara, CA 93140 | 805-252-9822
opalmaedailey@aol.com
Opal Mae Dailey, editor

Types: ebook, hardcover, offset paperback
Services: copyediting, design, manuscript evaluation, proofreading, substantive editing
Production time: six to nine months
Books per year: five to seven
Tip: "Turning recorded messages into book form for pastors is a specialty of ours. We do not accept any manuscript we would be ashamed to put our name on."

SERMON TO BOOK

424 W. Bakerview Rd., Ste. 105 #215, Bellingham, WA 98226 | 360-223-1877
info@sermontobook.com | *www.sermontobook.com*
Caleb Breakey, lead book director

Types: audiobook, ebook, offset paperback, POD
Services: author websites, copyediting, design, distribution, indexing, manuscript evaluation, marketing, online bookstore, packages of services, promotional materials, proofreading, substantive editing
Production time: seven to nine months
Books per year: 60
Tip: "Check out our materials at *SermonToBook.com*."

SOUTHERN WOMEN PUBLISHING

www.southernwomenpublishing.com
LaMonique Mac, publisher

Types: ebook, hardcover, POD
Services: copyediting, illustrations, marketing, online bookstore, packages of services, proofreading, substantive editing
Tip: "All submissions must adhere to our statement of faith."

SPRINKLE PUBLISHING

1675 Lucia Ln., Mansfield, OH 44907-2778 | 419-709-1435

Dr.Sprinkle@wsministries.ws | www.wsministries.ws/home/sprinkle-publishing

Dr. Wanda J. Sprinkle, CEO and editor

> **Types:** ebook, hardcover, offset paperback
> **Services:** à la carte options, copyediting, design, manuscript evaluation, online bookstore, packages of services, proofreading, substantive editing, royalty contracts
> **Production time:** seven months
> **Books per year:** five
> **Tip:** "Pray for confirmation from the Holy Spirit that Sprinkle Publishing can be your publisher." Requires authors to order a minimum of 100 copies, which is included in the publishing cost.

STONE OAK PUBLISHING

PO Box 2011, Friendswood, TX 77549 | 832-569-4282

stoneoakpublishing@gmail.com | stoneoakpublishing.com

Karen Porter, acquisitions

> **Types:** ebook, hardcover, offset paperback, POD
> **Services:** à la carte options, coaching, copyediting, design, distribution, ghostwriting, indexing, manuscript evaluation, marketing, packages of services, promotional materials, proofreading, substantive editing, royalty contracts
> **Production time:** six to eight months
> **Books per year:** 10
> **Tip:** "Send us a well-thought-out email detailing the information about your book."

TEACH SERVICES, INC.

11 Quartermaster Cir., Fort Oglethorpe, GA 30742-3886 | 800-367-1844

authoradvisor@TEACHServices.com | www.teachservices.com

Timothy Hullquist, author advisor

> **Types:** ebook, gift book, hardcover, offset paperback, picture book, POD
> **Services:** à la carte options, author websites, copyediting, design, distribution, indexing, manuscript evaluation, marketing, online bookstore, packages of services, promotional materials, proofreading, substantive editing, royalty contracts
> **Production time:** one to four months
> **Tip:** "We specialize in marketing our titles to Seventh-day Adventists."

THRILLING LIFE PUBLISHERS

PO Box 92522, Southlake, TX 76092 | 214-257-8716
info@thrillinglife.com | Thrillinglife.com
Victorya Rogers, publisher

> **Types:** ebooks, hardcover, POD
>
> **Services:** à la carte options, copyediting, design, distribution, manuscript evaluation, proofreading, substantive editing
>
> **Production time:** negotiable, typically two months
>
> **Books per year:** 8-12
>
> **Tip:** "We publish nonfiction Christian books. If you are, or strive to be, a Christian speaker, influencer, pastor, counselor, or life coach, with a heart for helping others find a relationship with Jesus, then we are a great choice for you. Our mission is helping our readers discover the thrilling life Christ offers in John 10:10. All books align with our Christian values and adherence to Scripture. We believe the Bible is living and breathing and our guidebook for life. See our website for previously published books on our label. Please submit your one-sheet book proposal, table of contents, and two chapters by email or standard mail for evaluation."

TMP BOOKS

3 Central Plaza, Ste. 307, Rome, GA 30161
info@tmpbooks.com | www.TMPbooks.com
Tracy Ruckman, publisher

> **Types:** audiobook, ebook, hardcover, picture book, POD
>
> **Services:** à la carte options, author websites, coaching, copyediting, design, manuscript evaluation, marketing, packages of services, promotional materials, proofreading, substantive editing
>
> **Production time:** six to nine months
>
> **Books per year:** five to ten
>
> **Tip:** "We work with each author individually, customizing our services to meet their needs. We've published beautiful books that started with notes on scraps of paper, from handwritten pages of legal pads, and even from fragments of an idea. We believe everyone has a story worth telling; our job is to get it to the publishable state, professionally and affordably. Check our website for client reviews."

TORCHBEARER PRESS

PO Box 306190, Nashville, TN 37230 | 877-474-2693

Torchbearer@rhboyd.com | rhboyd.com/pages/author-services
David Groves, director of publications
>   **Types:** ebooks, hardcover, offset paperback
>   **Services:** à la carte options, copyediting, design, proofreading
>   **Tip:** "Torchbearer Press requires a minimum print run of 2,500 books."

TRAIL MEDIA

PO Box 1285, Orange, CA 92856
admin@ChisholmTrailMedia.com | www.chisholmtrailmedia.com
Christine "CJ" Simpson, publishing director
>   **Types:** ebook, gift book, picture book, POD
>   **Services:** à la carte options, copyediting, manuscript evaluation, marketing, packages of services, promotional materials, proofreading, substantive editing
>   **Production time:** negotiable
>   **Tip:** "Our goal is to help new authors publish their work by coordinating the services needed with experts in the field and publishing in a co-op fashion under the Trail Media imprint, so 100% of the revenue generated goes to ministry of the authors. In many cases, we find scholarships and grants to help missionaries and those in the persecuted church. Trail Media is a ministry of modified tentmaking models."

TRILOGY CHRISTIAN PUBLISHING

PO Box A, Santa Ana, CA 92711 | 855-214-2665
www.trilogy.tv
Bryan Norris, director of publications
>   **Types:** ebook, hardcover, POD
>   **Services:** copyediting, design, illustrations, marketing, online bookstore, royalty contracts
>   **Tip:** "The Trinity Broadcasting Family of Networks is blazing a trail worldwide, with fresh, innovative programs that entertain, inspire, and change lives. In addition to the 8,000 cable and satellite affiliates that reach over 100 million homes across America and every inhabited continent, the TBN Family of Networks will continue to aggressively expand their reach as they deliver content across all social media and digital platforms. As part of your book release, TBN will use its social media platforms such as Facebook (1.8M followers), X (formerly Twitter) (138K followers) and Instagram (1.5M followers)

to promote it. From there, all of the social media strength of Trilogy Christian Publishing will be deployed."

VIDE PRESS

videpress.com

> **Types:** ebook, paperback
> **Services:** copyediting, design, distribution, marketing, proofreading
> **Tip:** "We are always searching for new voices, articulate Christian writers who have the courage to confront the issues challenging today's culture and our faith."

THE WELL PUBLISHERS

PMB #533, 520 Butternut Dr., Ste. 8, Holland, MI 49424 | 616-212-0151
thewellpublishers@gmail.com | *thewellpublishers.com*
Kathy Bruins, owner

> **Types:** audiobook, ebook, gift book, hardcover, offset paperback, POD
> **Services:** à la carte options, copyediting, design, distribution, manuscript evaluation, marketing, packages of services, proofreading, substantive editing
> **Production time:** 3–12 months
> **Books per year:** 10
> **Tip:** "Make your manuscript shine as much as possible (i.e., no spelling errors). Work as part of the team in getting your book published. Realize that this is a business."

WESTBOW PRESS

1663 Liberty Dr., Bloomington, IN 47403 | 844-714-3454
www.westbowpress.com

> **Types:** audiobook, ebook, gift book, hardcover, offset paperback, POD
> **Services:** book trailer, copyediting, design, distribution, illustrations, indexing, manuscript evaluation, marketing, packages of services, Spanish translation, substantive editing
> **Tip:** Independent publishing division of Thomas Nelson and Zondervan.

WILT AND WADE PUBLISHING

7911 S. 162nd St., Omaha, NE 68136 | 402-541-6997
publish@wiltandwade.com | *wiltandwade.com*
Tonya Ludwig, founder, CEO

> **Types:** audiobook, ebook, hardcover, offset paperback, picture

book, POD

Services: author websites, copyediting, design, distribution, manuscript evaluation, marketing, online bookstore, packages of services, promotional materials, proofreading, substantive editing, royalty contracts

Production time: four to six months

Books per year: five

Tip: "We encourage you to view your authorship as a business. Entrepreneurial efforts like marketing, investment, and growth are vital to developing a writing career. The results show when you are committed to your success. Remember, timing is everything. Quicker doesn't necessarily equal better. Take time to ensure that your work is of the quality you would expect to receive from any business where you purchase products. Your book is like any other product that receives a review. As the manufacturer of your product, seek to give your customer a top-notch experience."

WORD ALIVE PRESS

119 De Baets St., Winnipeg, MB R2J 3R9, Canada | 866-967-3782

publishing@wordalivepress.ca | *www.wordalivepress.ca*

Jen Jandavs-Hedlin, publishing consultant

Types: audiobook, ebook, gift book, hardcover, offset paperback, picture book, POD

Services: à la carte options, copyediting, design, distribution, indexing, manuscript evaluation, marketing, online bookstore, packages of services, promotional materials, royalty contracts

Production time: three to six months

Books per year: 100

Tip: "Start with a manuscript evaluation from a reputable editor or publisher. They will help you to identify and address any big-picture trouble spots prior to investing in copyediting or publishing."

XULON PRESS

555 Winderley Pl., Ste. 225, Maitland, FL 32751 | 407-339-4217

www.xulonpress.com

Donald Newman, executive director of publishing

Types: ebook, hardcover, offset paperback, POD

Services: à la carte options, book trailer, copyediting, design, ghostwriting, illustrations, manuscript evaluation, marketing, online bookstore, packages of services, promotional materials, substantive editing

Production time: three to six months

Note: See "Editorial Services" and "Publicity and Marketing Services" for help with these needs.

4

DESIGN AND PRODUCTION SERVICES

1DOLLARSCAN

2470 Winchester Blvd., Ste. A, Campbell, CA 95008 | 669-212-0185
contact@1dollarscan.com | *1dollarscan.com*

> **Contact:** email
> **Services:** document scanning, file conversion
> **Charges:** custom, flat fee
> **Credentials/experience:** "1DollarScan is the most affordable scanning/digitizing service in the world. Through innovative technology solutions and the best practices, we are able to create the lowest priced and most affordable service with the best quality in the business."

829 DESIGN | LINNÉ GARRETT

8749 Cortina Cir., Roseville, CA 95678-2940 | 408-410-8072
linne@829design.com | *www.829design.com*

> **Contact:** email, phone, website form
> **Services:** book-cover design, book-interior design, branding design, ebook conversion, graphic design, illustrations, marketing design, typesetting, website design
> **Charges:** custom, flat fee, hourly rate
> **Credentials/experience:** "For over two decades, our unwavering commitment to delivering exceptional creative design services has left a lasting impact on brands, ambitious startups, small businesses, and private clients around the globe. While custom book design remains one of our cherished specialties, our portfolio encompasses a wide spectrum of offerings. From brand strategy and identity design to publication design, user-centric digital experiences with bespoke web development, and comprehensive digital marketing services encompassing SEO and Google ads—we

deliver it all. Print design and brand collateral marketing are also part of our diverse expertise."

BACK·DOOR DESIGN

backdoordesign99@gmail.com | *backdoordesign99.wixsite.com/info*

Contact: email, website form

Services: book-cover design, book-interior design, ebook conversion, illustrations, typesetting

Charges: custom, flat fee

Credentials/experience: "At back • door DESIGN, our mission is to create high-quality book designs at DIY prices. We are all about book design, from front cover to back cover and everything in between. Adobe Certified Associate in Print & Digital Publication Using Adobe InDesign."

BBS PUBLISHING AND COMMUNICATIONS, LLC | PAMELA GOSSIAUX

734-846-0112

pam@pamelagossiaux.com | *BestsellingBookShepherd.com*

Contact: email

Services: book-cover design, book-interior design, ebook conversion, newsletter design, printing, social-media posts, website design

Charges: custom, flat fee, hourly rate

Credentials/experience: "Let me turn your fiction or nonfiction manuscript into a bestseller! Experienced book shepherd can help you with design, publication, distribution, and more. I've coached and promoted authors to Amazon, *USA Today* and *Wall Street Journal* bestsellers. Degrees in Creative Writing & English Language and Literature from University of Michigan. International bestselling author."

BELIEVERS BOOK SERVICES | DAVE SHEETS

2329 Farragut Ave., Colorado Springs, CO 80907 | 719-641-7862

dave@believersbookservices.com | *www.believersbookservices.com*

Contact: website form

Services: book-cover design, book-interior design, ebook conversion, illustrations, printing, typesetting, website design

Charges: custom

Credentials/experience: "Our team has decades of experience in traditional publishing (Tyndale, Multnomah, Harvest House, NavPress), book wholesaling (STL Distribution), book distribution

(Advocate Distribution Solutions), book printing (Bethany Press, Snowfall Press), book retailing (Glen Eyrie Bookstore), and independent publishing (Believers Press, BelieversBookServices). We know how to help our clients achieve their goals while maintaining control over their own book project. We have helped hundreds of authors successfully publish, both in the United States and around the world."

BETHANY PRESS INTERNATIONAL

6820 W. 115th St., Bloomington, MN 55438 | 888-717-7400
info@bethanypress.com | *www.bethanypress.com*

> **Contact:** email, website form
> **Service:** printing
> **Charges:** flat fee
> **Credentials/experience:** Printer for the majority of Christian publishing houses since 1997. "We partner with authors, ministries, and publishers to create, produce, and distribute millions of life-changing Christian books each year. We invest our proceeds in training and sending missionaries through Bethany International."

BLUE LEAF BOOK SCANNING | DON O'DANIEL

618 Crowsnest Dr., Ballwin, MN 63021 | 314-606-9322
blue.leaf.it@gmail.com | *www.blueleaf-book-scanning.com*

> **Contact:** email, website form
> **Services:** audiobook, document scanning, ebook conversion
> **Charges:** flat fee
> **Credentials/experience:** "We have been providing low-cost scanning services since 2008."

BREE ROSE CREATIVE | BREE BYLE

Grand Rapids, MI | 616-425-8816
breerosecreative@gmail.com | *www.BreeRoseCreative.com*

> **Contact:** email, website form
> **Services:** book-branding photography and marketing design, book-interior design, ebook conversion, illustrations, typesetting, website design
> **Charges:** flat fee
> **Credentials/experience:** "I worked in the interior design department at Baker Publishing Group for six years before starting my own business. I have since worked with several publishers (Zondervan, Lake Drive Books, BPG) and many independent authors to design

book interiors, create websites and landing pages, and take book-styling photos to be used for marketing."

BRIAN WHITE DESIGN | BRIAN WHITE
Lawrence, KS | 785-841-5500
brianwhite.design
>**Contact:** phone, website form
>**Services:** app design, book-cover design, graphic design, illustrations, logo design, website design
>**Charges:** flat fee, hourly rate
>**Credentials/experience:** Twenty years in the design/web design/ branding industry.

BROOKSTONE CREATIVE GROUP | JOHN HERRING
100 Missionary Ridge, Birmingham, AL 35242 | 302-514-7899
www.brookstonecreativegroup.com
>**Contact:** phone
>**Services:** book-cover design, book-interior design, logo design, printing, promotional materials, website design
>**Charges:** flat fee
>**Credentials/experience:** "Brookstone Creative Group is changing the landscape for how writers, authors, speakers, pastors, musicians, and other creatives navigate the ever-changing landscape of platform development. Through true and tested solutions, training, and community-building, Brookstone Creative Group guides their clients in the who, where, when, and how to inspirational success."

BUTTERFIELD EDITORIAL SERVICES | DEBRA L. BUTTERFIELD
4810 Gene Field Rd., Saint Joseph, MO 64506 | 816-752-2171
deb@debralbutterfield.com | *themotivationaleditor.com*
>**Contact:** email
>**Services:** book-cover design, book-interior design, ebook conversion
>**Charges:** flat fee
>**Credentials/experience:** "Over six years of experience."

CREATIVE CORNERSTONES | CAYLAH COFFEEN and GALADRIEL COFFEEN
Huntsville, AL | 318-553-1625
creativecornerstones@gmail.com | *creativecornerstones.com/pre-release-materials*

Contact: email, website form

Services: audiobook, book trailer, book-cover design, book-interior design, ebook conversion, illustrations, typesetting, website design

Charges: custom

Credentials/experience: "Creative Cornerstones is a team of creatives who can make your book stand out from the crowd. We can create all your designs in one place: book exterior, interior, and visual marketing. Galadriel is an artist with over 10 years of experience. She can bring your vision to life, creating a sharp, hyperrealistic digital cover, character illustrations, maps, and even audiobooks. She specializes in fantasy and sci-fi art and can make the inside of a book pop as much as the outside. Caylah is a designer with experience creating WordPress websites, book trailers, and illustrations for social media and has worked as a content creator for Monster Ivy Publishing and Eschler Editing. We'll create a plan for each design step with our knowledge of the industry, so you can focus on what you love: writing."

DESERT RAIN EDITING | GLENIECE LYTLE

PO Box 8163, Hualapai, AZ 86412 | 928-715-7125
desert.rain.editing@gmail.com | *desertrainediting.com*

Contact: website form

Services: book-interior design, ebook conversion, typesetting

Charges: flat fee, page rate

Credentials/experience: "I began the typesetting journey a few years ago when one of my editing clients was dissatisfied with her final printed book from a vanity publisher. I learned quickly and discovered how much I enjoy interior book design. Now, I look forward to taking my editing clients' final manuscripts and creating clean, elegant, and readable print-ready PDFs and EPUB ebook files that look as polished and professional as they read."

DESIGN CORPS | JOHN WOLLINKA

1370 Carlson Dr., Colorado Springs, CO 80910 | 719-260-0500
general@designcorps.us | *designcorps.us*

Contact: phone, website form

Services: book-cover design, book-interior design, ebook conversion, illustrations, typesetting

Charges: flat fee

Credentials/experience: "Design Corps has been serving the Christian community for over 20 years. Our publishing clients have ranged from big publishers (such as Zondervan and Moody Publishers) to self-publishers. We have a love for the word that we bring with extensive experience in design to covers, interiors, page composition, illustration, and production (printed books and ebooks)."

DIGGYPOD | KEVIN OSWORTH

301 Industrial Dr., Tecumseh, MI 49286 | 877-944-7844
kosworth@diggypod.com | *www.diggypod.com*

> **Contact:** phone, website form
> **Services:** book-cover design, printing
> **Charges:** custom
> **Credentials/experience:** "DiggyPOD has been printing books since 2001. All facets of the book printing take place in our facility."

EAH CREATIVE | EMILIE HANEY

PO Box 69, Taylorsville, IN 47280 | 661-904-9409
emilie.eahcreative@gmail.com | *www.eahcreative.com*

> **Contact:** email
> **Services:** book-cover design, book-interior design
> **Charges:** custom, flat fee
> **Credentials/experience:** "Emilie works with small and large traditional publishers, as well as independent authors to create vibrant and marketable covers and graphics. Over the last six years, her covers have been finalists for awards and allowed her opportunities to speak about cover design and other aspects of graphic design specifically for authors. She approaches each new project with the desire to make the best and most marketable cover that will be at home on the digital or physical shelf."

EDENBROOKE PRODUCTIONS | MARTY KEITH

615-415-1942
johnmartinkeith@hotmail.com | *www.edenbrookemusic.com/booktrailers*

> **Contact:** email, phone, website form
> **Service:** book trailer
> **Charges:** flat fee
> **Credentials/experience:** "Edenbrooke Productions believes your story deserves a unique soundtrack. We've produced music for everyone from CBS Television to Discovery Channel, and now we want to give your story the star treatment."

ERIN ULRICH CREATIVE | ERIN ULRICH

PO Box 80282, Simpsonville, SC 29680
hello@erinulrichcreative.com | erinulrichcreative.com

Contact: website form
Service: website design
Charges: flat fee
Credentials/experience: "In today's world, your website matters more than ever. You need an online space designed to help you reach your goals. Sometimes that's easier said than done. We're here to listen to what you hope to achieve and develop a website strategy that gets results. We have been designing and building WordPress sites for over 13 years. Our clients include writers, small-business owners, nonprofits, and more. Whether you're starting from scratch or ready to take your web presence to the next level, we want to partner with you to see your vision become a reality."

FINDLEY FAMILY VIDEO PUBLICATIONS | MARY C. FINDLEY

mjmcfindley@gmail.com | findleyfamilyvideopublications.com/the-design-in-your-mind

Contact: email
Services: book trailer, book-cover design, book-interior design, ebook conversion
Charges: flat fee
Credentials/experience: "Twenty plus years in publishing, including work for a university press and design and formatting for multiple indie authors. Many testimonials, affordable pricing, and multigenre examples are on the website."

FISTBUMP MEDIA, LLC | DAN KING

115 E. 4th Ave., Ste. 212, Mount Dora, FL 32757 | 941-681-8015
dan@fistbumpmedia.com | fistbumpmedia.com

Contact: email
Services: book-cover design, book-interior design, ebook conversion, website design
Charges: flat fee, hourly rate, page rate
Credentials/experience: "With our roots in building an online presence as a blogger-author and growing authentic social-media community, we are a digital marketing (and managed WordPress hosting) agency which knows how to grow a brand online from the ground up. We're WordPress specialists, and our goal is to help you manage the technical side of being online."

FIVE JS DESIGN | JOY A. MILLER

joy@fivejsdesign.com | fivejsdesign.com

Contact: email, website form
Services: book-cover design, book-interior design, ebook conversion, logo design, marketing graphics, typesetting
Charges: custom
Credentials/experience: "Over sixteen years' experience with book and graphic design. Have designed for self-published, traditionally published, and *New York Times* best-selling authors."

THE FOREWORD COLLECTIVE | MOLLY HODGIN

1726 Charity Dr., Brentwood, TN 37027 | 615-497-4322
info@theforewordcollective.com | www.theforewordcollective.com

Contact: email, phone, website form
Service: book-cover design
Charges: flat fee, hourly rate
Credentials/experience: "The Foreword Collective was founded by Molly Hodgin, a publishing professional with two decades of experience. Most recently, she served as the Associate Publisher for the Specialty Division of HarperCollins Christian Publishing, working to acquire and create gift books, children's books, and new media products with authors and brands."

HANNAH LINDER DESIGNS | HANNAH LINDER

hannah@hannahlinderdesigns.com | www.hannahlinderdesigns.com

Contact: email, website form
Services: book-cover design, book-interior design
Charges: custom, flat fee
Credentials/experience: "Hannah Linder Designs specializes in professional book-cover design with affordable prices. Having designed for both traditional publishing houses and individual authors, including *New York Times*, *USA Today*, national, and international bestsellers, Hannah understands the importance of an attractive book cover and the trends of today's industry. Also, Hannah is a *magna cum laude* Graphic Design Associates Degree graduate and an award-winning book-cover designer."

HISWAY | KIMBERLY MORRISON

133 Hudspeth Rd., Statesville, NC 28677 | 828-244-0183
kim@onlyhisway.com | onlyhisway.com

Contact: email

Services: book-cover design, book-interior design, ebook conversion, website design

Charges: custom

Credentials/experience: "I am a self-published author and speaker of seven books and numerous devotionals and operate a successful graphic design and content creation company specific to churches and Christian organizations."

INKSNATCHER | SALLY HANAN

429 S. Avenue C, Elgin, TX 78621 | 512-265-6403
inkmeister@inksnatcher.com | inksnatcher.com

Contact: email, phone, website form

Services: book trailer, book-cover design, book-interior design, ebook conversion, typesetting, website design

Charges: custom

Credentials/experience: "Sally Hanan, an author herself, started Inksnatcher in 2008 with just editing services. Today, Inksnatcher provides self-publishing authors with every service they need to produce and publish with excellence. Inksnatcher is an approved service provider with the Alliance of Independent Authors, the Christian Editor Connection, and Reedsy."

JAMIE FOLEY

Giddings, TX
jamie@jamiefoley.com | jamiefoley.com/typesetting

Contact: email

Services: book-interior design, typesetting

Charges: flat fee, hourly rate

Credentials/experience: "Specializing in efficient digital typesetting and custom interior-book design, Jamie has been working in the Christian publishing industry since 2008. Starting at Thomas Nelson, she is currently the typesetter at Enclave Publishing, Sky Turtle Press, and The Christian Writers Institute, and has served many independent authors, including the estate for the *New York Times* bestselling Christy novels. She also has art director experience, including press checks and printer relations."

JENNIFER EDWARDS COMMUNICATIONS | JENNIFER EDWARDS

2839 Sleeping Bear Rd., Montrose, CO 81401 | 916-768-4207
mail.jennifer.edwards@gmail.com | jedwardsediting.net

Contact: website form
Service: production management for self-publishing
Charges: flat fee
Credentials/experience: "I manage the production of printed/ digital books and consult with self-publishing authors through the publishing process. Includes working with cover and interior designers and illustrators to produce hardcovers, paperbacks, and ebooks. I have seven years of experience working on Amazon KDP and Ingram Spark to self-publish books."

JENNIFER WESTBROOK

14030 Connecticut Ave. #6813, Silver Spring, MD 20916
support@jenwestwriting.com | *www.jenwestwriting.com/web-design*

Contact: phone
Service: website design
Charges: custom, flat fee
Credentials/experience: "I build Wix websites that pack a punch, complete with all the must-haves you need to keep thriving online. As a copywriter and web designer with over eight years of experience, I create the right mix of words, design, and behind-the-scenes systems to make everything work together seamlessly so you can get next-level results."

JESSICA LINN EVANS, LLC | JESSICA LINN EVANS

jessicaevans915@gmail.com | *jessicalinnevans.com*

Contact: email, website form
Services: book-cover design, book-interior design, illustrations
Charges: custom
Credentials/experience: "BFA in studio art at University of Idaho. Art director/graphic designer experience. Traditional-mediums illustration and cover design for children's picture books and middle-grade novels. Interior design for children's picture books."

KELLIE BOOK DESIGN | KELLIE PARSONS

Unit 1, 23 Apara Way, Nollamara, WA 6061, Australia | 0412 591 687
kellie@kelliemaree.com | *instagram.com/kelliebookdesign*

Contact: email
Services: book-cover design, book-interior design, ebook conversion, typesetting
Charges: custom
Credentials/experience: "Bachelor degree in graphic and interactive

design. Eight years specialized experience in typesetting book and cover designs. Ten plus years' experience in design for print. Tools used include the Adobe Suite (print) and Vellum (for ebooks)."

LAUNCH MISSION CREATIVE | TRAVIS D. PETERSON

travis@launchmissions.com | *www.launchmissioncreative.com*

Contact: website form
Services: Amazon A+ content, book-cover design, book-interior design, Kickstarter graphics, printing, typesetting
Charges: custom
Credentials/experience: "Not only am I an award-winning Christian children's author myself, but also an award-winning print designer with over a decade of experience both in-house for a couple of internationally recognized ministries and as a freelancer. I hold a degree in Computer Graphics Technology from Purdue University."

LEMUEL MASSUIA STUDIO | LEMUEL MASSUIA

Brazil
lemuel@lemuelmassuia.com | *www.lemuelmassuia.com*

Contact: email, website form
Services: book-cover design, book-interior design, illustrations, videobook
Charges: flat fee, page rate
Credentials/experience: "Technologist diploma in publicity with specialization in arts and production, 20+ years of experience on art direction, illustration, graphic design, and storytelling."

MARTIN PUBLISHING SERVICES | MELINDA MARTIN

Palestine, TX | 903-948-4893
martinpublishingservices@gmail.com | *melindamartin.me*

Contact: phone
Services: book-cover design, book-interior design, ebook conversion, typesetting
Charges: flat fee
Credentials/experience: "More than five years of working with clients' manuscripts to achieve a design that is best for their platforms."

MISSION AND MEDIA | MICHELLE RAYBURN

11510 County Highway M, New Auburn, WI 54757
info@missionandmedia.com | *missionandmedia.com*

Contact: email
Services: book-cover design, book-interior design, ebook conversion, typesetting
Charges: flat fee, free consultation, hourly rate
Credentials/experience: "Michelle works with indie and self-published authors to design a quality book cover and interior. She also coaches those who want to create their own imprint with full control of their own publishing process. Her area of specialty is with Amazon KDP. Michelle has more than 20 years of experience on the writing and editing side of publishing. Portfolio and additional information are available on the website."

MOUNTAIN CREEK BOOKS, LLC | KARA STARCHER

PO Box 21, Chloe, WV 25235
kara@mountaincreekbooks.com | *mountaincreekbooks.com*

Contact: website form
Services: book-cover design, book-interior design, ebook conversion, typesetting
Charges: custom, flat fee
Credentials/experience: "BA in publishing; over 20 years of experience."

PAGE & PIXEL PUBLICATIONS | SUSAN MOORE

La Crosse, WI
pageandpixelpublications@gmail.com | *pageandpixelpublications.com*

Contact: email
Services: book trailer, book-cover design, book-interior design, ebook conversion, typesetting
Charges: hourly rate
Credentials/experience: "Are you preparing to self-publish? I can format your manuscript to give it that professional look within the parameters of your publishing house. The design would include the entire interior of your book. A digital, print-ready PDF of your book's completed interior layout is provided. I can convert your manuscript into the digital format that is readable on devices like Kindle, Nook, tablets, phones, computers, and notebooks, as well as generic brand e-readers. Working from your original document in Microsoft Word, InDesign, PDF, or other format, I will provide you with a digital file that you can upload to Amazon, Barnes and Noble, or other suppliers. Your finished product will feature a navigable table of contents and hyperlinked footnotes, as well as any graphic images that you choose to include."

PRAIRIE FALLS BOOKS | DEBRA L. BUTTERFIELD and TAMARA CLYMER

St. Joseph, MO
deb@prairiefallbooks.com | *prairiefallsbooks.com*

- **Contact:** website form
- **Services:** book-cover design, book-interior design, ebook conversion, website design
- **Charges:** flat fee
- **Credentials/experience:** "Our professional designers have a wide variety of experience in book design, interior layout, catalogs, and magazines in both freelance and traditional publishing."

PROFESSIONAL PUBLISHING SERVICES | CHRISTY CALLAHAN

912-388-1898
professionalpublishingservices@gmail.com |
professionalpublishingservicesus.weebly.com

- **Contact:** email
- **Services:** book-cover design, book-interior design, ebook conversion, typesetting
- **Charges:** custom
- **Credentials/experience:** "Christy graduated Phi Beta Kappa from Carnegie Mellon University, where she first learned how to use Adobe software. While she earned her MA in Intercultural Studies from Fuller Seminary, she edited sound files for distance-learning classes for the Media Center and designed ads as Women's Concerns Committee chairperson. Christy is an Adobe Certified Associate in Print & Digital Publication Using Adobe InDesign, leveraging her expertise as an editor and proofreader and extensive knowledge of *Chicago* style to create professional-looking book covers and interior layouts."

REDEMPTION PRESS | ATHENA DEAN HOLTZ

1602 Cole St., Enumclaw, WA 98022 | 360-226-3488
athena@redemption-press.com | *www.redemption-press.com*

- **Contact:** phone, website form
- **Services:** audiobook, website design
- **Charges:** flat fee
- **Credentials/experience:** "Our website partner helps authors create well-branded and effective websites with email marketing

integration, including a compelling lead magnet. We also offer both author- and professional-narrated audiobooks with full distribution. We don't list all our services on our website."

RICK STEELE EDITORIAL SERVICES | RICK STEELE
26 Dean Rd., Ringgold, GA 30736 | 706-937-8121
rsteelecam@gmail.com | *steeleeditorialservices.myportfolio.com*

Contact: email, website form
Services: book-interior design, ebook conversion, typesetting
Charges: page rate
Credentials/experience: "With decades of experience using page-layout software, Rick Steele Editorial Services has the skills to take your edited manuscript to printed-page format with a professional, attractive page layout. If you wish to publish your manuscript with Amazon's KDP or similar platform, I can help prepare your manuscript file for printer and ebook submission."

ROSEANNA WHITE DESIGNS | ROSEANNA WHITE
roseannamwhite@gmail.com | *www.RoseannaWhiteDesigns.com*

Contact: email, website form
Services: book-cover design, book-interior design, ebook conversion, illustrations, typesetting
Charges: custom, flat fee, hourly rate
Credentials/experience: "Roseanna has been designing and typesetting books for nearly ten years, combining her keen eye and artistic skills with her insider knowledge of the industry. As an author herself, she knows how important it is for the appearance of a book to match the words and strives to bring your story to life at a single glance. She has worked for publishing houses and independently for some of Christian fiction's top authors."

SCOTT LA COUNTE
Anaheim, CA | 714-404-7182
Roboscott@gmail.com | *scottdouglas.org/coaching*

Contact: website form
Services: book-cover design, book-interior design, ebook conversion
Charges: flat fee
Credentials/experience: "I've worked in publishing for over 20 years (both in traditional publishing and self-publishing). Over those years, I have helped indie publishers sell over 2,000,000 books."

SKWD ASSOCIATES FL, LLC | BRUCE SHANK

PO Box 471068, Celebration, FL 34747 | 407-966-4558
info@celebrationwebdesign.com | *celebrationwebdesign.com*

> **Contact:** email, phone, website form
> **Services:** marketing, SEO, website design
> **Charges:** custom, flat fee, hourly rate
> **Credentials/experience:** "Since 2002 Celebration Web Design
> has been passionate about sharing the gospel and enabling
> Christian authors and ministries through our expertise in website
> development, design, and online marketing. Our experienced team
> of designers and developers work closely with you to craft tailor-
> made websites that reflect your unique vision and message."

STORMHILL MEDIA | JIM CAMOMILE

15226 County Rd. 434, Lindale, TX 75771 | 512-914-8458
jim@stormhillmedia.com | *www.stormhillmedia.com*

> **Contact:** email, website form
> **Services:** book-cover design, website design
> **Charges:** custom, hourly rate
> **Credentials/experience:** "Award-winning author website designers and
> developers of MyBookTable for WordPress. Stormhill Media has over
> 10 years of experience invested in designing and building attractive
> and highly effective author websites that sell books and get noticed."

STORYWRAP.CA | LYSA

Saskatchewan, Canada
designer@storywrap.ca | *storywrap.ca*

> **Contact:** website form
> **Services:** advertising, book-cover design, book-interior design, graphics
> **Charges:** custom, flat fee
> **Credentials/experience:** "Storywrap.ca is a team of graphic designers
> with several years of experience. We are committed to offering
> quality design services at an affordable price for authors. We invite
> potential clients to browse our website; and if our design style is
> what you're looking for, get in touch with us to discuss your needs."

SUZANNE FYHRIE PARROTT

PO Box 571, Gleneden Beach, OR 97388
author@suzannefyhrieparrott.com | *www.SuzanneFyhrieParrott.com*

> **Contact:** website form

Services: book-cover design, book-interior design, ebook conversion, illustrations, typesetting

Charges: custom, flat fee

Credentials/experience: "With over 40 years of experience in graphic design, illustration, and advertising, Suzanne Parrott's design services include logos, book-cover design, book layout and formatting, ebook formatting and design. She prioritizes each client's specific needs, ensuring they receive the utmost attention and tailored solutions. Additionally, Parrott guides authors throughout the entire publication process, leveraging POD publishing sources like Ingram Spark and Amazon KDP. Her dedication to delivering high-quality work has been recognized through several awards for design excellence."

TINNSY WINNSY EDITORIAL AND DESIGN STUDIO | BRENDA WILBEE

7595 Birch Bay Dr. #2, Blaine, WA 98230 | 360-389-6895
Brenda@BrendaWilbee.com | *www.BrendaWilbee.com*

Contact: email

Services: book-cover design, illustrations, printing, typesetting

Charges: custom, flat fee, hourly rate

Credentials/experience: "I hold an MA in professional writing and a degree in graphic design. I taught college composition for seven years, commercial writing for twenty, and in the past have worked as a designer for an international company. Some of my clients include Habitat for Humanity, PageMill Press, DDA Publishing, Forever Books, Lauren Myers, Carol Lawrence, Lisa Weitkamp, Deanna Nowadnick, Scott Wyatt, and so many other writers just like you."

TLC BOOK DESIGN | TAMARA DEVER

Austin, TX
tamara@tlcbookdesign.com | *www.TLCBookDesign.com*

Contact: website form

Services: author coaching for self-publishers, book-cover design, book-interior design, ebook conversion, printing, typesetting

Charges: custom, flat fee, hourly rate

Credentials/experience: "We are a small body of believers bringing you 30+ years of experience producing books that have garnered more than 300 awards. Better than that, our clients are thrilled and often become like family. We're here to support you in creating your best books with editorial, design, printing, and coaching to meet your specific needs. There's nothing templated or cookie-cutter here, just personalized and personable service."

TWO WORDS PUBLISHING | CLATON BUTCHER

3213 W. Main St. #166, Rapid City, SD 57702 | 605-939-5913
cbutcher@twowordspublishing.com | *www.twowordspublishing.com*

Contact: email
Service: audiobook
Charges: hourly rate
Credentials/experience: "Two Words Publishing has published and/or produced audiobooks from most major Christian publishers, as well as authors and their agents. With an Audie (considered the Oscars of audiobooks), Earphones Award, Voice Arts Awards, and more, you can expect top-notch audiobook quality."

TYPEWRITER CREATIVE CO. | TARYN NERGAARD

support@typewritercreative.co | *www.typewritercreative.co*

Contact: email
Services: book-cover design, book-interior design, ebook conversion, illustrations, typesetting
Charges: flat fee
Credentials/experience: "Since 2018, Typewriter Creative Co. has helped more than 50 authors self-publish over 90 books with their professional design and marketing services."

VIVID GRAPHICS | LARRY VAN HOOSE

221 S. Main St., Ste. 200, Galax, VA 24333 | 276-233-0276
info@vivid-graphics.com | *www.vivid-graphics.com*

Contact: email, phone, website form
Services: book-cover design, book-interior design, ebook conversion, graphic design, website design
Charges: custom, flat fee, hourly rate
Credentials/experience: "Larry Van Hoose is the creative director for Vivid Graphics and has over 20 years of experience in design, writing, photography, and marketing."

YO PRODUCTIONS, LLC | YOLONDA SANDERS

7185 E. Main St., Unit 1543, Reynoldsburg, OH 43068 | 614-452-4920
info_4u@yoproductions.net | *www.yoproductions.net*

Contact: email, phone, website form

Services: book-cover design, book-interior design, ebook conversion, typesetting

Charges: custom, flat fee, hourly rate

Credentials/experience: "Yo Productions, LLC is a publishing consultant that helps authors get their work from paper to print. The company is owned by author and scholar, Yolonda Tonette Sanders, PhD, and provides clients with book-cover designs and formatting for digital and print works."

ZAQ DESIGNS & PUBLISHING | DOUG WEST

13518 Heritage Dr., Bonner Springs, KS 66012 | 913-827-2225
doug@zaqdesigns.com | *www.zaqdesigns.com*

Contact: email, website form

Services: audiobook, book trailer, book-cover design, book-interior design, ebook conversion, illustrations, printing, typesetting, website design

Charges: custom, flat fee, page rate

Credentials/experience: "We specialize in offering book design and production services. With more than 29 years of experience in graphic design, printing, and illustration, we ventured into the book design and publishing business in 2010. ZAQ Designs & Publishing is dedicated to providing high quality, stunning cover designs and production services. Don't hesitate to contact us and see what we can do for you!"

Note: See "Editorial Services" and "Publicity and Marketing Services" for help with these needs.

5

DISTRIBUTION SERVICES

AMAZON SELLER CENTRAL
sell.amazon.com

Amazon has two selling plans: individual for 99¢ per book and professional for $39.99 per month. Both plans have other selling fees as well. You can manage inventory, update pricing, communicate with buyers, contact support, and add new products all from the Seller Central website.

BCH FULFILLMENT & DISTRIBUTION
33 Oakland Ave., Harrison, NY 10528 | 914-835-0015
bookch@aol.com | www.bookch.com/home.taf

Provides exclusive fulfillment and distribution services, including relationships with wholesalers and bookstores, warehousing your books, taking orders from wholesalers and bookstores, fulfilling those orders, billing and collecting monies, processing returns, and getting your books into Ingram if you qualify. Fees vary, depending on the services.

MIDPOINT TRADE BOOKS
814 N. Franklin St., Ste. 100, Chicago, IL 60610 | 312-337-0747
frontdesk@ipgbook.com | www.midpointtrade.com/christian_marketplace

A full-service book distribution division of Independent Publishers Group. Provides warehousing, fulfillment, and catalog inclusion under Covenant Media Resources, an extension of sales and distribution services specifically tailored to meet the needs of the Christian marketplace. In addition to reaching the traditional CBA market, it has access to a wide range of general bookstores and wholesalers that successfully sell Christian and other likeminded titles.

PATHWAY BOOK SERVICE
34 Production Ave., Keene, NH 03431 | 800-345-6665
pbs@pathwaybook.com | www.pathwaybook.com

Provides warehousing, order fulfillment, and trade distribution. It is a longtime distributor to Ingram and Baker & Taylor, the vendors of choice for most bookstores. Pathway uploads new-title spreadsheets to Ingram and Baker & Taylor, as well as to *Amazon.com*, Barnes & Noble, and Books-A-Million on a weekly basis. Distribution outside of North America is available through Gazelle Book Services in the United Kingdom. Also provides the option of having Pathway add titles to its Amazon Advantage account, which is at a lower discount and often a lower shipping cost per book than individual accounts.

PUBLISHERS STORING AND SHIPPING

660 S. Mansfield, Ypsilanti, MI 48197 | 734-487-9720
pssc.com

Provides warehousing, call center, order fulfillment, and returns for single-title self-publishers to large publishing houses. Has a second facility at 46 Development Rd., Fitchburg, MA 01420; 978-345-2121.

PART 3

PERIODICAL PUBLISHERS

6

TOPICS AND TYPES

This chapter is not an exhaustive list of types of manuscripts and topics periodical editors are looking for, but it is a starting place for some of the more popular ones. For instance, almost all periodicals take manuscripts in categories like Christian living, so they are not listed here. Plus writers guidelines tend to outline general areas, not every specific type and topic an editor will buy.

COLUMNS
Almost an Author
Blue Ridge Christian News
Christian Courier
Christian Herald
Christian Leader
Holiness Today
HomeLife
InSite
Light
The Mother's Heart
Power for Living
Prayer Connect
Teachers of Vision
Words for the Way

CONTEMPORARY ISSUES
Anglican Journal
The Baptist Bulletin
Canadian Mennonite
Caring Magazine

Celebrate Life Magazine
The Christian Century
Christianity Today
Columbia
The Covenant Companion
Faith Today
Ministry
Now What?
Our Sunday Visitor
St. Anthony Messenger
The War Cry

DEVOTIONS
Brio
Faith on Every Corner
Focus on the Family Clubhouse
Mature Living
ParentLife
Power for Living
StarLight Magazine

ESSAYS
America
The Canadian Lutheran
The Christian Century
Commonweal
Ekstasis
Faith Today
Faithfully Magazine
Image
Love Is Moving
The Lutheran Witness
Our Sunday Visitor
Poets & Writers Magazine
U.S. Catholic
Writer's Digest

EVANGELISM
Baptist Standard
Blue Ridge Christian News
Christian Herald
Christian Leader
Evangelical Missions Quarterly
Just Between Us
Mature Living
Outreach
The War Cry

FAMILY
The Alabama Baptist
The Baptist Bulletin
Baptist Standard
Columbia
Creative Inspirations
Faith & Friends
Focus on the Family
Gems of Truth
HomeLife
Influence

Inspire a Fire
Joyful Living Magazine
Light
Mature Living
Ministry
The Mother's Heart
ParentLife
St. Anthony Messenger

FICTION
See Short Story.

FILLERS
Angels on Earth
Bible Advocate
Blue Ridge Christian News
Christian Herald
Focus on the Family Clubhouse
Focus on the Family Clubhouse Jr.
Guideposts
LIVE
The Mother's Heart
StarLight Magazine
Words for the Way

HOW-TO
Almost an Author
Baptist Standard
Blue Ridge Christian News
Cadet Quest
Canada Lutheran
Celebrate Life Magazine
Christian Herald
Christian Standard
Evangelical Missions Quarterly
Faith Today
Focus on the Family
Focus on the Family Clubhouse

HomeLife
Influence
InSite
The Journal of Adventist Education
Joyful Living Magazine
Just Between Us
Leading Hearts
Light
LIVE
The Lutheran Witness
Mature Living
Ministry
The Mother's Heart
Mutuality
Outreach
ParentLife
Parish Liturgy
Poets & Writers Magazine
Prayer Connect
Teachers of Vision
Words for the Way
The Writer
Writer's Digest
WritersWeekly.com
Writing Corner

INTERVIEWS

The Arlington Catholic Herald
The Baptist Bulletin
Baptist Standard
Brio
byFaith
Cadet Quest
Canada Lutheran
Celebrate Life Magazine
Charisma
The Christian Century
Christian Herald
Christianity Today

Columbia
The Covenant Companion
DTS Magazine
Evangelical Missions Quarterly
Faith & Friends
Faith Today
Faithfully Magazine
Focus on the Family
Focus on the Family Clubhouse
HomeLife
Influence
InSite
The Journal of Adventist Education
Joyful Living Magazine
Just Between Us
Leading Hearts
Light
LIVE
The Lutheran Witness
The Marketplace
Mature Living
Ministry
The Mother's Heart
Mutuality
Net Results
Outreach
ParentLife
Parish Liturgy
Poets & Writers Magazine
Prayer Connect
Teachers of Vision
Words for the Way
Writer's Digest

LEADERSHIP/MINISTRY

The Alabama Baptist
The Baptist Bulletin
Baptist Standard
Christian Leader

Evangelical Missions Quarterly
Holiness Today
Influence
InSite
Just Between Us
Ministry
Outreach
testimony/Enrich

MARRIAGE
The Baptist Bulletin
Boundless
Faith & Friends
Focus on the Family
Gems of Truth
HomeLife
Joyful Living Magazine
Mature Living
St. Anthony Messenger

NEWSPAPERS
Anglican Journal
The Arlington Catholic Herald
Blue Ridge Christian News
Christian Courier
Christian Herald
Good News
The Messianic Times

OPINION
Canadian Mennonite
The Christian Century
Christian Courier
Christianity Today
Commonweal
Faithfully Magazine
Love Is Moving

The Messianic Times
Relevant
U.S. Catholic

PARENTING
The Baptist Bulletin
Columbia
Faith on Every Corner
Focus on the Family
HomeLife
Just Between Us
Light
Mature Living
The Mother's Heart
ParentLife

PERSONAL EXPERIENCE
The Alabama Baptist
Almost an Author
Angels on Earth
Anglican Journal
The Baptist Bulletin
Bible Advocate
Blue Ridge Christian News
The Breakthrough Intercessor
Café
Canada Lutheran
Canadian Mennonite
Celebrate Life Magazine
Christian Leader
The Covenant Companion
Creation Illustrated
DTS Magazine
Faith & Friends
Faith on Every Corner
Friends Journal
Gather
Gems of Truth

Guide
Guideposts
Highway News
Holiness Today
Inspire a Fire
The Journal of Adventist Education
Joyful Living Magazine
Just Between Us
Leading Hearts
LEAVES
LIVE
The Lutheran Witness
Mature Living
The Mother's Heart
Mutuality
Now What?
Power for Living
Standard
Teachers of Vision
testimony/Enrich
Today's Christian Living
The War Cry
Words for the Way

POETRY
America
Bible Advocate
The Breakthrough Intercessor
The Christian Century
Christian Courier
Commonweal
Creative Inspirations
Ekstasis
Faith on Every Corner
Focus on the Family Clubhouse Jr.
Friends Journal
Gems of Truth
Image

Ink & Quill Quarterly
Inspire a Fire
LEAVES
LIVE
Love Is Moving
The Lutheran Witness
Power for Living
Sharing
Sojourners
StarLight Magazine
Teachers of Vision
Time Of Singing
U.S. Catholic
Words for the Way

PROFILES
See Interviews.

REVIEWS
The Alabama Baptist
Anglican Journal
byFaith
Canadian Mennonite
Caring Magazine
Celebrate Life Magazine
Charisma
The Christian Century
Christian Courier
Christian Herald
Christianity Today
Evangelical Missions Quarterly
Faith & Friends
Faith Today
HeartBeat
The Journal of Adventist Education
Leading Hearts
LEAVES
Light

Love Is Moving
The Marketplace
The Messianic Times
Ministry
The Mother's Heart
Mutuality
Sojourners
Time Of Singing
Words for the Way

SHORT STORIES

Beginner's Friend
Blue Ridge Christian News
Brio
Cadet Quest
Creation Illustrated
Explorers
Faith on Every Corner
Focus on the Family Clubhouse
Focus on the Family Clubhouse Jr.
Gems of Truth
Image
LIVE
Mature Living
Nature Friend
St. Anthony Messenger
Sharing
StarLight Magazine
Teachers of Vision
Youth Compass

SUNDAY SCHOOL
TAKEHOME PAPERS

Beginner's Friend
Explorers
Gems of Truth
Guide
LIVE

Our Little Friend
Power for Living
Primary Treasure
Standard
Youth Compass

TEACHING

The Baptist Bulletin
Bible Advocate
The Breakthrough Intercessor
byFaith
The Canadian Lutheran
Celebrate Life Magazine
DTS Magazine
Focus on the Family
Friends Journal
Holiness Today
Influence
The Lutheran Witness
Mature Living
The Messianic Times
Ministry
ParentLife
Parish Liturgy
Relevant
St. Anthony Messenger
Teachers of Vision

TESTIMONIES

Bible Advocate
Christian Leader
Faith & Friends
Friends Journal
Just Between Us
LEAVES
Peer
Today's Christian Living

7

ADULT MARKETS

THE ALABAMA BAPTIST

3310 Independence Dr., Birmingham, AL 35209 | 205-870-4720

news@thealabamabaptist.org | *thealabamabaptist.org*

Jennifer Davis Rash, editor-in-chief

> **Denomination:** Baptist
> **Parent company:** TAB Media Group
> **Type:** bimonthly print newsletter; circulation: 40,000
> **Audience:** denomination
> **Purpose:** to share news and information relevant to the members of Baptist churches in Alabama to help them better live out their faith in the current cultural landscape
> **Submissions:** Email only.
> **Types of manuscripts:** Bible studies, news, personal experience, reviews, true stories
> **Topics:** Christian living, current events, events, family, ministry, missions
> **Guidelines:** *thealabamabaptist.org/submissions/submission-policy*
> **Tip:** "Most articles and columns are assigned by the editorial staff, but unsolicited submissions from readers are reviewed as time allows."

AMERICA

106 W. 56th St., New York, NY 10019-3803 | 212-581-4640

www.americamagazine.org

Sam Sawyer, S.J., editor in chief

> **Denomination:** Catholic
> **Parent company:** America Media/Jesuit Conference of the United States and Canada
> **Type:** monthly digital and print magazine; circulation: 46,000
> **Audience:** primarily Catholic, two-thirds laypeople, college educated

Purpose: to provide a smart Catholic take on faith and culture
Submissions: Submit complete manuscript or query letter through the website. Unsolicited freelance: 100%. Responds in two weeks.
Types of manuscripts: articles, essays, poetry
Length: articles and essays, 800–2,000 words; poetry, 40 lines maximum
Topics: Christian living/spirituality, culture, trends
Rights: electronic, first
Payment: competitive rates, on acceptance
Guidelines: *americamedia.submittable.com/submit*
Tip: "We are known across the Catholic world for our unique brand of excellent, relevant, and accessible coverage. From theology and spirituality to politics, international relations, arts and letters, and the economy and social justice, our coverage spans the globe."

ANGELS ON EARTH

110 William St., Ste. 901, New York, NY 10038 | 212-251-8100
submissions@angelsonearth.org | *www.shopguideposts.org/angels-on-earth-magazine.html*
Colleen Hughes, editor-in-chief
Parent company: Guideposts
Type: bimonthly digital and print magazine; circulation: 550,000
Audience: general
Purpose: to tell true stories of heavenly angels and earthly ones who find themselves on a mission of comfort, kindness, or reassurance
Submissions: Email complete manuscript. Unsolicited freelance: 90%. Responds in two months or not interested.
Types of manuscripts: fillers, personal experience, recipes
Length: articles, 1,200–1,500 words; short features, 300–600 words
Topic: angels
Rights: all
Payment: $25-500, on publication
Kill fee: 20%
Manuscripts accepted per year: 40–60
Guidelines: *www.guideposts.org/writers-guidelines*
Sample: 7"x10" SASE with four stamps
Tip: "We are not limited to stories about heavenly angels. We also accept stories about human beings doing heavenly duties."

ANGLICAN JOURNAL

80 Hayden St., Toronto, ON M4Y 3G2, Canada | 416-924-9199

editor@national.anglican.ca | www.anglicanjournal.com

Tali Folkins, editor

Denomination: Anglican

Parent company: Anglican Church of Canada

Type: monthly digital and print newspaper; circulation: 123,000; advertising accepted

Audience: denomination

Purpose: to share compelling news and features about the Anglican Church of Canada and the Anglican communion and religion in general

Submissions: Email query first. Responds in two weeks.

Types of manuscripts: news, personal experience, reviews

Length: 500–1,000 words

Topics: Christian living/spirituality, denomination, events, issues

Rights: first

Payment: $75–100, on acceptance

Seasonal submissions: two months in advance

Preferred Bible version: NRSV

Guidelines: *anglicanjournal.com/about/posting-policy*

Sample: on the website

Tip: "Stories should be of interest to a national audience. They are usually about a national event or a local issue that reflects the larger picture."

THE ARLINGTON CATHOLIC HERALD

200 N. Glebe Rd., Ste. 600, Arlington, VA 22203 | 703-841-2590

editorial@catholicherald.com | www.catholicherald.com

Ann M. Augherton, managing editor

Denomination: Catholic

Parent company: Arlington, Virginia, Diocese

Type: weekly digital and print newspaper; circulation: 70,000; advertising accepted

Audience: denomination

Purpose: to support the church's mission to evangelize by providing news from a Catholic perspective

Submissions: Email query letter.

Types of manuscripts: feature articles, news, profiles

Sample: on the website

THE BAPTIST BULLETIN

244 S. Randall Rd. #1188, Elgin, IL 60123 | 888-588-1600

submissions@BaptistBulletin.org | baptistbulletin.org

Matt Olmstead, managing editor

Denomination: Baptist

Parent company: Regular Baptist Ministries/General Association of Regular Baptist Churches

Type: quarterly digital and print magazine; circulation: 5,300

Audience: Baptist church members

Purpose: to provide a "kitchen table" where church members gather to discuss important topics

Submissions: Email complete manuscript as attachment.

Types of manuscripts: personal experience, profiles, teaching

Length: 800–2,000 words

Topics: Christian living, denomination, discipleship, family, marriage, ministry, parenting

Rights: all

Preferred Bible version: NKJV

Guidelines: *baptistbulletin.org/write-for-us*

Tip: "The magazine is your gateway to articles addressing current issues from a Baptist perspective, inspiring stories about people who serve in unique ways, and exciting coverage of what's happening in Regular Baptist Ministries."

BAPTIST STANDARD

PO Box 941309, Plano, TX 75094 | 214-630-4571

www.baptiststandard.com

Ken Camp, managing editor, news, features, book reviews;
  kencamp@baptiststandard.com

Eric Black, editor, opinion articles, sermons; eric.black@baptiststandard.com

Denomination: Baptist

Parent company: Baptist Standard Publishing

Type: quarterly website

Audience: denomination

Purpose: to connect God's story and God's people through information, inspiration, and challenge

Submissions: Email complete manuscript as attachment.

Types of manuscripts: how-to, profiles

Length: articles, 750–1,000 words; book reviews, 250–500 words

Topics: evangelism, family, leadership, ministry, missions, Texas Baptist history

Guidelines: *www.baptiststandard.com/submissions*

Tip: "When we consider something for publication, we ask: Does a news story or opinion piece inform, inspire or challenge people to live like Jesus? If so, it passes the most general test for consideration. Does a news story involve Baptists, in general? If so, we consider it. Does a story involve or have importance to Baptists in Texas? If so, we consider it. Does it involve the Baptist General Convention of Texas and Texas Baptists? An almost automatic yes."

BIBLE ADVOCATE

PO Box 33677, Denver, CO 80233

bibleadvocate@cog7.org | baonline.org

Sherri Langton, associate editor

Denomination: Church of God (Seventh Day)

Parent company: General Conference of the Church of God (Seventh Day)

Type: bimonthly digital and print magazine; circulation: 13,000

Audience: denomination, general

Purpose: to advocate the Bible and represent the Church of God (Seventh Day)

Submissions: Email complete manuscript. Unsolicited freelance: 30–50%. Responds in 4–10 weeks.

Types of manuscripts: fillers, personal experience, poetry, teaching, testimonies

Length: 600–1,300 words

Topics: Christian living/spirituality, theme-related

Rights: electronic, first, onetime, reprint (with info on where/when previously published)

Payment: articles, $25–65; poems and fillers, $20; on publication

Manuscripts accepted per year: 10–20

Preferred Bible versions: NIV, NKJV

Theme lists: available on website

Guidelines: *baonline.org/write-for-us-2*

Sample: 9"x12" envelope with three stamps

Tip: "Please read past issues of the magazine before you submit and become familiar with our style. No snail mail submissions or PDFs. No Christmas or Easter manuscripts. We do not pay writers who live outside the US or Canada."

BLUE RIDGE CHRISTIAN NEWS

152 Summit Ave., Spruce Pine, NC 28777 | 828-765-6800

cathy@brcnews.com | blueridgechristiannews.com

Cathy Pritchard, editor

Parent company: The Ninevah Productions, Inc.

Type: monthly digital and print newspaper; circulation: 12,000; advertising accepted

Audience: people seeking to know more about God

Purpose: to share the good news of Jesus and other positive, uplifting, and good news from around the world

Submissions: Email only. Unsolicited freelance: 10%. Responds in one week.

Types of manuscripts: columns, fillers, how-to, personal experience, short stories

Length: 1,000 words

Topics: Christian living/spirituality, evangelism

Rights: all, electronic, first, reprint (with info on where/when previously published)

Payment: none

Manuscripts accepted per year: 100

Seasonal submissions: one month in advance

Preferred Bible versions: KJV, NKJV, NASB

Guidelines: not available

Sample: $3, email request

Tip: "Looking for positive, uplifting, good news."

BOUNDLESS

See entry in "Teen/Young Adult Markets."

THE BREAKTHROUGH INTERCESSOR

PO Box 121, Lincoln, VA 20160-0121 | 540-338-4131

breakthrough@intercessors.org | *www.intercessors.org*

Claudette Ammons, managing editor

Parent company: Breakthrough

Type: quarterly digital and print magazine; circulation: 4,000

Audience: adults interested in growing their prayer lives

Purpose: to encourage people to pray and equip them to do so more effectively

Submissions: Email or mail complete manuscript.

Types of manuscripts: personal experience, poetry, teaching

Length: 600–1,000 words

Topic: prayer

Rights: electronic, first, onetime

Payment: none

Guidelines: *www.intercessors.org/media/downloads/Guidelines%20*
&*%20PermissionForm.pdf*
Sample: on the website

byFAITH

1700 N. Brown Rd., Ste. 105, Lawrenceville, GA 30043 | 678-825-1005
editor@byfaithonlineonline.wpengine.com | *byfaithonline.com*
Richard Doster, editor

Denomination: Presbyterian
Parent company: Presbyterian Church in America
Type: quarterly digital and print magazine; advertising accepted
Audience: denomination
Purpose: to provide news of the Presbyterian Church in America, to equip readers to become a more active part of God's redemptive plan for the world, and to help them respond biblically and intelligently to the questions our culture is asking
Submissions: Email complete manuscript.
Types of manuscripts: news, profiles, reviews, teaching
Length: 500–3,000 words
Topics: Christian living/spirituality, culture, denomination, theology
Guidelines: *byfaithonline.com/about*
Tip: "Theologically, the writers are Reformed and believe the faith is practical and applicable to every part of life. Most of our writers (though not all) come from the PCA."

CAFÉ

See entry in "Teen/Young Adult Markets."

CANADA LUTHERAN

400-185 Carlton St., Winnipeg, MB R3C 3J1, Canada | 888-786-6707
editor@elcic.ca | *canadalutheran.ca*
Kenn Ward, editor
Rachel Genge, British Columbia Synod; csynodeditor@gmail.com
Wendy Christensen Grosfield, Synod of Alberta and the Territories;
  lwgros@telusplanet.net
Anno Bell, Saskatchewan Synod; clsaskeditor@gmail.com
Rev. R. David Lowe, Manitoba/Northwestern Ontario Synod;
  mnoeditor@gmail.com
Liz Zehr, Eastern Synod; ezehr@elcic.ca

Denomination: Lutheran
Parent company: Evangelical Lutheran Church in Canada
Type: monthly print magazine; circulation: 6,000+
Audience: denomination
Purpose: to engage the Evangelical Lutheran Church in Canada in a dynamic dialogue in which information, inspiration, and ideas are shared in a thoughtful and stimulating way
Submissions: Email only.
Types of manuscripts: documentary, how-to, personal experience, profiles
Length: 700–1,200 words
Topics: Christian living/spirituality, denomination, seasonal
Rights: onetime
Tip: "As much as is possible, the content of the magazine is chosen from the work of Canadian writers. The content strives to reflect the Evangelical Lutheran Church in Canada in the context of our Canadian society."

THE CANADIAN LUTHERAN

3074 Portage Ave., Winnipeg, MB R3K 0Y2, Canada | 800-588-4226
editor@lutheranchurch.ca | www.canadianlutheran.ca
Matthew Block, editor
Michelle Heumann, regional news
Denomination: Lutheran
Parent company: Lutheran Church–Canada
Type: bimonthly digital and print magazine; circulation: 12,000, hits: 10,000
Audience: denomination
Purpose: to inspire, motivate, and inform
Submissions: Email complete manuscript.
Types of manuscripts: essays, news, teaching
Topics: culture, denomination, theology
Rights: first
Payment: none
Guidelines: *www.canadianlutheran.ca/editors-and-submissions*
Sample: *issuu.com/thecanadianlutheran*
Tip: "All feature articles with doctrinal content must go through doctrinal review to ensure fidelity to the Scriptures. As a result, authors may occasionally be asked to rewrite some sections of their article before publication."

CANADIAN MENNONITE

490 Dutton Dr., Unit C5, Waterloo, ON N2L 6H7, Canada | 519-884-3810
submit@canadianmennonite.org | *www.canadianmennonite.org*
Will Braun, editor

Denomination: Mennonite
Parent company: Canadian Mennonite Publishing Service
Type: monthly digital and print magazine; circulation: 9,000; advertising accepted
Audience: denomination
Purpose: to educate, inform, inspire and foster dialogue on issues facing Mennonites in Canada
Submissions: Email query as attachment or in body of message. Gives assignments. Accepts simultaneous queries. Unsolicited freelance: 10%. Responds in three weeks. Also accepts submissions from children and teens.
Types of manuscripts: opinion, personal experience, reviews, sermons
Length: 750 words
Topics: theme-related
Rights: first
Payment: 12¢/word, on publication
Manuscripts accepted per year: few; primarily publishes the writing of correspondents and related organizations
Seasonal submissions: three months in advance
Preferred Bible version: none
Theme lists: available on website
Guidelines: *canadianmennonite.org/submissions*
Sample: on the website
Tip: "Our content is focused on the Mennonite experience in Canada. We do not usually take submissions from USA. If the writer is in Canada and has a suggestion for a topic of known interest to Mennonites, we'd like to hear about it." Assignments are given to known writers.

CARING MAGAZINE

30840 Hawthorne Blvd., Rancho Palos Verde, CA 90275 | 562-491-8343
caring@usw.salvationarmy.org | *caringmagazine.org*
Karen Gleason, senior editor
Hillary Jackson, managing editor; hillary.jackson@usw.salvationarmy.org

Denomination: The Salvation Army

Parent company: The Salvation Army Western Territory
Type: monthly digital magazine; circulation: 18,000
Audience: denomination in the territory
Purpose: to help people who care to make an impact for good
Submissions: Email query letter through the website.
Types of manuscripts: articles, reviews
Topics: denomination
Sample: *issuu.com/caringmagazine*
Tip: "Shares information from across The Salvation Army world, reports that analyze effective programs to identify the unique features and trends for what works, tips to help local congregations better engage in the issues of today, and influential voices on relevant (and sometimes controversial) matters."

CELEBRATE LIFE MAGAZINE

PO Box 6170, Falmouth, VA 22403 | 540-659-4171
clmag@all.org | *www.clmagazine.org*
Susan Ciancio, editor

Denomination: Catholic
Parent company: American Life League
Type: quarterly digital and print magazine; circulation: 7,500; advertising accepted
Audience: pro-life
Purpose: to inspire, encourage, and educate pro-life activists
Submissions: Email complete manuscript as attachment, or mail it. Unsolicited freelance: 25%. Responds in one to two months.
Types of manuscripts: how-to, interviews, personal experience, reviews, teaching
Length: 1,500 words maximum, including sidebars
Topics: ethics, issues
Rights: first
Payment: 10–25¢/word, on publication
Kill fee: sometimes
Manuscripts accepted per year: six
Seasonal submissions: six months in advance
Preferred Bible version: Jerusalem Bible
Guidelines: *www.clmagazine.org/submission-guidelines*
Sample: email for copy
Tip: "Current-events articles, holiday articles, and articles with appropriate photos or artwork get top priority in our processing procedure." See list of possible topics in the guidelines.

CHARISMA

600 Rinehart Rd., Lake Mary, FL 32746 | 407-333-0600
robert.caggiano@charismamedia.com | *www.charismamag.com*
Robert Caggiano, managing editor

> **Denomination:** Charismatic/Pentecostal
> **Parent company:** Charisma Media
> **Type:** monthly digital and print magazine; circulation: 207,000; advertising accepted
> **Audience:** passionate, Spirit-filled Christians
> **Purpose:** to empower believers for life in the Spirit
> **Submissions:** Email query letter. Unsolicited freelance: 20%. Responds in two to three months.
> **Types of manuscripts:** feature articles, interviews, profiles, reviews
> **Length:** 700–2,600 words
> **Topics:** Christian living/spirituality, Christmas, Easter, prayer, prophecy, seasonal, spiritual warfare
> **Rights:** all
> **Payment:** on publication
> **Seasonal submissions:** five months in advance
> **Preferred Bible version:** MEV
> **Guidelines:** *charismamag.com/about/write-for-us*
> **Sample:** on the website
> **Tip:** "Please take time to read—even study—at least one or two of our recent issues before submitting a query. Sometimes people submit their writing without ever having read or understood our magazine or its readers, and sometimes people will have read our magazine years ago and think it's the same as it has always been, but magazines undergo many changes through the years."

THE CHRISTIAN CENTURY

104 S. Michigan Ave., Ste. 1100, Chicago, IL 60603-5901 | 312-263-7510
submissions@christiancentury.org | *www.christiancentury.org*
Steve Thorngate, managing editor
Jill Peláez Baumgaertner, poetry; poetry@christiancentury.org
Dawn Araujo-Hawkins, news

> **Type:** monthly digital and print magazine; advertising accepted
> **Audience:** ecumenical, mainline ministers, educators, and church leaders
> **Purpose:** to explore what it means to believe and live out the Christian faith in our time

Submissions: Email query letter. Unsolicited freelance: 90%. Responds in four to six weeks.

Types of manuscripts: essays, humor, interviews, opinion, poetry, reviews

Length: articles, 1,500–3,000 words; poetry, to 20 lines

Topics: culture, issues, justice

Rights: all, reprint (with info on where/when previously published)

Payment: articles, $100–300; poems, $50; reviews, to $75; on publication

Manuscripts accepted per year: 150

Seasonal submissions: four months in advance

Preferred Bible version: NRSV

Guidelines: *www.christiancentury.org/submission-guidelines*

Sample: *www.christiancentury.org/magazine*

Tip: "Keep in mind our audience of sophisticated readers, eager for analysis and critical perspective that goes beyond the obvious. We are open to all topics if written with appropriate style for our readers."

CHRISTIAN COURIER

PO Box 124, Wainfleet, ON L0S 1V0, Canada | 800-275-9185

editor@christiancourier.ca | *www.christiancourier.ca*

Angela Reitsma Bick, editor-in-chief

Marlene Bergsma, features; features@christiancourier.ca

Adele Gallogly, reviews; reviews@christiancourier.ca

Maaike Vandermeer, poetry; maaike@christiancourier.ca

Denomination: Christian Reformed

Parent company: Reformed Faith Witness

Type: biweekly digital and print newspaper; circulation: 2,500; advertising accepted

Audience: general

Purpose: to connect Christians with a network of culturally savvy partners in faith for the purpose of inspiring all to participate in God's renewing work with His creation

Submissions: Email complete manuscript or query letter. Accepts simultaneous submissions. Responds in one to two weeks, only if accepted.

Types of manuscripts: columns, feature articles, news, opinion, poetry, reviews

Length: articles, 700–1,200 words; reviews, 750 words

Rights: onetime, reprint (with info on where/when previously published)

Payment: articles, $50–70; reviews, $30–70; poetry, $45; reprints, none; all CAD; on publication
Seasonal submissions: three months in advance
Preferred Bible version: NIV
Guidelines: *www.christiancourier.ca/write-for-us*
Sample: *www.christiancourier.ca/past-issues*
Tip: "Suggest an aspect of the theme which you believe you could cover well, have insight into, could treat humorously, etc. Show that you think clearly, write clearly, and have something to say that we should want to read. Have a strong biblical worldview and avoid moralism and sentimentality."

CHRISTIAN HERALD

PO Box 68526, Brampton, ON L6R 0J8, Canada | 905-874-1731
info@christianherald.ca | *christianherald.ca*
Fazal Karim, Jr., editor-in-chief

Type: monthly digital and print newspaper; circulation: 24,000; advertising accepted
Audience: Christians living in the Greater Toronto Area
Purpose: to keep the Christian community in the greater Toronto area informed and aware of news and events of interest
Submissions: Email query as attachment. Gives assignments. Unsolicited freelance: 10%. Responds in 30 days.
Types of manuscripts: columns, event coverage, fillers, how-to, interviews, news, profiles, reviews, sidebars
Length: 300–1,500 words; reviews, 150–300 words
Topics: business, education, evangelism, travel
Rights: first
Payment: 10–12¢/word, 30 days past publication
Kill fee: sometimes
Manuscripts accepted per year: six
Seasonal submissions: three months in advance
Preferred Bible version: no paraphrases
Theme lists: available on website
Guidelines: *www.christianherald.ca/writing-guidelines.html*
Sample: on the website
Tip: "'Resource Reviews' and 'Seven Question Interviews' are the easiest ways to get started." To get an assignment, contact editor by email indicating experience, areas of interest.

CHRISTIAN LEADER

PO Box 155, Hillsboro, KS 67063 | 620-947-5543
editor@usmb.org | *christianleadermag.com*
Connie Faber, editor

Denomination: Mennonite
Parent company: U.S. Conference of Mennonite Brethren Churches
Type: bimonthly digital and print magazine; circulation: 8,000
Audience: denomination
Purpose: to inspire, inform, educate and challenge church members and attendees, as well as to provide a "kitchen table" around which our diverse denomination can gather
Submissions: Email complete manuscript.
Types of manuscripts: columns, feature articles, personal experience, testimonies
Length: feature articles, 800–1,200 words; columns, 550 words
Topics: church planting, discipleship, evangelism, leadership
Rights: first
Payment: on publication
Guidelines: *christianleadermag.com/about-cl/cl-history*
Sample: on the website
Tip: "We give preference to writers who are from North American Mennonite Brethren congregations, ministries and educational institutions. We welcome articles by writers from within the Anabaptist and Mennonite family of denominations. Articles by Mennonite Brethren and those from other Mennonite writers that focus on personal experiences are encouraged. Please do not submit personal testimonies or stories unless you are a Mennonite Brethren or Mennonite writer."

CHRISTIAN STANDARD

16965 Pine Ln., Ste. 202, Parker, CO 80134 | 800-543-1353
cs@christianstandardmedia.com | *www.christianstandard.com*
Rick Cherok, managing editor

Denomination: Christian Churches, Churches of Christ
Parent company: Christian Standard Media
Type: bimonthly digital and print magazine
Audience: paid and volunteer leaders
Purpose: to leverage the power of our unity and to resource Christian churches to fulfill Christ's commission
Submissions: Only accepts query letter. Unsolicited freelance: 5%;

95% assigned. Responds in one to three months.
Types of manuscripts: Communion meditations for website, how-to
Length: maximum 1,800 words, prefers 500–1,200 words
Topics: theme-related
Rights: first, reprint (with info on where/when previously published)
Payment: $50–250, on acceptance
Kill fee: sometimes
Manuscripts accepted per year: 15
Seasonal submissions: six to eight months in advance
Preferred Bible version: NIV
Theme lists: available on website
Guidelines: *christianstandard.com/writersguidelines*
Sample: on the website
Tip: "Writers with journalism backgrounds who are interested in
covering stories, conducting interviews, and writing news articles
are invited to contact us about becoming a freelance general
assignment reporter. These reporters may develop their own
leads or they may write on assignment by editors; they should
be available to write news stories on relatively short notice. If
you are interested in being considered, please email us at *cs@
christianstandardmedia.com* and include your journalism education
and experience as well as several published clips."

CHRISTIANITY TODAY

465 Gundersen Dr., Carol Stream, IL 60188-2498 | 630-260-6200
editor@christianitytoday.com | *www.christianitytoday.com*
Ashley Hales, editorial director
Matt Reynolds, books editor; mreynolds@christianitytoday.com
Parent company: Christianity Today International
Type: monthly digital and print magazine; circulation: 100,000; hits:
3.5 million page views/month; advertising accepted
Audience: Christian leaders throughout North America
Purpose: to equip Christians to renew their minds, serve the church,
and create culture to the glory of God
Submissions: Query through the website; no attachments.
Unsolicited freelance: few. If no response in three weeks, assume
not interested.
Types of manuscripts: feature articles, interviews, opinion, profiles,
reviews
Length: 300–1,800 words
Topics: Christian living/spirituality, culture, issues

Rights: electronic, first
Payment: varies, on acceptance
Preferred Bible version: NIV
Guidelines: *help.christianitytoday.com/hc/en-us/articles/*
360047411253-How-do-I-write-for-CT
Sample: articles are on the website
Tip: "We are most interested in stories of Christians living out their
faith in unique ways that impact the world for the better and
communicate truth in a way that is deep, nuanced, and challenging."

COLUMBIA

1 Columbus Plaza, New Haven, CT 06510-3326 | 203-752-4398
columbia@kofc.org | *www.kofc.org/en/news-room/columbia/index.html*
Alton J. Pelowski, editor

Denomination: Catholic
Parent company: Knights of Columbus
Type: monthly digital and print magazine; circulation: 1.7 million
Audience: general Catholic family
Submissions: Email or mail query letter.
Types of manuscripts: feature articles, profiles
Length: 700–1,500 words
Topics: current events, family, finances, health, issues, parenting, trends
Rights: first
Payment: varies, on acceptance
Seasonal submissions: six months in advance
Guidelines: *www.kofc.org/en/news-room/columbia/guidelines.html*
Sample: link on the website

COMMONWEAL

475 Riverside Dr., Rm. 405, New York, NY 10115 | 212-662-4200
editors@commonwealmagazine.org | *www.commonwealmagazine.org*
Dominic Preziosi, editor
poetry, poetryeditor@commonwealmagazine.org

Denomination: Catholic
Type: monthly digital and print magazine; circulation: 20,000;
advertising accepted
Audience: liberal Catholics
Purpose: to provide a forum about faith, public affairs, and the arts,
centered on belief in the common good
Submissions: Email complete manuscript or query via email or

through the website. Responds in six to eight weeks.
Types of manuscripts: essays, news, opinion, poetry
Length: 750–5,000 words
Topics: literature and the arts, public affairs
Rights: all
Payment: varies, on publication
Manuscripts accepted per year: poems, 30
Guidelines: *commonweal.submittable.com/submit*
Sample: request by email
Tip: "Articles should be written for a general but well-educated audience. While religious articles are always topical, we are less interested in devotional and 'churchy' pieces than in articles which examine the links between 'worldly' concerns and religious beliefs. Articles fall into three categories:

- 'Short Takes,' running from 1,000–2,000 words, are brief, 'newsy' and reportorial, giving facts, information, and some interpretation behind the 'headlines of the day.'
- Feature articles, running from 2,500–5,000 words, are more reflective and detailed, bringing new information or a different point of view to a subject, raising questions, and/or proposing solutions to the dilemmas facing the world, nation, church, or individual.
- 'Last Word' columns, running from 750–1,500 words, are more personal reflections on some aspect of the human condition: spiritual, individual, political, or social."

THE COVENANT COMPANION
8303 W. Higgins Rd., Chicago, IL 60631 | 773-907-3328
Cathy.NormanPeterson@covchurch.org | *covchurch.org/stories-news*
Cathy Norman Peterson, editorial director

Denomination: Evangelical Covenant
Parent company: The Evangelical Covenant Church
Type: biannual print magazine; circulation: 5,000
Audience: denomination
Purpose: to connect Covenanters to one another and to challenge and inspire them in their faith
Submissions: Email or mail.
Types of manuscripts: news, personal experience, profiles
Length: 1,200–1,800 words
Topics: Christian living/spirituality, church, church outreach,

denomination, issues, justice

Rights: onetime

Payment: $35–100, two months after publication

Tip: "We are interested in what is happening in local churches, conferences, and other Covenant institutions and associations, as well as reports from missionaries and other staff serving around the world. Human interest stories are also welcome."

CREATION ILLUSTRATED

PO Box 141103, Spokane Valley, WA 99214 | 530-269-1424

ci@creationillustrated.com | creationillustrated.com

Jennifer Ish, associate editor

Parent company: Creation Illustrated Ministries, Inc.

Type: quarterly digital and print magazine; circulation: 15,000; advertising accepted

Audience: families, homeschoolers

Purpose: to help one get away to nature and reconnect to the knowledge, power, and beauty found in God's creation

Submissions: Email query as attachment or in body of message, with clips. Unsolicited freelance: 75%+. Responds in four weeks.

Types of manuscripts: articles, personal experience, short stories, travel

Length: 700–1,500 words

Topic: nature

Rights: first, reprint (with info on where/when previously published)

Payment: $75–100, 30 days past publication

Kill fee: sometimes

Manuscripts accepted per year: 32

Seasonal submissions: two to three months in advance

Preferred Bible versions: KJV, NKJV, NASB, ESV

Guidelines: *www.creationillustrated.com/writer-and-photo-guidelines*

Sample: *www.creationillustrated.com/free-digital-copy*

Tip: "Send a good query (helps us avoid repeating a subject recently covered) that is focused on one of the key features. Make sure it can be illustrated with stunning photographs, as each story is beautifully illustrated with many full-colored photos. Looking especially for articles about creatures, nature up close, children's stories that have nature and character-building lessons, and gardening."

CREATIVE INSPIRATIONS

PO Box 19051, Kalamazoo, MI 49009 | 269-348-5712

creativeinspirations01@gmail.com | www.cipoetrypublication.com

MJ Reynolds, publisher and editor
Type: bimonthly digital magazine
Audience: poets and people who appreciate poetry
Purpose: to publish inspirational poetry
Submissions: Email as attachment or in body of message, or mail. Unsolicited freelance: 100%. Responds in one to two weeks. Also accepts submissions from teens.
Type of manuscripts: poetry
Topics: Christian living/spirituality, family, nature
Rights: onetime
Payment: none
Manuscripts accepted per year: varies
Preferred Bible version: NIV
Guidelines: *www.cipoetrypublication.com/ci-news–info.html*
Sample: request by email
Tip: "Follow the submission guidelines."

DTS MAGAZINE
3909 Swiss Ave., Dallas, TX 75204 | 800-387-9673
magazine@dts.edu | voice.dts.edu/article
Neil Coulter, editor
Parent company: Dallas Theological Seminary (DTS)
Type: quarterly digital and print magazine; circulation: 35,000
Audience: evangelical laypeople, students, alumni, donors, and friends
Purpose: to apply biblical truth to life as a ministry to friends of Dallas Theological Seminary
Submissions: Email query letter.
Types of manuscripts: personal experience, profiles, teaching
Length: 1,500–2,000 words
Topics: Christian living/spirituality
Rights: first, reprint
Payment: $300, $100 for reprints, $50-100 for web articles
Seasonal submissions: six months in advance
Guidelines: *voice.dts.edu/magazine/editorial-policies*
Sample: *voice.dts.edu/magazine*
Tip: "*DTS Magazine* is a ministry of Dallas Theological Seminary. We prefer articles written by our alumni, faculty, students, staff, board members, donors and their families."

EKSTASIS
465 Gundersen Dr., Carol Stream, IL 60188 | 416-912-7454

editor@ekstasismagazine.com | *www.ekstasismagazine.com*

Conor Sweetman, senior editor

Parent company: Christianity Today International

Type: monthly digital magazine and newsletter + annual print magazine; circulation: 10,000; advertising accepted

Audience: intellectuals and creatives

Purpose: to revive the Christian imagination

Submissions: Email as attachment. Accepts simultaneous submissions. Unsolicited freelance: 30%. Responds in two months.

Types of manuscripts: essays, poetry

Length: 1,500–3,000 words

Topics: arts, faith, literature

Rights: first

Payment: $75, on publication

Kill fee: sometimes

Manuscripts accepted per year: 50

Theme lists: available on website

Guidelines: *www.ekstasismagazine.com/submit*

Sample: buy on website

Tip: "Connect with us if you would like to submit your work. We want to hear from readers, writers, artists, and thinkers. We publish essays that combine personal narrative with literary, theological, and artistic history. We publish poetry that speaks to the wide breadth of the Christ-infused core of everyday experience; all forms welcome."

EVANGELICAL MISSIONS QUARTERLY

PO Box 398, Wheaton, IL 60187 | 678-392-4577

EMQ-Editor@MissioNexus.org | *missionexus.org/emq*

Heather Pubols, editorial director

David Dunaetz, book review editor

Parent company: Missio Nexus

Type: quarterly digital journal

Audience: missionaries, mission agency executives, mission professors, missionary candidates, students, mission pastors, mission-minded church leaders, mission supporters, and agency board members

Purpose: to increase the effectiveness of the evangelical missionary enterprise

Submissions: Email complete manuscript as attachment through the website.

Types of manuscripts: how-to, profiles, reviews

Length: 2,000–3,000 words
Topics: church planting, culture, discipleship, evangelism, leadership, missions, trends
Rights: first
Guidelines: *missionexus.org/emq/submit-an-article-to-emq*
Tip: "We are not a scholarly journal written for academics, but desire material that is academically respectable, reflecting careful thought and practical application to missions professionals, and especially working missionaries. We like to see problems not only diagnosed, but solved either by way of illustration or suggestion."

FAITH & FRIENDS

The Salvation Army, 2 Overlea Blvd., Toronto, ON M4H 1P4, Canada | 416-422-6226
faithandfriends@salvationarmy.ca | *salvationist.ca/editorial/faith-and-friends*
Ken Ramstead, editor

Denomination: The Salvation Army
Parent company: The Salvation Army Canada and Bermuda
Type: bimonthly digital and print magazine; circulation: 14,600
Audience: general
Purpose: to show Jesus Christ at work in the lives of real people and to provide spiritual resources for those who are new to the Christian faith
Submissions: Email as attachment.
Types of manuscripts: personal experience, profiles, reviews, testimonies
Length: 600–900 words
Topics: Christian living/spirituality, family, marriage, theology
Rights: first, reprint
Payment: none
Preferred Bible version: TNIV
Guidelines: *salvationist.ca/files/salvationarmy/Magazines/Writers_Guidelines_2023/Writers_Guidelines_-_Faith_Friends_2023-08_.pdf*
Sample: on the website
Tip: "Looking for stories about people whose lives have been changed through an encounter with Jesus: conversion, miracles, healing, faith in the midst of crisis, forgiveness, reconciliation, answered prayers, and more. Profiles of people who have found hope and healing through their ministries, including prisoners, hospital patients, nursing-home residents, single parents in distress, addicts, the unemployed, or homeless."

FAITH ON EVERY CORNER

159 Hudson Cajah Mountain Rd., Hudson, NC 28638 | 828-305-8570
team@faithoneverycorner.com | *www.faithoneverycorner.com/magazine*
Karen Ruhl, publisher and editor in chief

Parent company: Faith On Every Corner, LLC
Type: monthly digital magazine; circulation: 35,000
Audience: families, seekers
Purpose: to reach as many people as we can with the Good News
Submissions: Email as attachment. Unsolicited freelance: 20%.
Responds in one week. Also accepts submissions from teens.
Types of manuscripts: devotions, personal experience, poetry, short stories
Length: 850–1,000 words
Topics: Christian living/spirituality
Rights: onetime
Payment: none
Manuscripts accepted per year: 400
Seasonal submissions: two months
Preferred Bible version: NIV
Theme lists: available via email
Guidelines: *www.faithoneverycorner.com/submission-guidelines.html*
Sample: on the website
Tip: "Looking for true Christian stories, devotions, poetry, life events that brought you to Christ."

FAITH TODAY

10 Huntingdale Blvd., Scarborough, ON M1W 2S5, Canada | 866-302-3362
editor@faithtoday.ca | *www.faithtoday.ca*
Bill Fledderus, senior editor
Karen Stiller, senior editor

Parent company: The Evangelical Fellowship of Canada
Type: bimonthly digital and print magazine; circulation: print, 20,000;
online, 9,500; advertising accepted
Audience: Canadian evangelicals
Purpose: to connect, equip, and inform Canada's four million
evangelical Christians from Anglican and Baptist to Pentecostal and
The Salvation Army
Submissions: Email query letter with clips. Unsolicited freelance: 10%.
Responds in one week.
Types of manuscripts: essays, feature articles, how-to, news,
profiles, reviews

Length: 350–1,800 words
Topics: church, issues, trends
Rights: electronic, first, onetime, reprint (with info on where/when previously published)
Payment: 30–40¢ CAD/word, on acceptance
Kill fee: sometimes
Manuscripts accepted per year: 100
Seasonal submissions: four months in advance
Guidelines: *www.faithtoday.ca/writers*
Sample: *www.faithtoday.ca/digital*
Tip: "What is the Canadian angle? How does your approach include diverse Canadian voices from different churches, regions, generations, etc.?"

FAITHFULLY MAGAZINE
397 Hillside Ave. #5154, Hillside, NJ 07205
contact@faithfullymagazine.com | *faithfullymagazine.com*

Parent company: Faithfully Media, LLC
Type: daily website; advertising accepted
Audience: ethnically diverse millennials and post-millennials
Purpose: to report on issues, conversations, and events impacting Christian communities of color for an ethnically inclusive audience
Submissions: Query first. Responds in three days or not interested.
Types of manuscripts: biography, essays, feature articles, news, opinion, profiles
Length: feature, essay, varies; opinion and analysis, 1,000–1,200 words; news and trends, 400–500 words; profile, historical biography, 500–800 words
Topics: wide variety
Rights: all, first
Payment: $20–200
Guidelines: *faithfullymagazine.com/submissions*
Sample: see website
Tip: "Although we work with new writers, our time limits us to working with writers whose clips show they are well-practiced in their craft."

FOCUS ON THE FAMILY
8605 Explorer Dr., Colorado Springs, CO 80920 | 800-232-6459
FocusMagSubmissions@family.com | *www.focusonthefamily.com/magazine*
Andrea Gutierrez, managing editor

Parent company: Focus on the Family
Type: bimonthly print magazine; circulation: 240,000
Audience: married parents with children in the home
Purpose: to support couples in their marriage and parents when training their children
Submissions: Email complete manuscript as attachment or in body of message. Unsolicited freelance: 20%. Responds in two to eight weeks.
Types of manuscripts: how-to, profiles, teaching
Length: 400–800 words
Topics: marriage, parenting
Rights: first
Payment: 25¢/word, $50 for short articles; on acceptance
Kill fee: always
Manuscripts accepted per year: 100
Seasonal submissions: nine months in advance
Preferred Bible version: ESV
Guidelines: *www.focusonthefamily.com/magazine/call-for-submissions*
Sample: articles are on the website; free subscription, email *HELP@focusonthefamily.com*
Tip: "Start with 'Hacks & Facts' for parenting, extended family, grandparenting, and adult kids. Find any calls for submissions on our site, and follow the directions for that specific article." Also buys articles on parenting and marriage for online. Length: 800–1,500 words. Email to *Rhonda.Robinson@fotf.org*.

FRIENDS JOURNAL

1501 Cherry St., Philadelphia, PA 19102 | 215-563-8629
martink@friendsjournal.org | *www.friendsjournal.org*
Martin Kelly, senior editor

Denomination: Quaker
Parent company: Religious Society of Friends
Type: monthly digital and print magazine
Audience: denomination
Purpose: to communicate Quaker experience in order to connect and deepen spiritual lives
Submissions: Email through the website.
Types of manuscripts: personal experience, poetry, profiles, teaching, testimonies
Length: 1,200–2,500 words; departments, around 1,500 or fewer
Topics: theme-related
Rights: first

Payment: none
Manuscripts accepted per year: poems, 22–33
Theme lists: available on website
Guidelines: *www.friendsjournal.org/submissions*
Sample: articles are on the website
Tip: "*Friends Journal* prefers articles with a constructive approach to spiritual seeking. We seek an open, curious and respectful tone even when discussing controversial subjects. We prefer articles rooted in the author's own experiences of the divine. Submissions should show an awareness of Friends' ways and concerns, as well as sensitivity to them."

GATHER

8765 W. Higgins Rd., Chicago, IL 60631 | 844-409-0576
gather@elca.org | *www.gathermagazine.org*
Elizabeth Hunter, editor

Denomination: Lutheran
Parent company: Women of the Evangelical Lutheran Church in America
Type: monthly digital and print magazine
Audience: Lutheran women
Purpose: to help readers grow in faith and engage in ministry and action
Submissions: Email query letter with clips as attachment or in body of message. Accepts simultaneous submissions. Responds only if interested.
Type of manuscripts: personal experience
Topics: theme-related
Rights: first, onetime, reprint (with info on where/when previously published)
Payment: on publication
Seasonal submissions: seven months in advance
Guidelines: *www.gathermagazine.org/write-for-gather*
Sample: article samples are on the website
Tip: "Please know that most of what we publish is assigned—we ask particular established authors to write on specific themes far in advance of publication. We publish very few articles that originated as unsolicited manuscripts or queries."

GEMS OF TRUTH

PO Box 4060, Overland Park, KS 66204 | 913-432-0331
sseditor@heraldandbanner.com | *heraldandbanner.com/product/gems-of-truth*

Arlene McGehee, Sunday school editor
Denomination: Church of God
Parent company: Herald and Banner Press
Type: weekly Sunday school take-home paper; circulation: 4,750
Audience: denomination
Purpose: to build character values without being preachy
Submissions: Email as attachment or in body of message, or mail. Unsolicited freelance: 50%. Responds in nine months.
Types of manuscripts: biography, personal experience, poetry, short stories
Length: 1,000–2,000 words
Topics: Christian living/spirituality, family, marriage, prayer
Rights: first, reprint
Payment: prose, .0005¢/word; poetry, 25¢/line; reprints, 50%; on publication
Manuscripts accepted per year: varies
Seasonal submissions: six months in advance
Preferred Bible version: KJV
Guidelines: by email
Sample: 9"x12" SASE with $3.50 postage
Tip: Looking for seasonal stories.

GOOD NEWS

PO Box 670368, Coral Springs, FL 33067 | 954-564-5378
ShellyP@goodnewsfl.org | www.goodnewsfl.org
Shelly Pond, editor
Parent company: Good News Media Group, LLC
Type: monthly digital and print newspaper; circulation: 80,000 print, 30,000 digital; advertising accepted
Audience: Dade, Broward, and Palm Beach, Florida, areas
Submissions: Query by email with clips.
Type of manuscripts: articles
Length: 500–800 words
Payment: 10¢/word
Sample: on the website

GUIDEPOSTS

110 William St., Ste. 901, New York, NY 10038 | 212-251-8100
submissions@guideposts.org | guideposts.org/guideposts-magazine
Evan Miller, senior editor

Parent company: Guideposts
Type: bimonthly digital and print magazine
Audience: general
Purpose: to inspire people to believe that all things are possible with faith, hope, and prayer; to encourage, inform, entertain, and tell true stories of personal change; to affirm the positive, unite rather than divide, and meet people where they are on their spiritual journeys
Submissions: Email complete manuscript. Unsolicited freelance: 40%. Responds in two months or not interested.
Type of manuscripts: personal experience
Length: articles, 1,500 words; department anecdotes, 50–250 words
Rights: all
Payment: $100–500, on acceptance
Kill fee: 20% but not to first-time freelancers
Manuscripts accepted per year: 40–60
Guidelines: *guideposts.org/tell-us-your-story*
Tip: "*Guideposts* magazine stories are about personal change. Narrators face challenges in their lives that they resolve through leaning on faith and God. The challenge can cover everything from relationships to life transitions—such as caregiving, divorce, retirement, or job loss—to life-threatening events. Our true stories deliver hope and inspiration with a clear spiritual point that readers can apply to everyday difficulties in their own lives. We want to be a source of spiritual well-being for our readers."

Short anecdotes similar to full-length articles for departments: "Someone Cares," stories of kindness and caring, *sc@guideposts.com*; "Mysterious Ways," "Family Room," "What Prayer Can Do." Also takes inspiring quotes for "The Up Side," *upside@guideposts.com*.

HEARTBEAT

PO Box 9, Hatfield, AR 71945 | 870-389-6196
heartbeat@cmausa.org | *cmausa.org/Resources/Heartbeat*
Misty Bradley, editor

Parent company: Christian Motorcyclists Association
Type: monthly digital and print magazine; circulation: 18,000
Audience: motorcyclists
Purpose: to inspire leaders and members to be the most organized, advanced, equipped, financially stable organization, full of integrity in the motorcycling industry and the Kingdom of God
Submissions: Email complete manuscript.

Types of manuscripts: articles, reviews
Topic: motorcycling
Payment: none

HIGHWAY NEWS

1525 River Rd., Marietta, PA 17547 | 717-426-9977
editor@tfcglobal.org | tfcglobal.org/highway-news-current-issue
Lynn Bolster, editor

> **Parent company:** TFC Global
> **Type:** monthly digital and print magazine; circulation: 18,000–20,000
> **Audience:** truck drivers and their families
> **Purpose:** to lead truck drivers, as well as the trucking community, to Jesus Christ and help them grow in their faith
> **Submissions:** Email complete manuscript. Unsolicited freelance: 10–20%.
> **Types of manuscripts:** news, personal experience
> **Length:** 800–1,000 words
> **Topic:** trucking life
> **Rights:** first, reprint
> **Payment:** none
> **Seasonal submissions:** six months in advance
> **Preferred Bible version:** ESV
> **Guidelines:** by email
> **Sample:** download from the website
> **Tip:** "Articles submitted for publication do not have to be religious in nature; however, they should not conflict with or oppose guidelines and principles presented in the Bible."

HOLINESS TODAY

17001 Prairie Star Pkwy., Lenexa, KS 66220 | 913-577-0500
holinesstoday@nazarene.org | www.holinesstoday.org
Nate Gilmore, content editor

> **Denomination:** Nazarene
> **Parent company:** Church of the Nazarene
> **Type:** bimonthly digital and print magazine; circulation: 8,000; advertising accepted
> **Audience:** denomination
> **Purpose:** to keep readers connected with the Nazarene experience and provide tools for everyday faith
> **Submissions:** Email complete manuscript as attachment. Unsolicited freelance: 30%. Also accepts submissions from children and teens.

Types of manuscripts: columns, personal experience
Length: 700–1,100 words
Topics: denomination, ministry, teaching
Rights: first, reprint (with info on where/when previously published)
Payment: $135, on publication
Kill fee: yes
Manuscripts accepted per year: six to eight
Preferred Bible version: NIV
Theme lists: available via email
Guidelines: by email
Tip: "We are always interested in hearing from Nazarene pastors, lay leaders, and experts in their fields. We are a Nazarene publication that wants our articles to be relevant and applicable to real-life scenarios and the world we live in."

HOMELIFE

200 Powell Pl., Ste. 100, Brentwood, TN 37027 | 615-251-2196
homelife@lifeway.com | *www.lifeway.com/en/product-family/homelife-magazine*
David Bennett, managing editor

Denomination: Baptist
Parent company: Lifeway Christian Resources/Southern Baptist Convention
Type: monthly print magazine; circulation: 140,000
Audience: parents
Purpose: to offer biblical and practical encouragement that champions life-changing discipleship, dynamic marriages, and effective parenting
Submissions: Email complete manuscript as attachment. Gives assignments. Unsolicited freelance: 20%. Responds only if interested.
Types of manuscripts: columns, how-to, narrative, sidebars
Length: 500, 750, 1,500 words
Topics: family, living on mission, marriage, parenting
Rights: first
Payment: $100–500, on acceptance
Kill fee: sometimes
Manuscripts accepted per year: 18
Seasonal submissions: six months in advance
Preferred Bible version: CSB
Guidelines: by email
Sample: on the website
Tip: "Be familiar with the magazine and the Faith-Family-Life format."

IMAGE

3307 Third Ave. W, Seattle, WA 98119 | 206-281-2988
mkenagy@imagejournal.org | *imagejournal.org*
Mary Kenagy Mitchell, executive editor
Lauren F. Winner, creative nonfiction editor; lwinner@imagejournal.org
Nick Ripatrazone, culture editor, media essays and reviews;
nripatrazone@imagejournal.org
Shane McCrae, poetry editor; shanemccrae@imagejournal.org
Melissa Pritchard, fiction editor; mpritchard@imagejournal.org

Type: quarterly digital and print journal; circulation: 4,000; advertising accepted
Audience: people interested in art and literature
Purpose: to foster contemporary art and writing that grapple with the mystery of being human by curating, cultivating, convening, and celebrating work that explores religious faith and spiritual questions
Submissions: Only accepts submissions through the website. Accepts simultaneous submissions. Unsolicited freelance: 3%. Responds in five months.
Types of manuscripts: essays, interviews, poetry, short stories
Length: 500–5,000 words
Topics: literature and the arts
Rights: first
Payment: $25/published page, $3/line for poetry; on publication
Kill fee: sometimes
Manuscripts accepted per year: 80
Guidelines: *imagejournal.org/journal/submit*
Sample: *imagejournal.org/store*
Tip: "We're looking for crafted literary work that's surprising, honest, and beautifully written."

INFLUENCE

1445 N. Boonville Ave., Springfield, MO 65802 | 417-862-2781
editor@influencemagazine.com | *influencemagazine.com*
Christina Quick, lead editor

Denomination: Assemblies of God
Parent company: The General Council of the Assemblies of God
Type: quarterly digital and print magazine; circulation: 33,000
Audience: pastors and other leaders
Purpose: to provide a Christ-centered, Spirit-empowered perspective

that propels people to engage their faith—as individuals, in community, and with the global Church

Submissions: Email query letter.
Types of manuscripts: how-to, profiles, teaching
Length: 700–1,000 words
Topics: ethics, family, leadership, ministry, worship
Rights: first
Guidelines: *influencemagazine.com/submission-guidelines*
Sample: *influencemagazine.com/en/issues*
Tip: "We'd love to hear more about your background in leadership and how that might connect to your pitch. Links to sites, social-media profiles, or other writing samples are encouraged. Reprints or excerpts are considered on a case-by-case basis, but original content is preferred."

INSITE

PO Box 62189, Colorado Springs, CO 80962-2189 | 888-922-2287
editor@ccca.org | www.ccca.org/ccca/Publications.asp
Jen Howver, editor

Parent company: Christian Camp and Conference Association
Type: bimonthly digital and print magazine; circulation: 8,800; advertising accepted
Audience: executive directors, board members, and staff at Christian camps and conference centers
Purpose: to maximize ministry for Christian camps and conference centers
Submissions: Email query letter as attachment. Gives assignments. Unsolicited freelance: 1%. Responds in two to four weeks.
Types of manuscripts: how-to, interviews, profiles, columns
Length: features, 1,500 words; columns, 400 words
Topics: business, camping ministry, faith development, facilities, leadership, legal, relationships, marketing, Gen Z, Gen Alpha, board/governance, fundraising
Rights: electronic, first, reprint (with info on where/when previously published)
Payment: features, $300; columns, $125; on publication
Kill fee: sometimes
Manuscripts accepted per year: one
Seasonal submissions: nine months in advance
Preferred Bible version: NIV
Guidelines: by email

Sample: request by email

Tip: "Have good samples of well-researched, well-written articles."

INSPIRE A FIRE

dianaflegal@gmail.com | inspireafire.com
Diana Flegal, senior editor
Eddie Jones, executive editor, WritersCoach.us@gmail.com

Parent company: Christian Devotions Ministry

Type: daily website; circulation: 38,000

Audience: Christians looking for encouragement and inspiration

Purpose: to deliver life-giving articles that inspire hope, convey God's truth, and accompany believers on their spiritual journeys

Submissions: Unsolicited freelance: 40%. Responds in one week.

Types of manuscripts: personal experience, poetry

Length: 1,500 words

Topics: Christian living, culture, family, relationships

Rights: first, reprint if retitled and reworded 25%

Payment: none

Theme lists: available on website

Guidelines: *inspireafire.com/submissions-guidelines*

Sample: on the website

Tip: "*Inspire a Fire* is looking for committed writers familiar with WordPress, or willing to learn, to post a monthly article in accordance with submission guidelines. If you would like to become a monthly contributor, email Diana or Eddie to schedule a phone call or Zoom interview."

THE JOURNAL OF ADVENTIST EDUCATION

12501 Old Columbia Pike, Silver Spring, MD 20904-6600 | 301-680-5069
mcgarrellf@gc.adventist.org | www.journalofadventisteducation.org
Faith-Ann McGarrell, editor

Denomination: Seventh-day Adventist

Parent company: General Conference of Seventh-day Adventists

Type: quarterly digital journal; circulation: 10,000–16,000; advertising accepted

Audience: educators and administrators

Purpose: to aid professional teachers and educational administrators worldwide, kindergarten to higher education

Submissions: Submit complete manuscript through the website. Unsolicited freelance: 10%. Responds in four to six weeks.

Types of manuscripts: how-to, personal experience, reviews, sidebars
Length: 1,500–4,000 words; book reviews, 900–1,500 words
Topic: Christian education
Rights: first, reprint (with info on where/when previously published)
Payment: varies, on publication
Manuscripts accepted per year: 32
Seasonal submissions: six months in advance
Preferred Bible version: NIV
Guidelines: *www.journalofadventisteducation.org/author-guidelines*
Sample: download from the website
Tip: "JAE accepts invited and freelance submissions from educators, educational administrators, and individuals working in education. Authors must be familiar with Adventist Christian education—its philosophy, structure, and historical foundations."

JOYFUL LIVING MAGAZINE

PO Box 311, Palo Cedro, CA 97073 | 530-227-9330
joyfullivingmagazineredding@gmail.com | *joyfullivingmagazine.com*
Cathy Jansen, editor in chief

Type: quarterly digital magazine; advertising accepted
Audience: general
Purpose: to share encouragement and hope, to help readers grow spiritually and emotionally, and to help them in their everyday lives with practical issues
Submissions: Email complete manuscript as attachment.
Types of manuscripts: how-to, personal experience, profiles, recipes
Length: 200–700 words
Topics: aging, Christian living/spirituality, depression, family, finances, health, marriage, singleness, work
Payment: none
Guidelines: *www.joyfullivingmagazine.com/writers-info*
Sample: *www.joyfullivingmagazine.com/issues*
Tip: "Articles need to be uplifting and encouraging for singles, seniors, young people, and families. Each article needs to inspire the reader to grow spiritually, emotionally, and help them in their everyday lives with very practical issues."

JUST BETWEEN US

777 S. Barker Rd., Brookfield, WI 53045 | 262-786-6478
submissions@justbetweenus.org | *www.justbetweenus.org*

Shelly Esser, executive editor

> **Type:** quarterly print magazine; circulation: 10,000
> **Audience:** women
> **Purpose:** to encourage and equip women for a life of faith and service
> **Submissions:** Email complete manuscript as attachment. Responds in six to eight weeks or not interested.
> **Types of manuscripts:** how-to, personal experience, testimonies
> **Length:** articles, 1,000–1,200 words; testimonies, 450 words
> **Topics:** Christian living/spirituality, evangelism, faith, finances, friendship, ministry, parenting, prayer, relationships, spiritual warfare
> **Payment:** none
> **Preferred Bible version:** NIV
> **Guidelines:** *justbetweenus.org/magazine/writers-guidelines*
> **Sample:** *justbetweenus.org/magazine-sample-issue*
> **Tip:** "Articles should be personal in tone, full of real-life anecdotes as well as quotes/advice from noted Christian professionals, and be biblically based. Articles need to be practical and have a distinct Christian and serving perspective throughout."

LEADING HEARTS

PO Box 6421, Longmont, CO 80501 | 303-835-8473
amber@leadinghearts.com | *leadinghearts.com*
Amber Weigland-Buckley, editor

> **Parent company:** Right to the Heart Ministries
> **Type:** bimonthly digital magazine; circulation: 10,000; advertising accepted
> **Audience:** women leaders
> **Purpose:** to encourage Christian women who lead hearts at home, work, community, and church
> **Submissions:** Assignment only; no unsolicited freelance. 50–60% assigned.
> **Types of manuscripts:** how-to, personal experience, profiles, reviews
> **Length:** articles, 800 words maximum; columns, 250–500 words
> **Topics:** theme-related
> **Rights:** first, reprint
> **Payment:** none
> **Preferred Bible version:** NIV
> **Theme lists:** not available
> **Guidelines:** *leadinghearts.com/writers-guidelines*
> **Sample:** download from the website
> **Tip:** To audition for an assignment, email an article of 1,200 words

maximum and a short résumé. Gives preferred consideration to members of AWSA.

LEAVES

PO Box 87, Dearborn, MI 48121-0087 | 313-561-2330
editor.leaves@mariannhill.us | *www.mariannhill.us/leaves.html*
Rev. Thomas Heier, editor-in-chief

Denomination: Catholic
Parent company: Marianhill Mission Society
Type: bimonthly print magazine; circulation: 10,000
Audience: Catholics, primarily in the Detroit, Michigan, area
Purpose: to promote devotion to God and testimony of His blessings
Submissions: Email or mail complete manuscript.
Types of manuscripts: personal experience, poetry, reviews, testimonies
Length: 250 words
Topics: Christian living/spirituality, prayer
Rights: first, reprint
Payment: none
Manuscripts accepted per year: 40
Preferred Bible version: RSV Catholic edition
Sample: articles are on the website
Tip: Greatest need is for personal testimonies.

LIGHT

901 Commerce St., Ste. 550, Nashville, TN 37203 | 615-244-2495
nicolet@erlc.com | *erlc.com/resources*
Lindsay Nicolet, editor

Denomination: Baptist
Parent company: The Ethics and Religious Liberty Commission/ Southern Baptist Convention
Type: biannual digital and print journal; circulation: 8,000; advertising accepted
Audience: church and ministry leaders
Purpose: to bear witness to the gospel by speaking to congregations and consciences with a thoroughly Christian moral witness
Submissions: Email complete manuscript as attachment. Unsolicited freelance: 10%. Responds in one week.
Types of manuscripts: columns, how-to, news, reviews
Length: 1,500 words
Topics: culture, ethics, family, justice, parenting, politics

Rights: all
Payment: depends on article and writer
Manuscripts accepted per year: 10
Preferred Bible version: CSB
Guidelines: not available
Sample: on the website
Tip: "Looking for articles tied to current events and focus on local church ministry."

LIVE

1445 N. Boonville Ave., Springfield, MO 65802-1894 | 417-862-2781
rl-live@gph.org | *myhealthychurch.com*
Wade Quick, editor

Denomination: Assemblies of God
Parent company: Gospel Publishing House
Type: weekly Sunday school take-home paper; circulation: 40,000
Audience: denomination
Purpose: to encourage Christians in living for God through stories that apply biblical principles to everyday problems
Submissions: Email as attachment. Unsolicited freelance: 100%. Responds in six weeks.
Types of manuscripts: fillers, how-to, personal experience, poetry, short stories
Length: articles, 200–1,200 words; poetry, 12–25 lines
Topics: Christian living/spirituality
Rights: first, reprint
Payment: 10¢/word for first rights, 7¢/word for reprint, $35–60 for poetry; on acceptance
Seasonal submissions: 18 months
Preferred Bible version: NLT
Guidelines: *myhealthychurch.com/store/startcat.cfm?cat=tWRITGUID*
Tip: "Stories should be encouraging, challenging, and/or humorous. Even problem-centered stories should be upbeat. Stories should not be preachy, critical, or moralizing. They should not present pat, trite, or simplistic answers to problems. No Bible fiction or sci-fi. Make sure the stories have a strong Christian element, are written well, have strong takeaways, but do not preach."

THE LUTHERAN WITNESS

1333 S. Kirkwood Rd., St. Louis, MO 63122-7226 | 800-248-1930
lutheran.witness@lcms.org | *witness.lcms.org*

Roy S. Askins, managing editor

Denomination: Lutheran
Parent company: The Lutheran Church Missouri Synod
Type: monthly print magazine; circulation: 120,000
Audience: denomination
Purpose: to interpret the contemporary world from a Lutheran perspective
Submissions: Email complete manuscript or query, or submit through the website. Responds in at least three months.
Types of manuscripts: Bible studies, essays, how-to, humor, personal experience, poetry, profiles, teaching
Length: 500, 1,000, or 1,500 words
Topics: theme-related
Rights: electronic, first
Payment: based on both article length and complexity and author's credentials, on acceptance
Preferred Bible version: ESV
Theme lists: available on website
Guidelines: *witness.lcms.org/contribute*
Sample: articles on the website
Tip: "Because of the magazine's long lead time, and because many features are planned at least six months in advance of the publication date, your story should have a long-term perspective that keeps it relevant several months from the time you submit it."

THE MARKETPLACE

595 Parkside Dr., Ste. 2, Waterloo, ON, Canada N2L 0C7 | 800-665-7026
mstrathdee@meda.org | *meda.org/marketplace*
Mike Strathdee, editor

Denomination: Mennonite
Parent company: Mennonite Economic Development Associates
Type: bimonthly digital magazine; circulation: 13,000
Audience: business people
Purpose: to explore the intersection of faith and business
Submissions: Email query letter.
Types of manuscripts: news, profiles, reviews
Topic: business
Sample: *www.meda.org/the-marketplace/issues*

MATURE LIVING

200 Powell Pl., Ste. 100, Brentwood, TN 37027-7707 | 615-251-2000

matureliving@lifeway.com | *www.lifeway.com/en/product-family/*
mature-living-magazine
Debbie Dickerson, managing editor

Denomination: Baptist
Parent company: LifeWay Christian Resources/Southern Baptist
Convention
Type: monthly print magazine
Audience: ages 55 and older
Purpose: to equip mature adults as they live a legacy of leadership,
stewardship, and discipleship
Submissions: Assignment only.
Types of manuscripts: devotions, how-to, personal experience,
puzzles, recipes, short stories, teaching
Topics: caregiving, evangelism, marriage, parenting, relationships,
theology
Preferred Bible version: CSB
Guidelines: by email
Sample: on the website
Tip: Email for possible assignment. Not accepting unsolicited
manuscripts or queries. Open for "Kicks and Grins," fun stories of
your grandkids, 25–125 words; challenging, biblical, word-search
puzzles; and crossword puzzles.

THE MESSENGER

440 Main St., Steinbach, MB R5G 1Z5, Canada | 204-326-6401
messenger@emconference.ca | *emcmessenger.ca*
Rebecca Roman, editor

Denomination: Mennonite
Parent company: Evangelical Mennonite Conference
Type: bimonthly digital and print magazine; circulation: 2,700
Audience: members and adherents of churches within the Evangelical
Mennonite Conference
Purpose: to inform concerning events and activities of the
denomination, instruct in godliness and victorious living, and
inspire to earnestly contend for the faith
Submissions: Email query letter. Unsolicited freelance: 50%.
Responds in two weeks.
Types of manuscripts: feature articles
Length: 800–1,500 words; columns, 500 words
Topics: wide variety

Rights: first
Payment: articles, 15¢/word; columns, $85; on publication
Kill fee: half payment
Manuscripts accepted per year: few, mostly assigned
Seasonal submissions: six months in advance
Preferred Bible version: NIV
Guidelines: *emcmessenger.ca/submission-guidelines*
Sample: *www.emcmessenger.ca/current-issue*
Tip: "Always query first. A lead article involves a mixture of teaching, interpretation, and opinion. Effective writers 'inform, instruct, and inspire.' They display an informed opinion, a balance in approach, a Christ-centered focus, and concern for the well-being of the Church. The writer is expected to observe and comment on conference trends and issues as deemed fit. The purpose of a lead article is not to create controversy, but to motivate thought and action."

THE MESSIANIC TIMES

50 Alberta Dr., Amhurst, NY 14226 | 866-612-7770
editor@messianictimes.com | *www.messianictimes.com*
Kayla Levy, editorial coordinator

Denomination: Messianic
Parent company: Times of the Messiah Ministries
Type: bimonthly digital and print newspaper; advertising accepted
Audience: Messianic community and Christians interested in Jewish roots of their faith
Purpose: to provide accurate, authoritative, and current information to unite the international Messianic Jewish community, teach Christians the Jewish roots of their faith, and proclaim that Yeshua is the Jewish Messiah
Submissions: Email query letter.
Types of manuscripts: news, opinion, reviews, teaching
Sample: on the website

MINISTRY

12501 Old Columbia Pike, Silver Spring, MD 20904 | 301-680-6518
ministrymagazine@gc.adventist.org | *www.ministrymagazine.org*
Pavel Goia, editor

Denomination: Seventh-day Adventist
Parent company: General Conference of Seventh-day Adventists
Type: monthly digital and print magazine; circulation: 18,000+

Audience: pastors, church leaders, church elders
Purpose: to deepen spiritual life, develop intellectual strength, and increase pastoral and evangelistic effectiveness of all ministers in the context of the three angels' messages of Revelation 14:6-12
Submissions: Email complete manuscript as attachment.
Types of manuscripts: Bible studies, how-to, reviews, teaching
Length: articles, 1,500–2,000 words; reviews, 600 words maximum
Topics: family, issues, ministry, pastoral/preaching, relationships, theology
Rights: all
Payment: determined on amount of research done and other work needed to prepare manuscript, on acceptance
Guidelines: *www.ministrymagazine.org/about/article-submission*
Sample: articles are on the website
Tip: "Because *Ministry*'s readership includes individuals from all over the world, you will want to use words, illustrations, and concepts that will be understood by readers in various parts of the world. Avoid illustrations that are understood in one country but may be confusing in others."

THE MOTHER'S HEART

PO Box 275, Tobaccoville, NC 27050 | 336-775-8519
KymAWright@gmail.com | *www.the-mothers-heart.com*
Kym A. Wright, publisher and editor

Parent company: alWright! Publishing
Type: bimonthly digital magazine; circulation: 100,000
Audience: moms at home, homeschoolers, large families, homesteaders, DIYers
Purpose: to serve and encourage mothers in the many facets of staying at home and raising a family
Submissions: Email query letter as attachment or in body of message. Gives assignments. Accepts simultaneous submissions. Unsolicited freelance: 20%. Responds in two months.
Types of manuscripts: columns, fillers, how-to, personal experience, reviews
Length: 750–1,000 and 1,250–1,750 words
Topics: adoption story, Christian living/spirituality, DYI, family, fostering, gardening, homeschooling, hospitality, organization, parenting, special needs, time management
Rights: electronic, first
Payment: $10–75 or 1/8-page ad, on publication

Manuscripts accepted per year: 30
Seasonal submissions: six months in advance
Preferred Bible version: any
Guidelines: *tmhmag.com/Writers%20Guidelines%202023-2026.pdf*
Sample: *tmhmag.com/subscribe.htm*
Tip: "Break in with an adoption story, homeschool, gardening, parenting, DIY." Email to get an assignment.

MUTUALITY

122 W. Franklin Ave., Ste. 610, Minneapolis, MN 55404 | 612-872-6898
mutuality@cbeinternational.org | *www.cbeinternational.org/primary_page/*
  mutuality-blogmagazine
Carrie Silveira, editor

Parent company: Christians for Biblical Equality
Type: quarterly print magazine plus weekly blog; circulation: 400; hits: 40,000
Audience: Christian leaders; women in ministry; seminary and university students; and laity interested in gender, the Bible, and issues of justice
Purpose: to provide inspiration, encouragement, and information on topics related to a biblical view of mutuality between men and women in the home, church, and world
Submissions: Email complete manuscript or query as attachment. Responds in one month or more.
Types of manuscripts: how-to, personal experience, reviews
Length: articles, 800–1,800 words; reviews, 500–800 words
Topics: theme-related
Rights: first
Payment: subscription
Preferred Bible version: NIV
Theme lists: available on website
Guidelines: *www.cbeinternational.org/content/write-mutuality*
Sample: *www.cbeinternational.org/content/mutuality-sample-issue*

NOW WHAT?

PO Box 33677, Denver, CO 80233
nowwhat@cog7.org | *nowwhat.cog7.org*
Sherri Langton, associate editor

Denomination: Church of God (Seventh Day)
Parent company: General Conference of the Church of God (Seventh Day)
Type: monthly digital magazine

Audience: seekers

Purpose: to address the felt needs of the unchurched

Submissions: Email complete manuscript. Unsolicited freelance: 100%. Responds in 4-10 weeks.

Type of manuscripts: personal experience

Length: 1,000-1,500 words

Topics: issues, salvation

Rights: electronic, first, reprint (with info on where/when previously published)

Payment: $25-65, on publication

Manuscripts accepted per year: 10-12

Preferred Bible version: NIV

Guidelines: *nowwhat.cog7.org/send-us-your-story*

Sample: on the website

Tip: "Avoid unnecessary jargon or technical terms. No Christmas or Easter pieces or fiction. Think how you can explain your faith, or how you overcame a problem, to a non-Christian. Use storytelling techniques, like dialogue, scenes, etc., with the conflict clearly stated."

OUR SUNDAY VISITOR

200 Noll Plaza, Huntington, IN 46750 | 260-356-8400

oursunvis@osv.com | *www.oursundayvisitor.com*

Fr. Patrick Briscoe, editor

Denomination: Catholic

Type: monthly print magazine

Audience: denomination

Purpose: to examine the news, culture, and trends of the day from a faithful and sound Catholic perspective—to see the world through the eyes of faith

Submissions: Submit complete manuscript or query letter through the website. Responds in four to six weeks.

Types of manuscripts: essays, interviews, news, profiles

Length: 500-1,350 words

Topics: denomination, issues

Payment: on acceptance

Preferred Bible version: RSV

Guidelines: *osv.submittable.com/submit*

Tip: "Especially interested in writers able to do news analysis (with a minimum of three sources) or news features."

OUTREACH

5550 Tech Center, Colorado Springs, CO 80919 | 800-991-6011, x3208
tellus@outreachmagazine.com | *www.outreachmagazine.com*
James P. Long, editor

Type: bimonthly print magazine; circulation: 31,000
Audience: pastors and church leadership, as well as laypeople who are passionate about outreach
Purpose: to further the Kingdom of God by empowering Christian churches to reach their communities for Jesus Christ
Submissions: Email or mail query letter with clips and cover letter. Responds in two months.
Types of manuscripts: how-to, profiles
Length: 200–2,500 words
Topics: church outreach, evangelism, ministry, small groups
Rights: first, reprint (with info on where/when previously published)
Payment: $700–1,000 for feature articles
Seasonal submissions: six months in advance
Guidelines: *www.outreachmagazine.com/magazine/3160-writers-guidelines.html*
Tip: "While most articles are assigned, we do accept queries and manuscripts on speculation. Please don't query us until you've studied at least one issue of *Outreach*. If you're interested in writing on assignment, submit a cover letter, published writing samples, résumé, and a list of topics you specialize in or are interested in covering. We keep these on file and do not respond to all writing queries or return writing samples."

PARENTLIFE

200 Powell Pl., Ste. 100, Brentwood, TN 37027-7707 | 615-251-2196
parentlife@lifeway.com | *www.lifeway.com/en/product-family/
parentlife-magazine*
Nancy Cornwell, content editor

Denomination: Baptist
Parent company: LifeWay Christian Resources/Southern Baptist Convention
Type: monthly print magazine
Audience: parents of children from birth to preteen
Purpose: to encourage and equip parents with biblical solutions that will transform families
Submissions: Email complete manuscript or query letter. Responds

in six to twelve months.

Types of manuscripts: devotions, how-to, sidebars, teaching

Length: 500–1,500 words

Topics: discipline, education, parenting, spiritual growth

Preferred Bible version: CSB

Guidelines: by email

Sample: order from the website

Tip: "Serves as a springboard for parents who may feel exasperated or overwhelmed with information by offering a biblical approach to raising healthy, productive children. Offers practical ideas and information for individual parents and couples."

PARISH LITURGY

16565 S. State St., South Holland, IL 60473 | 708-331-5485

acp@acpress.org | *www.americancatholicpress.org/parLit.html*

Rev. Michael Gilligan, executive director

Denomination: Catholic

Parent company: American Catholic Press

Type: quarterly print magazine; circulation: 1,500

Audience: parish priests, music directors, liturgy planners

Purpose: to provide material for each Sunday: themes, comments, petitions, and music suggestions

Submissions: Mail complete manuscript. Unsolicited freelance: 50%. Responds in two months.

Types of manuscripts: how-to, teaching

Length: 300 words

Topics: liturgy, music

Rights: all

Payment: variable, on publication

Kill fee: yes

Guidelines: not available

Sample: 9"x12" envelope with $2 postage

Tip: "We use articles on the liturgy only—period. Send us well-informed articles on the liturgy."

POWER FOR LIVING

4050 Lee Vance Dr., Colorado Springs, CO 80918 | 719-536-0100

Powerforliving@davidccook.com | *davidccook.org*

Karen Scalf Bouchard, managing editor

Parent company: David C Cook

Type: weekly Sunday school take-home paper
Audience: general, ages 50 and older
Purpose: to connect God's truth to real life
Submissions: Email complete manuscript.
Types of manuscripts: columns, devotions, interviews, personal experience, poetry
Length: features, 1,200–1,500 words; poems, 20 lines or fewer; columns, 750 words; devotions, 400 words
Topics: Christian living, holidays
Rights: first, onetime, reprint
Payment: $375 for articles, $50 for poems, $150 for columns, $100 for devotions; on acceptance
Manuscripts accepted per year: feature articles, 20; poems, 6–12; columns, 5–8; devotions, rare
Seasonal submissions: 12–18 months in advance
Preferred Bible versions: NIV, KJV
Guidelines: *davidccook.org/submissions-and-writer-guidelines*
Sample: buy from website
Tip: "Looking for inspiring stories and articles about famous and ordinary people whose experiences and insights show the power of Christ at work in their lives."

PRAYER CONNECT
PO Box 10667, Terre Haute, IN 47801 | 812-238-5504
prayerconnectmag@aol.com | *prayerleader.com/magazine*
Carol Madison, editor

Parent company: Church Prayer Leaders Network
Type: quarterly digital and print magazine; circulation: 2,000; advertising accepted
Audience: pastors and local-church prayer leaders
Purpose: to encourage and equip you in all aspects of prayer, but with the ultimate goal of developing our readers to be intercessors who pray for their friends and families, churches, communities, and the world effectively and with passion
Submissions: Email complete manuscript as attachment, or mail it. Unsolicited freelance: 15%. Responds in two to three weeks.
Types of manuscripts: columns, how-to, news, prayer guides, short ideas
Length: 250–1,500 words
Topics: prayer, revival
Rights: first, reprint (with info on where/when previously published)
Payment: 10¢/word after editing, 5¢/word for reprints; on publication

Kill fee: sometimes
Manuscripts accepted per year: 30–40
Preferred Bible version: NIV
Guidelines: *www.prayerleader.com/about-us/write-for-us*
Sample: *www.prayerleader.com/free-issue-pdfs*
Tip: "Short ideas, prayer tips, are the easiest way to break in at *Prayer Connect*." Usually gives assignments only to regular writers. If mailing a manuscript, send it with an SASE to *PrayerConnect* submissions, 9300 College View Rd. #227, Bloomington, MN 55437.

RELEVANT

See entry in "Teen/Young Adult Markets."

SHARING: A JOURNAL OF CHRISTIAN HEALING

PO Box 780909, San Antonio, TX 78278-0909 | 877-992-5222
sharing@OSLToday.org | *osltoday.org/sharing-magazine*
Jamie Ferger, editor

Parent company: International Order of St. Luke the Physician
Type: bimonthly digital and print magazine; circulation: 3,000
Audience: membership
Purpose: to empower God's people throughout the world with Jesus' healing ministry
Submissions: Email as attachment. Unsolicited freelance: 80%. Responds in one week.
Types of manuscripts: poetry, short stories
Length: 800–1,500 words
Topic: healing
Rights: all
Payment: none
Manuscripts accepted per year: 40–50
Theme lists: available via email
Guidelines: by email
Sample: request by email

SOJOURNERS

400 C St. NE, Washington, DC 20002 | 202-328-8842
queries@sojo.net | *sojo.net/magazine/current*
Julie Polter, editor
news, news@sojo.net
reviews, reviews@sojo.net

poetry, poetry@sojo.net

Type: bimonthly digital and print magazine; circulation: 19,000

Audience: community influencers

Purpose: to explore the intersections of faith, politics, and culture; uncover in depth the hidden injustices in the world around us; and tell the stories of hope that keep us grounded, inspired, and moving forward

Submissions: Email query letter in body of message. Responds in six to eight weeks.

Types of manuscripts: feature articles, poetry, reviews

Length: articles, 1,800–2,000 words; poetry, 25 lines maximum

Topics: Christian living/spirituality, culture, faith, justice, politics

Rights: all

Payment: poetry, $50; on publication

Guidelines: *sojo.net/magazine/write*

Sample: buy from website

SPORTS SPECTRUM

640 Plaza Dr., Ste. 110, Highlands Ranch, CO 80129 | 866-821-2971

jon@sportsspectrum.com | *sportsspectrum.com/magazine*

Jon Ackerman, managing editor

Parent company: Pro Athletes Outreach

Type: quarterly digital and print magazine; circulation: 4,000; advertising accepted

Audience: sports fans

Purpose: to share stories of sports persons displaying an athletic lifestyle pleasing to God

Submissions: Email query letter with clips as attachment. Gives assignments. Accepts simultaneous queries. Unsolicited freelance: 10%. Responds in one week.

Types of manuscripts: feature articles, interviews, profiles

Length: 1,500–2,000 words

Topic: sports

Rights: all

Payment: 15¢/word, on acceptance

Manuscripts accepted per year: two or three

Seasonal submissions: two to three months in advance

Preferred Bible version: NIV

Guidelines: not available

Sample: call the office

Tip: "Come with a story idea and plan for executing it."

ST. ANTHONY MESSENGER

28 W. Liberty St., Cincinnati, OH 45202-6498 | 513-241-5615

MagazineEditors@Franciscanmedia.org | *www.FranciscanMedia.org/*
st-anthony-messenger

Christopher Heffron, editorial director

Denomination: Catholic
Parent company: Franciscan Media
Type: monthly print magazine
Audience: family-oriented, majority are women ages 40–70
Purpose: to offer readers inspiration from the heart of Catholicism—
the Gospels and the experience of God's people
Submissions: Email query letter. Responds in eight weeks.
Types of manuscripts: profiles, short stories, teaching
Length: 2,000–2,500 words
Topics: church, education, family, issues, marriage, sacraments,
spiritual growth
Rights: first
Payment: 25¢/published word, on acceptance
Manuscripts accepted per year: short stories, 12
Seasonal submissions: one year in advance
Preferred Bible version: NAB
Guidelines: *www.franciscanmedia.org/writers-guidelines*
Sample: articles are on website

STANDARD

PO Box 843336, Kansas City, MO 4184-3336 | 816-931-1900

standard.foundry@gmail.com | *www.thefoundrypublishing.com/*
curriculum/adult.html

Jeanette Gardner Littleton, editor

Denomination: Nazarene
Parent company: The Foundry Publishing
Type: weekly Sunday school take-home paper; circulation: 40,000
Audience: denomination
Purpose: to encourage and inspire our audience and to reinforce
curriculum
Submissions: Only accepts email. Primarily assignment only.
Response time varies.
Types of manuscripts: personal experience
Length: 400 and 800–900 words
Topics: theme-related

Rights: all, first, reprint
Payment: $35 and $50, on acceptance
Manuscripts accepted per year: 104
Seasonal submissions: one year in advance
Preferred Bible version: NIV
Theme lists: available via email
Guidelines: by email
Sample: email request
Tip: "Writers should know basics of Wesleyan-Arminian theological perspective. Write to the theme list; please indicate which theme you're proposing it for. Nonfiction cannot be preachy. Put full contact information in the body of the manuscript, not only in the email. It helps to know if you're Nazarene or another Wesleyan/ holiness denomination." To get an assignment, send clips of personal-experience articles.

TEACHERS OF VISION

PO Box 981, Yorba Linda, CA 92885 | 714-719-0812
tov@christianeducators.org | *christianeducators.org/tov*
Dawn Molnar, managing editor
Lara Busold, assistant editorial manager

Parent company: Christian Educators
Type: triannual digital and print magazine; circulation: 13,500; advertising accepted
Audience: educators in public schools
Purpose: to provide biblically principled resources that encourage, equip, and empower Christian educators
Submissions: Email as attachment. Responds in three weeks. Also accepts submissions from children and teens.
Types of manuscripts: columns, how-to, personal experience, poetry, short stories, sidebars, trends
Length: 600–1,400 words
Topic: teaching
Rights: first, reprint
Payment: $100–200, on publication
Manuscripts accepted per year: 30
Seasonal submissions: six months in advance
Guidelines: *christianeducators.org/tov-write-for-us*
Sample: link on the website
Tip: "Most of our authors write for us because they have a passion for encouraging Christian educators. The stipend is not large enough

to motivate. Sometimes authors have the opportunity to push their own book as part of their feature."

TESTIMONY/ENRICH

2450 Milltower Ct., Mississauga, ON L5N 5Z6, Canada | 905-542-7400

testimony@paoc.org | testimony.paoc.org

Stacey McKenzie, editor

Denomination: Pentecostal
Parent company: Pentecostal Assemblies of Canada
Type: quarterly digital and print magazine; circulation: 2,200
Audience: general and leaders
Purpose: to celebrate what God is doing in and through the Fellowship, while offering encouragement to believers by providing a window into the struggles that everyday Christians often encounter
Submissions: Email query letter. Responds in six to eight weeks.
Types of manuscripts: interviews, personal experience, sidebars
Length: 800–1,000 words
Topics: Christian living/spirituality, denomination, discipleship, leadership
Rights: first
Seasonal submissions: four months in advance
Preferred Bible version: NIV
Guidelines: *testimony.paoc.org/submit*
Tip: "Our readership is 98% Canadian. We prefer Canadian writers or at least writers who understand that Canadians are not Americans in long underwear. We also give preference to members of this denomination, since this is related to issues concerning our fellowship."

TIME OF SINGING: A Journal of Christian Poetry

PO Box 5276, Conneaut Lake, PA 16316 | 814-439-0914

timesing@zoominternet.net | www.timeofsinging.com

Lora Zill, editor

Parent company: Wind & Water Press
Type: quarterly print journal; circulation: 200
Audience: those who love language and its expression through the art and craft of poetry
Purpose: to provide poets and readers a platform for thought-provoking and reflective work
Submissions: Email complete manuscript as attachment or in body of message, or mail it. Gives assignments for book reviews. Unsolicited

freelance: 95%. Responds in three months. Also accepts submissions from teens.

Types of manuscripts: poetry, reviews
Length: 40 lines maximum
Rights: first, onetime, reprint (with info on where/when previously published)
Payment: none
Manuscripts accepted per year: 150
Seasonal submissions: six months in advance
Preferred Bible version: any
Guidelines: *www.thebluecollarartist.com/time-of-singing*
Sample: $5 each, including postage (checks, money orders payable to Wind & Water Press)
Tip: "I assign book reviews of *Time Of Singing* poets. Please inquire for an assignment. I want poems that aren't afraid to take chances or think outside the theological box. Challenge my assumptions about faith, living the Christian life, and loving God. I prefer poems that don't try to provide answers but fearlessly wrestle with the questions. Trust your reader to 'get it.' It's really best to pick up a back issue to analyze to see what I like. I don't publish greeting-card style poetry or sermons that rhyme. I love fresh rhyme, free verse, and beg for forms."

TODAY'S CHRISTIAN LIVING

PO Box 5000, Iola, WI 54945 | 715-445-5000
michellea@jpmediallc.com | *www.todayschristianliving.org*
Michelle Adserias, editor

Parent company: JP Media, LLC
Type: bimonthly digital and print magazine; circulation: 12,000; advertising accepted
Audience: general, ages 45 and older
Purpose: to engage, equip, and encourage readers through inspirational true stories
Submissions: Email complete manuscript as attachment or in body of message. Accepts simultaneous submissions. Unsolicited freelance: 25%. Responds in two months.
Types of manuscripts: humor, ministry spotlights, personal experience, profiles, testimonies
Length: 700–1,500 words
Topics: Christian living/spirituality, humor, personal experience
Rights: all

Payment: $75–150, $25 for short humorous anecdotes; 45 days after publication

Kill fee: yes

Manuscripts accepted per year: 24

Seasonal submissions: six months in advance

Preferred Bible version: none

Guidelines: *todayschristianliving.org/writers-guidelines*

Sample: *todayschristianliving.org/free-digital-issue-with-newsletter-signup*

Tip: "'Turning Point' and 'Grace Notes' columns are good starting points. No particular topics." Prefers manuscripts attached as Word documents. No teaching articles, essays, poetry, or devotions.

U.S. CATHOLIC

205 W. Monroe St., Chicago, IL 60606 | 312-544-8169

submissions@uscatholic.org | *www.uscatholic.org*

Emily Sanna, managing editor

Denomination: Catholic

Parent company: Claretian Missionaries

Type: monthly digital and print magazine

Audience: denomination

Purpose: to explore the wisdom of the Catholic faith tradition and apply that faith to the challenges of 21st-century life

Submissions: Email complete manuscript. Responds in six to eight weeks.

Types of manuscripts: essays, feature articles, opinion, poetry, profiles

Length: articles, 800–3,500 words; reviews, 315 words

Topics: denomination

Rights: first

Payment: $75–500

Seasonal submissions: six months in advance

Guidelines: *uscatholic.org/writers-guide*

Tip: "*U.S. Catholic* does not consider submissions that have simultaneously been sent to any other publication or that have appeared elsewhere in any form, either in print or online. This includes articles published on personal blogs or excerpts from books, published or unpublished."

THE WAR CRY

615 Slaters Ln., Alexandria, VA 22314 | 703-684-5500

www.thewarcry.org

Lt. Colonel Lesa Davis, editor-in-chief

Denomination: The Salvation Army

Parent company: The Salvation Army in the United States

Type: monthly digital and print magazine; circulation: 185,000; advertising accepted

Audience: denomination and general public

Purpose: to represent the mission of The Salvation Army to proclaim the Gospel of Jesus Christ and serve human need in His name without discrimination

Submissions: Only submit through the website. Accepts simultaneous submissions. Unsolicited freelance: 50%. Responds in three to four weeks.

Types of manuscripts: personal experience, profiles

Length: articles, 800–1,250 words; news items and sidebars, 100–400 words

Topics: Christian living/spirituality, culture, discipleship, evangelism, issues, The Salvation Army, trends

Rights: first

Payment: 35¢/word, 15¢/word for reprints; on acceptance

Kill fee: sometimes

Manuscripts accepted per year: 40

Seasonal submissions: six months in advance

Preferred Bible version: NLT

Theme lists: available on website

Guidelines: *www.thewarcry.org/submission-guidelines*

Sample: on the website

Tip: "Some association/connection/explication of The Salvation Army is helpful when possible."

8

TEEN/YOUNG ADULT MARKETS

BOUNDLESS

8605 Explorer Dr., Colorado Springs, CO 80920 | 719-531-3400

editor@boundless.org | *www.boundless.org*

Lisa Anderson, director

Parent company: Focus on the Family
Type: website; hits per month: 300,000
Audience: single young adults in 20s and 30s
Purpose: to help Christian young adults grow up, own their faith, date with purpose, and prepare for marriage and family
Submissions: Only accepts query letter with clips. Responds only if interested.
Types of manuscripts: articles, blog posts
Length: articles, 1,200–2,000 words; blog posts, 500–800 words
Topics: adulthood, Christian living/spirituality, relationships
Rights: all
Preferred Bible version: ESV
Guidelines: *www.boundless.org/write-for-us*
Sample: see the website
Tip: "We don't typically publish unsolicited articles, but we are always open to considering new writers. If you think you've got what it takes to have your work published on *Boundless,* please feel free to send us a sample or two of your writing, a link to your blog, and a proposal of what you're interested in writing about."

BRIO

8605 Explorer Dr., Colorado Springs, CO 80920 | 719-531-3400

www.focusonthefamily.com/parenting/brio-magazine-2

Laura Pottkotter, managing editor

Parent company: Focus on the Family

Type: bimonthly print magazine; circulation: 47,000

Audience: teen girls

Purpose: to provide inspiring stories, fashion insights, fun profiles, and practical tips, all from a biblical worldview

Submissions: Email complete manuscript as attachment, or mail.

Types of manuscripts: articles, devotions, profiles, short stories

Length: profiles, 1,200–1,400 words; character trait, 650–750 words; entertainment/social media, 800–900 words; prayer, 200–300 words; relationships, 800–900 words; fiction, 1,200–1,300 words

Topics: beauty, culture, entertainment, fashion, health, prayer, relationships, seasonal, social media

Rights: first

Payment: minimum 30¢ per word, on acceptance

Guidelines: *media.focusonthefamily.com/brio/pdf/brio-writers-guidelines-2019.pdf*

Sample: on the website

Tip: Notice at the time of publication: "We are in the process of changing how we accept submissions. Please be patient with us as we move from writers guidelines to a call-for-submissions page. During this transition, we are not accepting unsolicited submissions at *submissions@briomagazine.com*." Check the website for updates.

CADET QUEST

See entry in "Children's Markets."

CAFÉ

8765 W. Higgins Rd., Chicago, IL 60631 | 800-638-3522

cafe@elca.org | *www.boldcafe.org*

Elizabeth McBride, editor

Denomination: Lutheran

Parent company: Women of the Evangelical Lutheran Church in America

Type: monthly website

Audience: Lutheran women ages 18–35

Purpose: to share stories written by bold, young women who write about faith, relationships, advocacy, and more

Submissions: Query letter with clips; simultaneous submissions accepted. Responds only if interested.

Type of manuscripts: personal experience

Length: 700–1,000 words

Topics: theme-related

Rights: first, onetime, reprint (with info on where/when previously published)
Payment: $20 per 100 published words, excluding biblical text
Seasonal submissions: seven months
Preferred Bible version: NRSV
Guidelines: *www.boldcafe.org/add-voice-boldcafe*
Sample: see the website
Tip: "We ask particular established authors to write on specific themes far in advance of publication. We publish very few articles that originated as unsolicited manuscripts or queries. Those we do accept are most likely to be accepted from Christian women (though we accept queries from men) that include stories about women or reflections that especially speak to young adult women."

CREATION ILLUSTRATED

See entry in "Adult Markets."

GUIDE

See entry in "Children's Markets."

LOVE IS MOVING

10 Huntingdale Blvd., Scarborough, ON M1W 2S5, Canada | 905-479-5885
info@loveismoving.ca | *www.loveismoving.ca*
Ilana Reimer, editor

Parent company: The Evangelical Fellowship of Canada
Type: triannual digital and print magazine; circulation: 10,000; advertising accepted
Audience: Canadian young adults
Purpose: to reflect a biblical concept of love and challenge readers to live out their faith with passion for Jesus and compassion for others
Submissions: Email complete manuscript or query letter. Unsolicited freelance: 20%. Responds in two to four days.
Types of manuscripts: essays, feature articles, opinion, poetry, reviews
Length: features, essays, 1,000–2,000 words; short opinion, news, reviews, 300–800 words
Topics: Christian living/spirituality, creativity, culture
Rights: electronic, first
Payment: features and essays, 20¢/word; short opinion, reviews, news, 15¢/word; poetry, $50
Manuscripts accepted per year: 100

Seasonal submissions: three months
Preferred Bible version: NIV
Theme lists: available on website
Guidelines: *loveismoving.ca/about/submit*
Sample: *loveismoving.ca/magazine-issues*
Tip: "We're looking for smart, thoughtful writers who are wrestling
   with timely topics in the Canadian Church and broader culture
   through the lens of their faith. Demonstrate your knowledge
   on the topic you're pitching and don't be afraid to show your
   enthusiasm!"

NATURE FRIEND

See entry in "Children's Markets."

PEER

615 Sisters Ln., Alexandria, VA 22314 | 703-684-5500
peer@usn.salvationarmy.org | *peermag.org*
Lt. Colonel Lesa Davis, editor-in-chief
   Denomination: The Salvation Army
   Parent company: The Salvation Army in the United States
   Type: monthly digital and print magazine; circulation: print 30,000,
      digital 34,000
   Audience: ages 16–22
   Purpose: to ignite a faith conversation that will deepen biblical
      perspective, faith, and holy living by addressing topics related to
      faith, community, and culture
   Submissions: Only accepts complete manuscript through the website.
      Responds in one week. Accepts submissions from teens.
   Types of manuscripts: articles, profiles, testimonies
   Length: 800 words
   Topics: Christian living/spirituality, culture, current events
   Rights: first, onetime
   Payment: 35¢/word, 15¢/word for reprints
   Preferred Bible version: NLT
   Guidelines: *peermag.org/contribute*
   Tip: "We are *always* welcoming new submissions from young writers.
      Do you love to write? Do you consider yourself an expert on a
      topic that would interest 16- to 22-year-olds? *Peer* is a national
      publication, and you can most certainly add the experience of
      writing for us on your résumé!"

RELEVANT

55 W. Church St., Ste. 211, Orlando, FL 32801 | 407-660-1411

submissions@relevantmediagroup.com | *relevantmagazine.com*

Emily Brown, managing editor

> **Type:** bimonthly digital magazine plus annual print; hits: five million
> **Audience:** ages 20s and 30s
> **Purpose:** to challenge people to go further in their spiritual journeys; live selflessly and intentionally; care about positively impacting the world around them; and find the unexpected places God is speaking in life, music, and culture
> **Submissions:** Email complete manuscript or query letter as attachment. Responds in one to two weeks or not interested.
> **Types of manuscripts:** interviews, opinion, teaching
> **Length:** 750–1,000 words
> **Topics:** Christian living/spirituality, culture, faith, justice
> **Payment:** none
> **Guidelines:** *relevantmagazine.com/write*
> **Sample:** on the website

TAKE 5 PLUS

See entry in "Devotional Booklets and Websites."

UNLOCKED

See entry in "Devotional Booklets and Websites."

YOUTH COMPASS

PO Box 4060, Overland Park, KS 66204 | 913-432-0331

sseditor@heraldandbanner.com | *heraldandbanner.com/product/youth-compass*

Arlene McGehee, Sunday school editor

> **Denomination:** Church of God
> **Parent company:** Herald and Banner Press
> **Type:** weekly Sunday school take-home paper
> **Audience:** grades 7–12
> **Purpose:** to apply Christian principles on junior high and high school level
> **Submissions:** Email as attachment or in the body of the message, or mail. Responds in nine months.
> **Types of manuscripts:** biography, short stories
> **Length:** 800–1,500 words
> **Topic:** Christian living
> **Rights:** first, reprint (with info on where/when previously published)

Payment: .005¢/word, .0025¢/word for reprints; on publication
Manuscripts accepted per year: varies
Seasonal submissions: six months
Preferred Bible version: KJV
Writers guidelines: by email
Sample: 9"x12" SASE with $3.50 postage
Tip: Looking for seasonal stories.

9

CHILDREN'S MARKETS

BEGINNER'S FRIEND

PO Box 4060, Overland Park, KS 66204 | 913-432-0331

sseditor@heraldandbanner.com | *heraldandbanner.com/product/beginners-friend*

Arlene McGehee, Sunday school editor

Denomination: Church of God
Parent company: Herald and Banner Press
Type: weekly Sunday school take-home paper; circulation: 575
Audience: ages 2–5
Purpose: to apply biblical truths to daily life in an understandable way
Submissions: Email as attachment or in body of message, or mail. Unsolicited freelance: 33%. Responds in one year.
Types of manuscripts: short stories
Length: 500–800 words
Topic: Christian life
Rights: first, reprint (with info on where/when previously published)
Payment: .005¢/word, .0025¢/word for reprints; on publication
Manuscripts accepted per year: 10
Seasonal submissions: six months in advance
Preferred Bible version: KJV
Writers guidelines: by email
Sample: 9"x12" SASE with $3.50 postage
Tip: Needs seasonal manuscripts most.

CADET QUEST

4695 44th St. SE, Ste. B-130, Kentwood, MI 49512 | 616-241-5616

submissions@CalvinistCadets.org | *www.calvinistcadets.org/cadet-quest-magazine*

Steve Bootsma, editor

Parent company: Calvinist Cadet Corps

Type: bimonthly print magazine; circulation: 5,800
Audience: boys ages 9–14
Purpose: to help boys grow more Christlike in all areas of life
Submissions: Email complete manuscript in body of message, or mail. Unsolicited freelance: 5–10%. Responds by four months before publication date. Accepts submissions from children and teens.
Types of manuscripts: cartoons, how-to, profiles, projects, puzzles, short stories
Length: fiction, 1,000–1,300 words; nonfiction, 1,500 words maximum
Topics: camping, Christian athletes, nature, sports, theme-related
Rights: all, first, reprint
Payment: articles, minimum 5¢/word; puzzles, varies; cartoons, $5–15
Manuscripts accepted per year: 20
Preferred Bible version: NIV
Theme lists: available on website
Guidelines: download from *www.calvinistcadets.org/cadet-quest-magazine*
Sample: download from website
Tip: "Looking for fun fiction, without being preachy, for preteen boys. It needs to have some action, and don't be cliché with a Jesus-always-wins type of ending."

CREATION ILLUSTRATED
See entry in "Adult Markets."

DEVOKIDS
See entry in "Devotional Booklets and Websites."

EXPLORERS
PO Box 4060, Overland Park, KS 66204 | 913-432-0331
sseditor@heraldandbanner.com | *heraldandbanner.com/product/explorers*
Arlene McGehee, Sunday school editor
Denomination: Church of God
Parent company: Herald and Banner Press
Type: weekly Sunday school take-home paper
Audience: grades 1–6
Purpose: to apply Christian principles to elementary students

Submissions: Email as attachment or in body of message, or mail. Responds in nine months.
Types of manuscripts: biography, puzzles, short stories
Length: 500–1,500 words
Rights: first, reprint (with info on where/when previously published)
Payment: .005¢/word, .0025¢/word for reprints; on publication
Manuscripts accepted per year: varies
Seasonal submissions: six months in advance
Preferred Bible version: KJV
Writers guidelines: by email
Sample: 9"x12" SASE with $3.50 postage
Tip: Looking for seasonal stories. Accepts serial stories.

FOCUS ON THE FAMILY CLUBHOUSE

8605 Explorer Dr., Colorado Springs, CO 80920 | 719-531-3400
focusonthefamily.com/clubhouse-magazine
Rachel Pfeiffer, editor

Parent company: Focus on the Family
Type: monthly print magazine; circulation: 90,000
Audience: ages 8–12
Purpose: to inspire, entertain, and teach Christian values to children
Submissions: Mail complete manuscript. Unsolicited freelance: 15%. Responds in three months. Accepts submissions from children and teens.
Types of manuscripts: activities, crafts, devotions, how-to, interviews, personality features of kids, quizzes, recipes, short stories
Length: fiction, 1,800–2,000 words; nonfiction, 400–500 or 800–1,000
Topics: apologetics, archaeology, Christian life
Rights: first
Payment: 15–25¢ per word, on acceptance
Kill fee: sometimes
Manuscripts accepted per year: 80
Seasonal submissions: eight months in advance
Preferred Bible version: HCSB
Guidelines: *focusonthefamily.com/clubhouse-magazine/about/submission-guidelines*
Sample: $4.99 at *store.focusonthefamily.com/clubhouse-magazine-single-issue*
Tip: "We are always looking for unique and interesting nonfiction stories and articles, especially stories about real-life kids. Every article should have a Christian angle, though it shouldn't be

overbearing. The concepts and vocabulary should be appropriate for our audience's ages."

FOCUS ON THE FAMILY CLUBHOUSE JR.

8605 Explorer Dr., Colorado Springs, CO 80920 | 719-531-3400
focusonthefamily.com/clubhouse-jr-magazine
Grace Kelley, associate editor

Parent company: Focus on the Family
Type: monthly print magazine; circulation: 50,000
Audience: ages 3–7
Purpose: to inspire, entertain, and teach Christian values to children
Submissions: Mail complete manuscript. Unsolicited freelance: 15%. Responds in three months. Accepts submissions from children and teens.
Types of manuscripts: activities, Bible stories retold, crafts, poetry, rebus stories, recipes, short stories
Length: fiction, 800–1,000 words; rebus stories, 200 words; nonfiction, 250–400 words
Topics: animals, Bible stories, Christian life, nature, science
Rights: first
Payment: 15–25¢ per word, on acceptance
Manuscripts accepted per year: 50
Seasonal submissions: eight months in advance
Preferred Bible version: NIrV
Guidelines: *www.focusonthefamily.com/clubhouse-jr-magazine/about/ submission-guidelines*
Sample: $4.99 at *store.focusonthefamily.com/clubhouse-magazine-single-issue*
Tip: "Read the magazine to learn our style and reading level. Aim at early and beginning readers. Rebus and Bible stories are a great way to break in."

GUIDE

PO Box 5353, Nampa, ID 83653-5353
guide.magazine@pacificpress.com | *www.guidemagazine.org*
Randy Fishell, editor

Denomination: Seventh-day Adventist
Parent company: Pacific Press Publishing Association
Type: weekly Sunday school take-home paper; circulation: 26,000
Audience: ages 10–14
Purpose: to show readers, through stories that illustrate Bible truth, how

to walk with God now and forever

Submissions: Mail complete manuscript or query via email, or submit either through the website. Unsolicited freelance: 75%; 20% assigned. Responds in four to six weeks. Accepts submissions from teens.

Types of manuscripts: biography, humor, personal experience, profiles, quizzes

Length: 450–850 words

Topics: adventure, Christian living/spirituality, missions, nature

Rights: first, reprint (with info on where/when previously published)

Payment: 7-10¢ per word, $25-40 for games and puzzles; on acceptance

Seasonal submissions: eight months in advance

Preferred Bible version: NKJV

Guidelines: *www.guidemagazine.org/writers-guidelines*

Tip: "Use your best short-story techniques (dialogue, scenes, a sense of plot) to tell a true story starring a kid ages 10–14. Bring out a clear spiritual/biblical message. We publish multipart true stories regularly, two to twelve parts. All topics indicated need to be addressed within the context of a true story."

KEYS FOR KIDS DEVOTIONAL

See entry in "Devotional Booklets and Websites."

NATURE FRIEND

4253 Woodcock Ln., Dayton, VA 22821 | 540-867-0764

editor@naturefriendmagazine.com | *www.naturefriendmagazine.com*

Kevin Shank, editor

Parent company: Dogwood Ridge Outdoors

Type: monthly print magazine; circulation: 10,000

Audience: ages 6–14, 80% are ages 8–12

Purpose: to increase awareness of God and appreciation for God's works and gifts, to teach accountability toward God's works, and to teach natural truths and facts

Submissions: Email complete manuscript as attachment. Simultaneous OK. Unsolicited freelance: 55%. Accepts submissions from children and teens.

Types of manuscripts: articles, crafts, experiments, photo features, profiles, projects, short stories

Length: 500–1,000 words

Topics: animals, astronomy, first aid, flowers, gardening, marine life, nature, photography, science, weather

Rights: all, first, reprint

Amount of payment: all rights, 10¢/edited word; first rights, 8¢/edited word; reprints, 5¢/edited word; on publication

Manuscripts accepted per year: 40–50

Seasonal submissions: four months in advance

Preferred Bible version: KJV only

Guidelines: *naturefriendmagazine.com/contributors/writers-guide-for-freelance-writers*

Sample: *naturefriendmagazine.com/sample-issues*

Tip: "While talking animals can be interesting and teach worthwhile lessons, we have chosen to not use them in *Nature Friend*. Excluded are puzzle-type submissions, such as 'Who Am I?'"

OUR LITTLE FRIEND

PO Box 5353, Nampa, ID 83653

anita.seymour@pacificpress.com | *primarytreasure.com*

Anita Seymour, managing editor

Denomination: Seventh-day Adventist

Parent company: Pacific Press Publishing Association

Type: weekly Sunday school take-home paper; circulation: 16,000

Audience: ages 1–5

Purpose: to teach about Jesus and the Christian life

Submissions: Email complete manuscript as attachment. Responds in one month.

Types of manuscripts: true stories

Length: one to two double-spaced pages

Topics: Christian living/spirituality, God's love, holidays, nature

Rights: electronic, onetime

Payment: $25–50, on acceptance

Manuscripts accepted per year: 52

Seasonal submissions: eight to nine months in advance

Preferred Bible versions: ICB, NIrV

Theme lists: available via mail with SASE

Guidelines: *www.primarytreasure.com/for-writers*

Tip: "Stories that are humorous, yet teach a spiritual lesson, rate high in this office because they rate high with kids."

PRIMARY TREASURE

PO Box 5353, Nampa, ID 83653

anita.seymour@pacificpress.com | *www.primarytreasure.com*

Anita Seymour, managing editor

Denomination: Seventh-day Adventist
Parent company: Pacific Press Publishing Association
Type: weekly Sunday school take-home paper; circulation: 14,000
Audience: ages 6–9
Purpose: to teach children about the love of God and the Christian life through true stories
Submissions: Email complete manuscript as attachment. Unsolicited freelance: 80%. Responds in one month.
Types of manuscripts: true stories
Length: four to five double-spaced pages
Topics: Christian living/spirituality, holidays, nature
Rights: electronic, onetime
Payment: $25–50, on acceptance
Manuscripts accepted per year: 104
Seasonal submissions: eight months in advance
Theme lists: available via mail with SASE
Guidelines: *www.primarytreasure.com/for-writers*
Tip: "We look for stories that avoid stereotypical roles for men and women. More than half of today's mothers work outside the home. Stories should reflect that some of the time. A more traditional lifestyle setting is OK too. We also want more stories with Dad as the adult character. We get plenty with Mom."

STARLIGHT MAGAZINE

704 W. Madison St., La Grange, KY 40031 | 704-578-0858
editor@starlightmagazine.com | *www.starlightmagazine.com*
Jean Hall, editor

Type: quarterly digital magazine with monthly bonus material; circulation: 425
Audience: ages 5–10
Purpose: to shine God's truth through children's literature
Submissions: Email complete manuscript as attachment. Unsolicited freelance: 90%. Responds in two weeks.
Types of manuscripts: Bible stories retold, biography, devotions, fillers, poetry, puzzles, quizzes, short stories, sidebars, trivia
Length: ages 5–7, 500 words; ages 8–10, 1,000 words
Topics: animals, Bible stories, Christian living, Christmas, creation, Easter, heavenly bodies, love of reading, nature, reading, school, science
Rights: electronic, reprint (with info on where/when previously published)

Payment: none

Manuscripts accepted per year: 100

Seasonal submissions: three months in advance

Preferred Bible versions: NIV, NLT

Theme lists: available on website

Guidelines: *starlightmagazine.com/starlight-magazine-writers-guidelines*

Sample: on the website

Tip: "We especially need contemporary fiction related to daily life for children." To get an assignment, email the editor.

10

WRITERS MARKETS

ALMOST AN AUTHOR

editor@almostanauthor.com | www.almostanauthor.com
Norma Poore, editor

Parent company: Serious Writer
Type: daily website; circulation: 1,000
Audience: aspiring writers
Purpose: to help writers learn craft, launch career, and build platform
Submissions: Email query letter with writing sample/link to blog posts; no attachments. Unsolicited freelance: 20%. Responds in one to two days.
Types of manuscripts: personal experience, columns, how-to, poetry, inspirational
Length: 400–900 words
Topics: encouragement, craft tips, suggestions for aspiring writers
Rights: onetime (unpublished)
Manuscripts accepted per year: 120 guest articles, 240 columns
Seasonal submissions: 30 days in advance
Preferred Bible version: none
Guidelines: *www.almostanauthor.com/submissions-3*
Sample: on the website
Tip: "We will accept articles for all genres and categories."

INK & QUILL QUARTERLY

1053 E. 1400 N, Milford, IN 46542 | 574-658-3960
wishesandjoy@gmail.com
Amy Schlabach, prose editor
Arielle C. Walters, poetry

Denomination: Anabaptist
Type: quarterly print magazine; circulation: 400; advertising accepted
Audience: Anabaptist poets and writers primarily

Purpose: to give inspiration to beginning and experienced writers alike

Submissions: Email complete manuscript as attachment, or mail. Cover letter required. Unsolicited freelance: 10%. Responds in one month.

Types of manuscripts: articles, poetry, writing exercises

Length: 600–800 words

Topics: literature appreciation, writing

Rights: first, reprint (with info on where/when previously published)

Payment: articles, $30; poetry, 50¢/line; on acceptance

Manuscripts accepted per year: 80

Seasonal submissions: three months in advance

Preferred Bible version: KJV

Guidelines: by email or mail with SASE

Sample: write or email *mjhofstetter@hotmail.com* and request a sample copy; back issues are $5 each

Tip: "We put a special emphasis on poetry, especially traditional verse forms with rhyme and meter. We currently need high-quality poetry of all kinds (nature, Christian living, devotional, personal, narrative, and the kinds of poems poets write for fun)."

POETS & WRITERS MAGAZINE

90 Broad St., Ste. 2100, New York, NY 10004-2272 | 212-226-3586

editor@pw.org | *www.pw.org*

Emma Komlos-Hrobsky, senior editor

Parent company: Poets & Writers, Inc.

Type: bimonthly print magazine; circulation: 100,000; advertising accepted

Audience: writers of poetry, fiction, and creative nonfiction

Purpose: to provide practical guidance for getting published and pursuing writing careers

Submissions: Email or mail query letter with clips. Responds in four to six weeks.

Types of manuscripts: essays, how-to, interviews, news, profiles

Length: 500–3,000 words

Topic: writing

Rights: all

Payment: $150–500, when scheduled for production

Seasonal submissions: four months in advance

Guidelines: *www.pw.org/about-us/submission_guidelines*

Sample: sold at large bookstores and online

Tip: Most open to "News & Trends," "The Literary Life," and "The Practical Writer."

WORDS FOR THE WAY

5042 E. Cherry Hills Blvd., Springfield, MO 65809 | 417-832-8409

ozarksACW@yahoo.com | *www.ozarksacw.org*

Jeanetta Chrystie, managing editor

> **Parent company:** Ozarks Chapter of American Christian Writers
> **Type:** monthly digital newsletter; circulation: 95; advertising accepted
> **Audience:** writers at all levels
> **Purpose:** to encourage and educate Christians to follow their call to write and learn to write well
> **Submissions:** Email complete manuscript or query letter. Unsolicited freelance: 95%. Responds in three weeks. Accepts submissions from teens.
> **Types of manuscripts:** columns, fillers, how-to, personal experience, poetry, reviews, sidebars
> **Length:** features, 600–900 words; general writing how-to, 400–600 words; sidebars, 200–400 words; reviews, 200–400 words; devotions, 250–500 words; poetry, 12–40 lines
> **Topic:** writing
> **Rights:** electronic, first, onetime, reprint (with info on where/when previously published)
> **Payment:** none
> **Manuscripts accepted per year:** 45
> **Seasonal submissions:** two months in advance
> **Preferred Bible version:** any
> **Guidelines:** *www.OzarksACW.org/guidelines.php*
> **Sample:** request by email
> **Tip:** "We want content that speaks to our Christian writers by teaching and encouraging them. Specific current needs: how to write in a specific genre (your choice), how to grow spiritually through writing, how to organize a book, how to handle taxes as a freelancer. Also, we need devotions for the website that encourage, inspire, and teach (not preach) Christians to follow their calling to write." Advertising is usually free.

THE WRITER'S CHRONICLE

440 Monticello Ave., Ste. 1802, PMB 73708, Norfolk, VA 23510-2670 | 240-696-7683

chronicle@awpwriter.org | *www.awpwriter.org/about/overview*

James Tate Hill, editor

> **Parent company:** The Association of Writers & Writing Programs

Type: quarterly digital magazine; advertising accepted

Audience: serious writers, writing students and teachers

Purpose: to provide diverse insights into the art of writing that are accessible, pragmatic, and idealistic for serious writers; articles are used as teaching tools

Submissions: Email query; submit complete manuscript through the website. Simultaneous OK. Unsolicited freelance: 90%. Responds in three months.

Types of manuscripts: essays, interviews, news, sidebars

Length: 5,000 words maximum

Topic: writing

Rights: electronic, first

Payment: $18 per 100 words, on publication

Tip: The magazine is published four times during the academic year. Submit only from February 1 through July 15. Also buys blog posts year round for *The Writer's Notebook,* 1,000–2,000 words, $100 per post.

WRITER'S DIGEST

4665 Malsbary Rd., Blue Ash, OH 45242

wdsubmissions@aimmedia.com | *www.writersdigest.com*

Amy Jones, editor-in-chief

Parent company: Active Interest Media

Type: bimonthly digital and print magazine; circulation: 60,000; advertising accepted

Audience: aspiring and professional writers

Purpose: to celebrate the writing life and what it means to be a writer in today's publishing environment

Submissions: Email query in body of message. Unsolicited freelance: 20%; 60% assigned. Responds in two to four months.

Types of manuscripts: essays, how-to, humor, profiles, sidebars

Length: 300–2,500 words

Topic: writing

Rights: electronic, first

Payment: 30–50¢ per word, on acceptance

Kill fee: 25%

Seasonal submissions: eight months in advance

Theme lists: available on website

Guidelines: *www.writersdigest.com/resources/submission-guidelines*

Sample: available at newsstands and through *www.writersdigestshop.com*

Tip: "Although we welcome the work of new writers, we believe the established writer can better instruct our readers. Please include your publishing credentials related to your topic with your submission."

WRITERSWEEKLY.COM

12441 N. Main St. #38, Trenton, GA 30752 | 305-768-0261

angela@writersweekly.com | writersweekly.com

Brian Whiddon, managing editor

Parent company: BookLocker.com

Type: weekly digital newsletter; circulation: 23,000

Audience: professional freelance writers

Purpose: to help professional writers find new markets and ways to increase their freelance income

Submissions: Only accepts query letter through the website or by email. Unsolicited freelance: 20%. Responds in one week.

Types of manuscripts: feature articles, how-to

Length: 600 words

Topics: marketing, writing

Rights: first, reprint

Payment: $60, on acceptance

Manuscripts accepted per year: 100

Guidelines: *writersweekly.com/writersweekly-com-writers-guidelines*

Sample: on the website

Tip: "Understand that we are not a publication about writing but earning income through writing. Proofread your query letter; spelling, capitalization, and punctuation errors leap out at us and tell us what we can expect from you as a writer. *Sell* us your idea; don't just say, 'I want to write about . . . .'"

WRITING CORNER

contests@writingcorner.com | writingcorner.com

Type: website

Audience: writers at all levels

Purpose: to provide concrete, useful advice from those who have been in the trenches and made a successful journey with their writing

Submissions: Email complete manuscript or query letter. Responds in two days.

Types of manuscripts: how-to

Length: 600–900 words

Topic: writing

Rights: onetime, reprint

Payment: none

Guidelines: *writingcorner.com/submission-guidelines*

Sample: on the website

Tip: "Our site visitors are from all areas of writing, so keep that audience in mind when writing for us."

PART 4

SPECIALTY MARKETS

11

DEVOTIONAL BOOKLETS
AND WEBSITES

Many of these markets assign all manuscripts. If there is no information listed on getting an assignment, request a sample copy and writers guidelines if they are not on the website. Then write two or three sample devotions to fit that particular format, and send them to the editor with a request for an assignment.

THE BRINK

114 Bush Rd., Nashville, TN 37217 | 800-877-7030

thebrink@randallhouse.com | *d6family.com/d6curriculum/adult*

David Jones, senior editor

Denomination: Free Will Baptist
Parent company: D6 Family Ministry
Audience: young adults
Type: print
Frequency: bimonthly
Submissions: Devotions are by assignment only to coordinate with the curriculum. Length: 200 words. Rights: all. Bible: ESV. Email for information on getting an assignment. For articles, email query with 100–200-word excerpt if available. Length: 1,000–1,500 words. Does not respond unless interested. Rights: first, reprint, onetime.
Guidelines: by email
Payment: varies
Tip: "We do not accept freelance devotions, but we do accept freelance articles on topics of faith, culture, young adult life, etc."

CHRIST IN OUR HOME

PO Box 1209, Minneapolis, MN 55440-1209 | 800-328-4648

afsubmissions@1517.media | *www.augsburgfortress.org/store/category/*
  286996/Devotionals
Heidi Hyland Mann
  Denomination: Evangelical Lutheran Church in America
  Parent company: Augsburg Fortress/1517 Media
  Audience: adults
  Type: print
  Frequency: quarterly
  Submissions: Assignments only. Submit sample devotions as
    explained in the guidelines. Length: 1190 characters, including
    spaces, maximum. Rights: all. Bible: NRSV. Also available in audio.
  Guidelines: download from *ms.augsburgfortress.org/downloads/*
    Submission%20Guidelines.pdf?redirected=true
  Tip: "*Christ in Our Home* is read by people in many nations, so avoid
    thinking only in terms of those who live in the U.S."

CHRISTIAN DEVOTIONS
377 Woodcrest Dr., Kingsport, TN 37663 | 423-384-4821
martin@christiandevotions.us | *ChristianDevotions.us*
Martin Wiles, managing editor
Cindy Sproles, executive editor
  Parent company: Christian Devotions Ministries
  Audience: adults
  Type: website
  Frequency: daily
  Submissions: Accepts freelance submissions of single devotions.
    Length: 400 words. Email as attached Word document. Rights:
    onetime. Bible: any.
  Guidelines: *www.christiandevotions.us/writeforus*
  Payment: none
  Tip: "We use the Hook, Book, Look, and Took method of developing
    devotions. See our guidelines for samples."

DEVOKIDS
WritersCoach.us@gmail.com | *devokids.com*
Eddie Jones, managing editor
  Parent company: Christian Devotions Ministries
  Audience: children
  Type: website
  Frequency: weekly

Submissions: Takes freelance submissions. Length: **75–250** words. Email as an attached Word document. Rights: onetime. Bible: NIV. Accepts submissions from children.

Guidelines: *devokids.com/write-for-us*

Payment: none

Tip: "We also need kid-friendly posts related to crafts, puzzles, coloring pages, games, fun activities, art, and photography. Share an easy and fun recipe for children."

DEVOTIONS

See *The Quiet Hour*.

FORWARD DAY BY DAY

412 Sycamore St., Cincinnati, OH 45202-4110 | 800-543-1813

editorial@forwardmovement.org | *www.forwardmovement.org*

Richelle Thompson, managing editor

Denomination: Episcopal

Parent company: Forward Movement

Audience: adults

Type: print

Frequency: quarterly

Submissions: Devotions are written on assignment. To get an assignment, send three sample meditations based on three of the following Bible verses: Psalm 139:21; Mark 8:31; Acts 4:12; Revelation 1:10. Responds in six weeks. Authors complete an entire month's worth of devotions. Length: 220 words, including Scripture, maximum. Also available on the website, by email, as a daily podcast, and a smartphone app.

Guidelines: *www.forwardmovement.org/Pages/About/Writers-Guidelines.aspx*

Payment: $300 for a month of devotions

Tip: "*Forward Day by Day* is not the place to score points on controversial topics. Occasionally, when the Scripture passage pertains to it, an author chooses to say something about such a topic. If you write about a hot-button issue, do so with humility and make certain your comment shows respect for persons who hold a different view."

FRUIT OF THE VINE

211 N. Meridian St., Ste. 101, Newberg, OR 97132 | 503-538-9775

ericmuhr@gmail.com | *www.barclaypress.com*
Eric Muhr, executive editor

Denomination: Quaker
Parent company: Barclay Press
Audience: adults
Type: print, website
Frequency: quarterly
Submissions: Accepts freelance submissions, one week at a time. Length: 250 words. Rights: onetime. Bible: NIV.
Guidelines: *www.barclaypress.com/s/Writer-Guidelines-for-Fruit-of-the-Vine.pdf*
Payment: none
Tip: "Effective devotionals usually contain examples or personal experiences to illustrate their themes. Such illustrations engage the reader and allow the work to be more persuasive. Devotionals often provide new insights on familiar ideas or passages or acquaint the reader with the unfamiliar. They are Bible-centered, challenging, and encouraging. We aim for content comprehensible and applicable to the diverse group of subscribers. Because poetry is its own unique genre and is not universally appreciated or understood, we prefer the use of prose."

INKSPIRATIONS ONLINE

PO Box 3847, Mooresville, NC 28117
tina@inkspirationsonline.com | *inkspirationsonline.com*
Tina Yeager, publisher

Audience: writers
Type: website
Frequency: weekly
Submissions: Accepts freelance submissions. Email as an attached Word document. Length: 300–400 words, including the prayer. Rights: first, reprint (with info about when and where it appeared), electronic. Bible: any.
Guidelines: *inkspirationsonline.com/submission-guidelines*
Payment: none
Tip: "Be sure the devotion centers on writing or a writer's life. Please read published content and submission guidelines."

KEYS FOR KIDS DEVOTIONAL

2060 43rd St. SE, Grand Rapids, MI 49508 | 888-224-2324

editorial@keysforkids.org | www.keysforkids.org
Courtney Lasater, editor

Parent company: Keys for Kids Ministries
Audience: children
Type: print, website
Frequency: quarterly
Submissions: Takes only freelance submissions. Rights: all. Length: 375 words, including short fiction story. Buys 30–40 per year. Seasonal four to five months in advance. Bible: NKJV. Also does a phone app.
Guidelines: *keysforkids.org/writersguidelines*
Payment: $30, on acceptance
Tip: "Include illustration in devotional story that uses a real-world object/situation to help kids understand a spiritual truth. Download free PDFs of past issues for sample stories at *www. keysforkids.org/pdf.*"

LIGHT FROM THE WORD

PO Box 50434, Indianapolis, IN 46250-0434 | 317-774-7900
submissions@wesleyan.org | www.wesleyan.org/communication/dailydevo
Susan LeBaron, publishing services director

Denomination: Wesleyan
Parent company: Wesleyan Publishing House
Audience: adults
Type: print, website
Frequency: quarterly
Submissions: Must be affiliated with The Wesleyan Church. Email three sample devotions to fit the format and request an assignment. Write "Devotion Samples" in the subject line. Length: 200–240 words. Rights: all. Bible: NIV.
Guidelines: *finelink.com/wphstoreretail/writers-guidelines.html*
Payment: $100 for seven devotions
Tip: "Writing must lead readers to discover a biblical truth and *apply* that truth to their lives."

LIVING FAITH

PO Box 292824, Kettering, OH 45429 | 800-246-7390
info@livingfaith.com | livingfaith.com
Pat Gohn, editorial director

Denomination: Catholic

Parent company: Bayard, Inc.
Audience: adults
Type: print
Frequency: quarterly
Submissions: Assignments only; email one or two samples and credentials to request an assignment. Bible: NAB.
Tip: "*Living Faith* provides daily reflections based on a Scripture passage from the daily Mass. With readings for daily Mass listed at the bottom of each devotion, this booklet helps Catholics pray and meditate in spirit with the seasons of the Church Year."

LIVING FAITH KIDS

PO Box 292824, Kettering, OH 45429 | 800-246-7390
editor@livingfaithkids.com | *www.livingfaith.com/kids*
Connie Clark, editor

Denomination: Catholic
Parent company: Bayard, Inc.
Audience: children
Type: print
Frequency: quarterly
Submissions: Assignments only; email samples and credentials to request an assignment.
Tip: "*Living Faith Kids* features daily devotions based on the daily Scripture readings from the Catholic Mass. Each quarterly issue helps children 8-12 develop the habit of daily prayer and build their relationship with Jesus and the Church."

LOVE LINES FROM GOD

128 Leyland Ct., Greenwood, SC 29649 | 864-554-3204
mandmwiles@gmail.com | *lovelinesfromgod.blogspot.com*
Martin Wiles, managing editor

Audience: adults
Type: website
Frequency: daily
Submissions: Accepts freelance submissions. Email as an attachment. Length: 300-400 words. Rights: first. Bible: NIV.
Guidelines: *lovelinesfromgod.blogspot.com/p/write-for-us_3.html*
Payment: none
Tip: "We are looking for devotions that encourage, not preach. Following the submission guidelines will result in a better chance of

having the submission accepted."

OPEN WINDOWS

200 Powell Pl., Ste. 100, Brentwood, TN 37027-7707 | 615-251-2000
openwindows@lifeway.com | *lifeway.com/en/product-family/open-windows-*
magazine?intcmp=lw%3Aopenwindows%3Asmerch
David Bennett, managing editor

    Denomination: Southern Baptist
    Parent company: Lifeway Christian Resources
    Audience: adults
    Type: print, website
    Frequency: quarterly
    Submissions: Assignment only. Length: 300 words. Buys first rights.
        Bible: KJV, CSB.
    Guidelines: by email
    Payment: $30–40
    Tip: "Writers must be conservative evangelicals."

THE QUIET HOUR and DEVOTIONS

4050 Lee Vance Dr., Colorado Springs, CO 80919
thequiethour@davidccook.com | *davidccook.org*
Karen Cain, editor

    Parent company: David C Cook
    Audience: adults
    Type: print
    Frequency: quarterly
    Submissions: *Devotions* and *The Quiet Hour* jointly publish new
        devotionals. By assignment only. Must have North American postal
        address for contract and payment. Length: 200 words. Rights: all.
        Bible: NIV, KJV.
    Guidelines: *davidccook.org/wp-content/uploads/Devotions-and-Quiet-*
        Hour-Writers-Guidelines.pdf
    Payment: $140 for seven
    Tip: "Submit spec devotional on a key verse you select in a Scripture
        passage of your choice. Begin with anecdotal opening then
        transition to relevant biblical insight and encouragement for a life
        of faith rooted in the key verse."

REFLECTING GOD

PO Box 419427, Kansas City, MO 64141 | 816-931-1900

dbrush@thefoundrypublishing.com | reflectinggod.com;
www.thefoundrypublishing.com/catalog/product/view/id/7767/s/
reflecting-god-rg-son24/category/19/
Duane Brush, editor

Denomination: Nazarene
Parent company: The Foundry Publishing
Audience: adults
Type: print, website
Frequency: quarterly
Submissions: Send a couple of sample devotions to fit the format and request an assignment. Length: 180–200 words. Also available as a podcast and by email.
Payment: $115 for seven
Tip: "Our purpose is the pursuit to embrace holy living. We want to foster discussion about what it means to live a holy life in the 21st century."

REJOICE!

718 N. Main St., Newton, KS 67114 | 316-281-4412
RejoiceEditor@MennoMedia.org | www.mennomedia.org/rejoice
April Yamasaki, editor

Denomination: Mennonite
Parent company: MennoMedia
Audience: adults
Type: print
Frequency: quarterly
Submissions: Devotions on assignment only. Length: 240–265 words. Rights: first, electronic. Bible: prefers NRSVue. Also accepts devotional articles, 700 words, eight per year; poems, free verse, light verse, 60 characters, eight per year, submit three maximum.
Payment: devotions, $100–125 for seven; articles, $50; poems, $25; on publication
Tip: "Don't apply for an assignment unless you are familiar with the publication and Anabaptist theology."

THE SECRET PLACE

1075 First Ave., King of Prussia, PA 19406 | 610-768-2084
thesecretplace@judsonpress.com | www.judsonpress.com
Katelyn Morgan, administrator

Denomination: American Baptist

Parent company: Judson Press
Audience: adults
Type: print
Frequency: quarterly
Submissions: Accepts freelance submissions; does not give assignments. Length: 250 words. Rights: first. Bible: NRSVue.
Guidelines: *www.judsonpress.com/Content/Site189/ BasicBlocks/10271GUIDELINES_00000124086.pdf*
Payment: $20 each
Tip: "Write for comfort, inspiration, and hope in people's everyday lives."

TAKE 5 PLUS

1445 N. Boonville Ave., Springfield, MO 65802 | 417-862-2781
wquick@ag.org | myhealthychurch.com
Wade Quick, team leader

Denomination: Assemblies of God
Parent company: Gospel Publishing House
Audience: teens
Type: print
Frequency: quarterly
Submissions: Assignment only. Request writers guidelines and sample assignment (unpaid) via email. After samples are approved, writers will be added to the list for assignments. Length: 210–235 words. Rights: all. Bible: NIV.
Payment: $25 each, on acceptance
Tip: "Study the publication before attempting the sample assignment."

THESE DAYS: Daily Devotions for Living by Faith

100 Witherspoon St., Louisville, KY 40202 | 800-624-2412
mlindberg@presbypub.com | www.thethoughtfulchristian.com/Pages/ Item/59264/These-Days.aspx

Denomination: Presbyterian
Parent company: Presbyterian Publishing Corporation
Audience: adults
Type: print
Frequency: quarterly
Submissions: Accepts freelance submissions. Length: 190 words. Rights: first. Bible version: NRSV.
Payment: $100 or $150 worth of books for seven
Tip: "Write thoughtful entries based on a Scripture passage, use

gender-inclusive language for God and humanity, and include a brief closing prayer."

UNLOCKED

2060 43rd St. SE, Grand Rapids, MI 49508 | 616-647-4500
editorial@unlocked.org | unlocked.org
Hannah Howe, editor

Parent company: Keys for Kids Ministries
Audience: teens
Type: print
Frequency: quarterly
Submissions: Accepts only freelance submissions. Submit through the website. Rights: all. Publishes devotional essays, 200–315 words (personal stories, book-of-the-Bible summaries, church history pieces, tough topics, etc.); fiction, 200–350 words (primarily looking for allegorical fiction, especially sci-fi and fantasy; sometimes accepts contemporary fiction stories with characters, situation, and dialogue that are not too young; when in doubt, write for an older audience, not a younger one); and poetry, 16–23 lines. Accepts teen writers. Bible: CSB, NIV, NLT, WEB. Also available on the website and as a podcast. Sample: *unlocked.org/about.*
Guidelines: *unlocked.org/writers-guidelines*
Payment: $30, on acceptance
Tip: "We recommend all interested writers sign up for our writer's newsletter for monthly updates and more details about the kinds of submissions we are looking for (topics, genres, etc.): *unlocked.org/writers-newsletter.*"

THE UPPER ROOM

1908 Grand Ave., Nashville, TN 37212 | 615-340-6000
ureditorial@upperroom.org | upperroom.org
Lindsay Gray, editorial director

Parent company: The Upper Room
Audience: adults
Type: print
Frequency: bimonthly
Submissions: Accepts freelance submissions. Length: 300 words, which include everything on the printed page. Rights: first, electronic. Bible: NIV, NRSV, CEB, KJV. Submit through the website form (preferred), by mail, or by email. Also available on

the website.

Guidelines: *submissions.upperroom.org/en/guidelines/meditations*

Payment: $30, on publication

Tip: "*The Upper Room* is meant for an international, interdenominational audience. We want to encourage Christians in their personal life of prayer and discipleship. We seek to build on what unites us and to connect Christians together in prayer around the world."

THE WORD IN SEASON

411 N. Washington Ave., Minneapolis, MN 55401 | 800-328-4648

rochelle@writenowcoach.com | *www.augsburgfortress.org*

Rochelle Melander, managing editor

Denomination: Evangelical Lutheran Church in America

Parent company: Augsburg Fortress/1517 Media

Audience: adults

Type: print

Frequency: quarterly

Submissions: Assignment only; gives assignments based on samples. Read the guidelines, and write three trial devotions. Length: total character count with spaces is 1190. Rights: all. Bible: NRSV. Also available as an Amazon ebook.

Guidelines: download from *ms.augsburgfortress.org/downloads/ Submission%20Guidelines.pdf?redirected=true*

Payment: $40

Tip: "Know Lutheran theology, especially the concept of grace."

12

DRAMA

CHRISTIAN PUBLISHERS, LLC

PO Box 248, Cedar Rapids, IA 52406 | 844-841-6387

editor@christianpub.com | www.christianpub.com

Audiences: adult, children, teens

Types: children's Christmas and Easter pageants, full-length musicals, full-length plays, one-act musicals, one-act plays

Submissions: Publishes plays for the Christian market, including but not limited to elementary through high school, adults, and youth groups. Submit complete script through the website form. Response time varies according to the time of the year.

Payment: 10% royalty, often to a fixed amount; no advance

Guidelines: *www.christianpub.com/default.aspx?pg=ag*

Tip: "Be sure your play builds. People have short attention spans, and if the story is too bogged down in excessive dialogue, or if the play wanders aimlessly, they will simply tune out. If the comedy or suspense doesn't build from scene to scene, if we're not involved with the main character(s) or the dramatic question, then the play isn't going anywhere."

CSS PUBLISHING COMPANY, INC.

5450 N. Dixie Hwy., Lima, OH 45807 | 419-227-1818

editor@csspub.com | www.csspub.com

Audiences: adult, children, teens

Types: monologues, one-act plays, reader's theatre, short skits, skit compilations

Submissions: Publishes five to ten skits per year. Receives 20–30 submissions per year. Length: 15 minutes. Primarily interested in Advent/Christmas/Epiphany, and Lent/Easter. Doesn't publish lengthy dramatic works. Email or mail query letter or complete script. Responds in six months. Simultaneous submissions OK.

Payment: negotiated, no advance

Guidelines: *store.csspub.com/page.php?Custom%20Pages=10*

Tip: "Content needs to be fresh and imaginative."

DRAMA MINISTRY

2814 Azalea Pl., Nashville, TN 37204 | 866-859-7622

service@dramaministry.com | *www.dramaministry.com*

Vince Wilcox, general manager

Audiences: adult, children, teens

Types: monologues, reader's theatre, short skits

Submissions: Open to all topics, including seasonal/holidays, for children, youth, and adults. Email or mail script. Buys all rights.

Guidelines: *www.dramaministry.com/faq*

ELDRIDGE CHRISTIAN PLAYS AND MUSICALS

PO Box 4904, Lancaster, PA 17604 | 850-385-2463

NewWorks@histage.com | *www.95church.com*

Susan Shore, senior editor

Audiences: adult, children, teens

Types: full-length musicals, full-length plays, monologues, one-act plays, reader's theatre, skit compilations

Submissions: Publishes 15 scripts per year; receives 300 submissions annually. Length: plays and musicals, minimum 30 minutes, maximum two hours. Submit complete script via email attachment with cover letter in the body of the message. Simultaneous OK. Responds in two months.

Payment: 50% royalty plus 10% copy sales, no advance

Guidelines: *95church.com/submission-guidelines*

Tip: "We like all kinds of plays and are always open to new ideas. Generally speaking, our customers like plays with more female than male roles or flexible casting in which roles can be played by either men or women. This is not a hard-and-fast rule, however. We like easy costuming and scenery, if possible, as many church budgets are limited."

WORDCRAFTS THEATRICAL PRESS

912 E. Lincoln, Tullahoma, TN 37388 | 615-397-8376
wordcraftspress@gmail.com | *wordcrafts.net*
Mike Parker, publisher

Audience: Adult

Types: full-length plays, one-act plays

Details: Publishes two to four plays per year. Receives 25 submissions. Email query letter or complete script, or submit through the website. Accepts simultaneous submissions. Responds in two to four weeks.

Payment: royalty, no advance

Guidelines: *www.wordcrafts.net/how-to-submit*

Tip: "Make sure your play is producible."

13

GIFTS AND GREETING CARDS

BLUE MOUNTAIN ARTS

Editorial Dept., PO Box 1007, Boulder, CO 80306 | 303-449-0536

editorial@sps.com | www.sps.com

Audience: adult

Product: greeting cards

Submissions: General card publisher with some inspirational cards. Not looking for rhymed poetry, religious verse, or one-liners. Length: 50–300 words. Buys all rights. Accepts freelance submissions by email (no attachments), website form, or mail. Responds in two months or not interested. Holiday deadlines: Christmas and general holidays, May 15; Valentine's Day, July 12; Easter, September 8; Mother's Day and graduation, October 13; Father's Day, December 7.

Guidelines: *www.sps.com/greeting-card-guidelines-submissions*

Tip: "Because our cards capture genuine emotions on topics such as love, friendship, family, missing you, and other real-life subjects, we suggest that you have a friend, relative, or someone else in your life in mind as you write. We are looking for new, original, and creative writings that do not sound like anything we have already published."

CHRISTIAN ART GIFTS

359 Longview Dr., Bloomingdale, IL 60108 | 800-521-7807

info@christianartpublishing.com | www.christianartgifts.com

Rob Teigen, vice president of publishing

Audiences: adult, children, teens

Products: box of blessings, coloring books, devotionals, gift books, gifts, journals, mugs

Submissions: Interested in devotionals, prayer books, seasonal books, and kids resources. Submit query through the website form. Buys all rights.

Payment: 10–14% royalty, sometimes offers advance

Guidelines: *christianartpublishing.com/get-started*

Tip: "Looking for devotionals, kids devotionals, prayer books, and thoughtful gift books."

DICKSONS, INC.

709 B Ave. E, Seymour, IN 47274 | 812-522-1308

submissions@dicksonsgifts.com | *www.dicksonsgifts.com*

Thom Hunter, director of product development

Audience: adult

Products: gifts

Submissions: Two to eight lines, maximum 16, suitable for plaques, bookmarks, etc. Email submission. Responds in three months. Subjects can cover any gift-giving occasion and Christian, inspirational, and everyday social-expression topics. Phrases or acrostics of one or two lines for bumper stickers are also considered. Buys reprint rights.

Payment: royalty, negotiable

Tip: Looking for religious verses.

ELLIE CLAIRE

6100 Tower Cir., Ste. 210, Franklin, TN 37067 | 615-932-7600

www.hachettebookgroup.com/imprint/hachette-nashville/worthy-books/
  ellie-claire-gifts/?lens=worthy-books

Jeana Ledbetter, associate publisher and acquisitions

Audience: adult

Products: devotionals, gift books, journals

Submissions: Submit through agents only. Buys all rights.

Payment: flat fee, royalty

Tip: "We operate in the gift market, and the writing will need to reflect that. We are not interested in Bible studies but in inspirational and encouraging devotions, funny stories with a spiritual component, and compilations from a Christian worldview."

INK & WILLOW

10807 New Allegiance Dr., Ste. 500, Colorado Springs, CO 80921 | 719-590-4999

info@waterbrookmultnomah.com | *waterbrookmultnomah.com/ink-and-willow*

Jamie Lapeyrolerie, acquisitions editor

Audience: adult

Products: coloring books, inspirational cards, journals, planners

Submissions: Takes submissions only from agents.

Tip: "Ink & Willow encompasses a line of interactive products that infuse contemplation and inspiration into the regular spiritual practice of creative-minded Christians, wherever they are in their faith journey. Each thoughtfully curated gift product is based in biblical truth and sparks a reminder of how God reveals beauty in the midst of our ordinary."

WARNER PRESS

2902 Enterprise Dr., Anderson, IN 46013 | 800-741-7721

editors@warnerpress.org | *www.warnerpress.org*

Robin Loisch, kids and family ministry editor

Audiences: adult, children

Products: greeting cards

Submissions: Themes include birthday, anniversary, baby congratulations, sympathy, get well, kid's birthday and get well, thinking of you, friendship, Christmas, praying for you, encouragement. Use a conversational tone with no lofty poetic language, such as *thee, thou, art*. Don't preach or use a negative tone. Strive to share God's love and provide a Christian witness. Length: average of four lines. Responds in six to eight weeks. Email as attachment. Buys all rights. Deadlines: everyday, July 31; Christmas, October 1.

Guidelines: *www.warnerpress.org/submission-guidelines*

Payment: $25–50

Tip: "Include your name, address, and email address with each page of submissions. We prefer email submissions with verses sent as an attachment. We seldom buy rhyming verse. Greeting cards are sold as boxed sets. No individual counter-line cards. Verses should be general enough that they would be appropriate to send to multiple people. Including a Scripture for your verse is also appreciated (KJV and NIV preferred)."

14

TRACTS

The following companies publish gospel tracts but do not have writers guidelines. If you are interested in writing for them, email or phone to find out if they currently are looking for submissions. Also check your denominational publishing house to see if it publishes tracts.

FELLOWSHIP TRACT LEAGUE
3733 Snook Rd., Morrow, OH 45152 | 513-494-1075
mail@fellowshiptractleague.org | *fellowshiptractleague.org*

GOSPEL TRACT SOCIETY, INC.
1105 S. Fuller, Independence, MO 64050 | 816-461-6086
gospeltractsociety@gmail.com | *www.gospeltractsociety.org*

TRACT ASSOCIATION OF FRIENDS
1501 Cherry St., Philadelphia, PA 19102
info@tractassociation.org | *tractassociation.org*
Writers must be Quakers.

15

BIBLE CURRICULUM

This list includes only the major, nondenominational curriculum publishers. If you are in a denominational church, also check its publishing house for curriculum products. Plus some organizations, like Awana and Pioneer Clubs, produce curriculum for their programs.

Since Bible curriculum is written on assignment only, you'll need to get samples for age groups you want to write for (from the company's website, large Christian bookstores, or your church) and study the formats and pieces. Look for editors' names on the copyright or contents pages of teachers manuals, or call the publishing house for this information.

Then write query letters to specific editors. Tell why you're qualified to write curriculum for them, include a sample of curriculum you've written or other sample of your writing, and ask for a trial assignment. Since the need for writers varies widely, you may not get an assignment for a year or more.

Some of these companies also publish undated, elective curriculum books that are used in a variety of ministries. Plus some book publishers publish lines of Bible-study guides. (See "Traditional Book Publishers.") These are contracted like other books with a proposal and sample chapters.

DAVID C COOK
4050 Lee Vance Dr., Colorado Springs, CO 80918 | 719-536-0100
davidccook.org/curriculum
 Type: Sunday school
 Imprints: The Action Bible, Bible-in-Life, Echoes, Gospel Light, HeartShaper, Scripture Press, SEEN Youth, Standard Lesson, Tru, Wonder Ink

GROUP PUBLISHING
1515 Cascade Ave., Loveland, CO 80538 | 800-447-1070
submissions@group.com | *www.group.com*

Types: Sunday school, vacation Bible school, children's worship

Imprints: BE BOLD, DIG IN, FaithWeaver NOW, Following Jesus, Hands-On Bible Curriculum, LIVE, Simply Loved, KidsOwn Worship, Play-n-Worship

PENSACOLA CHRISTIAN COLLEGE

PO Box 17900, Pensacola, FL 32522-7900 | 877-356-9385

www.joyfullifesundayschool.com

Type: Sunday school

Imprint: Joyful Life

UMI (URBAN MINISTRIES, INC.)

1551 Regency Ct., Calumet City, IL 60409-5448 | 800-860-8642

support@urbanministries.com | *urbanministries.com*

Types: Sunday school, vacation Bible school

UNION GOSPEL PRESS

19695 Commerce Pkwy., Cleveland, OH 44130 | 216-749-2100

editorial@uniongospelpress.com | *www.uniongospelpress.com*

Type: Sunday school, homeschool

Imprints: Christian Life Series, Illuminate Bible Series

16

MISCELLANEOUS

These companies publish a variety of books and other products that fall into the specialty-markets category, such as puzzle books, game books, children's activity books, craft books, charts, church bulletins, and coloring books.

BARBOUR PUBLISHING
See entry in "Traditional Book Publishers."

BEAMING BOOKS
See entry in "Traditional Book Publishers."

BROADSTREET PUBLISHING
See entry in "Traditional Book Publishers."

CF4K
See entry in "Traditional Book Publishers."

CREATIVE COMMUNICATIONS FOR THE PARISH
See entry in "Traditional Book Publishers."

CSS PUBLISHING GROUP, INC.
See entry in "Traditional Book Publishers."

DAVID C COOK
See entry in "Traditional Book Publishers."

GROUP PUBLISHING
1515 Cascade Ave., Loveland, CO 80538 | 970-669-3836

www.group.com/writer-submissions

Submissions: Looking for innovative children's ministry experts who are interested in being contract writers to contribute to books, online articles, and curriculum. Complete the online form to get a writer's assessment, then an assignment.

JUST FOR KIDS

2 Overlea Blvd., Toronto, ON M4H 1P4, Canada | 416-425-2111

justforkids@salvationarmy.ca | *salvationist.ca/editorial/just-for-kids/*
2024-back-issues

Abbigail Oliver, editor

Parent company: The Salvation Army in Canada and Bermuda
Audience: ages 5–12
Type: weekly activity page
Submissions: Puzzles that relate to a biblical story or concept, common themes (seasons, holidays, sports, animals, etc.), and Salvation Army distinctives (junior soldiers, Salvation Army flag, etc.); jokes and tongue twisters; general knowledge and Salvation Army trivia questions; news photo (junior soldier enrollment, achievement or recognition of a young person or group of young people, a corps activity for or by young people, etc.) with caption of 75 words maximum.
Payment: none
Bible: NIV
Guidelines: *salvationist.ca/files/salvationarmy/Magazines/Just-for-Kids-Guidelines.pdf*

PAULINE BOOKS AND MEDIA

See entry in "Traditional Book Publishers."

ROSE PUBLISHING

See entry in "Traditional Book Publishers."

ROSEKIDZ

See entry in "Traditional Book Publishers."

TORCHBEARER PRESS

See entry in "Traditional Book Publishers."

TWENTY-THIRD PUBLICATIONS

See entry in "Traditional Book Publishers."

WARNER PRESS

2902 Enterprise Dr., Anderson, IN 46013 | 800-741-7721
editors@warnerpress.org | *www.warnerpress.org*
Robin Loisch, kids and family ministry editor

Children's coloring and activity books: Most activity books focus on a Bible story or biblical theme, such as love and forgiveness. Ages range from preschool (ages 2–5) to upper elementary (ages 8–10). Include activities and puzzles in every upper-elementary book. Coloring-book manuscripts should present a picture idea and a portion of the story for each page. Deadlines: May 1 and October 1. Payment varies.

Children's teaching resources: Books with skits, science experiments, and crafts. Length: 48–144 pages. Activities must be interesting for kids, teach important biblical lessons, and be easy to use in a class. Payment varies.

Guidelines: *www.warnerpress.org/submission-guidelines*

PART 5

SUPPORT FOR WRITERS

17

LITERARY AGENTS

Asking editors and other writers is a great way to find a reliable agent. You may also want to visit *www.sfwa.org/other-resources/for-authors/writer-beware/agents* for tips on avoiding questionable agents and choosing reputable ones.

The general market has the Association of American Literary Agents (*aalitagents.org*), also known as AALA. To be a member, the agent must agree to a code of ethics. The website has a searchable list of agents. Some listings below indicate at least one agent belongs to the AALA. Lack of such a designation, however, does not indicate the agent is unethical; most Christian agents are not members.

AKA LITERARY MANAGEMENT

11445 Dallas Rd., Peyton, CO 80831 | 646-846-2478
submissions@akaliterary.com | akalm.net

Agent: Terrie Wolf

Agency: Established in 2009. Represents 52 clients. Member of Association of American Literary Agents. Responds in 8–12 weeks. Specializes in rights management, including transmedia, film, TV, and foreign.

Types of books: adult fiction, adult nonfiction, children's fiction, cookbook, general-market children's, general-market fiction, general-market nonfiction, home arts, teen/YA nonfiction, wellness, young adult

New clients: Open to all writers. First contact: email proposal, website form, referral from current client. Query via the instructions on the website through Submittable or Query Manager. Simultaneous OK.

Commission: 15%

Tip: "(1) Make sure we're open to submissions. Those received when our window is not open will be discarded. (2) Get to know us on social media. (3) Please provide well-formatted submissions that include your query, your quick synopsis, the first three chapters (or full manuscript for children's works or full proposal for nonfiction works), and take the time to help us understand why you would like to work with us."

ALIVE LITERARY AGENCY

5001 Centennial Blvd. #50742, Colorado Springs, CO 80908
admin@aliveliterary.com | www.aliveliterary.com

> **Agents:** Bryan Norman, Lisa Jackson, Rachel Jacobson, Kathleen Kerr, Carly Kellerman
> **Agency:** Established in 1989.
> **Types of books:** adult nonfiction
> **New clients:** Open only to well-established book writers. Contact through the website. Response time varies.
> **Commission:** 15%
> **Tip:** "We only accept manuscripts by request or referral."

AMBASSADOR LITERARY

PO Box 50358, Nashville, TN 37205 | 615-370-4700
wes@AmbassadorAgency.com | www.AmbassadorAgency.com

> **Agent:** Wes Yoder
> **Agency:** Established in 1997. Represents 20 clients. Also offers national media representation for select clients.
> **Types of books:** adult nonfiction
> **New clients:** Open only to well-established book writers. Contact by email with a full proposal. Responds in two weeks.
> **Commission:** 15%
> **Tip:** "Looking for great storytellers!"

AUTHORIZEME LITERARY FIRM

PO Box 1816, South Gate, CA 90280 | 310-508-9860
AuthorizeMeNow@gmail.com | www.AuthorizeMe.net/
authorizeme#literary_agency

> **Agent:** Dr. Sharon Norris Elliott
> **Agency:** Established in 2020. Represents 60+ clients. Other services: See entry in "Editorial Services."
> **Types of books:** Bible study, Christian living, devotionals, family, leadership, parenting, picture books, spiritual growth
> **New clients:** Open to writers from established to those seeking their

first contract. Contact: email with one-sheet. Responds in one to three months.

Commission: 15%

Tip: "Love Jesus; be teachable, patient, and humble; possess a strong desire to reach for excellence; smile a lot."

BANNER LITERARY

PO Box 1828, Winter Park, CO 80482

mike@mikeloomis.co | *www.mikeloomis.co*

Agent: Mike Loomis

Agency: Established in 2004. Represents 48 clients. Other services: See entries in "Editorial Services" and "Publicity and Marketing Services."

Types of books: adult nonfiction, business, inspiration, politics, self-help

New clients: Open to writers who have not published a book and self-published writers. Contact through email or website form. Responds in two weeks.

Commission: 15%

Tip: "Send your web address with query."

BBH LITERARY

david@bbhliterary.com | *www.bbhliterary.com*

Agents: David Bratt; Laura Bardolph, *laura@bbhliterary.com*

Agency: Established in 2021. Represents 30 clients. Other services: See entries in "Editorial Services" and "Publicity and Marketing Services."

Types of books: adult nonfiction

New clients: Open to all book writers. Contact: query letter via website form, referral from current client. Accepts simultaneous submissions. Responds in one week.

Commission: 15%

Tip: "Please tell us why your book has some urgency to its message. We are most interested in books that speak to real life in a complicated world with nuance and wisdom."

THE BINDERY

2727 N. Cascade Ave., Ste. 170, Colorado Springs, CO 80207

info@thebinderyagency.com | *www.thebinderyagency.com*

Agents: Alex Field, Andrea Heinecke, Trinity McFadden, Ingrid Beck, John Blase, Morgan Strehlow

Agency: Established in 2017. Represents 200+ clients with a particular focus on under-represented voices. Member of Association of American Literary Agents.

Types of books: adult fiction, adult nonfiction, biography, Christian living, cultural issues, culture, history, memoir, mental health, parenting, poetry, pop culture, psychology, relationships, self-help, social issues, spirituality

New clients: Open to all book writers. Initial contact: email, referral from current client. Query first according to the directions on the website. Accepts simultaneous submissions. Responds in 10–12 weeks or is not interested.

Commission: 15%

Tip: "Before sending a query, you can find out what each agent is seeking on the About page of our website. We will read every query to determine whether it's a fit for our agency. However, due to the volume of email queries we receive, we have to be incredibly selective; and, as a result, we won't reply to every submission. If one of our agents would like to read more of your manuscript or discuss your project with you, they will reach out to you directly."

THE BLYTHE DANIEL AGENCY, INC.

PO Box 64197, Colorado Springs, CO 80962-4197

blythe@theblythedanielagency.com | www.theblythedanielagency.com

Agents: Blythe Daniel; Stephanie Alton, *stephanie@ theblythedanielagency.com*

Agency: Established in 2005. Represents 115 clients. Sells to general-market too. Other services: See entry in "Publicity and Marketing Services."

Types of books: adult fiction, apologetics, business, Christian living, current events, devotionals, family, gift books, leadership, marriage, parenting, social issues, spiritual growth, women's issues

New clients: Open to all writers from those who have never been published through well-published ones. Contact: email proposal and three sample chapters. Responds in 8–12 weeks if interested.

Commission: 15%

Tip: "We want to work with authors who are open to feedback and suggestions and are willing to work hard. We are looking for writers who are saying something no one else is saying, are committed to becoming authors who are building their audience, and whom we can build a relationship with over time."

BOOKS & SUCH LITERARY MANAGEMENT
representation@booksandsuch.com | www.booksandsuch.com

Agents: Janet Kobobel Grant, *janet@booksandsuch.com;* Wendy
Lawton, *wendy@booksandsuch.com;* Rachel Kent, *rachel@
booksandsuch.com;* Cynthia Ruchti, *cynthia@booksandsuch.com;*
Barb Roose, *barb@booksandsuch.com;* Debbie Alsdorf, *debbie@
booksandsuch.com;* Jen Babakhan, *jen@booksandsuch.com*

Agency: Established in 1996. Represents 275 clients.

Types of books: adult fiction, adult nonfiction, children's fiction,
children's nonfiction, Christian living, devotionals, discipleship,
family, health/wellness, leadership, marriage, middle grade, ministry,
teen/YA fiction, teen/YA nonfiction

New clients: Open to writers who have not published a book. Contact
by email with query first. Responds in one month.

Commission: 15%

Tip: "We're especially interested in writers who have developed a social-
media presence and have a website."

CHRISTIAN LITERARY AGENT
PO Box 428, Newburg, PA 17257 | 717-423-6621

keith@christianliteraryagent.com | www.christianliteraryagent.com

Agent: Keith Carroll

Agency: Established in 2010. Represents 10–15 new clients annually.
Other service: writer coach.

Types of books: adult nonfiction

New clients: Open to first-time book authors and self-published
writers. Initial contact: phone, mail application form. Responds in
two to four weeks.

Commission: 10%

Fees: $90 administrative fee

Tip: "I try to help you make your material more of an effective read."

THE CHRISTOPHER FEREBEE AGENCY
submissions@christopherferebee.com | christopherferebee.com

Agents: Christopher Ferebee, Angela Scheff, Jana Burson, Jonathan Merritt

Agency: Established in 2011.

Types of books: adult fiction, adult nonfiction

New clients: Submit query letter and proposal as email attachment.
Responds in four weeks.

Tip: "As a small agency, we focus our efforts on a very select group of authors. Our primary focus and attention is always on existing client relationships. But we are looking for the right authors with important ideas."

C.Y.L.E. AGENCY (CYLE YOUNG LITERARY ELITE)

PO Box 1, Clarklake, MI 49230 | 330-651-1604
submissions@cyleyoung.com | *cyleyoung.com*

Agents: Cyle Young, Tessa Emily Hall, Del Duduit, Megan Burkhart, Bethany Jett, Antwan Houser, Andy Clapp

Agency: Established in 2018. Represents 80 clients. Member of Association of American Literary Agents. Specialty: children's and nonfiction. Acquires general-market books too.

Types of books: adult fiction, adult nonfiction, children's fiction, children's nonfiction, middle grade, teen/YA fiction, teen/YA nonfiction

New clients: Some of the agents are currently closed to queries and proposals except when meeting writers at a conference or an online writing event. Check the website to see who is open to submissions. Simultaneous submissions OK. Responds in three months or not interested.

Commission: 15%

Tip: "We look for projects with great writing, big ideas, and great platform."

DUNAMIS WORDS

www.cherylricker.com/dunamis-words

Agents: Cheryl Ricker

Agency: Established in 2015. Represents 15 clients.

Types of books: adult fiction, business, charismatic, Christian living, current events, devotionals, gift books, leadership, marriage, memoir, ministry, parenting, social issues, women's issues

New clients: Accepts queries—maximum of six pages—only through the website. If interested, will ask for more information and sample chapters.

Tip: "One's heart matters as much as one's calling and ability to write. These authors work diligently at growing their craft and tuning their antennae to the Creator and wellspring of life. From a deep abiding relationship with Christ flows the richest substance and wisdom."

EMBOLDEN MEDIA GROUP

PO Box 953607, Lake Mary, FL 32795
submissions@emboldenmediagroup.com | *emboldenmediagroup.com*

Agents: Jevon Bolden, Deidra Riggs, Rebekah Von Lintel, Kathy Green, Joylanda Jamison, Mytecia Myles

Agency: Established in 2017. Represents more than 50 clients. Also offers content development, editorial, writing coaching.

Types of books: adult fiction, adult nonfiction, African American, charismatic, children's fiction, children's nonfiction, Christian living, devotionals, health/wellness, leadership, memoir

New clients: Open to writers at every level, including self-published. Contact: email query, website form, or current client referral. Accepts simultaneous submissions. Responds in 8–12 weeks.

Commission: 15%

Tip: "Follow us and our agents on social media, keep up with the kind of authors we represent and themes that catch our hearts and eyes."

GARDNER LITERARY, LLC

gardnerliterary@gmail.com | *gardner-literary.com*

Agents: Rachelle Gardner, Kristy Cambron, Ashley Hong, Sherri Johnson, Candice Benbow

Agency: Established in 2021. Represents 100 clients.

Types of books: adult fiction (no fantasy), adult nonfiction, general-market fiction, general-market nonfiction

New clients: Open to any writer. First contact by email or QueryManager. Responds in fewer than 30 days.

Commission: 15%

Tip: "Visit our website, see the books and authors we represent, take a look at our submission guidelines."

THE GATES GROUP

sarah@the-gates-group.com | *www.the-gates-group.com*

Agent: Don Gates

Agency: Established in 2013. Represents more than 50 authors. Member of Association of American Literary Agents.

Types of books: nonfiction

New clients: Open only to well-established book writers and writers who currently have an agent. Initial contact: Email. Responds in two days.

Commission: 15%

GOLDEN WHEAT LITERARY

jessica@goldenwheatliterary.com | *goldenwheatliterary.com*

Agents: Jessica Schmeidler

Agency: Established in 2015. Also sells to the general-market.

Types of books: adult fiction, devotionals, general-market fiction, memoir, middle grade, picture books, teen/YA nonfiction

New clients: Email query letter and first three chapters, all in body of message; no attachments. If no response in six months, assume not interested.

Tip: "If our lack of response has been due merely to a time availability issue, then we have been known to respond to queries that have gone unanswered for six months or longer. So, if you do not wish to receive a response after a certain time, for your own sanity and/ or record-keeping reasons, please note that in your initial query. Likewise, if your manuscript is no longer available for consideration, please do remember to withdraw the submission."

ILLUMINATE LITERARY AGENCY

submissions@illuminateliterary.com | illuminateliterary.com

Agent: Jenni Burke

Agency: Established in 2006. Represents 30 clients. Specialty: faith-based nonfiction.

Types of books: Bible studies, business, children's fiction, Christian living, church and ministry, culture, devotionals, family, gift books, leadership, lifestyle, memoir, personal development, relationships, spiritual growth

New clients: Open to writers with a strong platform, clear writing, and a powerful message. Initial contact: website form, referral from current client, full proposal. Responds in one month.

Commission: 15%

Tip: "Please review our website thoroughly, including what Jenni is looking for; and follow submission guidelines closely. Fast Track option is available for client referrals and sizable platforms."

LINDA S. GLAZ LITERARY AGENCY

51670 Washington St., New Baltimore, MI 48047

linda@lindasglaz.com | lindasglaz.com

Agent: Linda S. Glaz

Agency: Established in 2022. Represents 35 clients.

Types of books: adult fiction, adult nonfiction, general-market fiction, general-market nonfiction

New clients: Open to most authors but primarily those met at conferences or referred by other authors. First contact: email with full proposal, referral through current client. Accepts simultaneous submissions. Responds in one month; after that feel free to nudge.

Commission: 15%

Tip: "Be sure you send your best work that is exactly what I ask for and only in genres that I represent."

LITERARY MANAGEMENT GROUP

150 Young Way, Richmond Hill, GA 31324 | 615-812-4445

brucebarbour@literarymanagementgroup.com | *www.literarymanagementgroup.com*

Agents: Bruce R. Barbour

Agency: Established in 1996. Represents 100 clients.

Types of books: adult nonfiction

New clients: Open only to previously published authors with traditional publishers. Contact: email proposal according to the website template and sample chapters. Accepts simultaneous submissions. Responds in four to six weeks.

Commission: 15%

Tip: "Proposals and sample chapters should not be formatted or sent as PDF. Simple Word or Google documents allow me to reply with comments."

MACGREGOR AND LEUDEKE COLLABORATIVE, LLC

www.macgregorandluedeke.com

Agents: Amanda Luedeke, *amanda@macgregorliterary.com;* Alina Mitchell, *alina@macgregorliterary.com;* Colleen Oefelein, *colleen@adventurewrite.com*

Agency: Established in 2006; rebranded in 2025. Member of Association of American Literary Agents. Represents 5–30 clients each.

Types of books: adult fiction, adult nonfiction, general-market fiction, general-market nonfiction

New clients: Open to working with anyone who has an established platform and compelling book idea. Initial contact: email full proposal, referral from a current client. Simultaneous submissions OK. Responds in four to six weeks.

Commission: 15%

Tip: "Read our agent bios to find out who is open to submissions and what they are looking for. Email submissions directly to agents."

MARY DEMUTH LITERARY

2150 Heather Glen Dr., Rockwall, TX 75087 | 214-475-9083

query@marydemuthliterary.com | *marydemuthliterary.com*

Agent: Mary DeMuth

Agency: Established in 2022; former agent with Books & Such Literary Management. Represents 42 clients. Other services: mentoring writers in platform and proposal writing.

Types of books: Christian living

New clients: Open to all writers. First contact: email query. Responds in one week.

Commission: 15%

Tip: "Read *MaryDeMuthLiterary.com* for all the instructions you need."

PAPE COMMONS

11327 Rill Pt., Colorado Springs, CO 80921

don@papecommons.com | papecommons.com

Agent: Don Pape

Agency: Established in 2021. Represents 50 clients.

Types of books: adult nonfiction, children's fiction, children's nonfiction

New clients: No self-published authors. Contact: referral from current client, website form. Responds in two to three days.

Commission: 15%

Tip: "Will want to review a proposal, with careful consideration of your social-media acumen as well as strong writing samples, before a conversation with the author."

THE SEYMOUR AGENCY

4100 Corporate Sq., Ste. 140, Naples, FL 34104 | 239-398-8209

julie@theseymouragency.com | www.theseymouragency.com

Agent: Julie Gwinn, *querymanager.com/JulieGwinn*

Agency: Established in 1992. Primarily a general-market agency; Julie handles the Christian books.

Types of books: adult fiction, adult nonfiction

New clients: Open to writers who have not published a book and self-published writers. First contact: email query with no attachments or Query Manager. Responds in three weeks to queries or not interested.

Commission: 15%

Tip: "Hone your craft. Take advantage of writers groups, critique partners, etc., to polish your manuscript into the best shape it can be."

THE STEVE LAUBE AGENCY

24 W. Camelback Rd. A-635, Phoenix, AZ 85013

info@stevelaube.com | www.stevelaube.com

Agents: Steve Laube, *krichards@stevelaube.com;* Tamela Hancock Murray, *ewilson@stevelaube.com;* Bob Hostetler, *rgwright@stevelaube.com;* Dan

Balow, *vseem@stevelaube.com;* Megan Brown, *jsanders@stevelaube.com;* Lynette Eason, *ehumphries@stevelaube.com*

Agency: Established in 2004. Represents more than 250+ clients. See website blog post by each agent for what he or she is looking for.

Types of books: adult fiction, adult nonfiction

New clients: Open to unpublished authors. Email proposal as attachment according to the guidelines on the website. Steve Laube also will take proposals by mail. Accepts simultaneous submissions. Responds in 8–12 weeks.

Commission: 15%; foreign, 20%

Tip: "Please follow the guidelines! Since your book proposal is like a job application, you want to present yourself in the most professional manner possible. Your proposal will be a simple vehicle to convey your idea to us and, ultimately, to a publisher. Don't call the office to pitch your book idea. We'd rather read the proposal."

WILLIAM K. JENSEN LITERARY AGENCY

119 Bampton Ct., Eugene, OR 97404 | 541-688-1612

queries@wkjagency.com | *www.wkjagency.com*

Agents: William K. Jensen, Teresa Evenson

Agency: Established in 2005. Represents more than 50 clients.

Types of books: adult nonfiction

New clients: Open to unpublished authors. Contact by email only; no attachments. See the website for complete query details. Accepts simultaneous submissions. Responds in one month or not interested.

Commission: 15%

Tip: "Due to the changes in book retailing over the last ten years, publishers will only accept authors with a robust social-media and/ or speaking platform. That being the case, we can only consider queries by writers with at least 20,000 online followers and/or a dynamic speaking ministry."

WINTERS & KING

2448 E. 81st St., Ste. 5900, Tulsa, OK 74137-4259 | 918-494-6868

alacourse@wintersking.com | *wintersking.com/practice-areas/ publishing-agent-services*

Agents: Thomas J. Winters, Alyssa M. LaCourse

Agency: Established in 1983. Represents 150 clients. Part of a law firm. Other services: legal review of publishing contracts, drafting of work-for-hire agreements to contract writer/editor services, copyright/trademark filing.

Types of books: adult fiction, adult nonfiction

New clients: Open to writers with a story to tell. Contact by email or website form. Responds in two weeks.

Commission: 15%

Tip: "Submissions should be carefully edited and free of typos. Accompanying manuscripts or sample chapters for presentation to publishers should be edited, typo-free, and basically print-ready."

WOLGEMUTH & WILSON

info@wolgemuthandwilson.com | wolgemuthandwilson.com

Agents: Austin Wilson, Erik Wolgemuth, Andrew Wolgemuth

Agency: Established in 1992. Represents 150+ clients. Responds in two weeks if interested.

Types of books: adult nonfiction, Bible notes, Bible studies, children's fiction, children's nonfiction

New clients: Open only to well-established authors or who are referred by a client. First contact: email query or referral. Simultaneous submissions OK.

Commission: 15%

Tip: "Real-life relational networks and online presence are important factors."

WORDSERVE LITERARY GROUP

700 Colorado Blvd. #318, Denver, CO 80206

admin@wordserveliterary.com | www.wordserveliterary.com

Agents: Greg Johnson, *Greg@wordserveliterary.com;* Keely Boeving, *Keely@wordserveliterary.com;* Emma Fulenwider, *Emma@ wordserveliterary.com;* Nick Harrison, *nick@wordserveliterary.com*

Agency: Established in 2003. Represents 175 clients. General-market nonfiction is limited to military, history, business, health, and wellness. Other service: movie options.

Types of books: adult fiction, adult nonfiction, Bible studies, children's fiction, children's nonfiction, general-market nonfiction, gift books

New clients: Open to writers who have not published a book yet and self-published writers. Contact: email query or referral from a current client. No simultaneous submissions. Responds in two to four weeks.

Commission: 15%

Tip: "Go to our website to learn more. Follow instructions on submissions."

WORDWISE MEDIA SERVICES

4083 Avenue L, Ste. 255, Lancaster, CA 93536

www.wordwisemedia.com/agency

Agents: Steven Hutson, David Fessenden, Michelle S. Lazurek

Agency: Established in 2011. Member of Association of American Literary Agents. Represents 60 clients.

Types of books: almost everything

New clients: Open to unpublished book authors. Contact: downloadable query form as email attachment. Accepts simultaneous submissions. Responds in one month; OK to nudge after then.

Commission: 15%, more for movie deals

Tip: "Follow directions carefully. Meet us at a conference. Specify the agent's name in the email subject line if you have a preference."

YATES & YATES

1551 N. Tustin Ave., Ste. 710, Santa Ana, CA 92705 | 714-480-4000

email@yates2.com | www.yates2.com

Agents: Sealy Yates, Matt Yates, Curtis Yates, Mike Salisbury, Karen Yates

Agency: Established in 1988. Represents fewer than 50 clients.

Types of books: adult nonfiction

New clients: No unpublished book authors. Contact: query through the website. Responds in one to two months. Other service: author coaching.

Commission: negotiable

Tip: "We serve passionate, articulate, gifted Christian communicators, using our strengths to guide, counsel and protect them, fiercely advocate for them, and help them advance life- and culture-transforming messages for the sake of the Kingdom."

18

WRITERS CONFERENCES AND SEMINARS

✏️ **Note**: This chapter is divided by states, international countries, and online, each section in alphabetical order. Many directors had not set dates and details for 2025 when this book went to print, so check the websites for up-to-date information.

ALABAMA

BLUE LAKE CHRISTIAN WRITERS CONFERENCE

Andalusia, AL | March 12–15 | *BLCWC.com*

Director: Susan Neal, 8500 Oakwood Ln., Andalusia, AL 36420; 850-393-3681; *SusanNeal@Bellsouth.net*

Description: "At Blue Lake Christian Writers Conference, you'll enjoy the depth and diversity of a large writers conference but with a personal touch that makes all the difference. For example, you'll receive 30-minutes of mentoring with faculty, not a short, 15-minute appointment. Whether you're just beginning your writing journey or are an established author, our conference caters to both fiction and nonfiction enthusiasts along with a poetry flare."

Faculty includes: agents, editors, publishers

Keynote speakers: Bob Hostetler, Jesse Florea, Linda Goldfarb

Scholarships: partial

Attendance: 100

Contest: Christian Indie Awards *(Christianaward.com)*, CAN

Marketing Awards *(ChristianAuthorsNetwork.com/marketing-award)*, and Living Water Awards for unpublished works

SOUTHERN CHRISTIAN WRITERS CONFERENCE

Leeds, AL (Birmingham area) | June | *southernchristianwriters.my.canva.site*

Director: Cheryl Wray, PO Box 3057, Hueytown, AL 35023; 205-534-0595; *scwritersconference@gmail.com*

Description: "The SCWC is a two-day conference for beginners or experienced writers that focuses on several genres: nonfiction books, magazines, fiction, grammar, business aspects, legal aspects, etc."

Faculty includes: agents, editors

Attendance: 160–200

ARIZONA

FAITH, HOPE, & LOVE CHRISTIAN WRITERS IN-PERSON CONFERENCE

Phoenix, AZ | September | *fhlchristianwriters.com/in-person-conference*

Director: Janet Tronstad, *Janet@fhlchristianwriters.com*

Description: Focused on writing and selling romantic fiction.

Faculty includes: agents, authors, editors

Attendance: 80–100

CALIFORNIA

VISION CHRISTIAN WRITERS CONFERENCE

Mt. Hermon, CA (near Santa Cruz) | April 11–15 | *vcwconf.com*

Director: Robynne Elizabeth Miller, 2850 S.W. Cedar Hills Blvd. #138, Beaverton, OR 97005; 530-217-8233; *director@vcwconf.com*

Description: "Four-day, all-inclusive Christian writing conference with over 50 teaching and track options for writers of all levels, both nonfiction and fiction. Agents, editors, publishers from a variety of agencies and houses, as well as world-class worship and speakers."

Special track: advanced writers

Faculty includes: agents, editors, publishers

Keynote speaker: Bill Myers

Scholarships: full, partial

Attendance: 200

Contest: Vision Award: Most Promising Writer (faculty-voted based on attendee with the most promising writing future), Best Submission (based on a themed submission)

WEST COAST CHRISTIAN WRITERS CONFERENCE

Roseville, CA (Sacramento area) plus online | fall | *www.westcoast christianwriters.com*

Director: Ginny L. Yttrup, 1750 Prairie City Rd., Ste. 130, #689, Folsom, CA 95630; 800-660-0747; *info@westcoastchristianwriters.com*

Description: "Connect, grow, and belong. The West Coast Christian Writers conference and community equips and encourages writers for the journey."

Special tracks: advanced writers, speaking, teens

Faculty includes: agents, editors, publishers

Keynote speaker: Barb Roose

Scholarships: partial

Attendance: 250

Contest: WCCW Writing Contest and Goldie Awards

COLORADO

REALM MAKERS WINTER CREATIVITY SUMMIT

Colorado Springs, CO | March 17–21 | *www.realmmakers.com/winter-retreat*

Director: Rebecca Minor, *becky@realmmakers.com*

Description: "The Realm Makers Winter Creativity Summit seeks to gather writers of all experience levels in an encouraging, intimate setting where they can learn from a master writer and experience fellowship along the way. Writers will enjoy time gaining new skills, as well as opportunities to focus on the manuscript of their choosing."

Keynote speaker: Allen Arnold

Attendance: 40

WRITE IN THE SPRINGS

Colorado Springs, CO | March 28–29 | *acfwcosprings.net/wits-2025*

Director: Susan G. Mathis, 3820 N. 30th St., Colorado Springs, CO 80904; *info@acfwcosprings.com*

Description: "Write in the Springs is a small, personal, in-depth Christian writers conference at Glen Eyrie Conference Center."

Special tracks: advanced writers, teens

Faculty includes: editors, agents, publishers

Keynote speaker: Angela Hunt
Scholarships: partial
Attendance: 75

FLORIDA

FLORIDA CHRISTIAN WRITERS CONFERENCE
Leesburg, FL | October | *Word-Weavers.com/FloridaEvents*

Directors: Eva Marie Everson and Taryn Souders, PO Box 520224, Longwood, FL 32752; 407-209-4141; *FCWCManager@aol.com*

Description: "Florida Christian Writers Conference offers 10 continuing classes, approximately 60 one-hour workshops, five 3-hour workshops, special workshops (Book Proposal Studio, The 1000-Books-a-Month Workshop, etc.), VIP breakfasts (with speakers), a yearly genre-focused intensive, and a keynote speaker. Writers of all levels are welcome."

Special tracks: advanced writers, speaking
Faculty includes: agents, editors, publishers
Scholarships: full, partial
Attendance: 250
Contest: See website for details.

GEORGIA

WRITING FOR YOUR LIFE
Atlanta, GA | May | *writingforyourlife.com/conferences*

Director: Kate Rademacher, 320 Curlicue Rd., Sewanee, GA 37375; 919-357-0099; *wfylinfo@gmail.com*

Description: "Writing for Your Life is committed to offering a wide variety of useful resources and services to support spiritual writers. We offer in-person writing conferences and online events and videos featuring leading spiritual writers and publishing-industry experts. Authors discuss and teach about various aspects of spiritual writing. Industry experts offer advice on how to get published and how to market."

Special tracks: advanced writers, pastors
Faculty includes: agents, editors, publishers
Scholarships: partial
Attendance: 100

ILLINOIS

WRITE TO PUBLISH CONFERENCE

Wheaton, IL (Chicago area) | June 10–13 | *writetopublish.com*

Director: Dan Balow, 304 E. Forest Ave., Wheaton, IL 60187; 630-464-1377; *dan@christianwritersinstitute.com*

Description: "No matter where you are in your writing career—beginning the journey to becoming a published writer, exploring the process of becoming a working writer, or an experienced professional desiring to stay connected and growing—the Write to Publish Conference is your key to reaching those goals."

Faculty includes: agents, editors, publishers

Keynote speaker: Tim Challies

Scholarships: full, partial

Attendance: 300

INDIANA

TAYLOR UNIVERSITY PROFESSIONAL WRITERS CONFERENCE

Upland, IN | July 25–26 with intensive track July 24–25 | *taylorprofessionalwritersconference.weebly.com*

Director: Linda K. Taylor, 1846 Main St., Upland, IN 46989; 765-998-5591; *taylorpwrconference@gmail.com*

Description: "This conference is for all types of writers—beginners who have never been to a conference, teens (16+) who want to explore their desire to write, older folks who finally want to put pen to paper, and even seasoned writers who just want to soak in some training and be around other writers. This is a perfect conference to begin or continue your writing journey."

Special track: advanced writers

Faculty includes: agents, editors

Keynote speaker: Zena Dell Lowe

Attendance: 90

IOWA

CEDAR FALLS CHRISTIAN WRITERS CONFERENCE

Cedar Falls, IA | June 12–14 | *cfcwc.org*

Director: Mary Portzen, 439 N. Division St., Cedar Falls, IA 50613; 563-235-9408; *cfcwconference@gmail.com*

Description: "We welcome new writers, established writers, and everyone interested in the writer's craft. Our purpose is to glorify God and His Son Jesus Christ through all we do as we encourage others in the craft of writing."

Faculty includes: editors, publishers

Keynote speaker: Michelle Rayburn

Scholarships: partial

Attendance: 30

KENTUCKY

KENTUCKY CHRISTIAN WRITERS CONFERENCE

Elizabethtown, KY | October | *www.kychristianwriters.com*

Director: Gregg Bridgeman, PO Box 2719, Elizabethtown, KY 42702; *info@kychristianwriters.com*

Description: "Our purpose is to provide an annual, interdenominational event to equip and encourage writers in their quest for publication. The conference provides a safe environment where writers can discover their gifts and share their work."

Faculty includes: agents, editors, publishers

Attendance: 75

LOUISIANA

ACFW CONFERENCE

New Orleans, LA | September 4–7 | *www.acfw.com/conference*

Director: Robin Miller, PO Box 101066, Palm Bay, FL 32910-1066; *director@acfw.com*

Description: "Continuing education sessions and workshop electives specifically geared for five levels of fiction-writing experience from beginner to advanced." Note: This conference changes location every year.

Special track: advanced writers
Faculty includes: agents, editors, publishers
Scholarships: full
Attendance: 500
Contest: The Genesis Contest is for unpublished writers whose Christian fiction manuscript is completed. The Carol Awards honor the best of Christian fiction from the previous calendar year.

MICHIGAN

MARANATHA WOMEN'S WRITING RETREAT

Muskegon, MI | January 17–20 | *maranathamichigan.org/event/womens-christian-writers-retreat*

> **Director:** Shayne Moore, 4759 Lake Harbor Rd., Norton Shores, MI 49441; 231-798-2161; *info@maranathamichigan.org*
> **Description:** "Maranatha Writers exists to build Christ's church by fostering the development of Christian women writers through transformational biblical teaching, worship, and fellowship in order to serve God and others through our call to write."
> **Keynote speaker:** Dawn Anderson
> **Scholarships:** partial
> **Attendance:** 80

REALM MAKERS WRITERS CONFERENCE

Grand Rapids, MI | July 18–20 | *www.realmmakers.com/annual-conference*

> **Director:** Becky Minor, *becky@realmmakers.com*
> **Description:** "Realm Makers is a writers conference for Christian authors writing in the genres of fantasy, science fiction, or horror. Agents and editors from both Christian publishing and the general market can be found at Realm Makers." Note: This conference changes location every year.
> **Special tracks:** advanced writers, teens
> **Faculty includes:** agents, editors, publishers
> **Scholarships:** full, partial
> **Attendance:** 460

SPEAK UP CONFERENCE

Grand Rapids, MI | July 10–12 | *speakupconference.com*

> **Director:** Bonnie Emmorey, 1320 N. Topeka, Wichita, KS 67214;

316-882-9400; *bonnie@speakupconference.com*

Description: "The Speak Up Conference is a three-day event where Christian communicators gather to learn how to spread the gospel and build up the body of Christ through speaking and writing."

Faculty includes: agents, editors, publishers

Scholarships: partial

Attendance: 250

Contest: "Writers who meet deadlines, follow submission guidelines, and submit to the editing process will be chosen for inclusion in a book published by Living Parables, an imprint of EABooks Publishing, making them published authors. Authors can purchase books at a reduced rate and keep the profit from their sales."

THE WELL CONFERENCE FOR CREATIVES

Grand Rapids, MI | June 5–7 | *seeyouatthewell.net*

Director: Victoria Chapin, PMB #533, 520 Butternut Dr., Ste. 8, Holland, MI 49424; 616-886-8636; *victoriaatthewell@gmail.com*

Description: "Come and be equipped and refreshed as you network with our creative community."

Special tracks: advanced writers, speaking

Faculty includes: agents, editors, publishers

Keynote speakers: Linda Goldfarb, Dr. Sharon Elliot

Scholarships: full, partial

Attendance: 150

Contest: Oasis Awards for unpublished Christian fiction and nonfiction manuscripts, devotionals, play scripts, and screenplays. Winners will receive The Well OASIS Award and a publishing prize for their submitted work. For more info: *seeyouatthewell.net/ contests/oasis-awards*.

MISSOURI

EVANGELICAL PRESS ASSOCIATION ANNUAL CONVENTION

Branson, MO | May 4–6 | *epaconvention.com*

Director: Lamar Keener, PO Box 1787, Queen Creek, AZ 85142; 480-868-2466; *director@evangelicalpress.com*

Description: "Annual media convention for editors, writers, designers, and all content creators for Christian print and digital magazine platforms." Note: This conference changes location every year.

Faculty includes: editors

Attendance: 200

Contest: Freelance writers with EPA membership may submit articles and/or blog entries into Awards of Excellence and Higher Goals in Journalism

HEART OF AMERICA CHRISTIAN WRITERS CONFERENCE

Kansas City, MO | November | *www.HACWN.org*

Director: Jeanette Littleton, 3706 N.E. Shady Lane Dr., Gladstone, MO 64119; 816-459-8016; *HACWN@earthlink.net*

Description: "Our goal is to help new and advanced writers continue to hone their craft and network with editors and others."

Faculty includes: agents, editors, publishers

Attendance: 100

NEW YORK

RENEW—SPIRITUAL RETREAT FOR WRITERS AND SPEAKERS

Speculator, NY | April 25–27 | *reNEWwriting.com*

Director: Rachel Britton, 978-758-9574, *info@renewwriting.com*

Description: "reNEW is a community of Christ-following writers and speakers, both beginners and seasoned, growing inwardly so we can be effective outwardly."

Special track: speaking

Scholarships: partial

Attendance: 100

NORTH CAROLINA

ASHEVILLE CHRISTIAN WRITERS CONFERENCE

Asheville, NC | February 21–23 | *www.ashevillechristianwritersconference.com*

Director: Cindy Sproles, 377 Woodcrest Dr., Kingsport, TN 37663; 423-384-4821; *cindybootcamp@gmail.com*

Description: "We are an intentionally small conference catering to all levels of writers. We're perfect for new and first-time writers."

Special track: advanced writers

Faculty includes: agents, editors, publishers

Keynote speakers: Bob Hostetler, Eva Marie Everson, Edie Melson
Scholarships: full, partial
Attendance: 121 maximum
Contest: Sparrow Award Book Contest for unpublished manuscripts

BLUE RIDGE MOUNTAINS CHRISTIAN WRITERS CONFERENCE

Black Mountain, NC | May 26–30 | *www.BlueRidgeConference.com*

> **Director:** Edie Melson, 604 S. Almond Dr., Simpsonville, SC 29681; 864-373-4232; *ediegmelson@gmail.com*
> **Description:** "This is a multidiscipline conference that caters to writers of all levels. In addition to outstanding craft/industry instruction, there is a strong focus on preparing spiritually to follow God as He directs our words for His glory."
> **Special tracks:** advanced writers, speaking, teens
> **Faculty includes:** agents, editors, publishers
> **Scholarships:** partial
> **Attendance:** 550
> **Contests:** Selah Awards (industry-wide published books), Directors' Choice Awards (for former attendees and those in attendance at the 2025 event), Foundation Awards (restricted to unpublished writers who are attending the 2025 event)

MOUNTAINSIDE NOVELIST RETREAT

Black Mountain, NC | November | *www.BlueRidgeConference.com/ mountainside-retreats*

> **Director:** Edie Melson, 604 S. Almond Dr., Simpsonville, SC 29681; 864-373-4232; *ediegmelson@gmail.com*
> **Description:** "Through small-group instruction and hands-on exercises from bestselling writers, the craftsman is able to focus on building strengths from challenges. Writers developing all levels of their careers will benefit from one-on-one consultations, brainstorming, and instruction. This event is a guided intensive where all participants have the opportunity to practice what they're learning under experienced team leaders."
> **Attendance:** 40

SHE SPEAKS CONFERENCE

Charlotte, NC | July 24–25 | *shespeaksconference.com*

> **Director:** Lisa Allen, 630 Team Rd. #100, Matthews, NC 28105; 704-849-2270; *shespeaks@Proverbs31.org*

Description: Speaking and writing tracks. For women only.
Special track: speaking
Faculty includes: agents, editors
Attendance: 700

OKLAHOMA

MINICON
Edmond, OK | April 19 | *okchristianfictionwriters.com*
   Director: Kristy Werner, 5817 S. Fairgrounds Rd., Stillwater, OK
   74074; 405-714-2935; *authors@okchristianfictionwriters.com*
   Description: "One-day writer's conference. VIP luncheon with
   speakers is available."
   Attendance: 25

OREGON

CASCADE CHRISTIAN WRITERS CONFERENCE
Canby, OR (Portland area) | June 22–25 | *oregonchristianwriters.org*
   Director: Julie Bonn Blank, PO Box 22, Gladstone, OR 97027; 541-
   760-2322; *business@cascadechristianwriters.org*
   Description: "A multi-day conference with a focus on improving
   craft, fellowship with other writers, and increasing publishing
   opportunities. We write for both Christian and secular publishers/
   publications."
   Special tracks: advanced writers, teens
   Faculty includes: agents, editors, publishers
   Scholarships: partial
   Attendance: 200
   Contest: Cascade Awards with multiple opportunities to enter
   and gain invaluable feedback from three experienced writing/
   publishing judges; opens in January

CASCADE CHRISTIAN WRITERS FALL ONE-DAY CONFERENCE
Tualatin, OR (Portland area) | October | *www.oregonchristianwriters.org*
   Director: Julie Bonn Blank, PO Box 22, Gladstone, OR 97027;
   business@oregonchristianwriters.org
   Description: "A one-day conference with a focus on improving

craft, fellowship with other writers, and increasing publishing opportunities. We write for both Christian and secular publishers/publications."

Faculty includes: agents
Keynote speaker: Cynthia Ruchti
Attendance: 100+

CASCADE CHRISTIAN WRITERS SPRING ONE-DAY CONFERENCE

Salem, OR | March 8 | *cascadechristianwriters.org*

Director: Julie Bonn Blank, PO Box 22, Gladstone, OR 97027; *business@cascadechristianwriters.org*

Description: "A one-day conference with a focus on improving craft, fellowship with other writers, and increasing publishing opportunities. We write for both Christian and secular publishers/publications."

Faculty includes: agents
Keynote speaker: Melanie Dobson
Attendance: 100+

PENNSYLVANIA

MONTROSE CHRISTIAN WRITERS CONFERENCE

Montrose, PA | July 14–18 | *www.montrosebible.org*

Director: Marsha Hubler, 1833 Dock Hill Rd., Middleburg, PA 17842; 570-837-0002; *marshahubler@outlook.com*

Description: "In a family atmosphere at the restored home and conference center of evangelist R.A. Torrey, the conference always offers a faculty of best-selling authors, agents, editors, and publishers who present classes for beginners as well as published authors, teaching fiction, nonfiction, children's fiction and nonfiction, marketing, poetry, music, drama, and numerous subgenres. Private critiques are always offered, as well as works-in-progress sessions."

Special tracks: advanced writers, teens
Faculty includes: agents, editors, publishers
Scholarships: partial
Attendance: 70
Contest: The Shirley Brinkerhoff Scholarship Fund offers $200 to the best entry of a 300-piece submission based on the year's theme.

ST. DAVIDS CHRISTIAN WRITERS' CONFERENCE

Meadville, PA | June 18–22 | *www.stdavidswriters.com/conference*

Director: Sue Boltz, 724-359-8500, *registrar@stdavidswriters.com*
Faculty includes: agents, editors
Scholarships: full, partial
Attendance: 45
Contests: See detailed list on the website.

SOUTH CAROLINA

CAROLINA CHRISTIAN WRITERS CONFERENCE

Greer, SC | March 7–8 | *CarolinaChristianWritersConference.com*

Director: Linda Gilden, PO Box 85, Moore, SC 29369; *info@ carolinachristianwritersconference.com*
Description: "Focus is on learning to write to reach others with the love of Jesus. Special features include 'Lighting Learning,' panel discussions for all levels of writers, one-on-one appointments with publishers, editors, and agents.

Pastors Day is Thursday, March 6 for pastors and ministry leaders. This is separate to help pastors to learn how to create books and articles from the research they have done for their sermons and Sunday school lessons. Publishers and editors will be there to assist them."
Special tracks: pastors, teens, speaking
Faculty includes: agents, editors, publishers
Scholarships: full, partial
Attendance: 150
Contest: Kudos contest for book and article writers, published and unpublished

TENNESSEE

MID-SOUTH CHRISTIAN WRITERS CONFERENCE

Collierville, TN (Memphis area) | March 14–15 | *midsouthchristianwriters.com*

Director: Beth Gooch, 346 Landen Cir., Byhalia, MS 38611; 901-277-5525; *beth@bethgooch.com*
Description: "Mid-South Christian Writers Conference is an affordable, one-day conference, with a balance of fiction and nonfiction. We also have optional add-on workshops the day before

the conference."
Special track: advanced writers
Faculty includes: agents, editors
Keynote speakers: Bethany Jett, Jessica Patch
Scholarships: partial
Attendance: 100

WASHINGTON

NORTHWEST CHRISTIAN WRITERS RENEWAL

Bellevue, WA | April or May | *nwchristianwriters.org/Conference*

Director: Athena Dean Holtz, *renewal@nwchristianwriters.org*
Description: "This conference is where writers, editors, and
publishers can connect, network, and collaborate. Conferees will
sharpen their skills, learn strategies, and form connections to boost
their success on the writing journey."
Faculty includes: agents, editors, publishers
Scholarships: full
Attendance: 130

AUSTRALIA

OMEGA WRITERS CONFERENCE

online | September | *omegawriters.com.au/events*

Director: Penny Reeve, *info@omegawriters.org*
Description: "Omega Writers Conference offers focused craft
workshops, genre groups, networking opportunities, as well as
sessions on essential skills for writers like time management,
psychology marketing, and more. Participants also benefit from
the opportunity for one-on-one appointments with editors, agents,
and publishers and walk away with friendships and Christian
encouragement, unlike any other conference in Australia."
Attendance: 70

CANADA

INSCRIBE CHRISTIAN WRITERS' FELLOWSHIP CONFERENCE

Fort Qu'Appelle, SK, Canada | September | *inscribe.org/fall-conference*

Director: Box 68025, Edmonton, AB T6C 4N6, Canada; *president@ inscribe.org*

Description: "InScribe's fall conference features a seasoned author, publisher, or other expert as the keynote speaker; plus we offer a variety of workshop topics and presenters. It's a weekend where writers—whether they are seasoned or beginning—can connect for fellowship, encouragement, and support."

Scholarships: partial

Contest: See *www.inscribe.org/contests.*

ONLINE

ACFW VIRGINIA ROYAL WRITERS VIRTUAL CONFERENCE

November 7–8 | *acfwvirginia.com/writers-conference*

Director: Kelly Goshorn, 1019B Edwards Ferry Rd. #1159, Leesburg, VA 20176; 540-454-4144; *acfwvirginia@gmail.com*

Description: "The Royal Writers Conference strives to provide stellar teaching by industry professionals at an affordable price to extend every writer's knowledge of the business and craft of writing, fill them with inspiration, and provide the tools needed to write for God's glory."

Special track: advanced writers

Faculty includes: agents, editors, publishers

Attendance: 260

CASCADE CHRISTIAN WRITERS CONFERENCE

See entry in Oregon.

FAITH, HOPE, & LOVE CHRISTIAN WRITERS VIRTUAL CONFERENCE

spring | *fhlchristianwriters.com/virtual-conference*

Director: *vp@fhlchristianwriters.com*

Description: For writers of Christian romance and women's fiction

with romantic elements.
Attendance: 160

MT ZION RIDGE PRESS ONLINE WRITING CONFERENCE

May 1-3 | *mzrpchristianwritingconference.com*

Director: Penny McGinnis, 4280 Hickory Park Ln., Batavia, OH 45103; 937-402-0782; *penny.frost.mcginnis@gmail.com*
Description: "The online conference with an in-person experience."
Faculty includes: agents, editors, publishers
Attendance: 60

PENCON

May 7-9 | *PENCONeditors.com*

Director: Denise Loock, *director@PENCONeditors.com*
Description: "PENCON is the only annual conference for Christian editors and proofreaders. Our goal is to provide networking, education, and inspiration for Christians in the publishing industry."
Faculty includes: editors, publishers
Scholarships: full, partial
Attendance: 75

PUBLISHING IN COLOR

April | *publishingincolor.com*

Director: Joyce Dinkins, PO Box 150, Grand Junction, MI 49056; *JoyceDinkinsPublishing@gmail.com*
Description: "Publishing in Color is a bridge for Black and Indigenous People of Color (BIPOC) striving to publish content that shares biblical truths with everyone. Through its conferences and network, PIC helps connect creatives with publishers addressing historic underrepresentation."
Faculty includes: agents, editors, publishers
Keynote speaker: Joyce Dinkins
Scholarships: full
Attendance: 100

SHE WRITES FOR HIM 3-DAY CHALLENGES

varies | *www.ultimate3daychallenge.com*

Director: Carol Tetzlaff, 1602 Cole St., Enumclaw, WA 98022; 360-

226-3488; *carol@redemption-press.com*

Description: "We offer a number of different 3-day challenges on Devotional Writing, Children's Book Writing, Writing Your Hard Story, and more. Live Zoom training with recordings available later, downloadable materials, mentoring, and support. Special published compilation opportunities are offered as bonuses."

Faculty: editors, publishers

Attendance: 100–200

STORY EMBERS SUMMIT

May | *storyembers.org/summit*

Director: Brianna Storm Hilvety, *brianna@storyembers.org*

Description: "The Story Embers Summit is a 3-day virtual event where Christian authors and editors give actionable advice on how to exceed readers' expectations, develop authentic characters, convey resonant themes, and other topics focused on either craft or mindset, all with a strong faith component."

Faculty includes: agents, editors

Keynote speakers: Chris Fabry, Colleen Coble

Scholarships: full, partial

Attendance: 120

WEST COAST CHRISTIAN WRITERS CONFERENCE

See entry in California.

WRITE HIS ANSWER CONFERENCE

August 6–9 | *colorado.writehisanswer.com*

Director: Marlene Bagnull, 951 Anders Rd., Lansdale, PA 19446; 267-436-2503; *mbagnull@aol.com*

Description: "The 28th Colorado and 42nd Greater Philly Christian Writers Conference combine into one huge online conference with faculty of more than 60 editors, agents, and authors. All the features of an in-person conference, including 7 keynotes, 9 learning labs, 9 continuing sessions, and 63 workshops. Everything is live—no prerecords. For no additional charge, conferees will have access to over 100 hours of video replays through the end of the year. In addition to small-group breakouts, round tables, critique groups, 6 panels, and preconference events, conferees get 3 free appointments with editors or agents."

Faculty includes: agents, editors, publishers

Scholarships: partial

Attendance: 300

Contest: Poetry (12–30 lines) or prose (500–800 words) on our conference theme, "Write His Answer"—not only how He is calling you to "write His answer" but also what you have found to be His answer in the struggles you have faced as you have sought to "live His answer." Published and not-yet published writers are judged in separate categories. This is a win-win contest since everyone who enters receives their choice of a free ebook, either *Sleeping Near the Ark* or *Write His Answer: A Bible Study for Christian Writers*.

WRITE2IGNITE MASTER CLASSES

April and September | *write2ignite.com*

Director: Jean Matthew Hall, 704 W. Madison St., Ware Shoals, SC 29692; 704-578-0858; *jeanmatthewhall@outlook.com*

Description: "Master Classes are designed to educate, inspire, and encourage Christian writers of literature for children and young adults."

Faculty includes: agents, editors

Attendance: 30

19

WRITERS ORGANIZATIONS AND GROUPS

Note: In addition to the groups listed here, check the writers organizations for new groups in your area and information about starting a group.

WRITERS ORGANIZATIONS

540 WRITERS COMMUNITY
540writerscommunity.com
> **Contact:** Becky Antkowiak, PO Box 133, Sutherland, VA 23885; *becky@540writerscommunity.com*
> **Services:** "Free, stellar education accessible to every writer. We offer educational sessions, writing accountability, peer-to-peer feedback, 24/7 Write-in Zoom, and more—all online, free, and accessible."
> **Members:** 1,700+
> **Membership fee:** none

AMERICAN CHRISTIAN FICTION WRITERS
acfw.com
> **Contact:** Robin Miller, PO Box 101066, Palm Bay, FL 32910-1066; *director@acfw.com*
> **Services:** Email loop, genre Facebook pages, online courses, critique groups, and local and regional chapters. Sponsors contests for published and unpublished writers and conducts the largest Christian fiction writers conference annually.
> **Members:** 2600+
> **Membership fee:** $75 to join, $49/year to renew

CHRISTIAN AUTHORS NETWORK

ChristianAuthorsNetwork.com

> **Contact:** Susan U. Neal, 850-393-3681, *contact@ christianauthorsnetwork.com*
>
> **Services:** "CAN is a group of traditionally published Christian authors who have joined together in a supportive association to spread the news about books to book lovers everywhere. We operate as a cooperative, Christ-centered marketing organization, to encourage and teach one another, and get the word out about CAN authors' books to readers, retailers, and librarians. Membership is open to authors with two or more published books. One must be a Christian book published by a traditional royalty-paying publisher (with no financial input by the author), whose books are currently available in publication (in any and all formats) at the date of the membership application."
>
> **Members:** 140
>
> **Membership fee:** $90/year

CHRISTIAN INDIE AUTHOR NETWORK

www.christianindieauthors.com

> **Contact:** Mary C. Findley, 918-805-0669, *mjmcfindley@gmail.com*
>
> **Services:** Provides a readers site to connect independently published books to readers, several Facebook groups for both authors and readers, and book promotion opportunities.
>
> **Members:** 400+
>
> **Membership fee:** none

THE CHRISTIAN PEN: PROOFREADERS AND EDITORS NETWORK

www.TheChristianPEN.com

> **Contact:** Jayna Baas, *director@TheChristianPEN.com*
>
> **Services:** "The Christian PEN: Proofreaders and Editors Network provides aspiring, beginning, established, and professional editors and proofreaders with networking, community, and industry discounts. If you are an editor or proofreader, or are thinking about becoming one, join this community of like-minded professionals who share our knowledge and experience with one another."
>
> **Members:** 200
>
> **Membership fee:** $30-$90/year

FAITH, HOPE, & LOVE CHRISTIAN WRITERS

fhlchristianwriters.com

> **Contact:** Lori Altebaumer, *president@fhlchristianwriters.com*
>
> **Services:** "To promote excellence in Christian fiction and/or fiction written from a Christian worldview. To help Christian writers establish their careers and to provide continuing support for writers within the fiction-publishing industry. We accomplish this stated purpose through our email groups, our online programs, our contests and awards, etc."
>
> **Membership fee:** $35

INSPIRE CHRISTIAN WRITERS

www.inspirewriters.com

> **Contact:** Damon J. Gray, *communications@inspirewriters.com*
>
> **Services:** "Through Inspire you'll find a community of writers working together to achieve writing and publication goals. By taking advantage of our online and in-person critique groups, you'll give and receive feedback and grow in your craft. We offer web-based and local training through workshops and conferences to help you navigate publishing decisions, create your online presence, and polish your writing until it shines. You'll have opportunities to network with other writers—multipublished as well as those just starting out." Sponsors the Vision Christian Writers Conference at Mt. Hermon.
>
> **Members:** 150
>
> **Membership fee:** $50/year

REALM MAKERS

www.realmmakers.com

> **Contact:** Scott Minor, *scott@realmmakers.com*
>
> **Services:** "Realm Makers supports writers and artists who create science fiction and fantasy in their journeys from idea to marketplace. Whether participating artists wish to gear their content for inspirational or mainstream audiences, Realm Makers seeks to encourage them from a faith-friendly perspective." Offers a membership program, where authors can connect throughout the year, critique one another's work, and participate in periodic webinars to keep their writing and marketing toolkits sharp. Sponsors the Realm Makers conference and Realm Makers Winter Creativity Summit.

Members: 100
Membership fee: ranges from $4.99/month or $49.99/year to $24.99/month or $249.99/year

WORD WEAVERS INTERNATIONAL, INC.
www.Word-Weavers.com

Contact: Eva Marie Everson, CEO, *WordWeaversInternational@aol. com*
Services: Local traditional chapters and Zoom online pages for manuscript critiquing. Sponsors Florida Christian Writers Conference.
Members: 1,200
Membership fee: $55/year, traditional or online; $75/year, traditional plus online; teens: $45/year, traditional or online; $65/year, traditional plus online

WORDGIRLS
www.kathycarltonwillis.com/wordgirls

Contact: Kathy Carlton Willis, 956-642-6319, *kathy@kathycarltonwillis.com*
Services: "WordGirls is a special sisterhood of writing support for women writing from a biblical worldview (whether for the faith market or general market). Services include one-on-one coaching, topical monthly video sessions, writing accountability, prayer support, and more. In-person and virtual getaways are hosted several times a year. Sessions offer how-tos for the nonwriting side of the writing business, as well as honing writing skills. From want-to-be a writer to the multipublished, experienced professional, WordGirls helps each writer get to the next step of her writing journey. Membership is limited in order to customize services to the needs of the group. WordGirls is a group of fun, female believers from across America who are serious about writing."
Members: 30-40
Membership fee: $300/year

NATIONAL AND INTERNATIONAL ONLINE GROUPS

ACFW BEYOND THE BORDERS
www.facebook.com/groups/ACFWBeyondtheBorders

   Contact: Iola Goulton, *BeyondBorders@acfwchapter.com*
   Members: 100, in all countries outside the US
   Membership fee: national fee
   Affiliation: American Christian Fiction Writers

ACFW KIDLIT
www.acfwkidlit.com, www.facebook.com/groups/acfwkidlit

   Contact: Bettie Boswell, *acfwkidlit@acfwchapter.com*
   Members: 100
   Membership fee: national fee plus $10/year
   Affiliation: American Christian Fiction Writers

ACFW QIP AUTHORS
www.facebook.com/groups/ACFWQIPAuthors

   Contact: Hallee Bridgeman
   Qualifications: For Qualified Independently Published fiction writers
      who are current ACFW members.
   Members: 35
   Membership fee: national fee
   Affiliation: American Christian Fiction Writers

WORD WEAVERS ONLINE GROUPS

   Meetings: online via Zoom, times vary, two hours
   Contact: Susan Simpson, *SimpsonCircle@gmail.com*
   Members: 375
   Membership fee: national fee
   Affiliation: Word Weavers

ALABAMA

WORD WEAVERS NORTH ALABAMA
www.facebook.com/groups/936711453176211

   Meetings: email for location, Hartsell; third Thursdays, 10:00 a.m.–
      noon

Contact: Bonita McCoy, *byvette.mccoy@gmail.com*
Members: 7
Membership fee: national fee
Affiliation: Word Weavers

ARIZONA

ACFW ARIZONA/CHRISTIAN WRITERS OF THE WEST

www.christianwritersofthewest.com

Meetings: Denny's Restaurant, 3315 N. Scottsdale Rd., Scottsdale;
second Saturdays, noon–2:00 p.m.
Contact: Pamela Tracy, *arizona@acfwchapter.com*
Members: 30
Membership fee: national fee plus $15/year
Affiliation: American Christian Fiction Writers

MESA CHRISTIAN WRITERS

Meetings: Redemption Gilbert Church, 1820 W. Elliot Rd., Gilbert;
second Mondays, 9 a.m.–noon
Contact: Peggy Morris, 480-710-6861, *peggysuemor29@gmail.com*
Members: 20
Membership fee: none

READY WRITERS PSALM 45:1

www.facebook.com/ReadyWritersPsalm451

Meetings: email for location, Sierra Vista; second Saturdays, 2:00–
3:30 p.m.
Contact: Charity Plumb, 520-255-3020, *cplumbwrites@gmail.com*
Members: 10
Membership fee: none

WORD WEAVERS NORTHERN ARIZONA

Meetings: Verde Community Church, 102 S. Willard, Cottonwood;
second Saturdays, 9:30–11:30 a.m.
Contact: Barry Jones, *VisualClarity@protonmail.com*
Membership fee: national fee
Affiliation: Word Weavers

WORD WEAVERS SOUTHEAST ARIZONA

Meetings: Pantano Christian Church, 1755 S. Houghton Rd., Tuscan; third Saturdays, 10:00 a.m.–noon
Contact: Charity Plumb, *cplumbwrites@gmail.com*
Membership fee: national fee
Affiliation: Word Weavers

ARKANSAS

ACFW NW ARKANSAS

www.facebook.com/groups/127662834752320

Meetings: Springdale; first Mondays, 5:30 p.m.
Contact: Robyn Hook, *NWArkansas@acfwchapter.com*
Members: 20
Membership fee: national fee
Affiliation: American Christian Fiction Writers

CALIFORNIA

WORD WARRIORS

www.facebook.com/wordwarriorswriters

Meetings: online; first Tuesdays September–June, 7:00 p.m.
Contact: Debbie Jones Warren, *debbiencj@aim.com*
Members: 10
Membership fee: none

WORD WEAVERS VENTURA COUNTY

Meetings: Lucky Llama Coffee Shop, 5100 Carpinteria Ave., Carpinteria; third Mondays, 9:00–11:00 a.m.
Contact: Norma Bennett, *normajeanbennett@gmail.com*
Membership fee: national fee
Affiliation: Word Weavers

COLORADO

ACFW COLORADO SPRINGS

acfwcosprings.net

Meetings: B.R.A.V.E. Church plus online, 3337 N. Academy Blvd., Colorado Springs; first Saturdays, 10:00–11:30 a.m.

Contact: Susan G. Mathis, *info@acfwcosprings.com*

Services: Sponsors the Write in the Springs Conference.

Members: 60

Membership fee: national fee plus $25/year

Affiliation: American Christian Fiction Writers

HIGHLANDS RANCH CREATIVES

www.facebook.com/groups/1509730649342640

Meetings: 9912 Sylvestor Rd., Highlands Ranch; first Thursdays, 6:30 p.m.

Contact: Mike Klassen, *mklassen@illumifymedia.com*

Membership fee: none

Affiliation: Writers on the Rock

WOLF CREEK CHRISTIAN WRITERS NETWORK

wolfcreekwriters.com

Meetings: Grace in Pagosa and Zoom, 1044 Park Ave., Community Room, Pagosa Springs; Mondays except holidays, 9:00–11:00 a.m.

Contact: Cathy McIver, 970-946-3554, *allynschuylerink@gmail.com*

Members: 35

Membership fee: $40/year

WORD WEAVERS PIKES PEAK

www.facebook.com/groups/415291469231448

Meetings: Springs Church, 1515 Auto Mall Loop, Colorado Springs; third Saturdays, 9:00–noon

Contact: Tez Brooks, *tezwrites@gmail.com*

Members: 20

Membership fee: national fee

Affiliation: Word Weavers

WORD WEAVERS WESTERN SLOPE

www.facebook.com/groups/568085077249557

Meetings: email for location, Grand Junction; fourth Saturdays, 10:00 a.m.–noon

Contact: Templa Melnick, *templa.melnick@gmail.com*
Members: 10
Membership fee: national fee
Affiliation: Word Weavers

WRITERS ON THE ROCK ARVADA
www.facebook.com/groups/281086379291783
> **Meetings:** email or call for location, Arvada; last Thursdays, 6:30–
> 8:30 p.m.
> **Contact:** Sue Roberts, 303-467-0286, *srobertswithjoy@yahoo.com*
> **Membership fee:** none
> **Affiliation:** Writers on the Rock

WRITERS ON THE ROCK CASTLE ROCK
www.facebook.com/groups/193369214634778
> **Meetings:** Phillip Miller Library, 100 S. Wilcox St., Castle Rock; third
> Mondays, 6:30 p.m.
> **Contact:** Amber Baughman, *amberjbaughman@gmail.com*
> **Membership fee:** none
> **Affiliation:** Writers on the Rock

WRITERS ON THE ROCK COLORADO SPRINGS
www.facebook.com/groups/1916955675297782
> **Meetings:** Penrose Library, 20 N. Cascade Ave., Colorado Springs;
> second Thursdays, 6:30 p.m.
> **Contact:** April Musekamp, 719-650-1480
> **Membership fee:** none
> **Affiliation:** Writers on the Rock

WRITERS ON THE ROCK LAKEWOOD
www.writersontherock.com/groups
> **Meetings:** Green Mountain Recreation Center, 13198 W. Green
> Mountain Dr., Lakewood; fourth Tuesdays, 7:00-8:30 p.m.
> **Contact:** Amy Young, *amy.young@swissmail.org*
> **Membership fee:** none
> **Affiliation:** Writers on the Rock

WRITERS ON THE ROCK NORTH METRO DENVER
www.facebook.com/groups/1110986532338485
> **Meetings:** Crossroads Church, 10451 Huron St., Northglenn; first

Mondays, 6:30–8:30 p.m.
Contact: Marla Lindstrom Bentroth, *tellyourstorytoo@msn.com*
Membership fee: none
Affiliation: Writers on the Rock

WRITERS ON THE ROCK NORTHERN COLORADO

www.facebook.com/groups/445776855860806

Meetings: Panera Bread, 1550 Fall River Dr., Loveland; third
Thursdays, 7:00–8:30 p.m.
Contact: Jen Grams, *jennygrams@gmail.com*
Membership fee: none
Affiliation: Writers on the Rock

DELAWARE

DELMARVA CHRISTIAN WRITERS' ASSOCIATION

www.facebook.com/groups/219751814716191

Meetings: third Saturdays, 9:00 a.m.–noon
Members: 20
Membership fee: none

FLORIDA

ACFW CENTRAL FLORIDA

www.facebook.com/CFACFW

Meetings: third Saturdays
Contact: Kelly Underwood, *centralflorida@acfwchapter.com*
Membership fee: national fee
Affiliation: American Christian Fiction Writers

SUNCOAST CHRISTIAN WRITERS GROUP

Meetings: The Haus Coffee Shop, 12199 Indian Roacks Rd., Largo;
third Wednesdays, 10:00 a.m.
Contact: Elaine Creasman, 727-251-3756, *emcreasman@aol.com;*
contact her before attending first meeting
Members: 10–20
Membership fee: none

WORD WEAVERS BREVARD COUNTY

Meetings: Freedom Christian Center, 7250 Lake Andrew Dr., Melbourne; second Saturdays, 10:00 a.m.–noon
Contact: Sally Friscea, *sfriscea@gmail.com*
Members: 11
Membership fee: national fee
Affiliation: Word Weavers

WORD WEAVERS CLAY COUNTY

www.facebook.com/groups/WordWeaversClayCounty

Meetings: Panera Bread, 1510 County Rd. 220, Fleming Island; second Saturdays, 9:00–11:30 a.m.
Contact: Evelyn Collins, *wawacollins5@gmail.com*
Members: 9
Membership fee: national fee
Affiliation: Word Weavers

WORD WEAVERS DESTIN

Meetings: email for location, Destin; second Saturdays, 9:30 a.m.
Contact: Alice Murray, *pstyre@aol.com*
Members: 17
Membership fee: national fee
Affiliation: Word Weavers

WORD WEAVERS GAINESVILLE

Meetings: email for location, Gainesville; second Sundays, 2:00–4:30 p.m.
Contact: Lori Roberts, *authorLorilynRoberts@gmail.com*
Members: 6
Membership fee: national fee
Affiliation: Word Weavers

WORD WEAVERS JENSEN BEACH

www.facebook.com/groups/851396695481639

Meetings: Coastal Style Kitchens, conference room, 11274 Business Park Pl., Jensen Beach; third Saturdays, 9:30 a.m.–noon
Contact: Penny Cooke, *LifeCoachPenny@yahoo.com*
Membership fee: national fee
Affiliation: Word Weavers

WORD WEAVERS LAKE COUNTY

www.facebook.com/groups/1790245144535020

> **Meetings:** Leesburg Public Library, 100 E. Main, Leesburg; third Saturdays, 9:15 a.m.–noon
> **Contact:** Mike Anderson, *andersonwriter@gmail.com*
> **Members:** 25
> **Membership fee:** national fee
> **Affiliation:** Word Weavers

WORD WEAVERS MOUNT DORA

www.facebook.com/groups/351333987985122

> **Meetings:** Trinity Church, 890 Abrams Rd., Eustis; third Thursdays, 6:30–9:00 p.m.
> **Contact:** Joy Morris, *JoyBells16@icloud.com*
> **Membership fee:** national fee
> **Affiliation:** Word Weavers

WORD WEAVERS OCALA CHAPTER

> **Meetings:** Belleview Public Library, 13145 S.E. County Hwy. 484, Belleview; second Fridays, 10:00 a.m.–12:30 p.m.
> **Contact:** Yeny Rowley, *yenyrowley@yahoo.com*
> **Members:** 10+
> **Membership fee:** national fee
> **Affiliation:** Word Weavers

WORD WEAVERS ORLANDO

www.facebook.com/groups/216603998394619

> **Meetings:** Calvary Chapel, 5015 Goddard Ave., Orlando; second Saturdays, 10:00 a.m.–12:30 p.m.
> **Contact:** Julie Payne, *info@juliamargaretauthor.com*
> **Members:** 60
> **Membership fee:** national fee
> **Affiliation:** Word Weavers

WORD WEAVERS PENSACOLA

> **Meetings:** Hillcrest Baptist Church, 800 E. Nine Mile Rd., Pensacola; second Tuesdays, 5:30–8:00 p.m.
> **Contact:** Gretchen Huesmann, *Pastor@MyLivingWord.com*
> **Members:** 9
> **Membership fee:** national fee
> **Affiliation:** Word Weavers

WORD WEAVERS SANFORD
Meetings: 8224 Emerald Forest Ct., Sanford; second Tuesdays, 10:00 a.m.–noon
Contact: Suzanne Bennett, *SuzyB3699@hotmail.com*
Membership fee: national fee
Affiliation: Word Weavers

WORD WEAVERS SARASOTA
Meetings: 6807 48th Ter. E, Bradenton; third Sundays, 2:00–4:00 p.m.
Contact: Deb Entsminger, *Navgirladventures@gmail.com*
Members: 4
Membership fee: national fee
Affiliation: Word Weavers

WORD WEAVERS SOUTH FLORIDA
www.facebook.com/groups/132148070172748
Meetings: Gracepoint Church, 5590 N.E. 6th Ave., Fort Lauderdale; second Saturdays, 9:00 a.m.–noon
Contact: Patricia Hartman, *Patricia@PatriciaHartman.net*
Members: 15
Membership fee: national fee
Affiliation: Word Weavers

WORD WEAVERS TAMPA
Meetings: 1901 S. Village Ave., Tampa; first Saturdays, 9:30 a.m.–noon
Contact: Carol Pierce, *sharroncosby@gmail.com*
Members: 30
Membership fee: national fee
Affiliation: Word Weavers

WORD WEAVERS TREASURE COAST
www.facebook.com/groups/480150568723000
Meetings: First Church of God Vero Beach, 1105 58th Ave., Vero Beach; first Saturdays, 9:30 a.m.–noon
Contact: Del Bates, *Del@DelBates.com*
Members: 10
Membership fee: national fee
Affiliation: Word Weavers

WORD WEAVERS VOLUSIA COUNTY
www.facebook.com/groups/227447203952675

Meetings: Faith Church, 4700 S. Clyde Morris Blvd., Port Orange; first Mondays, 7:00 p.m.
Contact: Donna Tinsley, *ThornRose7@aol.com*
Members: 18
Membership fee: national fee
Affiliation: Word Weavers

GEORGIA

ACFW GEORGIA

acfwnga.wordpress.com, www.facebook.com/groups/acfwga

Meetings: Zoom and in person in July, second Tuesdays, 6:30 p.m.
Contact: Janette Melson, *georgia@acfwchapter.com*
Members: 52
Membership fee: national fee plus $15/year
Affiliation: American Christian Fiction Writers

CHRISTIAN AUTHORS GUILD

www.christianauthorsguild.org

Meetings: Sojourn Woodstock, 8816 Main St., Woodstock; first Mondays, 7:00 p.m.
Contact: Deborah Crawford, *deborahrdcrawford@gmail.com*
Members: 30
Membership fee: $30/year

WORD WEAVERS BROOKHAVEN

www.facebook.com/groups/200656040663612

Meetings: Westminster Presbyterian Church, 1438 Sheridan Rd. NE, Atlanta; second Saturdays, 10:00 a.m.–12:30 p.m.
Contact: Maria Gosa, *MariposaArt@Live.com*
Members: 13
Membership fee: national fee
Affiliation: Word Weavers

WORD WEAVERS COLUMBUS

www.facebook.com/groups/541016626433688

Meetings: Barnes & Noble Bookstore, 5555 Whittlesey Blvd., Ste. 1800, Columbus; third Mondays, 6:30–8:30 p.m.
Contact: Terri Miller, *wordweaverscolumbus@gmail.com*
Members: 8

Membership fee: national fee
Affiliation: Word Weavers

WORD WEAVERS CONYERS

www.facebook.com/groups/638509006538934

Meetings: Bethel Christian Church, 1930 Bethel Rd. NE, Conyers; third Saturdays, 10:00 a.m.–noon
Contact: Terri Webster, *TerriJWebster@gmail.com*
Members: 8
Membership fee: national fee
Affiliation: Word Weavers

WORD WEAVERS GREATER ATLANTA

Meetings: 4541 Vendome Pl. NE, Roswell; first Saturdays, 9:30 a.m.–noon
Contact: Kathleen Metzger, *mkmetzger45@hotmail.com*
Members: 15
Membership fee: national fee
Affiliation: Word Weavers

WORD WEAVERS MACON–BIBB

www.facebook.com/groups/173188826644758

Meetings: Central City Church, 621 Foster Rd., Macon; second Sundays, 3:00–5:30 p.m.
Contact: Robin Dance, *RobinDance.me@gmail.com*
Members: 45
Membership fee: national fee
Affiliation: Word Weavers

WORD WEAVERS VALDOSTA

Meetings: Corinth Baptist Church, 4089 Corinth Church Rd., Lake Park; third Saturdays, 2:00–4:00 p.m.
Contact: Christy Adams, *ChristyAdams008@gmail.com*
Membership fee: national fee
Affiliation: Word Weavers

ILLINOIS

ACFW CHICAGO

www.facebook.com/acfwchicago

Meetings: Calvary Community Church, 1000 Springinsguth Rd., Schaumburg; second Fridays, 6:30–8:30 p.m.
Contact: Lori Davis, *chicago@acfwchapter.com*
Members: 20
Membership fee: national fee plus $35/year
Affiliation: American Christian Fiction Writers

WORD WEAVERS CHAMPAIGN–URBANA
www.facebook.com/groups/941611857298603

Meetings: Champaign Public Library, 200 W. Green St., Champaign; fourth Mondays, 10:00 a.m.–noon
Contact: Lesley Dzik, *LesleyDzik@gmail.com*
Members: 8
Membership fee: national fee
Affiliation: Word Weavers

WORD WEAVERS GREATER PEORIA
www.facebook.com/groups/664318908999620

Meetings: Central Life Church, 1100 Hamilton St., Pekin; fourth Saturdays, 3:00–5:00 p.m.
Contact: Laurie Walters, *vyzyn1228@gmail.com*
Membership fee: national fee
Affiliation: Word Weavers

WORD WEAVERS LAND OF LINCOLN

Meetings: Liberty Baptist Church, 2105 Sheridan Rd., Pekin; second Saturdays, 10:00 a.m.–noon
Contact: Rita Klundt, *RitaKlundt@ymail.com*
Members: 10
Membership fee: national fee
Affiliation: Word Weavers

WORD WEAVERS ON THE BORDER

Meetings: Panera Bread, 254 E. Rollins Rd., Round Lake; fourth Thursdays, 7:00–8:30 p.m.
Contact: Mark Drinnenberg, *WritingsbyMark@gmail.com*
Members: 10
Membership fee: national fee
Affiliation: Word Weavers

INDIANA

ACFW INDIANA
www.acfwindiana.com
Meetings: various places in Indiana and Zoom, four to six times per year
Contact: Rebecca Reed, *acfwindianachapter@gmail.com*
Members: 40
Membership fee: national fee plus $15/year
Affiliation: American Christian Fiction Writers

HEARTLAND CHRISTIAN WRITERS
www.facebook.com/HeartlandChristianWriters?mibextid=LQQJ4d
Meetings: Mount Pleasant Christian Church, 381 N. Bluff Rd.,
Greenwood; third Mondays, 10:00 a.m.
Contact: Joyce Long, 317-306-0284, *joyce.e.long@gmail.com*
Members: 10

WORD WEAVERS INDY
Meetings: Carmel-Clay Public Library, 425 E. Main St., Carmel;
third Tuesdays, 6:30–8:30 p.m.
Contact: Mandy Young, *wwindychap@gmail.com*
Membership fee: national fee
Affiliation: Word Weavers

IOWA

WORD WEAVERS DES MOINES
www.facebook.com/groups/495808943830132
Meetings: Union Park Baptist Church, 821 Arthur Ave., Des Moines;
last Mondays, 6:30–8:30 p.m.
Contact: Judy Hagey, *Judy.Hagey@gmail.com*
Members: 12
Membership fee: national fee
Affiliation: Word Weavers

KANSAS

HEART OF AMERICA CHRISTIAN WRITERS NETWORK
www.hacwn.org
>**Meetings:** Colonial Presbyterian Church, 12501 W. 137th St.,
>   Overland Park; second Thursdays, 7:00 p.m.
>**Contact:** Karen Morerod, *HACWN@earthlink.net*
>**Members:** 150
>**Membership fee:** active member, $35/year; professional member,
> $45/year

KENTUCKY

ACFW LOUISVILLE
www.facebook.com/groups/1876813595891979
>**Meetings:** Louisville; fourth Saturdays
>**Contact:** Crystal Caudill, *acfwlouisville@gmail.com*
>**Members:** 50
>**Affiliation:** American Christian Fiction Writers

WORD WEAVERS BOONE COUNTY
www.facebook.com/groups/349709925923088
>**Meetings:** email for location; first Saturdays, 10:30 a.m.–12:30 p.m.
>**Contact:** Karisa Moore, *karisam660@gmail.com*
>**Members:** 15
>**Membership fee:** national fee
>**Affiliation:** Word Weavers

LOUISIANA

ACFW LOUISIANA
www.facebook.com/ACFWLouisiana
>**Meetings:** Barksdale Baptist Church, 1714 Jimmie Davis Hwy.,
>   Bossier City; last Saturdays, 11:00 a.m.
>**Contact:** Charles Sutherland, *louisiana@acfwchapter.com*
>**Membership fee:** national fee
>**Affiliation:** American Christian Fiction Writers

SOUTHERN CHRISTIAN WRITERS
scwguild.com
>**Meetings:** Gospel Bookstore and Zoom, 91 Westbank Expy., Gretna; third Saturdays except November and December, 10:30 a.m.
>**Contact:** Teena Myers, *scwg@cox.net*
>**Members:** 23
>**Membership fee:** none; premium members with extra benefits, $50/year

MICHIGAN

ACFW GREAT LAKES
acfwgreatlakes.wordpress.com, www.facebook.com/groups/ 527572863929168
>**Meetings:** various locations; fourth Saturdays, 10:00 a.m.
>**Contact:** Beth Foreman, *acfwgreatlakes@gmail.com*
>**Members:** 35
>**Membership fee:** national fee plus $10/year
>**Affiliation:** American Christian Fiction Writers

WORD WEAVERS WEST MICHIGAN
>**Meetings:** City on a Hill, 100 Pine St., Zeeland; first and third Tuesdays, noon–2:00 p.m.
>**Contact:** Gene Koon, *koongene@gmail.com*
>**Members:** 10
>**Membership fee:** national fee
>**Affiliation:** Word Weavers

MINNESOTA

ACFW MINNESOTA N.I.C.E.
www.facebook.com/ACFW.MN.NICE
>**Meetings:** Ridgewood Church, 4420 County Rd. 101, Minnetonka; fourth Sundays, 6:00–8:00 p.m.
>**Contact:** Linda Arrowood, *acfw.mn.nice@gmail.com*
>**Members:** 25
>**Membership fee:** national fee plus $25/year
>**Affiliation:** American Christian Fiction Writers

MINNESOTA CHRISTIAN WRITERS GUILD
www.mnchristianwriters.com
> **Meetings:** Oak Knoll Lutheran Church, 600 Hopkins Xrd.,
> Minnetonka; second Mondays, September–May, 7:00-8:30 p.m.
> **Contact:** Jason Sisam, *info@mnchristianwriters.com*
> **Members:** 50
> **Membership fee:** $90/year or $25/meeting

MISSISSIPPI

MID–SOUTH CHRISTIAN WRITERS ROUNDTABLE
www.facebook.com/groups/145426569547064
> **Meetings:** various locations, Memphis metro area; third Saturdays
> **Contact:** William G. Hill, 901-212-8020
> **Members:** 10
> **Membership fee:** none

MISSOURI

ACFW MOZARKS
www.facebook.com/MozArksACFW
> **Meetings:** The Library Center, 4653 S. Campbell Ave., Springfield;
> third Saturdays, 10:30 a.m.
> **Contact:** Erin Miffin, 417-251-1587, *mozarks@acfwchapter.com*
> **Members:** 10
> **Membership fee:** national fee plus $10/year
> **Affiliation:** American Christian Fiction Writers

ACFW ST. LOUIS
acfwstl.wordpress.com
> **Meetings:** Festus Public Library, 400 W. Main St., Festus; second
> Saturdays, 11:30 a.m.
> **Contact:** Karen Sargent, 573-450-0514, *stlouis@acfwchapter.com*
> **Members:** 18
> **Membership fee:** national fee plus $25/year
> **Affiliation:** American Christian Fiction Writers

OZARKS CHAPTER OF AMERICAN CHRISTIAN WRITERS
www.OzarksACW.org
> **Meetings:** University Heights Baptist Church and Zoom, 1010 S. National, Springfield; second Saturdays, September–May, 10:00 a.m.–noon
> **Contact:** Dr. Jeanetta Chrystie, 417-832-8409, *OzarksACW@yahoo.com*
> **Members:** 50
> **Membership fee:** $20/year; couple, $30; newsletter only, $10

NEBRASKA

MY THOUGHTS EXACTLY WRITERS
mythoughtsexactlywriters.wordpress.com
> **Meetings:** Keene Memorial Library, 1030 N. Broad St., Fremont; third Mondays, 6:30–8:00 p.m.
> **Contact:** Cheryl, *mythoughtse@gmail.com*
> **Membership fee:** none

NEW JERSEY

ACFW NY/NJ
www.facebook.com/groups/955365637934907
> **Meetings:** Grace Bible Chapel, 100 Oakdale Rd., Chester; first Saturdays October–June, 10 a.m.-noon; critique groups at other times
> **Contact:** Cherlyn Gatto, *nynj@acfwchapter.com*
> **Members:** 65
> **Membership fee:** national fee plus $20/year
> **Affiliation:** American Christian Fiction Writers

NORTH JERSEY CHRISTIAN WRITERS GROUP
www.njcwg.blogspot.com
> **Meetings:** varies, email *njcwgroup@gmail.com* for location, North Haledon; first Saturdays except holidays, 10:00 a.m.-noon
> **Contact:** Barbara Higby, *bhigby9323@gmail.com*
> **Members:** 10
> **Membership fee:** none

NEW YORK

WORD WEAVERS NEW HAVEN
Meetings: 245 Sundown Rd., Fulton; third Thursdays, 9:00 a.m.–noon
Contact: Mary Curcio, *mathmary56@gmail.com*
Membership fee: national fee
Affiliation: Word Weavers

WORD WEAVERS WESTERN NEW YORK
Meetings: 2458 Rush Mendon Rd., Honeoye Falls; third Wednesdays, 6:00–9:00 p.m.
Contact: Karen Rode, 585-571-7124, *karen.a.rode@gmail.com*
Members: 7
Membership fee: national fee
Affiliation: Word Weavers

NORTH CAROLINA

ACFW NORTH CAROLINA
www.facebook.com/groups/336801510020700
Meetings: Raleigh
Contact: Vince Vezza, *northcarolina@acfwchapter.com*
Membership fee: national fee
Affiliation: American Christian Fiction Writers

WORD WEAVERS CHARLOTTE
Meetings: Charlotte Mecklenburg Library South County Regional, 5801 Rea Rd., Charlotte; first Saturdays, 10:00 a.m.–noon
Contact: Brandie Muncaster, *Brandie.Muncaster@gmail.com*
Members: 15
Membership fee: national fee
Affiliation: Word Weavers

WORD WEAVERS HENDERSONVILLE
www.facebook.com/groups/746784416992918
Meetings: 125 Mountain Valley Dr., Hendersonville; fourth Thursdays, 1:30–3:30 p.m.
Contact: Fred Von Kamecke, *FVonKamecke@comcast.net*
Members: 5

Membership fee: national fee
Affiliation: Word Weavers

WORD WEAVERS HICKORY–NEWTON

www.facebook.com/groups/2328785447421711

> **Meetings:** Southwest Library, 2944 S. Hwy. 127, Hickory; first
> Saturdays, 10:00 a.m.
> **Contact:** Norma Poore, *hickorynewtonwordweavers@gmail.com*
> **Members:** 7
> **Membership fee:** national fee
> **Affiliation:** Word Weavers

WORD WEAVERS MAGGIE VALLEY

facebook.com/groups/2374738259340596

> **Meetings:** Long's Chapel, 133 Old Clyde Rd., Waynesville; third Thursdays
> **Contact:** Linda Summerford, *Juleps2@yahoo.com*
> **Members:** 10
> **Membership fee:** national fee
> **Affiliation:** Word Weavers

WORD WEAVERS PIEDMONT TRIAD

> **Meetings:** 510 Holyoke Rd., Pleasant Garden; third Saturdays, 10:00
> a.m.–noon
> **Contact:** Renee Leonard Kennedy, *Reneeleonardkennedy@gmail.com*
> **Members:** 10
> **Membership fee:** national fee plus $50/year
> **Affiliation:** Word Weavers

WORD WEAVERS WILMINGTON

> **Meetings:** Calvary Baptist Church, 423 23rd St., Wilmington; second
> Tuesdays, 6:30 p.m.
> **Contact:** Laurel Senick, *LSenick6@gmail.com*
> **Members:** 5
> **Membership fee:** national fee
> **Affiliation:** Word Weavers

WORD WEAVERS WINSTON–SALEM

www.facebook.com/groups/268156771940401

> **Meetings:** 1038 Pine Place Dr., Germanton; second Saturdays, 9:30–
> 11:30 a.m.
> **Contact:** Diane Virginia Cunio, *Diane@dianevirginia.com*

Membership fee: national fee
Affiliation: Word Weavers

OHIO

ACFW OHIO
facebook.com/groups/220166801456380

Meetings: online; first Saturdays, 10:00 a.m.
Contact: Victor Hess, 504-258-2199, *ohio@acfwchapter.com*
Members: 32
Membership fee: national fee plus $12/year
Affiliation: American Christian Fiction Writers

COLUMBUS CHRISTIAN WRITERS ASSOCIATION
www.facebook.com/profile.php?id=100057586834554

Meetings: Zoom; second Sundays, 3:00-5:00 p.m.
Contact: Mina R. Raulston, 614-507-7893, *m_raulston@hotmail.com*
Members: 5
Membership fee: none

DAYTON CHRISTIAN SCRIBES
www.facebook.com/DaytonChristianScribes

Meetings: Kettering Seventh-day Adventist Church, 3939
Stonebridge Rd., Kettering; fourth Thursdays, 7:00-9:00 p.m.
Contact: Kim D. Villalva, 512-680-8729, *Kdanisk@yahoo.com*
Members: 20
Membership fee: $15/year

MIDDLETOWN AREA CHRISTIAN WRITERS/M.A.C. WRITERS
middletownwriters.blogspot.com

Meetings: Healing Word Assembly of God, 5303 S. Dixie Hwy.,
Franklin; second Tuesdays, 7:00-8:30 p.m.
Contact: Donna J. Shepherd, 513-373-5671, *donna.shepherd@
gmail.com*
Members: 25
Membership fee: $30/year or $5/meeting

WORD WEAVERS KNOX COUNTY

www.facebook.com/groups/1440083346651013

> **Meetings:** 303 S. Edgewood Rd., Mount Vernon; third Sundays,
> 3:00–5:00 p.m.
> **Contact:** Steve Feazel, *SteveFeazel@gmail.com*
> **Membership fee:** national fee
> **Affiliation:** Word Weavers

WORD WEAVERS NORTHEAST OHIO

> **Meetings:** Good Shepherd Villa, 726 Center St., Ashland; first
> Thursdays, 6:30–8:30 p.m.
> **Contact:** Cherie Martin, *kitties395@yahoo.com*
> **Members:** 10
> **Membership fee:** national fee
> **Affiliation:** Word Weavers

OKLAHOMA

ACFW OKLAHOMA CITY

www.okchristianfictionwriters.com

> **Meetings:** New Hope Church of Christ, 700 W. 2nd St., Edmond;
> third Saturdays, 1:00–3:00 p.m.
> **Contact:** Kristy Werner, *authors@okchristianfictionwriters.com*
> **Members:** 35
> **Membership fee:** national fee plus $20/year
> **Affiliation:** American Christian Fiction Writers

FELLOWSHIP OF CHRISTIAN WRITERS

fellowshipofchristianwriters.org

> **Meetings:** Kirk of the Hills Presbyterian Church, 4102 E. 61st St.,
> Tulsa; second Tuesdays, 6:30–8:00 p.m.
> **Contact:** Cheryl Barker, *cheryl@cherylbarker.net*
> **Members:** 33
> **Membership fee:** $30

WORDWRIGHTS

www.wordwrightsok.com

> **Meetings:** The Last Drop Coffee Shop, 5425 N. Lincoln Blvd.,
> Oklahoma City; second Saturdays, 10:00 a.m.

Contact: *info@wordwrightsok.com*
Members: 30
Membership fee: $20/year

OREGON

CASCADE CHRISTIAN WRITERS
cascadechristianwriters.org
> **Meetings:** Portland metro area and Salem
> **Contact:** President, *president@oregonchristianwriters.com*
> **Services:** Offers private Facebook page for networking and discussion, newsletter, prayer support, conference discounts, and monthly virtual workshops and discussion groups. Sponsors two Saturday conferences and a summer coaching conference each year.
> **Membership fee:** $55/year; 30 and younger, $40/year

PENNSYLVANIA

LANCASTER CHRISTIAN WRITERS
lancasterchristianwriters.org
> **Meetings:** Petra Church and online, 565 Airport Rd., New Holland; third Saturdays every other month, 9:30 a.m.–noon
> **Contact:** Cheryl Weber, email through the website
> **Membership fee:** none

WORD WEAVERS HARRISBURG
facebook.com/groups/wordweaversharrisburg
> **Meetings:** Living Water Community Church, 206 Oakleigh Ave., Harrisburg; second Saturdays, 1:30–3:30 p.m.
> **Contact:** Mae Spradley, *Mae@2c1ministries.org*
> **Members:** 7
> **Membership fee:** national fee
> **Affiliation:** Word Weavers

WRITE HIS ANSWER CRITIQUE GROUPS
writehisanswer.com/critiquegroups
> **Meetings:** online; every other Thursday, 10:00 a.m. and alternating Thursdays, 8:00 p.m.

Contact: Marlene Bagnull, 267-436-2503, *mbagnull@aol.com*
Members: 15 each group
Membership fee: none

SOUTH CAROLINA

ACFW SOUTH CAROLINA LOWCOUNTRY
facebook.com/profile.php?id=100083299843252
Meetings: Seacoast Church, 750 Long Point Rd., Mt. Pleasant; fourth
  Saturdays, 10:00 a.m.–noon
Contact: Laurie Larsen, *sclowcountry@acfwchapter.com*
Members: 14
Membership fee: national fee plus $20/year
Affiliation: American Christian Fiction Writers

ACFW UPSTATE SC
acfwupstatesc.wordpress.com
Meetings: Cross Roads Baptist Church, 705 Anderson Ridge Rd.,
  Greer; second Saturdays, 10:00 a.m.–1:00 p.m.
Contact: Christine Boatwright, *upstatesc@acfwchapter.com*
Members: 30
Membership fee: national fee plus $20/year
Affiliation: American Christian Fiction Writers

WORD WEAVERS AIKEN
Meetings: Trinity United Methodist Church, 2724 Whiskey Rd.,
  Aiken; second Tuesdays, 7:00–9:00 p.m.
Contact: Lee Allen-Russ, *AikenWordWeavers@gmail.com*
Members: 5
Membership fee: national fee
Affiliation: Word Weavers

WORD WEAVERS CHARLESTON
www.facebook.com/groups/2112701302307131
Meetings: St John's Parish Church, Resurrection Hall, 1811 Paulette
  Dr., Johns Island; third Saturdays, 10:00 a.m.–noon
Contact: Timothy Griggs, *timothygriggs@gmail.com*
Members: 25
Membership fee: national fee
Affiliation: Word Weavers

WORD WEAVERS LEXINGTON, SC

LexingtonWordWeavers.com

Meetings: Trinity Baptist Church, 2003 Charleston Hwy., Cayce; second Mondays, 6:45–9:00 p.m.

Contact: Jean Wilund, *Jwilund@icloud.com*

Members: 40

Membership fee: national fee

Affiliation: Word Weavers

WRITING 4 HIM

Meetings: Spartanburg First Baptist Church, The Hanger Room 215, 250 E. Main St., Spartanburg; second Thursdays, 9:45 a.m.

Contact: Linda Gilden, *linda@lindagilden.com*

Members: 20

Membership fee: none

TENNESSEE

ACFW KNOXVILLE

www.facebook.com/groups/341397182924371

Meetings: Parkway Baptist Church, 401 S. Peters Rd., Knoxville; second Tuesdays online; in–person twice/year

Contact: Mary Ostrander, *knoxville@acfwchapter.com*

Members: 20

Membership fee: national fee

Affiliation: American Christian Fiction Writers

ACFW MEMPHIS

facebook.com/groups/699561666820044

Meetings: M.R. Davis Library, 8554 Northwest Dr., Southaven; online and in-person

Contact: Shannon Leach, *memphis@acfwchapter.com*

Members: 32

Membership fee: national fee plus $20/year

Affiliation: American Christian Fiction Writers

ACFW MIDDLE TENNESSEE

www.facebook.com/groups/250177678658399

Meetings: Nashville; first Saturdays, 10:00 a.m.–noon

Contact: Sheila Stovall, *midtennessee@acfwchapter.com*
Members: 40
Membership fee: national fee plus $24/year
Affiliation: American Christian Fiction Writers

WORD WEAVERS KNOXVILLE
www.facebook.com/groups/336414403544597
> **Meetings:** Pleasant Grove Baptist Church, 3736 Tuckaleechee Pike, Maryville; third Saturdays, 9:30 a.m.-noon
> **Contact:** Les Burnette, 865-679-3370, *LesBurnette@gmail.com*
> **Members:** 12
> **Membership fee:** national fee
> **Affiliation:** Word Weavers

WORD WEAVERS NASHVILLE
www.facebook.com/groups/1321489534609537
> **Meetings:** Goodletsville Public Library, 205 Rivergate Pkwy., Goodlettsville; second Saturdays, 10:00 a.m.-noon
> **Contact:** Kim Aulich, *KAAfterGodsOwnHeart@gmail.com*
> **Members:** 10
> **Membership fee:** national fee
> **Affiliation:** Word Weavers

WORD WEAVERS SOUTH MIDDLE TENNESSEE
www.facebook.com/share/g/RD2upBcGBdW4dcv4
> **Meetings:** Edgemont Baptist Church, 150 Fairfield Pike, Shelbyville; third Saturdays, 10:00 a.m.
> **Contact:** Amanda West, *awestwrites@outlook.com*
> **Members:** 10
> **Membership fee:** national fee
> **Affiliation:** Word Weavers

TEXAS

67 WRITERS
roaringwriters.org/groups-locations
> **Meetings:** A H Meadows Library, Bluebonnet Room, 922 S. 9th St., Midlothian; second Saturdays except December, 2:00-3:45 p.m.
> **Contact:** Jan Johnson, email through website

Membership fee: none
Affiliation: Roaring Writers

ACFW ALAMO CITY
www.facebook.com/groups/243114107289
>**Meetings:** La Madeleine, 722 Northwest Loop 410, San Antonio; second Saturdays, 10 a.m.–noon
>**Contact:** Allison Pittman, *alamocity@acfwchapter.com*
>**Members:** 15
>**Membership fee:** national fee
>**Affiliation:** American Christian Fiction Writers

ACFW DFW READY WRITERS
facebook.com/DFWReadyWriters
>**Meetings:** George W. Hawkes Public Library, 100 S. Center St. #327, Arlington, also online 3/4 of the time; second Saturdays, 10:30 a.m.–noon
>**Contact:** Paula Peckham, 817-454-5218, *acfwdfw@gmail.com*
>**Members:** 43
>**Membership fee:** national fee plus $25 and $3/online meeting
>**Affiliation:** American Christian Fiction Writers

ACFW THE WOODLANDS/WRITERS ON THE STORM
wotsacfw.blogspot.com
>**Meetings:** The Woodlands; third Saturdays
>**Contact:** Linda Kozar, *wotsacfw@gmail.com*
>**Members:** 40
>**Membership fee:** national fee plus $20/year, $10 for 70+
>**Affiliation:** American Christian Fiction Writers

CHRISTIAN WRITERS WORKSHOP/Denton
>**Meetings:** 802 Thomas St., Denton; every Monday, 1:00–3:00 p.m.
>**Contact:** Nancy McMinn, 254-339-3060, *reitahawthorne2@gmail.com*
>**Members:** 26
>**Membership fee:** $5

CHRISTIAN WRITERS WORKSHOP/Woodway
roaringwriters.org/groups-locations
>**Meetings:** First Woodway Baptist Church, Room 210–211, 101 N. Ritchie Rd., Woodway; Sundays, 5:30–7:00 p.m., mid-January to the

first week in April and mid-September through the end of October
Contact: Michelle Ruddell, *mruddell21@gmail.com*
Affiliation: Roaring Writers

HEART AND SOUL WRITERS
roaringwriters.org/groups-locations
> **Meetings:** Alsbury Baptist Church, 500 N.E. Alsbury Blvd., Burleson;
> third Tuesdays 7:00-9:00 p.m.
> **Contact:** Lisa Bell, email through the website
> **Membership fee:** none
> **Affiliation:** Roaring Writers

INSPIRATIONAL WRITERS ALIVE! CENTRAL HOUSTON
www.centralhoustoniwa.com
> **Meetings:** various places in Houston, email for location; second
> Thursdays, 7:00-9:00 p.m.
> **Contact:** Connie Parks, 281-627-3011, *connie1.4@juno.com*
> **Members:** 15
> **Membership fee:** $20/year

INSPIRATIONAL WRITERS ALIVE! NORTHWEST HOUSTON
www.centralhoustoniwa.com
> **Meetings:** email for location, Houston; second Wednesdays, 2:00 p.m.
> **Contact:** Martha Roddy, 281-859-4208, *magnolia7787@gmail.com*
> **Members:** 15
> **Membership fee:** $20/year

LIVING WATERS
roaringwriters.org/groups-locations
> **Meetings:** Hood County Library, Pecan Room, 222 N. Travis,
> Granbury; second Fridays, 2:00-4:00 p.m.
> **Contact:** Lisa Bell, email through the website
> **Membership fee:** none
> **Affiliation:** Roaring Writers

ROARING WRITERS MENTORING WITH FRANK BALL
roaringwriters.org/roaring-writers-mentoring
> **Meetings:** Roaring Lambs, upstairs conference room and Zoom, 17110
> Dallas Pkwy., Ste. 284, Dallas; third Saturdays, 9:30 a.m.-12:30 p.m.
> **Contact:** Frank Ball, *fball@RoaringLabs.org*

Membership fee: $35 per session, $110 for four-session season
Affiliation: Roaring Writers

ROCKWALL CHRISTIAN WRITERS GROUP
www.facebook.com/groups/rockwallchristianwritersgroup

Meetings: Redeemer Rockwall Annex, 303 E. Rusk St., Rockwall;
first Mondays, 7:00–9:00 p.m.
Contact: Leslie Wilson, 214-505-5336, *leslieporterwilson@gmail.com*
Members: 15–20 in person, 380+ on Facebook page
Membership fee: none
Affiliation: Roaring Writers

WACO CHRISTIAN WRITERS WORKSHOP
facebook.com/groups/374145049720167

Meetings: First Woodway Baptist Church, 101 Ritchie Rd.,
Woodway; Sundays September–November, January–April, 5:30–
7:00 p.m.
Contact: Michelle Ruddell, 254-749-1740, *mruddell21@gmail.com*
Members: 50
Membership fee: none

WITNESS WRITERS
roaringwriters.org/groups-locations

Meetings: email for location and days, Plainview
Contact: Carole Bell, *caroleabell@gmail.com*
Membership fee: none
Affiliation: Roaring Writers

VIRGINIA

ACFW VIRGINIA
acfwvirginia.com

Meetings: Blacksburg, Chesapeake, Leesburg; see website for days
and times; plus monthly Zoom webinars
Contact: Deena Adams, *acfwvirginia@gmail.com*
Members: 75
Membership fee: national fee plus $15/year
Affiliation: American Christian Fiction Writers

WORD WEAVERS WOODBRIDGE

Meetings: Chinn Library Community Room, 13065 Chinn Park Dr., Woodbridge; last Saturdays, 10:00 a.m.–noon
Contact: Lauren Craft, *laurenchristianauthor@gmail.com*
Members: 4
Membership fee: national fee
Affiliation: Word Weavers

WASHINGTON

VANCOUVER CHRISTIAN WRITERS

Meetings: email for address, Vancouver; first Mondays, 9:00 a.m.
Contact: Jon Drury, 510-909-0848, *jondrury2@yahoo.com*
Members: 8
Membership fee: none
Affiliation: Cascade Christian Writers

WISCONSIN

ACFW WI SOUTHEAST

www.facebook.com/wiseacfw

Meetings: Brookfield Library, four times/year and Zoom rest of year, 1900 N. Calhoun Rd., Brookfield; first Thursdays, 6:30–8:30 p.m.
Contact: Laura DeNooyer Moore, *wisconsinSE@acfwchapter.com*
Members: 25
Membership fee: national fee plus $25/year
Affiliation: American Christian Fiction Writers

PENS OF PRAISE CHRISTIAN WRITERS

www.susanmarlene.com/writers--pens

Meetings: 4Given Coffee Shop, 1034 S. 18th St., Manitowoc; third Mondays, 1:30–3:00 p.m.
Contact: Susan Marlene Kinney, 920-242-3631, *susanmarlenewrites@gmail.com*
Members: 10
Membership fee: none

WORD AND PEN CHRISTIAN WRITERS

wordandpenchristianwriters.com

> **Meetings:** St. Thomas Episcopal Church, April–November; Zoom, January–March, 226 Washington St., Menasha; second Mondays, 7:30 p.m.
> **Contact:** Chris Stratton, 920-739-0752, *gcefsi@new.rr.com*
> **Members:** 16
> **Membership fee:** $10/year

WORD WEAVERS ST. CROIX

> **Meetings:** First Congregational Church of Christ, 110 N. 3rd St., River Falls; second Saturdays, 10:00 a.m.–noon
> **Contact:** Erin Maruska, *erin.maruska@gmail.com*
> **Membership fee:** national fee
> **Affiliation:** Word Weavers

AUSTRALIA AND NEW ZEALAND

NEW ZEALAND CHRISTIAN WRITERS

www.nzchristianwriters.org

> **Meetings:** various places, see website
> **Contact:** Justin St. Vincent, *president@nzchristianwriters.org*
> **Services:** "NZ Christian Writers is a nationwide collective of over 330 authors, bloggers, editors, lyricists, poets, publishers, songwriters, storytellers, and writers throughout New Zealand. Along with our bimonthly magazines and competitions, we offer inspiring seminars and writers retreats to encourage, inspire, and upskill people in their writing. NZ Christian Writers' vision is to encourage and inspire Christian writers throughout New Zealand. We welcome both beginner and experienced writers to join us."
> **Members:** 330+

OMEGA WRITERS

omegawriters.com.au

> **Meetings:** virtual, every other month
> **Contact:** Karen Roper, *membership@omegawriters.org*
> **Services:** Australian group with local and online chapters across the country and New Zealand. See the website for locations. Also sponsors an annual conference and the CALEB Award to

recognize the best in Australasian Christian writing, published and unpublished.

Members: 160
Membership fee: $60/year
Affiliation: Omega Writers

CANADA

INSCRIBE CHRISTIAN WRITERS' FELLOWSHIP
inscribe.org

Contact: Barbara Fuller, *president@inscribe.org*
Services: Canadian group with chapters across the country. See the website for locations. Also sponsors workshops, a fall conference, and contests and produces the quarterly magazine *FellowScript* that is included with membership.
Members: 160
Membership fee: varies, see website

MANITOBA CHRISTIAN WRITERS ASSOCIATION

Meetings: Bleak House, 1637 Main St., Winnipeg; first Saturdays September–June, 1:00–3:30 p.m.
Contact: Frieda Martens, 204-770-8023, *friedamartens1910@gmail.com*
Members: 18
Membership fee: $30
Affiliation: InScribe Christian Writers' Fellowship

THE WORD GUILD
www.thewordguild.com

Contact: Box 77001, Markham ON L3P 0C8, Canada; 800-969-9010, *info@thewordguild.com*
Services: "The Word Guild is a growing community of Canadian writers, editors, speakers, publishers, booksellers, librarians and other interested individuals who are Christian. From all parts of Canada and many denominational and cultural backgrounds, we affirm a common statement of faith and are united in our passion for the written word." Sponsors regional chapters across Canada and contests and awards for Canadian Christian writers.
Members: 325
Membership fee: $65/year; professional, $105; student, $30

20

EDITORIAL SERVICES

Entries in this chapter are for information only, not an endorsement of editing skills. Before hiring a freelance editor, ask for references if they are not posted on the website; and contact two or three to help determine if this editor is a good fit for you. You may also want to pay for an edit of a few pages or one chapter before hiring someone to edit your complete manuscript.

A LITTLE RED INK | BETHANY KACZMAREK
115 1st St., Somerset, WI 54025 | 715-907-5144
contact@bethanykaczmarek.com | *www.bethanykaczmarek.com/little-red-ink2*
   Contact: website
   Services: copyediting, manuscript evaluation, substantive/
     developmental editing
   Types of manuscripts: adult, middle grade, novels, teen/YA
   Charges: hourly rate
   Credentials/experience: "An ACFW Editor of the Year finalist (2015),
     Bethany enjoys working with both traditional and indie authors.
     Several of her clients are award-winning and best-selling authors,
     though she does work with aspiring authors as well. She has edited
     speculative fiction for Enclave Fiction and Gilead, and general fiction
     for Sunrise Publishing."

A LITTLE RED INK | ERYNN NEWMAN
1 Fairway One, Taylors, SC 29687 | 919-229-1357
ErynnNewman@gmail.com | *www.ALittleRedInk.com*
   Contact: email, website
   Services: copyediting, proofreading, substantive/developmental editing
   Types of manuscripts: adult, novels, teen/YA
   Charges: hourly rate
   Credentials/experience: "I specialize in helping authors find their

unique voice, deepening point of view, and bringing characters to life. I'm an unapologetic grammar nerd, but I don't take anything (except the Oxford Comma) too seriously. I have edited over 100 published novels including several *NYT* and *USA Today* best sellers, have authored two award-winning novels of my own, and won the National Readers' Choice Award and the Rita Award for editing."

AB WRITING SERVICES, LLC | ANN BYLE
www.annbylewriter.com/ab-writing-services
Contact: website
Services: articles, back-cover copy, book coaching, consulting, copyediting, discussion questions for books, ghostwriting, manuscript evaluation, press releases
Types of manuscripts: adult, articles, book proposals, devotionals, nonfiction books, novels, query letters
Charges: hourly rate
Credentials/experience: "Ann's experience includes years as a newspaper copy editor, freelance journalist for newspapers and magazines including *Publishers Weekly*, writing her own books including *Christian Publishing 101*, and co- and ghost-writing book projects."

ABOVE THE PAGES | PAM LAGORMARSINO
abovethepages@gmail.com | *www.abovethepages.com*
Contact: email, website
Services: copyediting, discussion questions for books, manuscript evaluation, proofreading, substantive/developmental editing
Types of manuscripts: adult, articles, Bible studies, book proposals, curriculum, devotionals, easy readers, gift books, middle grade, nonfiction books, novels, query letters, short stories, teen/YA
Charges: custom, flat fee, word rate
Credentials/experience: "Pam Lagomarsino has owned and operated Above the Pages since early 2015 when she established it as a business. Pam has edited, proofread, or beta-read Christian nonfiction books, devotionals, sermons, Bible studies, homeschool curriculum, children's books, and Christian fiction. Additional experience includes working in a rural library, writing frequent articles for area newspapers, being a sales rep of children's books, and home teaching her children through high school. Her college coursework included English, literature, library science, and child development. Whether you need a light proofread, substantive revision, copyedit, manuscript review, or anything in between, I will

work alongside you to help you create a captivating piece that will engage, inspire, or educate your readers."

ACEVEDO WORD SOLUTIONS, LLC | JENNE ACEVEDO
editor@jenneacevedo.com | *www.jenneacevedo.com*

Contact: email

Services: back-cover copy, copyediting, discussion questions for books, project management, proofreading, substantive/developmental editing, writing coach

Types of manuscripts: adult, Bible studies, book proposals, curriculum, devotionals, gift books, middle grade, nonfiction books, query letters, teen/YA

Charges: hourly rate, word rate

Credentials/experience: "Consultant for private and corporate clients, proofreader for publishers. Cofounder of Christian Editors Association, former director of The Christian PEN, former director of PENCON, member of Christian Editor Connection, instructor for The PEN Institute, Editors' Choice Award judge. Founder and former director of Chandler Writers' Group."

AMBASSADOR COMMUNICATIONS | CLAIRE HUTCHINSON
13733 W. Gunsight Dr., Sun City West, AZ 85375 | 812-390-7907
clairescreenwriter@gmail.com | *www.clairehutchinson.net*

Contact: email

Services: coauthoring, copyediting, proofreading, screenwriting, substantive/developmental editing, writing coach

Types of manuscripts: scripts

Charges: flat fee

Credentials/experience: "M.A. English, Professional Program in Screenwriting UCLA, produced and award-winning screenwriter and producer and script analyst."

AMI EDITING | ANNETTE IRBY
editor@AMIediting.com | *www.AMIediting.com*

Contact: email

Services: copyediting, critiquing, manuscript evaluation (fiction only), proofreading, substantive/developmental editing

Types of manuscripts: novellas, novels, short stories

Charges: page rate

Credentials/experience: "Annette spent 5 years working as an acquisitions editor for a Christian book publisher. She has more than

20 years of experience editing freelance in the CBA marketplace. Her clients have included several well-known authors and publishers. She is a long-time member of ACFW and has served as a judge for their contests, including final-round evaluation. As a fiction author herself, she has published books of various lengths. Over the years, her writing has achieved top-three status in competitions, as well as placing first in BRMCWC's 2019 Selah Contest. In 2009, she founded Seriously Write, a co-hosted blog, which ran for 10 years with active participation from the Christian writing community. See her editing website for testimonials."

ANDREA MERRELL

60 McKinney Rd., Travelers Rest, SC 29690 | 864-616-5889
AndreaMerrell7@gmail.com | www.AndreaMerrell.com

> **Contact:** email, website
> **Services:** back-cover copy, copyediting, proofreading
> **Types of manuscripts:** adult, articles, devotionals, nonfiction books, novels, short stories
> **Charges:** hourly rate
> **Credentials/experience:** "Professional freelance editor. Associate editor for Christian Devotions Ministries and former associate editor for LPC Books. Member of The Christian PEN: Proofreaders and Editors Network."

ANN KROEKER, WRITING COACH

ann@annkroeker.com | annkroeker.com/writing-coach

> **Contact:** email, website
> **Services:** writing coach
> **Types of manuscripts:** adult, articles, blog posts, book proposals, nonfiction books, query letters, social-media content
> **Charges:** flat fee, hourly rate, word rate
> **Credentials/experience:** "A writing coach, author, speaker, and host of the *Ann Kroeker, Writing Coach* podcast, Ann works with clients one-to-one, through programs and courses like The Art & Craft of Writing, and through Your Platform Matters (YPM), her platform membership program. Her website has landed on *The Write Life*'s annual '100 Best Websites for Writers' list six years in a row thanks to years of valuable writing-related content. She leverages over three decades of experience in the writing and publishing world to support writers looking for input and confidence to advance their careers. Ann's clients have achieved personal goals, landed

contracts, hit bestseller lists, and won awards. She's presented at conferences, retreats, and summits; coauthored *On Being a Writer: 12 Simple Habits for a Writing Life that Lasts*; and authored *Not So Fast: Slow-Down Solutions for Frenzied Families* and *The Contemplative Mom*."

ARMOR OF HOPE WRITING & PUBLISHING SERVICES | DENISE M. WALKER

info@armorofhopewritingservices.com | *www.armorofhopewritingservices.com*

Contact: email
Services: copyediting, proofreading, writing coach
Types of manuscripts: Bible studies, board/picture books, devotionals, easy readers, nonfiction books
Charges: flat fee, word rate
Credentials/experience: "I have been in business for over five years and have copyedited and/or proofread 100+ nonfiction, children's picture books, and easy readers. In addition, I serve as a writing coach, assisting nonfiction authors with organizing and developing their thoughts. I am also a full-service nonfiction self-publishing coach and an author of middle grades/YA fiction, women's Christian fiction, and Bible literacy journals. I have attended several book writing and editing workshops. I am also certified in middle grades English language arts and have taught English for over 20 years."

AUTHOR AS ENTREPRENEUR | MICHAEL L. WHITE

PO Box 8277, Mobile, AL 36689 | 251-643-6985
mwhite@authorasentrepreneur.com | *www.authorasentrepeneur.com*

Contact: email, website
Services: back-cover copy, proofreading, substantive/developmental editing
Types of manuscripts: articles, Bible studies, nonfiction books, novels, poetry
Charges: custom
Credentials/experience: "Dual B.S. degree in English and history from Troy University. Master of Divinity degree from Emory University's Candler School of Theology. 40+ years as a freelance writer. 27+ years of experience as a pastor before retiring. Retired with 30+ years of service as a Chaplain Assistant and a Chaplain in the U.S. Army and Alabama Army National Guard. 17+ years of experience as the founder and managing editor for the independent Christian publishing company, Parson Place Press."

AUTHORIZEME LITERARY FIRM, LLC | DR. SHARON NORRIS ELLIOTT

9514 Dorothy Ave., South Gate, CA 90280 | 310-508-9860

AuthorizeMeNow@gmail.com | *lifethatmatters.net*

Contact: email

Services: back-cover copy, coauthoring, copyediting, discussion questions for books, ghostwriting, manuscript evaluation, proofreading, substantive/developmental editing, writing coach

Types of manuscripts: adult, articles, Bible studies, board/picture books, book proposals, curriculum, devotionals, easy readers, gift books, middle grade, nonfiction books, novels, poetry, query letters, short stories

Charges: custom

Credentials/experience: "Over 35 years of experience in this business as an author, editor, writer, and speaker; AuthorizeMe business growing and in successful operation since 2008."

AUTHORS WHO SERVE | RACHEL HILLS

rachel@authorswhoserve.com | *authorswhoserve.com*

Contact: website

Services: coauthoring, copyediting, ghostwriting, manuscript evaluation, substantive/developmental editing, writing coach

Types of manuscripts: adult, articles, devotionals, nonfiction books, novels, query letters, short stories, teen/YA

Charges: flat fee, word rate

Credentials/experience: "Because Jesus came to serve (Matthew 20:28), any author who serves via their writing follows in His steps. I would love to serve you. I have 25 years' experience, a bachelor's degree, certificates in copyediting, developmental editing, and ghostwriting, along with training in book coaching. I monitor publishing trends to better assist you. How can I serve you today?"

AVODAH EDITORIAL SERVICES | CHRISTY DISTLER

www.avodaheditorialservices.com

Contact: website

Services: copyediting, manuscript evaluation, proofreading, substantive/developmental editing

Types of manuscripts: adult, devotionals, easy readers, nonfiction books, novels, picture books, poetry, short stories

Charges: word rate

Credentials/experience: "Educated at Temple University and

University of California–Berkeley. Thirteen years of editorial experience, both as an employee and a freelancer. Currently works mostly for publishing houses but accepts freelance work as scheduling allows."

BANNER LITERARY | MIKE LOOMIS
mike@mikeloomis.co | *www.MikeLoomis.co*

Contact: email, website

Services: back-cover copy, book-contract evaluation, coauthoring, copyediting, discussion questions for books, ghostwriting, manuscript evaluation, substantive/developmental editing, writing coach

Types of manuscripts: articles, book proposals, devotionals, nonfiction books, query letters

Charges: custom, flat fee

Credentials/experience: "I have ghostwritten two *NYT* bestsellers, and advised internationally-known authors. But I truly enjoy helping aspiring authors develop their books, brands, and business."

BARBARA KOIS
barbara.kois@gmail.com

Contact: email

Services: back-cover copy, copyediting, ghostwriting, manuscript evaluation, proofreading, substantive/developmental editing, writing coach

Types of manuscripts: adult, Bible studies, devotionals, gift books, middle grade, nonfiction books, novels, short stories, teen/YA

Charges: hourly rate, word rate

Credentials/experience: "Barbara has worked as a writer, ghostwriter, editor, teacher, coach, corporate communication consultant and journalist, and served as Writer in Residence at Tyndale House Publishers. She has written or co-written ten books, published more than 600 articles in the *Chicago Tribune*, and edited more than 250 books for various publishers and authors. Barbara has helped dozens of writers to prepare for the publication of their books, including both those who have published with traditional publishers and those who have chosen to self-publish. Her goals include making writing clear, memorable and even humorous where appropriate."

BBH LITERARY | DAVID BRATT
david@bbhliterary.com | *www.bbhliterary.com/developmental-editing*

Contact: email, website

Services: manuscript evaluation, substantive/developmental editing
Types of manuscripts: academic, articles, book proposals, nonfiction books, query letters
Charges: hourly rate
Credentials/experience: "Twenty-one years editing for Eerdmans Publishing; Ph.D. in American religion (Yale University, 1999)."

BECCA WIERWILLE EDITING AND COACHING SERVICES
becca@beccawierwille.com | beccawierwille.com/editing-services
Contact: email, website
Services: copyediting, manuscript evaluation, proofreading, substantive/developmental editing, writing coach
Types of manuscripts: adult, book proposals, devotionals, easy readers, middle grade, novels, query letters, short stories, teen/YA
Charges: word rate
Credentials/experience: "Becca Wierwille is a freelance editor and writing coach who has worked with writers of various genres and experience levels. As a former newspaper reporter and avid critique group member, she has years of experience doing edits at every level. She loves partnering with authors to help make their stories shine and focuses on editing clean fiction, with a specialization in middle grade and YA. Her editing portfolio and testimonials are available upon request."

BESTSELLING BOOK SHEPHERD | PAMELA GOSSIAUX
pam@pamelagossiaux.com | BestsellingBookShepherd.com
Contact: email
Services: back-cover copy, coauthoring, copyediting, discussion questions for books, ghostwriting, manuscript evaluation, proofreading, substantive/developmental editing, writing coach
Types of manuscripts: adult, articles, Bible studies, board/picture books, book proposals, devotionals, easy readers, gift books, middle grade, nonfiction books, novels, query letters, short stories, teen/YA
Charges: custom, flat fee, hourly rate, packages
Credentials/experience: "30 years experience writing, editing, journalism, book PR. Dual degree in Creative Writing & English Language and Literature from University of Michigan. International bestselling author. Have coached and promoted authors to Amazon, *USA Today* and *Wall Street Journal* bestsellers."

BOOKHOUND EDITING | KATY SCHLOMACH
katy@bookhoundediting.com | *www.bookhoundediting.com*

Contact: email
Services: copyediting, manuscript evaluation, proofreading
Types of manuscripts: adult, novels, teen/YA
Charges: flat fee, packages, word rate
Credentials/experience: "Katy Schlomach specializes in line editing, copyediting, and proofreading fiction, particularly the romance, speculative, and suspense genres. She helps authors create captivating stories by removing any hindrance between the author's intent and the reader's perception. She has a BA in communication (with a concentration in technical writing), completed training courses through Edit Republic and The PEN Institute, and is a member of the Christian Editor Connection. This turned her love of language into a career that allows her to work with authors to make their stories clear, consistent, and compelling for readers. See her website for more information about her services, testimonials of her work, and articles with self-editing tips."

BREAKOUT EDITING | DORI HARRELL
doriharrell@gmail.com | *doriharrell.wixsite.com/breakoutediting*

Contact: email
Services: copyediting, proofreading, substantive/developmental editing, website text
Types of manuscripts: adult, articles, devotionals, middle grade, nonfiction books, novels, picture books, query letters, short stories, teen/YA
Charges: word rate
Credentials/experience: "Dori is a multiple-award-winning writer and a highly experienced editor who freelance edits full time and has edited more than 300 novels and nonfiction books. Breakout authors final in awards or win awards almost every year! She edits for publishers, including Gemma Halliday Publishing and Kregel Publications, and as an editor, she releases more than twenty books annually."

BROOKSTONE CREATIVE GROUP | JOHN HERRING
100 Missionary Ridge, Birmingham, AL 35242 | 302-514-7899
www.brookstonecreativegroup.com

Contact: website

Services: book proposals, copyediting, ghostwriting, one-sheets,
proofreading, substantive/developmental editing, writing coach
Types of manuscripts: books of all kinds and all ages
Charges: flat fee
Credentials/experience: "Brookstone Creative Group is changing
the landscape for how writers, authors, speakers, pastors,
musicians, and other creatives navigate the ever-changing
landscape of platform development. Through true and tested
solutions, training, and community-building, Brookstone Creative
Group guides their clients in the who, where, when, and how to
inspirational success."

BUTTERFIELD EDITORIAL SERVICES | DEBRA L. BUTTERFIELD

4810 Gene Field Rd., Saint Joseph, MO 64506 | 816-752-2171
deb@debralbutterfield.com | *themotivationaleditor.com*
   Contact: email
   Services: copyediting, mentoring, substantive/developmental editing
   Types of manuscripts: adult, book proposals, devotionals, nonfiction
   books, novels
   Charges: word rate
   Credentials/experience: "Fourteen years experience freelance
   editing. Ten years as an editor for CrossRiver Media Group
   traditional publisher, and now holds the position of editorial
   director."

C. S. LAKIN, COPYEDITOR AND WRITING COACH | SUSANNE LAKIN

20406 Tiger Tail Rd., Grass Valley, CA 95949 | 530-200-5466
cslakin@gmail.com | *www.livewritethrive.com*
   Contact: email, website
   Services: back-cover copy, coauthoring, copyediting, critiquing,
   manuscript evaluation, proofreading, substantive/developmental
   editing, writing coach
   Types of manuscripts: adult, Bible studies, book proposals,
   devotionals, easy readers, gift books, middle grade, nonfiction
   books, novels, picture books, poetry, query letters, short stories,
   teen/YA
   Charges: flat fee, hourly rate
   Credentials/experience: "For nearly two decades I've helped more
   than 6,000 writers learn the skills and techniques to become

masterful writers. Whether you have a spark of an idea for a book and have never attempted writing fiction or you've written multiple novels and need to level-up your craft to greater mastery, you will greatly benefit from my coaching and mentoring. Services include copyediting, proofreading, manuscript and outline critiques, story brainstorming, coaching, and mentoring."

CATHY STREINER

Cathy@thecorporatepen.com | thecorporatepen.com

    Contact: email

    Services: back-cover copy, coauthoring, copyediting, discussion questions for books, proofreading, substantive/developmental editing, writing coach

    Types of manuscripts: academic, adult, articles, Bible studies, devotionals, easy readers, gift books, middle grade, nonfiction books, novels, scripts, short stories, technical material, teen/YA

    Charges: custom, flat fee, hourly rate, word rate

    Credentials/experience: "Author of a Christian novel, I have experience with the start-to-finish self-publishing process. I also have extensive experience working with writers who need editing and proofreading services as well as limited coaching with constructive feedback."

CELTICFROG EDITING | ALEX MCGILVERY

22-121 Ferry Rd., Clearwater, BC V0E 1N2, Canada | 250-819-4275
thecelticfrog@gmail.com | celticfrogediting.com

    Contact: email, website

    Services: manuscript evaluation, substantive/developmental editing, writing coach

    Types of manuscripts: academic, adult, devotionals, easy readers, middle grade, nonfiction books, novels, short stories, teen/YA

    Charges: flat fee

    Credentials/experience: "I'm an author, content editor and publisher. After writing some four hundred reviews over a couple decades, I moved over to content editing and have worked with dozens of authors and hundreds of books. I also do manuscript assessments."

CHERI FIELDS EDITING

Cherifieldsediting@gmail.com | Cherifields.com

    Contact: email, website

    Services: discussion questions for books, manuscript evaluation, substantive/developmental editing, writing coach

Types of manuscripts: articles, Bible studies, easy readers, middle grade, nonfiction books, picture books, teen/YA

Charges: flat fee, word rate

Credentials/experience: "I'm a graduate from the Institute of Children's Literature, have passed my gold level certification with The PEN Institute for nonfiction and children's editing. I am the managing editor for The Creation Club website (since 2019) and am currently earning my Master's degree in Biblical Counseling from Faith Bible Seminary. While many of my clients are early in their writing careers, you can see various finished books my clients have published by visiting my website. My specialty is to come alongside those who either need or want to go the self-publishing route, as I have done with my own books."

CHRISTIAN COMMUNICATOR MANUSCRIPT CRITIQUE SERVICE | SUSAN TITUS OSBORN

3133 Puente St., Fullerton, CA 92835 | 714-313-8651

susanosb@aol.com | *www.christiancommunicator.com*

Contact: email, phone, website

Services: back-cover copy, book-contract evaluation, coauthoring, copyediting, discussion questions for books, ghostwriting, manuscript evaluation, proofreading, writing coach

Types of manuscripts: academic, adult, articles, Bible studies, book proposals, curriculum, devotionals, easy readers, gift books, middle grade, nonfiction books, novels, picture books, poetry, query letters, scripts, short stories, technical material, teen/YA

Charges: hourly rate, page rate

Credentials/experience: "Our critique service, comprised of 14 professional editors, has been in business for almost 40 years. We are recommended by ECPA, the Billy Graham Association, and a number of publishing houses and agents."

CHRISTIAN EDITOR CONNECTION

PO Box 9243, Brea, CA 92822

director@ChristianEditor.com | *www.ChristianEditor.com*

Contact: website

Services: copyediting, ghostwriting, indexing, manuscript evaluation, proofreading, substantive/developmental editing, writing coach

Types of manuscripts: academic, adult, articles, Bible studies, board/ picture books, book proposals, curriculum, devotionals, easy readers, gift books, middle grade, nonfiction books, novels, poetry, query letters, short stories, technical material, teen/YA

Charges: hourly rate, page rate, word rate

Credentials/experience: "Christian Editor Connection is a matchmaking service that connects Christian authors, project managers, agents, and publishers with vetted, professional Christian editors."

CHRISTIANBOOKPROPOSALS.COM | SALLY CRAFT
scraft@ecpa.org | *ChristianBookProposals.com*

Contact: website

Services: online proposal-submission service

Types of manuscripts: books of all kinds and all ages

Charges: $98 for six months

Credentials/experience: "Operated by the Evangelical Christian Publishers Association (ECPA), it is the only manuscript service created by the top Christian publishers looking for unsolicited manuscripts in a traditional, royalty-based relationship. It allows authors to submit their manuscript proposals in a secure, online format for review by editors from publishing houses that are members of ECPA."

CLAIRE KOHLER
clairekohlerbooks@yahoo.com | *www.clairekohlerbooks.com/services*

Contact: website

Services: copyediting, proofreading

Types of manuscripts: devotionals, novels

Charges: word rate

Credentials/experience: "I worked as an English teacher in a public school for two years before becoming an online English teacher to students overseas. I completed a rigorous proofreading course in 2022 and have worked as a professional editor since then. I am also a published author with two books and a third in progress."

COLLABORATIVE EDITORIAL SOLUTIONS | ANDREW BUSS
info@collaborativeeditorial.com | *collaborativeeditorial.com*

Contact: email

Services: copyediting, proofreading

Types of manuscripts: academic, adult, articles, Bible studies, devotionals, nonfiction books, technical material

Charges: hourly rate, page rate

Credentials/experience: "I'm a professional editor with more than five years of full-time experience working with authors and scholarly publishers such as InterVarsity Press, Reformation Heritage, P&R Publishing, Georgetown University Press, and Baylor University Press. Although I primarily work in the genre of scholarly nonfiction, I'm always keen to work with creative and thoughtful authors, whatever the topic or genre. I'm a member of the Editorial Freelancers Association and the Society of Biblical Literature."

COMMUNICATION ASSOCIATES | KEN WALKER

729 Ninth Ave. #331, Huntington, WV 25701 | 304-525-3343
kenwalker33@gmail.com | *www.KenWalkerWriter.com*

Contact: email
Services: back-cover copy, coauthoring, discussion questions for books, ghostwriting, substantive/developmental editing
Types of manuscripts: adult, articles, Bible studies, devotionals, nonfiction books
Charges: flat fee, hourly rate
Credentials/experience: "Started freelancing in 1983 and went full-time in 1990. Experienced ghostwriter and developmental book editor. Have been doing more book editing the past nine years. Written, edited or contributed to more than 90 books."

CREATIVE CORNERSTONES | CAYLAH COFFEEN

creativecornerstones@gmail.com | *creativecornerstones.com/editing-2*

Contact: email, website
Services: back-cover copy, copyediting, ghostwriting, manuscript evaluation, substantive/developmental editing, writing coach
Types of manuscripts: adult, articles, novels, scripts, teen/YA
Charges: hourly rate, word rate
Credentials/experience: "Caylah Coffeen will give you the tools you need to make your fantasy or sci-fi novel shine! Don't be one in millions of 3 star books. Caylah will give your story a health checkup (manuscript evaluation), help you write characters that make readers laugh and cry (developmental edit), and make your turns of phrase clear and compelling (line edit). A member of the Editorial Freelancers Association, she has several years of freelance editing experience and also works with Monster Ivy Publishing and Eschler Editing. She is the founder of Creative Cornerstones, a book publishing services company which guides authors at each stage in the publishing journey: writing, design, and sales. Our team

326

will take your story from 'great,' and elevate it to unforgettable."

CREATIVE EDITORIAL SOLUTIONS | CLAUDIA VOLKMAN
cvolkman@mac.com

Contact: email

Services: back-cover copy, book-contract evaluation, copyediting, discussion questions for books, ghostwriting, indexing, manuscript evaluation, proofreading, substantive/developmental editing, writing coach

Types of manuscripts: adult, Bible studies, devotionals, gift books, nonfiction books, novels

Charges: flat fee, word rate

Credentials/experience: "I have more than 35 years of experience in the publishing world, most of it in Christian and Catholic trade publishing. Now as owner of Creative Editorial Solutions, I offer author coaching, developmental editing, and copyediting to entrepreneurs, coaches, speakers, and authors."

CREATIVE ENTERPRISES STUDIO | MARY HOLLINGSWORTH
1507 Shirley Way, Ste. A, Bedford, TX 76022-6737 | 817-312-7393
ACreativeShop@aol.com | *www.creativeenterprisesltd.com*

Contact: email

Services: coauthoring, copyediting, discussion questions for books, ghostwriting, manuscript evaluation, proofreading, substantive/developmental editing

Types of manuscripts: adult, book proposals, curriculum, devotionals, easy readers, gift books, middle grade, nonfiction books, novels, picture books, short stories, teen/YA

Charges: custom

Credentials/experience: "CES is a publishing services company, hosting more than 150 top Christian publishing freelancers. We work with large, traditional Christian publishers on books by best-selling authors. We also produce custom, first-class books on a turnkey basis for independent authors, ministries, churches, and companies."

DENICA MCCALL EDITING
denica@denicamccall.com | *denicamccall.com/editing-services*

Contact: email, website

Services: copyediting, manuscript evaluation, proofreading, substantive/developmental editing

Types of manuscripts: adult, devotionals, easy readers, middle grade, nonfiction books, novels, picture books, poetry, short stories, teen/YA

Charges: word rate

Credentials/experience: "I have a copyediting badge and a developmental editing badge from Editorial Arts Academy. I've also worked as an intern for Twenty Hills Publishing and an editing intern for Quill and Flame Publishing. I have been writing fiction for over sixteen years and poetry for most of my life, and I have stories and poems published in several anthologies. For the past two years, I have worked with several individual authors and a couple small publishers as an editor."

DENISE HARMER

1695 Dorothea Ave., Fallbrook, CA 92028 | 760-505-0531

dharmeredits@gmail.com | *www.deniseharmer.weebly.com*

Contact: email

Services: copyediting, proofreading

Types of manuscripts: novels, short stories, teen/YA

Charges: word rate

Credentials/experience: "Denise Harmer specializes in copyediting and proofreading fiction and creative nonfiction. She started her editing experience in 1990 editing court transcripts, and over the last fifteen years she has had the privilege of working with several bestselling Christy and Carol Award-winning authors to help make their books the best that they can be."

DESERT RAIN EDITING | GLENIECE LYTLE

PO Box 8163, Hualapai, AZ 86412 | 928-715-7125

desert.rain.editing@gmail.com | *desertrainediting.com*

Contact: email, website

Services: copyediting, proofreading, substantive/developmental editing

Types of manuscripts: Bible studies, devotionals, memoir, nonfiction books

Charges: word rate

Credentials/experience: "I edit memoir, devotionals, Bible studies, and Christian living books, as well as health and wellness and business books from a Christian perspective for self-publishing authors. Every editing project has taught me something new about the art of editing, the craft of writing, and life in general. I am a silver member of the Christian PEN: Proofreaders and Editors Network and use the current versions of the *Chicago Manual of Style, Merriam-Webster's Collegiate Dictionary,* and the *Christian Writer's Manual of Style* for my substantive and line/copy editing decisions. At Desert Rain Editing, I look forward to partnering with each client, turning the vision they held for their seedling manuscript and nurturing it to become a fully bloomed book."

DONE WRITE EDITORIAL SERVICES | MARILYN A. ANDERSON

127 Sycamore Dr., Louisville, KY 40223 | 502-244-0751
shelle12@aol.com

Contact: email, phone

Services: copyediting, proofreading, substantive/developmental editing, writing coach

Types of manuscripts: academic, adult, articles, Bible studies, book proposals, children, curriculum, devotionals, gift books, nonfiction books, novels, poetry, query letters, short stories, technical material

Charges: hourly rate

Credentials/experience: "I am qualified by both bachelor's and master's degrees in English. I am also qualified because I have tutored more than thirty English/writing students since 2004. Most of them have been English-language learners. Also, I have taught English/writing as a classroom teacher. I have additionally conducted business-project editing for several corporations over the years. I currently copyedit for nonfiction and fiction independent writers, as well as for publishers and a few Christian ministries and am in the process of mentoring several other writers/editors. I copyedit both books (such as memoirs) and doctoral dissertations, theses, and other academic journal articles and papers.

"I offer a free sample edit, and my rates are both reasonable and competitive. I am a Gold charter member of The Christian PEN proofreaders and editors' network, along with a tested member of the Christian Editor Connection."

ECHO CREATIVE MEDIA | BRENDA NOEL and DAWN SHERILL-PORTER

108 Springfield Dr., Smyrna, TN 37167 | 615-223-0754
echocreativemedia.com

Contact: email

Services: copyediting, discussion questions for books, ghostwriting, proofreading, substantive/developmental editing

Types of manuscripts: adult, articles, book proposals, curriculum, devotionals, easy readers, gift books, nonfiction books, picture books, short stories, teen/YA

Charges: flat fee, hourly rate

Credentials/experience: "More than 20 years of experience in the Christian publishing industry."

EDIT RESOURCE, LLC | ERIC STANFORD

19265 Lincoln Green Ln., Monument, CO 80132 | 719-290-0757

info@editresource.com | *www.editresource.com*

Contact: email

Services: back-cover copy, book proposals, coauthoring, copyediting, discussion questions for books, ghostwriting, indexing, manuscript evaluation, proofreading, substantive/developmental editing, writing coach

Types of manuscripts: adult, Bible studies, book proposals, curriculum, devotionals, middle grade, nonfiction books, novels, query letters, teen/YA

Charges: depends on the service

Credentials/experience: "Owners Eric and Elisa have a combined 40 years of experience and have worked with numerous bestselling authors and books. They also represent a team of other top writing and editing professionals."

EDIT WITH CLAIRE | CLAIRE TUCKER

PO Box 3072, Ladysmith, KwaZulu Natal 3370, South Africa

editor@editwithclaire.com | *www.editwithclaire.com*

Contact: email

Services: back-cover copy, copyediting, proofreading

Types of manuscripts: adult, devotionals, nonfiction books, novels, short stories

Charges: word rate

Credentials/experience: "I am a detail-oriented editor who loves to work with authors to achieve excellence. I am also a gold member of the Christian PEN (an association for Christian editors and proofreaders) and a member of the Christian Editor Connection. My experience includes a wide range of genres from fantasy to contemporary fiction and nonfiction, and some of my clients have gone on to finalize in and win various awards. Most importantly, I am a Bible-believing Christian who strives to live out 1 Corinthians 10:31 in my life and work."

EDITING BY LUCY | LUCY CRABTREE

editingbylucy@gmail.com | editingbylucy.com

Contact: email, website

Services: copyediting, discussion questions for books, manuscript evaluation, proofreading, substantive/developmental editing

Types of manuscripts: academic, adult, articles, Bible studies, devotionals, gift books, nonfiction books, novels, teen/YA

Charges: word rate

Credentials/experience: "I have been a communications professional since 2007—at a national syndicate, a public university, and even an art museum. So when I say I've edited a little bit of everything ... I do mean everything! Crossword puzzles, faculty manuscripts, advice columns, political commentaries, comic strips, university websites, grant proposals, promotional copy—you name it, I've (probably) read it."

EDITING GALLERY, LLC | CAROL L. CRAIG

2622 Willona Dr., Eugene, OR 97408 | 541-735-1834

kf7orchid@gmail.com | www.editinggallery.com

Contact: email

Services: back-cover copy, coauthoring, ghostwriting, manuscript evaluation, substantive/developmental editing, writing coach

Types of manuscripts: adult, book proposals, easy readers, middle grade, novels, picture books, query letters, scripts, teen/YA

Charges: hourly rate

Credentials/experience: "Fiction author with over 25 years of editorial experience. I have worked with numerous award-winning, best-selling fiction authors who have published with Bethany House, Revell, Guideposts, Avon, Bantam Books, HarperCollins, Random House, Beaufort, Ballantine, Midnight Ink, Thomas Dunn, Lake Union Publishing, Soho Press, etc."

EDITING INSIDERS | JANYRE TROMP

janyre@editinginsiders.com | www.editinginsiders.com

Contact: email

Services: back-cover copy, coauthoring, manuscript evaluation, substantive/developmental editing, writing coach

Types of manuscripts: adult, articles, Bible studies, book proposals, devotionals, nonfiction books, novels, query letters, short stories

Charges: hourly rate, word rate

Credentials/experience: "Award-winning nonfiction and fiction editor with more than 20 years of experience in acquiring, editing, and marketing books. I've edited more than 200 books written by new and seasoned authors. With an additional 10 years of experience in book marketing, I've written and edited marketing copy for a traditional publisher and had a hand in producing copy for several Indie authors. I adore working with writers and equipping them to make their manuscripts the best they can be."

eDITMORE EDITORIAL SERVICES | TAMMY DITMORE

501-I S. Reino Rd. #194, Newbury Park, CA 91320 | 805-630-6809
tammy@editmore.com | *www.editmore.com*

Contact: email
Services: copyediting, discussion questions for books, manuscript evaluation, proofreading, substantive/developmental editing, writing coach
Types of manuscripts: academic, adult, articles, Bible studies, curriculum, devotionals, gift books, nonfiction books, teen/YA
Charges: hourly rate
Credentials/experience: "Tammy Ditmore offers editing, proofreading, and coaching services to publishers, authors, businesses, organizations, and scholars. Two of her Christian authors recently won Benjamin Franklin awards from the Independent Book Publishers Association, and one of those authors has worked with Tammy while publishing dozens of articles in national and international periodicals and websites. An editor for more than 40 years, Tammy specializes in nonfiction, with an emphasis on Christian and spiritual topics, personal histories, current events, and material on aging and Alzheimer's disease."

EDITOR WORLD, LLC | PATTI FISHER

info@editorworld.com | *www.editorworld.com*

Contact: email, website
Services: copyediting, ghostwriting, proofreading, substantive/developmental editing
Types of manuscripts: academic, adult, articles, Bible studies, book proposals, curriculum, devotionals, gift books, middle grade, nonfiction books, novels, poetry, short stories, technical material, teen/YA
Charges: word rate
Credentials/experience: "Editor World provides an on-demand team

of native English writers and editors with extensive experience. Our writers and editors provide writing, rewriting, and editing/proofreading services for clients. Individual writer profiles can be viewed at *www.editorworld.com/writers* and individual editor profiles can be viewed at *www.editorworld.com/editors.*"

ELOQUENT EDITS | DENISE ROEPER

1025 Third St., Port Orange, FL 32129 | 386-290-4117
denise.eloquentedits@gmail.com | *www.eloquentedits.com*

Contact: email, website
Services: copyediting, proofreading, substantive/developmental editing
Types of manuscripts: academic, easy readers, memoir, middle grade, novels, short stories, teen/YA
Charges: word rate
Credentials/experience: "Fiction is my passion. I love to read it. I love to edit it. My clients will receive my full attention when I work on their creation."

EXEGETICA PUBLISHING | CATHY CONE

312 Greenwich #112, Lee's Summit, MO 64082
editor@exegeticapublishing.com | *exegeticapublishing.com/editing*

Contact: website
Services: copyediting, manuscript evaluation, proofreading, substantive/developmental editing
Types of manuscripts: academic, articles, Bible studies, curriculum, devotionals, nonfiction books
Charges: flat fee
Credentials/experience: "Exegetica editorial staff have more than 30 years editing experience with diverse media and publishers."

EXTRA INK EDITS | MEGAN EASLEY-WALSH

Ireland
Megan@ExtraInkEdits.com | *www.ExtraInkEdits.com*

Contact: email
Services: back-cover copy, copyediting, discussion questions for books, manuscript evaluation, proofreading, substantive/developmental editing, writing coach
Types of manuscripts: academic, adult, articles, Bible studies, devotionals, easy readers, gift books, middle grade, nonfiction books, novels, picture books, poetry, query letters, short stories, teen/YA

Charges: flat fee, word rate

Credentials/experience: "Megan Easley-Walsh, PhD History, is an author of historical fiction, a researcher, and a writing consultant and editor at Extra Ink Edits. She is an award-winning writer and has taught college writing in the UNESCO literature city of Dublin, Ireland. She is a dual American and Irish citizen and lives in Ireland with her Irish husband. Megan is a Professional Member of the Irish Writers' Centre, a Full Member of the Irish Writers' Union, a member of the Historical Novel Society, a Full Member of ACES: The Society for Editing, a member of the Irish Association of Professional Historians, and a member of the American Historical Association. Additionally, she was shortlisted for the 2021 Hammond House International Literary Prize in Poetry."

FAITH EDITORIAL SERVICES | REBECCA FAITH

PO Box 184, Novelty, OH 44072 | 330-898-6365

rebecca@faitheditorial.com | *www.faitheditorial.com*

Contact: email, website

Services: copyediting, manuscript evaluation, proofreading

Types of manuscripts: academic, adult, articles, Bible studies, book proposals, curriculum, devotionals, medical, nonfiction books, technical material

Charges: hourly rate

Credentials/experience: "My experience editing in the Christian market includes six years as managing editor for a Christian nonprofit, another eight years editing/transcribing content for a global Christian ministry, and copyediting nonfiction Christian books and devotionals. In addition I have eleven years experience editing technical, engineering, medical, and educational material for university presses, journal publishers, and independent clients. I hold membership in the EFA, the Christian PEN (Gold), and the Christian Editor Connection."

FAITHWORKS EDITORIAL & WRITING, INC. | NANETTE THORSEN SNIPES

PO Box 1596, Buford, GA 30518 | 770-945-3093

nsnipes@bellsouth.net | *www.faithworkseditorial.com*

Contact: email, website

Services: copyediting, manuscript evaluation, proofreading, work-for-hire projects

Types of manuscripts: adult, articles, business materials, devotionals, easy readers, gift books, memoir, middle grade, nonfiction books, picture books, poetry, query letters, short stories

Charges: hourly rate, page rate

Credentials/experience: "Member: The Christian PEN (Proofreaders & Editors Network), Christian Editor Connection, Christian Editor Network. Proofreader for corporate newsletters, thirteen years. Published writer for more than twenty-five years. Published hundreds of articles in magazines and stories in more than sixty compilation books, including Guideposts, B&H, Regal, and Integrity. Twelve years of editorial experience in both adult and children's short fiction and books, memoirs, short stories, devotions, articles, business. Rates are generally by page but, under specific circumstances, by the hour. Editorial clients have published with such houses as Zondervan, Tyndale, and Revell."

FINAL TOUCH PROOFREADING & EDITING | HEIDI MANN

mann.heidi@gmail.com | *www.FinalTouchProofreadingAndEditing.com*

Contact: email

Services: copyediting, proofreading

Types of manuscripts: devotionals, middle grade, nonfiction books, picture books, teen/YA

Charges: flat fee, hourly rate

Credentials/experience: "In addition to my editing expertise, I bring experience as a Lutheran pastor and seminary training in Bible and theology."

THE FOREWORD COLLECTIVE | MOLLY HODGIN

1726 Charity Dr., Brentwood, TN 37027 | 615-497-4322

info@theforewordcollective.com | *www.theforewordcollective.com*

Contact: email, website

Services: back-cover copy, book-contract evaluation, coauthoring, discussion questions for books, ghostwriting, manuscript evaluation, substantive/developmental editing, writing coach

Types of manuscripts: adult, apps, board/picture books, book proposals, cookbooks, devotionals, easy readers, gift books, middle grade, nonfiction books, novels, query letters, style books, teen/YA

Charges: flat fee, hourly rate

Credentials/experience: "Molly Hodgin has over twenty years of publishing experience in acquiring and editing gift books, cookbooks, style books, devotionals, trade nonfiction books, YA and middle grade fiction, and children's picture books and board books.

Her specialty is helping authors craft a book proposal that will stand out to land them an agent or publishing deal. She has also written, ghost written, and co-authored over seventy-five books.

"If Molly isn't the right fit for your book, well, The Foreword Collective also employs a number of highly experienced industry professionals from all areas of Christian publishing. Whether you are an experienced author looking for editorial help or brand building or a new author who wants to make the leap into traditional publishing, The Foreword Collective is here to help!"

FRENCH AND ENGLISH COMMUNICATION SERVICES | DIANE GOULLARD

3104 E. Camelback Rd., PMB 124, Phoenix, AZ 85016-4502 | 602-870-1000
RequestFAECS2008@cox.net | *frenchandenglish.com*

> **Contact:** email, phone, website
> **Services:** copyediting, English to French translation, French to English translation, proofreading
> **Types of manuscripts:** academic, adult, articles, Bible studies, book proposals, curriculum, devotionals, easy readers, gift books, middle grade, nonfiction books, novels, poetry, query letters, scripts, short stories, technical material, teen/YA
> **Charges:** custom, flat fee, hourly rate, page rate, word rate
> **Credentials/experience:** "Experience + academic + occupational training. MA, BA, Certificates, Experience, Skills."

FULL CIRCLE EDITS | TANYA MINNICK

1150 S. Kansas Rd., Orrville, OH 44667 | 330-317-6603
Fullcircle.edits@gmail.com | *www.facebook.com/profile.php?id=100069299295315*

> **Contact:** email
> **Services:** back-cover copy, copyediting, proofreading, substantive/developmental editing
> **Types of manuscripts:** adult, articles, book proposals, curriculum, devotionals, easy readers, gift books, middle grade, nonfiction books, novels, picture books, short stories, technical material, teen/YA
> **Charges:** custom, page rate
> **Credentials/experience:** "Freelance experience in editing memoirs, devotionals, and children's story books—but willing to branch out to other areas as well. Participated in several book launch teams, with a focus on editing. Background in teaching English, applied linguistics,

and language acquisition with extensive knowledge of grammar and syntax. Full Circle Edits provides 'noteworthy proofing that makes you stand out.'"

GINNY L. YTTRIP'S WORDS FOR WRITERS | GINNY L. YTTRUP

3575 Arden Way #1093, Sacramento, CA 95864 | 916-276-7359

ginny@wordsforwriters.net | *wordsforwriters.net*

Contact: email

Services: manuscript evaluation, substantive/developmental editing, writing coach

Types of manuscripts: adult, book proposals, devotionals, memoir, nonfiction books, novels, query letters

Charges: word rate

Credentials/experience: "Ginny L. Yttrup is the author of seven novels, including *Words,* which won the Christy Award for Best First Novel and was a Christy finalist for Best Contemporary Standalone. A developmental editor and coach, Ginny is the founder of Words for Writers, which offers inspiration and instruction for writers."

THE GRAMMAR QUEEN | RENEE GARRICK

1503 S. Park St., Red Wing, MN 55066 | 651-327-9686

renee@thegrammarqueen.net | *TheGrammarQueen.net*

Contact: email, phone, website

Services: copyediting, proofreading, substantive/developmental editing

Types of manuscripts: Bible studies, devotionals, memoir, nonfiction books

Charges: hourly rate

Credentials/experience: "Since 2014 I've edited 7 books and proofed 3 more for TRISTAN Publishing in Minneapolis, MN; 3 of the editing projects have won a total of 4 awards. During the same time period, I've also edited for more than a dozen self-publishing authors and personal historians, along with providing services for 4 books for one 'boutique' publisher."

HANEMANN EDITORIAL | NATALIE HANEMANN

1865 Gunner Ln., Chapel Hill, TN 37034

nathanemann@gmail.com | *www.nataliehanemann.com*

Contact: website

Services: coauthoring, ghostwriting, substantive/developmental editing, writing coach

Types of manuscripts: academic, nonfiction books, novels

Charges: custom

Credentials/experience: "After working in publishing for 20 years doing many forms of editing, I've honed my skillset to co-authoring, ghostwriting, and coaching. Will do developmental edits if it's a challenging manuscript that needs massive work (I'm a sucker for problem-solving!). Preferred categories include Catholic or Orthodox, academic (i.e. books with lots of footnotes and citations), social justice (poverty, disenfranchised people groups) and novels (adventure, general, historical, women's, biblical). Not accepting projects that are 'light reads' or strictly 'entertaining.' I like books that are well-thought out with deep messages that promote social change . . . or change of heart."

HEATHER KLEINSCHMIDT
hi@theseworthywords.com | *www.theseworthywords.com*

Contact: email, phone

Services: back-cover copy, coauthoring, copyediting, discussion questions for books, ghostwriting, indexing, manuscript evaluation, proofreading, substantive/developmental editing, writing coach

Types of manuscripts: academic, adult, articles, curriculum, nonfiction books, technical material

Charges: flat fee, word rate

Credentials/experience: "For a 10% discount, use 'CWMG' in your email subject line (or mention that this is where you found me)! Nonfiction: I specialize in emotionally nuanced or complicated topics—or issues that are just generally difficult to articulate. Genres I work in include Health & Wellness, Psychology & Mental Health, Business & Finance. Academic: I've worked with universities and researchers to create high-impact curricula and research communications for both general and academic audiences."

HEATHER PUBOLS
heather.pubols@gmail.com | *heatherpubols.com/editing-services*

Contact: phone, website

Services: copyediting, substantive/developmental editing

Types of manuscripts: academic, articles, Bible studies, nonfiction books, technical material

Charges: hourly rate

Credentials/experience: "More than 20 years of editorial experience working in corporate communications for Christian missions organizations. Freelance editor since 2018."

HENRY MCLAUGHLIN
921 Silver Streak Dr., Saginaw, TX 76131 | 817-703-9875
henry@henrymclaughlin.org | *www.henrymclaughlin.org*
> **Contact:** phone, website
> **Services:** coauthoring, ghostwriting, manuscript evaluation, substantive editing & rewriting
> **Types of manuscripts:** adult, book proposals, novels, short stories
> **Charges:** page rate
> **Credentials/experience:** "Over 20 years as a novelist, coach/mentor, editor, teacher. Prize winning novelist. Successful ghostwriter. Teaching the craft at conferences, workshops, writers groups. Coaching and editing several clients to publication."

HISWAY | KIMBERLY MORRISON
133 Hudspeth Rd., Statesville, NC 28677 | 828-244-0183
kim@onlyhisway.com | *www.onlyhisway.com*
> **Contact:** email
> **Services:** back-cover copy, coauthoring, commercials, ghostwriting, radio scripts, substantive editing & rewriting
> **Types of manuscripts:** adult, Bible studies, devotionals, gift books, nonfiction books, novels, poetry, short stories
> **Charges:** project rate
> **Credentials/experience:** "Self-published author of seven Christian fiction books, devotionals, book trailers, radio scripts, commercials, and back cover blurbs for myself and other authors."

HONEST EDITING | WILLIAM CARMICHAEL
PO Box 2437, Sisters, OR 97759
www.honestediting.com
> **Contact:** website
> **Services:** copyediting, manuscript evaluation, proposal creation, substantive/developmental editing
> **Types of manuscripts:** academic, adult, Bible studies, book proposals, devotionals, easy readers, gift books, middle grade, nonfiction books, novels, query letters, teen/YA
> **Charges:** flat fee
> **Credentials/experience:** "A professional editor with years of experience in Christian editing is assigned." A division of Writer's Edge Service.

INKSNATCHER | SALLY HANAN
429 S. Avenue C, Elgin, TX 78621 | 512-265-6403
bookhelp@inksnatcher.com | *inksnatcher.com*

> **Contact:** email, website
> **Services:** back-cover copy, coauthoring, copyediting, discussion questions for books, ghostwriting, manuscript evaluation, proofreading, substantive/developmental editing
> **Types of manuscripts:** adult, devotionals, nonfiction books, novels
> **Charges:** custom
> **Credentials/experience:** "A full-service provider for self-publishing authors, Inksnatcher is a vetted and verified member of the Alliance of Independent Authors, the Christian Editor Connection, and Reedsy. Sally is also a self-published author of five books in multiple genres and coauthor of two."

THE INKY BOOKWYRM | GINA KAMMER
1054 Deer Ridge Ct. NW, Lonsdale, MN 55046 | 507-381-1887
ginakammer@inkybookwyrm.com | *www.inkybookwyrm.com*

> **Contact:** website
> **Services:** copyediting, manuscript evaluation, proofreading, query/submissions coaching, substantive/developmental editing, writing coach
> **Types of manuscripts:** adult, easy readers, middle grade, novels, query letters, teen/YA
> **Charges:** monthly fee, word rate
> **Credentials/experience:** "Gina Kammer specializes in editing and book coaching for science fiction and fantasy. She is a former Capstone editor and Bethany Lutheran College writing/journalism instructor with 10+ years of experience in fiction and children's nonfiction. Using brain science hacks, hoarded craft knowledge, and solution-based direction, this book dragon helps science-fiction and fantasy authors get their stories—whether on the page or still in their heads—ready to enchant their readers."

INSPIRATION FOR WRITERS, INC. | SANDY TRITT
1527 18th St., Parkersburg, WV 26101 | 304-428-1218
IFWeditors@gmail.com | *Inspirationforwriters.com/editorial-services*

> **Contact:** email, mail, phone
> **Services:** copyediting, ghostwriting, manuscript evaluation, proofreading, substantive/developmental editing, writing coach

Types of manuscripts: academic, adult, articles, Bible studies, book proposals, devotionals, gift books, memoir, middle grade, nonfiction books, novels, query letters, short stories, teen/YA

Charges: word rate

Credentials/experience: "Since 1998, Inspiration for Writers has provided editing and writing services for hundreds of clients. Our editors are all published writers (including *NY Times* bestselling) and are active in the writing world. We believe in treating our clients with dignity and honesty—and 90% of our business is repeat business. We love our clients and they love us."

JAMES PENCE EDITING

1551 County Road 4109, Greenville, TX 75401 | 214-460-0390

jamespence919@gmail.com | *jamespence.com/writing-services*

Contact: email

Services: coauthoring, copyediting, manuscript evaluation, proofreading, substantive/developmental editing, writing coach

Types of manuscripts: nonfiction books, novels

Charges: flat fee, word rate

Credentials/experience: "Discover the writer within you with James Pence's expert guidance. As an experienced author, collaborator, and editor, James will help you bring your book-length project to fruition. Having authored ten books, many of which were published by major publishers such as Osborne/McGraw-Hill, Tyndale, Kregel, Baker, and Thomas Nelson (as a ghostwriter), James possesses a diverse range of writing skills across various genres, including fiction, nonfiction memoir, how-to, Christian living, and self-help."

JAMIE CHAVEZ

jamie.chavez@gmail.com

Contact: email

Services: copyediting, substantive/developmental editing

Types of manuscripts: nonfiction books, novels

Charges: flat fee

Credentials/experience: "Jamie Chavez worked for more than ten years in the Christian publishing industry (and more than twenty as a freelance copywriter) before she found her niche as an independent writer and editor in 2004. Specializing in content and line/copy editing, Chavez counts many national publishing houses as clients, many authors and agents as friends, and spends her days in the swanky second-floor office in the pink house with the green door making good books better."

JAMI'S WORDS | JAMI BENNINGTON
jami@jamiswords.com | jamiswords.com
- **Contact:** email, website
- **Services:** copyediting, manuscript evaluation, proofreading
- **Types of manuscripts:** adult, Bible studies, curriculum, devotionals, middle grade, nonfiction books, novels, picture books, short stories, teen/YA
- **Charges:** flat fee, hourly rate, word rate
- **Credentials/experience:** "After spending over twenty years as a teacher of language arts, Jami launched her editing business in 2017. She is a graduate of UC San Diego's copyediting certificate program, is a fan of continuing education, and is a member of The Christian PEN."

JEANETTE GARDNER LITTLETON, PUBLICATION SERVICES
3706 N.E. Shady Lane Dr., Gladstone, MO 64119-1958 | 816-459-8016
jeanettedl@earthlink.net | www.linkedin.com/in/jeanette-littleton-b1b790101
- **Contact:** email
- **Services:** back-cover copy, book-contract evaluation, copyediting, discussion questions for books, indexing, manuscript evaluation, proofreading, substantive/developmental editing
- **Types of manuscripts:** adult, articles, Bible studies, book proposals, curriculum, devotionals, gift books, nonfiction books, novels, query letters, short stories, technical material, teen/YA
- **Charges:** flat fee, hourly rate, page rate
- **Credentials/experience:** "I've been a full-time editor and writer for more than thirty years for a variety of publishers. I've written five thousand articles and edited thousands of articles and dozens of books. Please see my profile at LinkedIn."

JEANETTE HANSCOME
jeanettehanscome.com
- **Contact:** website
- **Services:** manuscript evaluation, sensitivity reader for blind/visually impaired characters or issues, writing coach
- **Types of manuscripts:** articles, devotionals, gift books, middle grade, nonfiction books, novels, short stories
- **Charges:** flat fee, hourly rate
- **Credentials/experience:** "Jeanette Hanscome has written twelve

books, hundreds of articles and devotions (including ghostwriting for *Guideposts*), and contributed to numerous devotional and story collections. Her writing experience includes work-for-hire, traditionally published, co-authored, and self-published titles. She has coached and edited in a variety of genres."

JENNIFER EDWARDS COMMUNICATIONS

2839 Sleeping Bear Rd., Montrose, CO 81401 | 916-768-4207
mail.jennifer.edwards@gmail.com | *jedwardsediting.net*

Contact: email

Services: back-cover copy, coauthoring, copyediting, discussion questions for books, manuscript evaluation, proofreading, self-publishing consulting, substantive/developmental editing, writing coach

Types of manuscripts: academic, adult, Bible studies, book proposals, curriculum, devotionals, nonfiction books, query letters

Charges: hourly rate

Credentials/experience: "Jennifer Edwards has been a professional editor, author coach, and self-publishing and book production consultant for 13 years. She has worked with authors represented by publishers such as Penguin Random House, Redemption Press, Lexham Press, PTLB Publishing, and BMH Publishing, as well as over 100 self-publishing authors. Jennifer has a master's degree in Biblical Studies & Theology from Western Seminary and is a standing Gold member of the Christian Editors & Proofreaders Network (PEN)."

JESSICA SNELL BOOK SERVICES

jessicasnelledits@gmail.com | *jessicasnell.com/editing*

Contact: email

Services: coauthoring, copyediting, discussion questions for books, ghostwriting, manuscript evaluation, proofreading, substantive/developmental editing

Types of manuscripts: academic, adult, articles, Bible studies, devotionals, nonfiction books, novels, poetry, short stories, teen/YA

Charges: flat fee, hourly rate

Credentials/experience: "I am a member of the Christian Editor Connection (CEC) and a gold member of the Christian PEN (Proofreaders and Editors Network). I've also presented workshops at PENCON, the annual conference for Christian editors and proofreaders. I have almost a decade of professional experience, and I love helping authors polish their books so that their own voices shine through in a clear and compelling way."

JHWRITING+ | NICOLE HAYES

www.jhwritingplus.com

Contact: website

Services: coauthoring, copyediting, discussion questions for books, ghostwriting, manuscript evaluation, proofreading, substantive/developmental editing, writing coach

Types of manuscripts: adult, articles, curriculum, devotionals, gift books, nonfiction books, novels, poetry, short stories, technical material, teen/YA

Charges: flat fee, word rate

Credentials/experience: "Bachelor's degree in English; PhD in education. Although I do most writing, editing, and proofreading projects, my niche is creative nonfiction (engaging, dramatic, factual prose). I have been writing and editing for more than twenty-five years."

JOANNE CREARY

joanne8340@gmail.com

Contact: email

Services: copyediting, substantive/developmental editing, writing coach

Types of manuscripts: academic, articles, nonfiction books

Charges: custom, hourly rate, page rate

Credentials/experience: "I have extensive experience as a freelance editor, especially for academic book publishers, and as a newspaper feature writer. I'm also a trained Christian life coach passionate about helping you realize your dream! I'd love to bring this experience to help you polish your article or nonfiction book manuscript for publication. Contact me for a free 20-minute consultation."

JOHN SLOAN, LLC

830 Grey Eagle Cir. N, Colorado Springs, CO 80919 | 719-888-0365
jsjohnsloan@gmail.com | *johnsloaneditorial.wordpress.com*

Contact: email, website

Services: coauthoring, substantive/developmental editing, writing coach

Types of manuscripts: academic, adult, Bible studies, devotionals, easy readers, gift books, nonfiction books, short stories, teen/YA

Charges: flat fee, hourly rate, word rate

Credentials/experience: "I have worked in publishing and editorial roles for 40 years, with Multnomah Press and HarperCollins

Christian Publishing, Zondervan. I am offering my services for freelance work in the areas of book development, collaboration, writer coaching, book doctoring, macro editing, content editing. I have worked with a broad spectrum of book and author types: I have edited the literary and general market works of authors like Philip Yancey and Frederick Buechner; the popular issues volumes of writers like Chuck Colson; the high visibility authors like Lee Strobel and Ben Carson; the broader market authors and pastors like John Ortberg and Mark Batterson; and I've worked in the area of the popular academic works."

JOT OR TITTLE EDITORIAL SERVICES | SAMUEL RYAN KELLY

sam@jotortittle.com | *jotortittle.com*

> **Contact:** email, phone
> **Services:** copyediting, manuscript evaluation, proofreading, substantive/developmental editing, writing coach
> **Types of manuscripts:** academic, adult, articles, Bible studies, devotionals, nonfiction books, novels, short stories
> **Charges:** hourly rate
> **Credentials/experience:** "Sam has a double BA in English and biblical and religious studies and an MA in theology. He specializes in academic writing and has a background in biblical languages, but he likes to bring his expertise to a variety of projects. In addition to his freelance work, Sam does research for pastors and churches at Docent Research Group and serves as an associate editor with Wordsmith Writing Coaches."

JOY MEDIA | JULIE-ALLYSON IERON

PO Box 413, Mt. Prospect, IL 60056

j-a@joymediaservices.com | *www.joymediaservices.com*

> **Contact:** email
> **Services:** back-cover copy, coauthoring, copyediting, discussion questions for books, ghostwriting, manuscript evaluation, substantive/developmental editing, writing coach
> **Types of manuscripts:** adult, articles, Bible studies, book proposals, devotionals, gift books, nonfiction books, novels, query letters, teen/YA
> **Charges:** hourly rate
> **Credentials/experience:** "Julie was a mentor/master craftsman with the Jerry B. Jenkins Christian Writers Guild. She mentored more than 100 professional writers through Guild studies. Her students reached their writing goals of signing publishing contracts and seeing

articles published. Julie was lead writer for the Guild's Writing Essentials and Apprentice curriculum in 2010. She works with late-teen through senior-adult writers of Christ-centered materials."

JUDITH ROBL

PO Box 802, Lyons, KS 67554 | 620-257-3143

jrlight620@yahoo.com | *www.judithrobl.com/editing-2*

> **Contact:** email
>
> **Services:** back-cover copy, copyediting, discussion questions for books, proofreading, writing coach
>
> **Types of manuscripts:** adult, Bible studies, devotionals, gift books, novels, query letters, short stories
>
> **Charges:** custom
>
> **Credentials/experience:** "Educated as a secondary English teacher decades ago, I've edited for people for many years. My first major accomplishment in editing was published in 2010. I use *The Chicago Manual of Style* unless another style guide is required. A sample edit lets me see if the author and I are a good fit and allows me to determine the appropriate fee. While perfection in writing is the goal, it must be done with absolute respect for the author's voice."

KAREN APPOLD

kappold@msn.com

> **Contact:** email
>
> **Services:** copyediting, ghostwriting, proofreading
>
> **Types of manuscripts:** academic, articles, curriculum, devotionals
>
> **Charges:** flat fee, hourly rate, word rate
>
> **Credentials/experience:** "I am an award-winning journalist with a BA from Penn State University in English (Writing). I have more than 30 years of professional editorial experience. I mainly write on healthcare/medical and retail, but welcome Christian-themed work."

KARI BARLOW EDITING SERVICES

731 Cornell Ave., Pensacola, FL 32514 | 850-830-0796

karibarlow.com

> **Contact:** email, phone, website
>
> **Services:** back-cover copy, copyediting, discussion questions for books, ghostwriting, manuscript evaluation, proofreading, substantive/developmental editing
>
> **Types of manuscripts:** academic, adult, articles, Bible studies, curriculum, devotionals, easy readers, gift books, middle grade,

nonfiction books, novels, picture books, query letters, short stories

Charges: custom, hourly rate, word rate

Credentials/experience: "Since graduating from UNC-Chapel Hill with a journalism degree, I have focused my entire career on crafting the written word. Simply put, I am at my professional best when helping individuals and organizations identify and share their best messages. I am skilled at managing projects for multiple clients simultaneously, using project management software, content management systems, and videoconferencing platforms to track progress and communication and spur collaboration. My experience includes writing new copy for rebranded websites, corporate blogging, editing manuscripts at all stages of the publishing process and writing and editing articles, op-eds, press releases, and research reports."

KATHY IDE WRITER SERVICES

Kathy@KathyIde.com | www.KathyIde.com

Contact: email

Services: coauthoring, copyediting, ghostwriting, manuscript evaluation, proofreading, substantive/developmental editing, writing coach

Types of manuscripts: adult, articles, Bible studies, book proposals, curriculum, devotionals, gift books, nonfiction books, novels, query letters, screenplays, scripts, short stories, technical material, teen/YA

Charges: hourly rate

Credentials/experience: "Kathy Ide is the author of *Proofreading Secrets of Best-Selling Authors* and *Editing Secrets of Best-Selling Authors* and the editor/compiler of the Fiction Lover's Devotional series. She's been a professional freelance editor for 20+ years, and in 2022 started proofreading screenplays for Pinnacle Peak/PureFlix. Kathy owns Christian Editor Network, parent organization to the four divisions she founded: The Christian PEN: Proofreaders and Editors Network, The PEN Institute, PENCON, and Christian Editor Connection. CEN sponsors the Editors' Choice Award."

KATIE PHILLIPS CREATIVE SERVICES

1500 E. Tall Tree Rd. #6206, Derby, KS 67037-6033 | 316-293-9202

katie@katiephillipscreative.com | www.katiephillipscreative.com

Contact: email

Services: back-cover copy, branding, copyediting, substantive/developmental editing, writing coach

Types of manuscripts: adult, book proposals, middle grade, novels, query letters, short stories, teen/YA

Charges: hourly rate, word rate

Credentials/experience: "Edited six award-finalist novels in multiple categories, including the winners of the Realm Award for Book of the Year, Reader's Choice, and Fantasy. Instructor for The Author Conservatory, run by bestselling and award-winning authors Brett Harris and Kara Swanson. Over ten years industry experience writing and editing both fiction and non-fiction. Bachelor of Arts in Journalism."

KIM PETERSON

1114 Buxton Dr., Knoxville, KY 37922

petersk.ktp@gmail.com | *naturewalkwithgod.wordpress.com/about-kim*

Contact: email

Services: back-cover copy, copyediting, create brochures and newsletters, discussion questions for books, manuscript evaluation, proofreading, substantive/developmental editing, write curriculum/lesson plans, writing coach

Types of manuscripts: academic, adult, articles, Bible studies, blog posts, book proposals, curriculum, devotionals, easy readers, gift books, middle grade, nonfiction books, novels, poetry, query letters, short stories, technical material, teen/YA

Charges: hourly rate

Credentials/experience: "College writing instructor (30+ years), freelance writer (40+ years), freelance editor (15 years), conference speaker (16 years), contest judge (11 years), and former agent's fiction reader (9 years). MA in print communication."

KRISTEN STIEFFEL

kristen@kristenstieffel.com | *www.kristenstieffel.com*

Contact: website

Services: coauthoring, copyediting, ghostwriting, manuscript evaluation, proofreading, substantive/developmental editing, writing coach

Types of manuscripts: novels, short stories, teen/YA

Charges: flat fee, word rate

Credentials/experience: "Kristen Stieffel specializes in Sci-Fi and Fantasy and has edited more than 80 books for more than 60 clients in her 20-plus years as a freelancer. Kristen is also a writing instructor—teaching is her primary gift, so she approaches editing as an opportunity to educate. Her writing includes the fantasy novel *Alara's Call* and a steampunk book, *Tales of the Phoenix*."

KUNDE ED | KATHY KUNDE
kathyjkunde@gmail.com

Contact: email

Services: back-cover copy, copyediting, discussion questions for books, indexing, proofreading, substantive/developmental editing

Types of manuscripts: academic, adult, articles, Bible studies, book proposals, curriculum, devotionals, gift books, nonfiction books, query letters

Charges: custom

Credentials/experience: "My experience as a copy editor has allowed me to work alongside pastor authors and their teams to publish relevant nonfiction books, newsletters, articles, devotionals. I am in prayer about each work because I see myself as a servant of the King to further the Heavenly Kingdom. In addition, as a school administrator, I have been responsible for the transmission of professional letters, public notices, school newsletters, state reports and much more. As an English teacher, my habit is to review text until it speaks with excellence. I consider it an honor to partner with linguistic artists."

LEE WARREN COMMUNICATIONS
9212 Manderson St., Omaha, NE 68134

leewarrenjr@outlook.com | *www.leewarren.info/editing*

Contact: email

Services: copyediting, proofreading

Types of manuscripts: articles, devotionals, gift books, nonfiction books, novels

Charges: word rate

Credentials/experience: "Lee Warren has fifteen years of experience in the Christian publishing industry as a contract editor for various publishers, including Barbour Publishing, Electric Moon Publishing, Bold Vision Books and others. He's also on staff with The Christian Communicator Manuscript Critique Service."

LESLIE L. MCKEE EDITING
lmckeeediting@gmail.com | *lmckeeediting.wixsite.com/lmckeeediting*

Contact: email

Services: back-cover copy, copyediting, discussion questions for

books, proofreading, substantive/developmental editing
Types of manuscripts: adult, Bible studies, devotionals, easy readers, middle grade, nonfiction books, novels, poetry, short stories, teen/YA
Charges: flat fee, page rate, word rate
Credentials/experience: "Freelance editor and proofreader with various publishing houses (large and small) since 2012. I work with traditionally published and self-published/indie authors. I'm a member of The Christian PEN and American Christian Fiction Writers. See my website for details on services offered, as well as testimonials and a portfolio."

LESLIE SANTAMARIA
PO Box 195861, Winter Springs, FL 32719
www.lesliesantamaria.com
Contact: website
Services: copyediting, manuscript evaluation, proofreading, substantive/developmental editing, writing coach
Types of manuscripts: children's magazines, easy readers, middle grade, picture books, teen/YA
Charges: page rate
Credentials/experience: "Leslie Santamaria specializes in children's literature. With over 200 pieces published in periodicals, including *Highlights for Children, Pockets,* and *Spider,* and a picture book, Leslie earned a Master of Fine Arts in Creative Writing for Children from Spalding University. Her debut middle grade novel with a major publisher is scheduled for 2026. A longtime freelance editor for publishers, businesses, ministries, and individuals, she is a frequent contest judge and workshop presenter. Leslie has coached many writers to publication and would love to help you too."

LIBBY GONTARZ
libbygontarz@gmail.com | libbygontarz.com
Contact: email, phone
Services: copyediting, substantive/developmental editing
Types of manuscripts: adult, articles, Bible studies, curriculum, devotionals, nonfiction books
Charges: custom, page rate, word rate
Credentials/experience: "After a career of teaching and nationwide educational training, I accepted a curriculum development position at an educational publishing company. Writing lessons and assessments gradually led into editing. Since 2015, I have focused on Christian

nonfiction, editing for various publishers and individuals. Earned 2022 Excellence in Editing award for copyediting winning book, *On Wings Like Eagles*. Worked on editing team for two other award-winning books—a devotional and a business book. Your project deserves professional editing!"

LIFE LAUNCH ME | JANE RUBIETTA

9030 Federal Ct., Des Plaines, IL 60016 | 847-363-6364
jane@lifelaunchme.com | *www.LifeLaunchMe.com*

Contact: email, phone
Services: coauthoring, copyediting, discussion questions for books, ghostwriting, manuscript evaluation, proofreading, substantive/developmental editing, writing coach
Types of manuscripts: adult, articles, book proposals, devotionals, nonfiction books, novels, query letters
Charges: hourly rate
Credentials/experience: "The author of 21 books and hundreds of articles and devotionals, Jane has helped launch many writing careers as a writing coach and editor. Her writing savvy and marketing background help writers find their own voices and progress in their callings. She can turn one idea into 100 articles and numerous books."

LIGHTNING EDITING SERVICES | DENISE LOOCK

699 Golf Course Rd., Waynesville, NC 28786 | 908-868-5854
denise@lightningeditingservices.com | *www.lightningeditingservices.com*

Contact: email, website
Services: coauthoring, copyediting, discussion questions for books, ghostwriting, manuscript evaluation, proofreading, substantive/developmental editing
Types of manuscripts: adult, articles, Bible studies, book proposals, devotionals, nonfiction books, teen/YA
Charges: flat fee, hourly rate
Credentials/experience: "Former high school English teacher and college instructor Denise Loock is a general editor for Iron Stream Media and also accepts freelance projects. With thirty years of experience in the academic world coupled with ten years in the publishing industry, she helps writers produce books that attract publishers and engage readers."

LISA BARTELT

lmbartelt@gmail.com | lisabartelt.com/the-work

Contact: website

Services: back-cover copy, coauthoring, copyediting, manuscript evaluation, proofreading

Types of manuscripts: nonfiction books, novels

Charges: hourly rate

Credentials/experience: "20 years of experience including 8 years as a newspaper editor/reporter, 4 years as a contest judge for a well-known writing organization, ACFW contest judging, 2 co-authored books, avid reader of all kinds of books, middle school reading teacher's aide."

LISSA HALLS JOHNSON EDITORIAL

lissahallsjohnson@gmail.com | lissahallsjohnson.com

Contact: email

Services: copyediting, substantive/developmental editing

Types of manuscripts: adult, novels, short stories, teen/YA

Charges: hourly rate

Credentials/experience: "I have 35+ years of writing and editing experience on both sides of the publishing desk, so I understand what a writer needs personally and editorially. I have taught conference seminars on how to write and/or edit. I have written 20 published books. Most of my written work has been in the form of novels, although I have also written (and edited) nonfiction, articles, short stories, and radio dramas as well as pre-writing chapters for other writers. Some of the books I have edited have won awards and/or starred *Publisher's Weekly* reviews."

LITTLE FOXES EDITING | LAUREN SIMONIC

littlefoxesediting.godaddysites.com

Contact: website

Services: back-cover copy, coauthoring, copyediting, discussion questions for books, ghostwriting, proofreading, substantive/developmental editing, writing coach

Types of manuscripts: academic, articles, Bible studies, curriculum, devotionals, gift books, nonfiction books, poetry, short stories, technical material

Charges: custom, flat fee, hourly rate, word rate

Credentials/experience: "Lauren Simonic has been a freelance editor and writer since 1996 specializing in Christian nonfiction. She holds a degree in Literature and Journalism from the University of North Florida and has worked extensively with self-publishing new authors and traditional Christian publishers. Lauren has expertise with memoir, self-help, devotionals, theological works, curricula, articles, Bible studies and more. Her desire is to help authors catch all the little problems that spoil the finished presentation of the message God put in their heart to proclaim—to catch 'the little foxes that spoil the vines' (Song of Sol. 2:15)."

LOGOS WORD DESIGNS, LLC | LINDA L. NATHAN
PO Box 735, Maple Falls, WA 98266-0735 | 360-599-3429
linda@logosword.com | *www.logosword.com*

Contact: email, website
Services: back-cover copy, copyediting, manuscript evaluation
Types of manuscripts: adult, articles, Bible studies, devotionals, gift books, nonfiction books, novels, short stories, teen/YA
Charges: custom, flat fee, hourly rate, word rate
Credentials/experience: "Owner and Managing Editor Linda Nathan has over 30 years of experience as an independent freelance writer, editor, and publishing consultant, working with authors and institutions on a wide range of projects. She currently is semi-retired and takes only select projects. Linda is a former Gold Member of the Christian PEN and a former freelance staff editor with Redemption Press. She has a B.A. in Psychology from the University of Oregon and master's level work in that area, as well as 10 years of experience in the legal field as a paralegal, legal secretary, and notary public. She has managed Logos Word Designs since 1992."

LOUISE M. GOUGE, COPYEDITOR
900 Jamison Loop #105, Kissimmee, FL 34744 | 407-694-5765
Louisemgouge@aol.com | *louisemgougeauthor.blogspot.com*

Contact: email
Services: copyediting, substantive/developmental editing
Types of manuscripts: novels
Charges: word rate
Credentials/experience: "Louise M. Gouge is a retired college English professor and the author of twenty-eight novels. For editing, she utilizes *CMOS* and *CWMoS*. Copyediting includes checking grammar, punctuation, spelling, and phrasing. Substantive editing includes making sure character arcs are

balanced, the story is well-paced, and the conclusion is satisfying. Checking a client's research will raise the cost, the amount depending upon how much research is required. Novel editing $2,000–3,000, depending on word count and services required."

LUCIE WINBORNE

116 Hickory Rd., Longwood, FL 2750-2708 | 321-439-7743
lwinborne704@gmail.com | *www.bluetypewriter.com*

Contact: website
Services: copyediting, proofreading
Types of manuscripts: adult, devotionals, middle grade, nonfiction books, novels, poetry, short stories, teen/YA
Charges: hourly rate
Credentials/experience: "Conversant with *Chicago Manual of Style, Merriam-Webster Collegiate Dictionary,* Google Docs and Microsoft Word, with experience in fiction, nonfiction, educational, and business documents. Demonstrated adherence to deadlines and excellent communication and organizational skills."

MEGHAN STOLL EDITING

meghanbielinski.wordpress.com

Contact: website
Services: copyediting, manuscript evaluation, substantive/ developmental editing
Types of manuscripts: devotionals, nonfiction books, novels
Charges: hourly rate, word rate
Credentials/experience: "For the past six years, I've been helping independent authors bring their books to a high level of excellence. It's a great joy to aid them in producing works that are true to their vision and valuable and enjoyable to their audience. Please see my website for more information."

MG LITERARY SERVICES | MEGAN GERIG

mgliteraryservices@gmail.com | *mgliteraryservices.com*

Contact: website
Services: copyediting, proofreading, substantive/developmental editing
Types of manuscripts: middle grade, teen/YA
Charges: word rate
Credentials/experience: "I am a proofreader for Enclave Publishing and have also performed several developmental edits for a Penguin

Random House imprint. I've also worked with several incredible self-published and aspiring authors to bring their manuscripts to the next level. Client testimonials are available on my website."

MICHELLE MILLER PROOFREADING

diligentanalyzer@michellemillerproofreading.com | michellemillerproofreading.com

Contact: email
Services: proofreading
Types of manuscripts: Bible studies, devotionals, gift books, middle grade, nonfiction books, novels, short stories, teen/YA
Charges: word rate
Credentials/experience: "I have been proofreading for three years and am currently a proofreader for a small publishing house. With two courses completed, I strive to keep my skills up-to-date."

MIDWEST PROOFREADING SERVICES | TRACY ADAMS

midwest-proofreading-services.com

Contact: website
Services: copyediting, proofreading
Types of manuscripts: adult, articles, easy readers, middle grade, novels, short stories, teen/YA
Charges: word rate
Credentials/experience: "I am a passionate proofreader and copy editor, dedicated to helping authors create clean and polished manuscripts. With a keen eye for detail and a love for language, I thrive on refining written content to ensure clarity and coherence. Throughout my career, I have honed my skills in grammar, punctuation, and style, allowing me to meticulously polish texts across various genres and industries. My commitment to maintaining the author's voice while enhancing readability has earned me a reputation for delivering exceptional results. I find immense satisfaction in collaborating with writers, offering insightful suggestions and constructive feedback to bring their stories to life in the most impactful way. If you're seeking a meticulous proofreader and copy editor to elevate your work, I am eager to embark on this rewarding partnership with you."

MISSION AND MEDIA | MICHELLE RAYBURN

info@missionandmedia.com | www.missionandmedia.com

Contact: email
Services: copyediting, discussion questions for books, ghostwriting,

proofreading, substantive/developmental editing

Types of manuscripts: Bible studies, nonfiction books

Charges: flat fee, hourly rate, word rate

Credentials/experience: "Michelle Rayburn has been a freelance writer for more than 20 years and has edited for Christian publishers as well as for indie authors. Has also worked in the marketing and public relations industry. Michelle has an MA in ministry leadership and has published hundreds of articles and Bible studies as well as five books. She specializes in Christian living, Bible study, humor, and self-help."

MOUNTAIN CREEK BOOKS | KARA STARCHER

PO Box 21, Chloe, WV 25235 | 330-705-3399

mountaincreekbooks.com

Contact: website

Services: copyediting, ghostwriting, manuscript evaluation, proofreading, substantive/developmental editing, writing coach

Types of manuscripts: academic, adult, Bible studies, curriculum, devotionals, middle grade, nonfiction books, novels, teen/YA

Charges: flat fee, word rate

Credentials/experience: "BA in Publishing; 20+ years of editing and publishing experience for independent authors and small presses."

NOBLE CREATIVE, LLC | SCOTT NOBLE

PO Box 131402, St. Paul, MN 55113 | 651-494-4169

snoble@noblecreative.com | *www.noblecreative.com*

Contact: email

Services: copyediting, ghostwriting, manuscript evaluation, proofreading, substantive/developmental editing, writing coach

Types of manuscripts: adult, articles, book proposals, curriculum, devotionals, nonfiction books, query letters

Charges: flat fee

Credentials/experience: "Nearly twenty years of experience as an award-winning journalist, writer, editor, and proofreader. More than 1,000 published articles, many of them prompting radio and television appearances. Won several awards from Evangelical Press Association. Worked with dozens of published authors and other public figures, as well as first-time authors and small businesses. Have a BA and MS from St. Cloud State University and an MA from Bethel Seminary."

NOVEL IMPROVEMENT EDITORIAL SERVICES | JEANNE MARIE LEACH

PO Box 25663, Silverthorne, CO 80498

jeanne@novelimprovement.com | novelimprovement.com

Contact: website

Services: ghostwriting, manuscript evaluation, substantive/ developmental editing, writing coach

Types of manuscripts: book proposals, memoir, novels, query letters, short stories, teen/YA

Charges: flat fee

Credentials/experience: "Jeanne Marie Leach is a multi-published fiction author, speaker, mentor, and freelance editor specializing in fiction and memoirs. She is past coordinator and current Gold Member of The Christian PEN: Proofreaders and Editors Network and a member of the Christian Editor Connection. She has been editing for seventeen years and has edited over 160 books, of which many have gone on to win awards and make it to bestseller's lists."

OASHEIM EDITING SERVICES, LLC | CATHY OASHEIM

cathy@cathyoasheim.com

Contact: email

Services: copyediting, discussion questions for books, manuscript evaluation, proofreading, substantive/developmental editing, writing coach

Types of manuscripts: academic, articles, Bible studies, curriculum, devotionals, devotions, doctoral dissertations/theses, nonfiction books, novels, query letters, short stories, technical material

Charges: custom, flat fee, hourly rate, page rate, word rate

Credentials/experience: "Cathy is a professional freelance editor since 2012, blogger, and writing coach who specializes in nonfiction, true fiction, and fiction for Indy authors. She has judged over 1,000 Indie books for the Next Generation Indie Book Awards since 2016. Her services also include academic editing and fact checking for doctoral candidates (all have passed their boards), and blogs. A BS degree in Applied Psychology from Regis University allows Cathy to 'Refine Your Masterpiece.' Earlier engineering and military experiences support highly technical work and complex storytelling to get the rough draft manuscript out of the head, to the heart, and out of the plume to a polished product for the readers.

"Organizations: Author Alliance of Independent Authors, Journal Storage, National Association of Independent Writers & Editors,

Nonfiction Authors Association, Toastmasters International—
Distinguished Toastmaster, and The Christian PEN Proofreaders
and Editors Network—Silver Member."

PAGE & PIXEL PUBLICATIONS | SUSAN MOORE

pageandpixelpublications@gmail.com | *pageandpixelpublications.com*
> **Contact:** email
> **Services:** back-cover copy, coauthoring, copyediting, discussion
> questions for books, ghostwriting, indexing, manuscript evaluation,
> proofreading, substantive/developmental editing
> **Types of manuscripts:** academic, adult, articles, Bible studies, book
> proposals, curriculum, devotionals, easy readers, gift books, middle
> grade, nonfiction books, novels, poetry, query letters, scripts, short
> stories, technical material, teen/YA
> **Charges:** hourly rate
> **Credentials/experience:** "Whether your project requires extensive
> reworking or simple proofreading, with more than 30 years
> of editing experience I can put that professional edge on your
> publication. Your full length manuscript or article can be edited
> for continuity and grammar to industry standards so that it's
> ready to submit to your publisher. If your manuscript is only in the
> idea stage and you can't get started . . . If you suspect you need
> additional assistance beyond traditional editing . . . If you have a
> project or assignment that you just can't get to . . . If your research
> is complete but you don't know where to go from there—let's talk. I
> am accepting freelance assignments on a variety of topics."

PENCIL SHAVINGS | CHRISTINA FENNELL

christinajfennell@gmail.com | *lifeofawriter2.wixsite.com/pencilshavings*
> **Contact:** email
> **Services:** copyediting, substantive/developmental editing, writing
> coach
> **Types of manuscripts:** board/picture books, middle grade, scripts,
> teen/YA
> **Charges:** custom, word rate
> **Credentials/experience:** "Christina Fennell has a Bachelor's
> degree in English and nine years of experience editing a variety of
> genres. She specializes in editing children's books ranging from
> picture books to YA. She is a member of the Editorial Freelancers
> Association."

PERPEDIT PUBLISHING INK | BECKY LYLES

PO Box 190246, Boise, ID 83719 | 208-562-1592
beckylyles@beckylyles.com | *www.beckylyles.com*
> **Contact:** email
> **Services:** copyediting, ghostwriting, manuscript evaluation,
> proofreading, writing coach
> **Types of manuscripts:** adult, articles, Bible studies, book proposals,
> devotionals, nonfiction books, novels, query letters, short stories,
> teen/YA
> **Charges:** flat fee, hourly rate, word rate
> **Credentials/experience:** "15 years creating/proofing/editing articles,
> newsletters and magazines for government and corporate entities
> and 15 years freelance-editing fiction and nonfiction, including
> Bible studies, white papers, résumés, novels and short stories."

PICKY, PICKY INK | SUE MIHOLER

1075 Willow Lake Rd. N, Salem, OR 97303 | 503-393-3356
suemiholer@comcast.net
> **Contact:** email
> **Services:** back-cover copy, copyediting, proofreading
> **Types of manuscripts:** academic, articles, Bible studies, curriculum,
> devotionals, nonfiction books
> **Charges:** hourly rate
> **Credentials/experience:** "Sue Miholer has been a freelance line
> editor for more than 20 years on a part-time basis. Her business
> name is Picky, Picky Ink because early on a managing editor
> told her she was really "picky," which she took as a compliment.
> She specializes in nonfiction manuscripts and is not afraid to
> take on Bible study materials that will have her running all over
> *biblegateway.com* to be sure verses are quoted properly. Her client
> list is more than 50 names long, and she has edited multiple books
> for several of her clients."

PRAIRIE FALLS BOOKS | DEBRA L. BUTTERFIELD and TAMARA CLYMER

4810 Gene Field Rd. #2, St. Joseph, MO 64506 | 816-752-2171
prairiefallsbooks.com
> **Contact:** website
> **Services:** back-cover copy, copyediting, proofreading, substantive/
> developmental editing

Types of manuscripts: adult, articles, board/picture books, book proposals, devotionals, easy readers, gift books, middle grade, nonfiction books, novels, short stories, teen/YA

Charges: word rate

Credentials/experience: "An award-winning editorial team with decades of experience in Christian writing, editing, and publishing."

PRATHERINK LITERARY SERVICES | VICKI PRATHER

20 Parkview Rd., Clinton, MS 39056 | 601-573-4295

pratherINK@gmail.com | pratherink.wordpress.com

Contact: email

Services: coauthoring, copyediting, discussion questions for books, proofreading

Types of manuscripts: academic, articles, Bible studies, curriculum, devotionals, easy readers, gift books, middle grade, nonfiction books, novels, poetry, scripts, short stories, teen/YA

Charges: custom, flat fee, hourly rate, word rate

Credentials/experience: "I've been assisting first-time and experienced authors since 2014 in taking their writing to the next level, whether that means general advice or proofreading or being by their side through publishing. My first love is Christian works of any kind. I've authored and coauthored curriculums, Bible studies, and memoirs, as well as children's books & fiction. Before transitioning into freelance work, I wrote procedures manuals in my secretarial years, then taught writing skills and study skills and Bible to middle schoolers for a decade. If I'm *not* right for your editing needs, I'll tell you!"

PROFESSIONAL PUBLISHING SERVICES | CHRISTY CALLAHAN

professionalpublishingservices@gmail.com | professionalpublishingservicesus.weebly.com

Contact: website

Services: copyediting, discussion questions for books, French to English translation, French-language editing, manuscript evaluation, proofreading, substantive/developmental editing

Types of manuscripts: academic, adult, articles, Bible studies, curriculum, devotionals, easy readers, gift books, middle grade, nonfiction books, novels, teen/YA

Charges: custom

Credentials/experience: "Christy graduated Phi Beta Kappa from Carnegie Mellon University and then earned her MA in Intercultural Studies from Fuller Seminary. A gold member of The Christian PEN:

Proofreaders and Editors Network and certified by the Christian Editor Connection and Reedsy, she also completed the 40-hour Foundational Course (Christian track) with the Institute for Life Coach Training."

PWC EDITING | PAUL W. CONANT
527 Bayshore Pl., Dallas, TX 75217-7755 | 214-289-3397
pwcediting@gmail.com | PWC-editing.com

    Contact: website
    Services: copyediting, proofreading, substantive/developmental editing
    Types of manuscripts: academic, adult, articles, Bible studies, business materials, devotionals, nonfiction books, novels, poetry, short stories, technical material, textbooks
    Charges: hourly rate, word rate
    Credentials/experience: "Book editor since '94; textbook editor for 1.5 years; academic editor since 2001; gold member of The Christian PEN (Proofreaders and Editors Network); copyeditor for Christian Editing & Design, Redemption Press, and Baker Books."

READ. WRITE. PRAY. CARE, LLC | MARTI PIEPER
246 Maple Grove Rd., Seneca, GA 29678 | 352-409-3136
marti@martipieper.com | www.martipieper.com

    Contact: website
    Services: copyediting, ghostwriting, manuscript evaluation, substantive/developmental editing
    Types of manuscripts: adult, articles, book proposals, curriculum, devotionals, nonfiction books, query letters
    Charges: custom
    Credentials/experience: "I have served as ghostwriter/collaborative writer for eight traditionally published books, including a CBA bestseller, and edited many more. I have written and edited for both print and digital magazines, all of these in the Christian market."

REBECCA LUELLA MILLER'S EDITORIAL SERVICES
rluellam@yahoo.com | rewriterewordrework.wordpress.com

    Contact: email, website
    Services: back-cover copy, copyediting, manuscript evaluation, proofreading, substantive/developmental editing, writing coach
    Types of manuscripts: academic, adult, articles, devotionals, middle grade, nonfiction books, novels, query letters, short stories, teen/YA

Charges: page rate, word rate

Credentials/experience: "I became an editor as a direct result of my work as a critique partner. Behind that were the thirty years I spent as an English teacher evaluating student writing. Since 2004 I have had the privilege of working with numerous traditionally published authors, self-published authors, and aspiring authors alike."

REFINE SERVICES, LLC | KATE MOTAUNG

kate@refineservices.com | www.refineservices.com

Contact: email

Services: copyediting, proofreading

Types of manuscripts: academic, adult, articles, Bible studies, board/ picture books, book proposals, curriculum, devotionals, easy readers, gift books, middle grade, nonfiction books, novels, poetry, query letters, scripts, short stories, teen/YA

Charges: word rate

Credentials/experience: "Kate Motaung is the owner of Refine Services, LLC. She has been offering copyediting services since 2015 and enjoys serving a variety of authors. Visit *refineservices. com/reviews* to read testimonials from past clients."

REFINED PEN EDITS, LLC | JESSICA BOUDREAUX

jessica@refinedpenedits.com | www.refinedpenedits.com

Contact: email, website

Services: copyediting, manuscript evaluation, proofreading, substantive/developmental editing

Types of manuscripts: adult, novellas, novels, short stories, teen/YA

Charges: word rate

Credentials/experience: "10+ years studying writing. Certificates in editing courses from The PEN Institute (TPI). Continuing education with TPI, The Editorial Freelancers Association (EFA), and The Christian Writers Institute (CWI). Member of American Christian Fiction Writers (ACFW), The Christian PEN, and EFA. My goal is to create and support stories that glorify God and bring delight to his people."

REVISIONS BY RACHEL, LLC | RACHEL E. BRADLEY

1512 Lynhaven Ave., Richmond, VA 23224 | 866-872-3253

editor@RevisionsbyRachel.com | www.RevisionsbyRachel.com

Contact: email

Services: back-cover copy, coauthoring, copyediting, ghostwriting, indexing, manuscript evaluation, proofreading, substantive/developmental editing

Types of manuscripts: adult, Bible studies, curriculum, nonfiction books, novels, teen/YA

Charges: custom, flat fee, hourly rate, word rate

Credentials/experience: "Rachel holds a BS degree in Paralegal Studies from Northeastern State University in Oklahoma. She graduated *summa cum laude* in 2006 and has been awarded the Advanced Certified Paralegal designation by the National Association of Legal Assistants. She is a gold member of the Christian PEN: Proofreaders and Editors Network, is an established freelance editor with the Christian Editor Connection, is an instructor with the PEN Institute, and has served as a judge for the Excellence in Editing Award and as faculty for PENCON, the only conference for editors in the Christian market."

RICK STEELE EDITORIAL SERVICES

26 Dean Rd., Ringgold, GA 30736 | 706-937-8121
rsteelecam@gmail.com | *steeleeditorialservices.myportfolio.com*

Contact: email, website

Services: back-cover copy, book-contract evaluation, copyediting, manuscript evaluation, proofreading, substantive/developmental editing, writing coach

Types of manuscripts: academic, adult, articles, Bible studies, book proposals, curriculum, devotionals, gift books, middle grade, nonfiction books, novels, query letters, scripts, short stories, technical material, teen/YA

Charges: flat fee

Credentials/experience: "Rick Steele has adeptly managed the workflow of scores of titles for two different publishing houses, working with both fledgling and experienced authors along the way. While in different editorial capacities at AMG Publishers for over twenty years, the publishing house launched five different Bible study brands plus several fiction lines along with Christian living books, study Bibles, and reference works. Rick has traveled extensively to writer's conferences all over the United States, teaching workshops and helping writers with their craft. Since 2017, Rick has been using his skills and expertise to help clients achieve their publishing objectives."

ROBIN L. REED

1857 Alcan Dr., Medford, OR 97504 | 541-301-0869

robin@robinlreed.com | robinlreed.com

> **Contact:** email
> **Services:** copyediting, proofreading
> **Types of manuscripts:** academic, adult, Bible studies, curriculum, devotionals, easy readers, middle grade, nonfiction books, novels, short stories, teen/YA
> **Charges:** word rate
> **Credentials/experience:** "I'm an experienced editor who specializes in helping independent authors get their books into print with the highest possible quality. My priority is to preserve and strengthen my clients' original writing voice and support them through the editing process. I've received training through the PEN Institute and Proofread Anywhere as well as earning a master's degree in history from UC Riverside."

SARA ELLA EDITING AND COACHING

saraellawrites@gmail.com | saraella.com

> **Contact:** email
> **Services:** back-cover copy, copyediting, manuscript evaluation, proofreading, substantive/developmental editing, writing coach
> **Types of manuscripts:** adult, middle grade, novels, query letters, teen/YA
> **Charges:** word rate
> **Credentials/experience:** "Multi-published author of 6 young adult novels with Thomas Nelson/HarperCollins and Enclave Publishing. High school creative writing instructor. Three years of experience as a professional copywriter and proofreader. Experienced workshop instructor and keynote speaker for writing conferences across the country. Editor for Enclave Publishing. Freelance editor for 7+ years. Five years of experience as a social media coach and assistant."

SARA LAWSON

1509 Garfield Ave., South Pasadena, CA 91030 | 530-933-9838

sararereelawson@gmail.com | www.sarasbooks.com

> **Contact:** website
> **Services:** copyediting, substantive/developmental editing
> **Types of manuscripts:** Bible studies, devotionals, middle grade, novels, teen/YA

Charges: custom, word rate

Credentials/experience: "Sara Lawson has over 10 years of freelance editing experience working with fiction, nonfiction, and magazine articles of all lengths. She has also served within quite a few different Christian denominations, so she understands a variety of ministry contexts. She loves to help writers because she believes that everyone has a story to tell and no one should have to let technical writing abilities get in the way of telling that story."

SARAH HAMAKER WRITERS COACH

sarah@sarahhamaker.com | sarahhamakerfiction.com

Contact: email, website

Services: coauthoring, copyediting, discussion questions for books, ghostwriting, manuscript evaluation, proofreading, writing coach

Types of manuscripts: adult, articles, Bible studies, easy readers, middle grade, nonfiction books, novels, teen/YA

Charges: custom, flat fee, hourly rate, word rate

Credentials/experience: "I specialize in helping clients finish their current work-in-progress as well as editing their final drafts. I also have a heart to encourage writers to fulfill their calling from God to write."

SARAH HAYHURST EDITORIAL, LLC

1441 Haynescrest Ct., Grayson, GA 30017 | 470-825-2905

sarah@sarahhayhurst.com | www.sarahhayhurst.com

Contact: email, website

Services: copyediting, proofreading, substantive/developmental editing

Types of manuscripts: articles, Bible studies, curriculum, devotionals, nonfiction books, short stories

Charges: word rate

Credentials/experience: "Sarah is a gold-level member of The Christian PEN and Christian Editor Network with whom she passed extensive testing and demonstrated expertise in the substantive editing, copyediting, and proofreading of both fiction and nonfiction manuscripts. Sarah has over ten years of editing experience and started her editorial company in 2014."

SCRIBELANCE | VALARI WESTEREN

valari.westeren@scribelance.com

Contact: email

Services: copyediting, proofreading

Types of manuscripts: academic, adult, Bible studies, nonfiction books

Charges: word rate

Credentials/experience: "Valari helps Christian authors and scholars become authoritative voices in their fields with meticulous copy editing that Grammarly can't provide. Her academic studies have spanned both English and theology, and her skills have served academic Christian presses such as B&H Academic, debut authors publishing under Wipf&Stock, theology professors submitting PhD-level work, and various smaller Christian presses that publish memoirs and Bible studies. She is very knowledgeable of Scripture and double-checks all biblical references according to the chosen English translation(s)."

SCRIPTS4C.COM | DAVID M. HYDE

2245 Q St., Rio Linda, CA 95673 | 916-261-1816

scripts4c@icloud.com | *Scripts4c.com*

Contact: website

Services: copyediting, manuscript evaluation, novel adaptation, substantive/developmental editing

Types of manuscripts: scripts

Charges: flat fee

Credentials/experience: "Kairos Prize, multi-optioned, produced screenwriter."

SCRIVEN COMMUNICATIONS | KATHIE SCRIVEN

22 Ridge Rd. #220, Greenbelt, MD 20770 | 240-542-4602

KathieScriven@yahoo.com | *www.linkedin.com/in/kathie-scriven-46981037*

Contact: email, phone

Services: back-cover copy, coauthoring, copyediting, discussion questions for books, ghostwriting, manuscript evaluation, proofreading, substantive/developmental editing, writing coach

Types of manuscripts: academic, adult, articles, Bible studies, book proposals, devotions, easy readers, gift books, middle grade, nonfiction books, poetry, query letters, short stories, technical material, teen/YA

Charges: custom

Credentials/experience: "I specialize in offering editing and coaching services related to self-publishing and marketing books. Have completed over 95 nonfiction Christian book-editing assignments. Former editor of three Christian publications and freelance writer for mostly secular publications. Bachelor's degree in Mass Communication (concentration in journalism) from Towson University. I'm happy to send anyone interested a document that goes over my background, credentials and the services I offer in greater detail. Discount for those in full-time ministry."

SPEAK WRITE PLAY | ETHLEEN SAWYERR

225 DeMott Ln., Ste. 206, Somerset, NJ 08873 | 732-908-2211
editing@speakwriteplay.com | speakwriteplay.com

Contact: website

Services: copyediting, manuscript evaluation, proofreading, substantive/developmental editing

Types of manuscripts: adult, articles, Bible studies, devotionals, easy readers, middle grade, nonfiction books, novels, picture books, poetry, short stories

Charges: word rate

Credentials/experience: "We are a team of experienced manuscript editors and book translators who accompany authors and writers along the publication process. Books we've edited and/or translated have gone on to win notable awards and recognition. With years of experience and training under our proverbial belts, our aim is to help clients sharpen their craft as they release quality content to domestic and international audiences."

STICKS AND STONES | JAMIE CALLOWAY-HANAUER

snsedits@gmail.com | www.snsedits.com

Contact: email

Services: book-contract evaluation, coauthoring, copyediting, discussion questions for books, ghostwriting, manuscript evaluation, proofreading, substantive/developmental editing, writing coach

Types of manuscripts: adult, articles, book proposals, curriculum, devotionals, easy readers, middle grade, nonfiction books, novels, poetry, query letters, short stories, teen/YA

Charges: flat fee

Credentials/experience: "Jamie has eighteen years of experience in the editing field. Previously a full-time public interest attorney who also edited part-time, she is now the owner/operator of Sticks and Stones, where she specializes in academic, legal, and faith-based fiction and nonfiction for adults and teens; ghostwriting; and proposal and query review and development."

SUE A. FAIRCHILD, EDITOR

sueafairchild74@gmail.com | *www.sueafairchild.wordpress.com*

> **Contact:** email, website
> **Services:** back-cover copy, copyediting, discussion questions for books, manuscript evaluation, proofreading, substantive/developmental editing, writing coach
> **Types of manuscripts:** Bible studies, devotionals, gift books, middle grade, nonfiction books, novels, short stories, teen/YA
> **Charges:** hourly rate
> **Credentials/experience:** "Elk Lake Publishing Inc. editor (content, line, proofreading) since 2018, Gold member editor of The Christian PEN since 2021, have worked with both freelance clients and through publishing houses, bachelor of arts degree in graphic design (book formatting skills)."

SUSAN HOBBS EDITING

shobbs20@gmail.com | *www.susan-hobbs-editing.com*

> **Contact:** email
> **Services:** copyediting, manuscript evaluation, proofreading
> **Types of manuscripts:** articles, Bible studies, devotionals, nonfiction books
> **Charges:** word rate
> **Credentials/experience:** "As an editor, my primary goals are to preserve the author's voice and ensure the text is clear, concise, and compelling. My experience includes devotionals, memoirs, and other nonfiction works. I believe every writer deserves an editor that will be a cheerleader, challenger, and champion for their book."

SUSAN KING EDITORIAL SERVICES

1113 Brookside Dr., Nashville, TN 37069 | 615-202-6019

susankingedits.com

> **Contact:** website
> **Services:** coauthoring, copyediting, discussion questions for books, ghostwriting, manuscript evaluation, proofreading, substantive/ developmental editing, writing coach
> **Types of manuscripts:** academic, adult, articles, Bible studies, book proposals, devotionals, gift books, nonfiction books, novels, poetry, query letters, short stories, teen/YA
> **Charges:** hourly rate
> **Credentials/experience:** "Of my more than 30 years in the industry,

I served 24 years as an editor for *The Upper Room,* the world's premier daily devotional guide reaching 3 million subscribers in 100 countries and 35 languages. For the past 21 years, I have trained writers at over one hundred Christian writers' conferences in the U.S. and Canada. My professional life has also included teaching freshman English, American literature, and feature-writing classes at Lipscomb University, Biola University, and Abilene Christian University for a total of 27 years. Currently, I am the compiler and editor of the Short and Sweet anthology series."

SARA R. TURNQUIST

255 Alonzo Pl., Cunningham, TN 37052 | 407-288-7416
sara@saraturnquist.com | *saraturnquist.com/editing-rates*

> **Contact:** email
> **Services:** copyediting, proofreading, substantive/developmental editing
> **Types of manuscripts:** novels, short stories, teen/YA
> **Charges:** word rate
> **Credentials/experience:** "I first became an editor when I worked with Clean Reads (a medium sized publishing house out of Alabama). One of the editors on staff trained and honed my editing skills for content, developmental, line, and copy editing as well as proofing. Then I became an editor for that publishing house, editing science fiction, dystopian, contemporary romance, historical romance, historical time slip, and many other genres and subgenres. Since becoming a freelance editor, I have continued working in these genres and expanded into other subgenres of Clean and Christian Romance."

TANDEM SERVICES | JENNIFER CROSSWHITE

PO Box 220, Yucaipa, CA 92399 | 414-465-2567
jennifer@tandemservicesink.com | *www.tandemservicesink.com*

> **Contact:** email, website
> **Services:** back-cover copy, copyediting, copywriting, manuscript evaluation, proofreading, substantive/developmental editing, writing coach
> **Types of manuscripts:** adult, devotionals, middle grade, nonfiction books, novels, teen/YA
> **Charges:** custom, flat fee
> **Credentials/experience:** "Jennifer Crosswhite is owner and CEO of Tandem Services. Her experience spans both sides of the

publishing desk, from author to former managing editor of a Big 5 publisher for over 20 years. She and her team have worked with hundreds of authors at every stage to help them tell the story of their heart."

THREE FATES EDITING | SARAH GRACE LIU and VALERIE DIMINO

28 Close Hollow Dr., Hamlin, NY 14464

sarah.grace@threefatesediting.com | *www.threefatesediting.com*

Contact: website

Services: copyediting, ghostwriting, manuscript evaluation, proofreading, substantive/developmental editing

Types of manuscripts: academic, adult, Bible studies, middle grade, nonfiction books, novels, poetry, short stories, teen/YA

Charges: word rate

Credentials/experience: "I have an MA in Creative Writing and have run my own editing business since 2012. My true specialization is speculative fiction. For nonfiction, I am more comfortable with progressive texts."

TINSY WINSY EDITORIAL AND DESIGN STUDIO | BRENDA WILBEE

7959 Birch Bay Dr. #2, Blaine, WA 98230 | 360-389-6895

Brenda@BrendaWilbee.com | *BrendaWilbee.com*

Contact: email

Services: manuscript evaluation, substantive/developmental editing, writing coach

Types of manuscripts: adult, devotionals, memoir, nonfiction books, novels

Charges: custom, flat fee, hourly rate, page rate, word rate

Credentials/experience: "I hold a BA in Creative Writing, an MA in Professional Writing, and a degree in Graphic Design. I've written hundreds of articles and ten books, six of which were bestsellers, selling over 700,000 copies. For 17 years I wrote devotionals for Guideposts. My background includes teaching college composition and workshops on all aspects of writing at conferences. Some of my editorial and design clients include Edirol, Habitat for Humanity, Whatcom Community College, PageMill Press, DDA Publishing, Forever Books, and writers of fiction and nonfiction— just like yourself."

TISHA MARTIN EDITORIAL, LLC
www.tishamartin.com

Contact: website

Services: back-cover copy, copyediting, discussion questions for books, ghostwriting, manuscript evaluation, proofreading, self-publishing packages, substantive/developmental editing, writing coach

Types of manuscripts: adult, articles, curriculum, deaf subject matter, devotionals, gift books, memoir, nonfiction books, novels, query letters, scripts, teen/YA

Charges: custom, hourly rate, word rate

Credentials/experience: "I partner with brilliant, insightful authors to write and edit their best stories. Fiction, nonfiction, and creative memoir. Themes: redemption, faith, love, relationships, inspiration, leadership. Encouraging is my middle name. Joy and peace are my superpowers. Together, we work from a place of rest and grace, dedication and determination, patience and prayer."

TRAILBLAZE EDITORIAL SERVICES | SARAH BARNUM
sarah@trail-blazes.com | trail-blazes.com

Contact: email, website

Services: coauthoring, copyediting, manuscript evaluation, substantive/developmental editing

Types of manuscripts: adult, articles, Bible studies, devotionals, gift books, nonfiction books, short stories

Charges: word rate

Credentials/experience: "Sarah Barnum is an award-winning writer and editor. She holds a bachelor's degree with highest honors and serves as the Administrative Director for the West Coast Christian Writers. Sarah's short stories have been featured in multiple anthologies, and two memoirs she coauthored earned a Selah Award and the 2022 Christian Editor Connection's Excellence in Editing award, respectively."

TURN THE PAGE CRITIQUES | CINDY THOMSON
PO Box 298, Pataskala, OH 43062 | 614-354-3904
cindyswriting@gmail.com | cindyswriting.com/index.php/critique-service

Contact: website

Services: critiquing, manuscript evaluation, proofreading

Types of manuscripts: articles, book proposals, novels, query letters

Charges: flat fee

Credentials/experience: "Published author both traditionally and independently of fiction and non-fiction, author of numerous magazine articles, and a former mentor with the Jerry B. Jenkins Christian Writers Guild, I can help you get a solid footing as you prepare to publish."

WHALIN & ASSOCIATES | W. TERRY WHALIN

170 Ambroise, Newport Coast, CA 92657 | 949-423-2188

terry@terrywhalin.com | terrywhalin.blogspot.com

Contact: email

Services: coauthoring, discussion questions for books, ghostwriting, substantive/developmental editing

Types of manuscripts: adult, book proposals, devotionals, gift books, nonfiction books

Charges: flat fee

Credentials/experience: "Terry has written more than sixty books for traditional publishers, including one book that has sold more than 100,000 copies. He has written for more than fifty publications and worked in acquisitions at three publishing houses."

WORDMELON, INC. | MARGOT STARBUCK

308-B Northwood Cir., Durham, NC 27701 | 919-321-5440

wordmelon@gmail.com | www.margotstarbuck.com

Contact: email

Services: book coach, coauthoring, discussion questions for books, ghostwriting, manuscript evaluation, substantive/developmental editing, writing coach

Types of manuscripts: adult, book proposals, devotionals, nonfiction books, query letters

Charges: flat fee, word rate

Credentials/experience: "Margot, a graduate of Westmont College and Princeton Theological Seminary, has written dozens of books, including 2 *New York Times* bestsellers. She's passionate about helping writers get published."

WORDPOLISH EDITORIAL SERVICES | YVONNE KANU

yvonne@wordpolish.net | www.wordpolish.net

Contact: email, website

Services: copyediting, discussion questions for books, manuscript evaluation, proofreading, writing coach

Types of manuscripts: academic, Bible studies, devotionals, easy readers, nonfiction books, novels, short stories, teen/YA

Charges: word rate

Credentials/experience: "Over 10 years of experience in publishing, business communication, and technical writing. BA degree in English, and certificates in Editing, Publishing, and Technical Writing."

WORDPRO COMMUNICATION SERVICES | LIN JOHNSON

6525 Emerald Hill Ct., Ste. 104, Indianapolis, IN 46237-3098 | 847-296-3964

ljohnson@wordprocommunications.com | *wordprocommunications.com*

Contact: email

Services: back-cover copy, book-contract evaluation, copyediting, discussion questions for books, proofreading, small-group Bible study guides

Types of manuscripts: adult, Bible studies, curriculum, devotionals, nonfiction books

Charges: flat fee, hourly rate

Credentials/experience: "I've worked in Christian publishing for more than four decades as an in-house and freelance Bible curriculum editor and writer; award-winning writer of more than 70 books and hundreds of articles, devotions, and reviews; former managing editor of *Christian Communicator, Advanced Christian Writer,* and *Church Libraries;* and freelance editor and proofreader for traditional and independent publishing houses, organizations, and authors. Clients have praised me for being accurate, detailed, thorough, and deadline oriented.

"In addition, I've trained thousands of writers at conferences, as an adjunct writing instructor at Taylor University, and in international settings. I have an English minor from Adrian College, a BA in Christian education from Cedarville University, a BA in Bible-theology from Moody Bible Institute, and an MS in adult and continuing education from National-Louis University."

WRITE BY LISA | LISA THOMPSON

200 Laguna Dr. S, Litchfield Park, AZ 85340 | 623-258-5258

writebylisa@gmail.com | *www.writebylisa.com*

Contact: website

Services: back-cover copy, copyediting, discussion questions for books, ghostwriting, manuscript evaluation, proofreading, substantive/developmental editing, writing coach

Types of manuscripts: academic, adult, articles, Bible studies, board/picture books, book proposals, curriculum, devotionals, easy readers, middle grade, nonfiction books, novels, query letters, short stories, teen/YA

Charges: flat fee, hourly rate, word rate

Credentials/experience: "I have a degree in elementary education and a minor in English and Spanish. I have been editing since 2009. Nearly everything I edit is Christian content. I also subcontract for a fairly large Christian publisher and several smaller indie publishers in addition to editing for many Christian leaders, pastors, and lay people."

WRITE CONCEPTS, LLC | ALICE B. CRIDER

590 Highway 105 #107, Monument, CO 80132 | 719-651-0160
editoralicecrider@gmail.com | *www.alicecrider.com*

Contact: email, website

Services: back-cover copy, coauthoring, discussion questions for books, ghostwriting, manuscript evaluation, substantive/developmental editing, writing coach

Types of manuscripts: adult, book proposals, nonfiction books, novels

Charges: custom

Credentials/experience: "I am a freelance editor with 25+ years of experience in traditional book publishing, including eight years in a division of Random House. I have served in various editorial capacities in Christian publishing—including editor, literary agent, and director of acquisitions and development. I specialize in non-fiction, developmental, content, and line editing. I am skilled at analyzing a manuscript's strengths and weaknesses, and at suggesting improvements and revisions. I am also a certified life coach and author coach with 15+ years of experience in helping individuals and authors achieve their dreams and goals."

THE WRITE FLOURISH | TIM and NOLA PASSMORE

nola@thewriteflourish.com.au | *www.thewriteflourish.com.au*

Contact: email

Services: copyediting, manuscript evaluation, mentoring, proofreading, substantive/developmental editing

Types of manuscripts: academic, adult, articles, book proposals, devotionals, memoir, nonfiction books, novels, poetry, short stories, teen/YA

Charges: hourly rate

Credentials/experience: "Tim and Nola Passmore each have more than 20 years of experience as university academics. Nola also has a degree in creative writing. They founded The Write Flourish in 2014 and have edited a wide range of manuscripts across a variety of styles and genres. They have also had many of their own short pieces published including fiction, poetry, devotions, memoir, nonfiction and academic articles. They would love to help you add the right flourish to your manuscript."

WRITE HIS ANSWER MINISTRIES | MARLENE BAGNULL

951 Anders Rd., Lansdale, PA 19446 | 267-436-2503
mbagnull@aol.com | *writehisanswer.com/editingmentoring*

Contact: email
Services: copyediting, manuscript evaluation, proofreading, substantive/ developmental editing
Types of manuscripts: adult, articles, devotionals, nonfiction books, novels
Charges: flat fee, hourly rate
Credentials/experience: "More than forty years of experience in publishing, leading critique groups, and directing writers conferences; author of fourteen books and more than a thousand sales to Christian periodicals; editor, typesetter, and publisher of twelve Ampelos Press books."

WRITE JUSTIFIED | JUDY HAGEY

10628 Sharon Cir., Urbandale, IA 50322 | 386-562-7192
judy.hagey@gmail.com | *judyhagey.com*

Contact: email
Services: back-cover copy, copyediting, proofreading, writing coach
Types of manuscripts: academic, adult, Bible studies, devotionals, nonfiction books, novels
Charges: word rate
Credentials/experience: "Freelance editor with more than a dozen years of experience editing and proofreading for Christian publishers, self-publishing/independent authors, and academics with projects ranging from Christian nonfiction, Bible studies, and devotionals to adult and middle grade novels. Currently nonfiction managing editor for Elk Lake Publishing, Inc. Proficient in *CMS* and *CWMS*. Professional memberships include ACES, Christian Editors Association (CEA), and Gold Member of Christian Editor Connection. I can ensure your manuscript uses the right word at the right time in the right way."

WRITE NOW EDITING | KARIN BEERY

PO Box 31, Elk Rapids, MI 49629 | 231-350-0226

karin@writenowedits.com | *www.writenowedits.com*

Contact: email

Services: ghostwriting, manuscript evaluation, substantive/ developmental editing, writing coach

Types of manuscripts: nonfiction books, novels, query letters

Charges: word rate

Credentials/experience: "Turning good manuscripts into great books, Karin is a multi-award-winning author and editor with experience in traditional and self-publishing, freelance editing, and editing for publishers. She's an active member of the Christian Editors Association, including the Christian Editor Connection, and the National Association of Independent Writers and Editors. Her book *How to Edit Your Novel: Practical Tips for Strengthening Your Story* is a 2024 Selah Award winner and Golden Scroll runner-up."

WRITE PATHWAY EDITORIAL SERVICES | ANN KNOWLES

annknowles03@aol.com | *write-pathway.blogspot.com*

Contact: email

Services: coauthoring, copyediting, ghostwriting, proofreading, Spanish translation, transcription, writing coach

Types of manuscripts: adult, articles, book proposals, curriculum, devotionals, easy readers, gift books, middle grade, nonfiction books, novels, picture books, poetry, query letters, short stories, teen/YA

Charges: custom

Credentials/experience: "Retired educator, MA in education, certified ESL and Spanish; ESL training consultant for public schools and community colleges. I joined The Christian PEN: Proofreaders and Editors Network in 2005 and started Write Pathway in 2007. I have taken numerous courses from The Christian PEN, American Christian Fiction Writers, Write Integrity Press, and Christian Writers International."

WRITE WAY | PEGGYSUE WELLS

3419 E. 1000 N, Roanoke, IN 46783 | 260-433-2817

peggysuewells@gmail.com | *www.PeggySueWells.com*

Contact: email, website

Services: back-cover copy, book proposals, coauthoring, discussion questions for books, ghostwriting, substantive/developmental editing, writing coach

Types of manuscripts: adult, articles, Bible studies, book proposals, curriculum, devotionals, easy readers, gift books, middle grade, nonfiction books, novels, picture books, query letters, scripts, short stories, teen/YA

Charges: custom, flat fee, hourly rate

Credentials/experience: "Bestselling author of 34 books, collaborator of many more. I also polish manuscripts to be publish-ready, draft proposals, and prepare manuscripts to publish independently."

WRITE WAY COPYEDITING, LLC | DIANA SCHRAMER

diana@writewaycopyediting.com | *www.writewaycopyediting.com*

Contact: email

Services: copyediting, manuscript evaluation

Types of manuscripts: Bible studies, devotionals, gift books, memoir, nonfiction books, novels

Charges: word rate

Credentials/experience: "I started my business in 2010 and have copyedited 100+ book-length manuscripts and have reviewed 200+ manuscripts. In addition, I have copyedited and reviewed front- and back-cover copy as well as business-related documents and blogs."

WRITERS' COACH | EDDIE JONES and DIANA FLEGAL

2333 Barton Oaks Dr., Raleigh, NC 27614

writerscoach.us@gmail.com | *writerscoach.us*

Contact: email, website

Services: back-cover copy, book-contract evaluation, coauthoring, discussion questions for books, ghostwriting, manuscript evaluation, proofreading, substantive/developmental editing, writing coach

Types of manuscripts: adult, Bible studies, board/picture books, book proposals, devotionals, easy readers, gift books, middle grade, nonfiction books, novellas, query letters, scripts, short stories, teen/YA

Charges: custom, flat fee, monthly fee

Credentials/experience: "Do you need help with your novel or nonfiction project? Do you have a book idea but are not sure where to start? Book your free Introductory Coaching Session at *writerscoach. us*. With 30-plus years of experience in Christian publishing (agenting, editing, book publishing), our team can help you turn your stories, talks, sermons, life lessons, and podcasts into a book."

WRITER'S EDGE SERVICE, LLC

PO Box 310, Sisters, OR 97759

www.writersedgeservice.com

  Contact: website
  Services: manuscript evaluation
  Types of manuscripts: academic, adult, Bible studies, book proposals, devotionals, easy readers, gift books, middle grade, nonfiction books, novels, teen/YA
  Charges: $99
  Credentials/experience: "Manuscripts evaluated by professional Christian editors who've worked for major publishers." If the manuscript is approved, it's referred to more than 75 traditional publishers in the monthly or bimonthly newsletter.

WRITER'S TABLET PUBLISHING | TERRI WHITMIRE

3155 Hembree Trace Dr., Marietta, GA 30062 | 770-331-4326

Twhitmire@writerstablet.org | *www.Writerstablet.org*

  Contact: website
  Services: back-cover copy, copyediting, discussion questions for books, ghostwriting, indexing, manuscript evaluation, proofreading, substantive/developmental editing, writing coach
  Types of manuscripts: academic, adult, articles, Bible studies, curriculum, devotionals, easy readers, middle grade, nonfiction books, novels, picture books, poetry, scripts, short stories, teen/YA
  Charges: page rate
  Credentials/experience: "Writers Tablet has been helping aspiring writers become authors for over seven years, including three bestselling authors. With well over 60 years of combined experience, the Writers Tablet team consists of highly sought-after editors, publishers, poets, illustrators, and graphic artists who are industry experts. As a Christian assisted self-publishing agency, we pray with and for your project and attribute all of our success to our Father in heaven. With certifications in literature, editing, and graphic artists, the Writers Tablet team has received numerous awards, accolades, and recognition for its service to the writing community."

WRITING PURSUITS | KATHRESE MCKEE

27708 Tomball Pkwy., PMB 107, Tomball, TX 77375

kmckee@writingpursuits.com | *www.writingpursuits.com*

  Contact: website

Services: copyediting, manuscript evaluation, substantive/ developmental editing

Types of manuscripts: adult, middle grade, novels, short stories, teen/YA

Charges: flat fee, hourly rate

Credentials/experience: "Kathrese McKee has edited fiction professionally since 2014 in the following genres: urban and paranormal fantasy, fairytale retellings, dystopian and military science fiction, women's fiction, and contemporary and historical romance. She hosts the *Writing Pursuits* podcast and writes and produces a weekly newsletter, *Writing Pursuits Tips for Authors.*"

YO PRODUCTIONS, LLC | YOLONDA SANDERS

7185 E. Main St., Unit 1543, Reynoldsburg, OH 43068 | 614-452-4920

info_4u@yoproductions.net | *www.yoproductions.net*

Contact: email, phone, website

Services: back-cover copy, coauthoring, copyediting, discussion questions for books, ghostwriting, manuscript evaluation, proofreading, substantive/developmental editing, writing coach

Types of manuscripts: academic, adult, articles, Bible studies, curriculum, devotionals, easy readers, gift books, middle grade, nonfiction books, novels, poetry, query letters, scripts, short stories, technical material, teen/YA

Charges: custom, flat fee, hourly rate, word rate

Credentials/experience: "More than twenty years of professional editing and writing experience, editor and writer for a national publication."

21

PUBLICITY AND MARKETING SERVICES

THE ADAMS GROUP | GINA ADAMS
6688 Nolensville Rd. 108-149, Brentwood, TN 37027 | 615-776-1590
gina@adamsprgroup.com | *www.adamsprgroup.com*
   Contact: email, phone, website form
   Services: public relations, publicity campaigns, press releases, press-release distribution, press-kit creation, contributed content, video production
   Books: all genres
   Charges: flat fee
   Credentials/experience: "Honored by the prestigious Communicator Awards in 2019, 2020, and 2022, The Adams Group has represented faith-based authors for over three decades. Gina received her B.S. degree in business and marketing from Murray State University. She is a member of the National Religious Broadcasters and the Evangelical Press Association and serves on the Publicity Committee for the Arts of Southern Kentucky. Gina has also earned an Expert Rating Certification in Social Media Marketing and is a Hootsuite Certified Professional in Social Marketing."

ANCHOR PROJECT MANAGEMENT | MELISSA CLUTTER
PO Box 574, Anoka, MN 55303
melissa@anchorprojectmanagement.com | *www.anchorprojectmanagement.com*
   Contact: email, website form
   Services: support for launching new books and products, from prelaunch to post-release
   Books: no preference, previous experience with nonfiction and children's
   Charges: flat fee, hourly rate
   Credentials/experience: "Owner, Melissa Clutter, has more than

a decade of experience in managing projects and events, such as conferences, film festivals, new brand launches, and concerts. Melissa has skills and a keen understanding of the value of social media and email marketing."

APRICOT SERVICES | PETE FORD
Michigan
pete@apricotservices.com | *apricotservices.com*
- **Contact:** website form
- **Services:** digital platform audit, website design, social-media content, digital advertising, audience engagement, email marketing
- **Books:** nonfiction, fiction
- **Charges:** custom
- **Credentials/experience:** "We specialize in fostering meaningful digital connections, storytelling, and community-building to empower Christian authors and nonprofit organizations. Whether you're seeking to engage readers or launch a book, we're dedicated to serving your audience with tailored strategies that resonate and endure."

AUDRA JENNINGS PR | AUDRA JENNINGS
2609 Sandy Ln., Corsicana, TX 75110 | 903-874-8363
ajenningspr@gmail.com | *www.audrajennings.com*
- **Contact:** email
- **Services:** publicity, blog tours, social-media management, graphics packages
- **Specialty:** Christian books to Christian media
- **Books:** nonfiction, fiction, children's
- **Charges:** flat fee, hourly rate
- **Credentials/experience:** "I have worked as a publicist in the Christian market since 2002. For 16 years, I worked for two different agencies before going freelance on my own and have worked with every major Christian publisher over the years."

BANNER CONSULTING | MIKE LOOMIS
mike@mikeloomis.co | *www.mikeloomis.co*
- **Contact:** email, website form
- **Services:** book-launch planning, branding, article curation and placement, web development, PR
- **Specialty:** branding and marketing strategy
- **Books:** nonfiction
- **Charges:** custom

Credentials/experience: "I've worked with internationally known brands and *New York Times* bestsellers. I've helped clients get breakthrough PR, speaking engagements, and bestseller lists."

BBH LITERARY | LAURA BARDOLPH and DAVID BRATT
616-319-1641
bbhliterary.com/publicity
Laura Bardolph, laura@bbhliterary.com
David Bratt, david@bbhliterary.com

Contact: email, website form
Services: book publicity
Books: nonfiction
Charges: flat fee
Credentials/experience: "Nine years on staff in the marketing department at Eerdmans Publishing, with roles that included publicist, publicity manager, and director of marketing and publicity."

BBS PUBLISHING AND COMMUNICATIONS, LLC | PAMELA GOSSIAUX
734-846-0112
pam@pamelagossiaux.com | *BestsellingBookShepherd.com*

Contact: website form
Services: marketing, newsletters, blurbs, press kits, blogs, social media, and more
Specialty: bestseller campaigns
Books: fiction, nonfiction
Charges: custom, flat fee, hourly rate, package rates
Credentials/experience: "I've promoted authors to Amazon, *USA Today,* and *Wall Street Journal* bestsellers. I have dual degrees in Creative Writing and English Language and Literature from University of Michigan and am a speaker and international bestselling author."

BLUE RIDGE READER CONNECTIONS | EDIE MELSON
604 S. Almond Dr., Simpsonville, SC 29681 | 864-373-4232
ediegmelson@gmail.com | *blueridgereaderconnections.com*
Debb Hackett, brreaderconnection@gmail.com
Darlene Franklin, brreaderconnection@gmail.com
Heather Kreke, brreaderconnection@gmail.com

Contact: website form

Services: connecting authors to readers

Books: all clean reads in all genres

Charges: flat fee

Credentials/experience: "Our aim is to create a place for readers and book clubs to take their reading experience deeper. This is more than opening a new book. This is where you can find new authors or rediscover old favorites and interact with them, check out new writers, and hear about upcoming releases." BRRC falls under the Blue Ridge Mountains Christian Writers Conference.

THE BLYTHE DANIEL AGENCY, INC. | BLYTHE DANIEL and STEPHANIE ALTON

PO Box 64197, Colorado Springs, CO 80962-4197

www.theblythedanielagency.com/publicity-campaigns

Blythe Daniel, blythe@theblythedanielagency.com

Stephanie Alton, stephanie@theblythedanielagency.com

Contact: email

Services: range of publicity campaigns utilizing broadcast and print media and the Internet, including blogs, podcasts, articles, TV and radio interviews, book reviews, and book launches

Specialty: placing different genres of books with appropriate media and also with clients we represent who have media platforms; our relationships as literary agents of authors who interview guests has given us additional opportunities

Books: adult nonfiction, children's nonfiction and fiction, some adult fiction

Charges: custom

Credentials/experience: "Blythe Daniel managed the publicity for Thomas Nelson, a division of Harper Collins Christian Publishing, for 7 years and led the publicity team in media relations. She has almost 30 years of experience managing relationships with traditional media and is also an author and conducts her own publicity and marketing campaigns as well for clients. Stephanie Alton leads the launch teams and blog network for the agency's marketing clients."

BROOKSTONE CREATIVE GROUP | JOHN HERRING

100 Missionary Ridge, Birmingham, AL 35242 | 888-811-9934

www.brookstonecreativegroup.com

Contact: website form

Services: Amazon optimization, social-media assessment and consulting, video interviews, email and digital marketing, search-engine optimization, Facebook and Google ad management

Books: all

Charges: custom, flat fee

Credentials/experience: "Brookstone Creative Group is changing the landscape for how writers, authors, speakers, pastors, musicians, and other creatives navigate the ever-changing landscape of platform development. Through true and tested solutions, training, and community-building, Brookstone Creative Group guides their clients in the who, where, when, and how to inspirational success."

CELEBRATE LIT PUBLICITY | SANDRA BARELA and DENISE BARELA

45459 Stockton St., Beaumont, CA 92223 | 909-520-8603

Publicityservices@celebratelit.com | *www.celebratelit.com*

Denise Barela, editor.deniseb@gmail.com

Contact: email

Services: book tours, epic book-launch promos, review blasts, coaching, social-media-building promos, sidebar ads

Specialty: book tours, book launches

Books: any Christian or clean fiction and nonfiction

Charges: flat fee

Credentials/experience: "Our ministry began in 2015. We complete between 28 and 35 promos a month and have over 700,000 views per book tour on average. Both Denise and Sandra have master's degrees in English, which include marketing classes. We have scholarships available."

CHOICE MEDIA & COMMUNICATIONS | HEATHER ADAMS

404-423-8411

hello@choicemediacommunications.com | *www.choicemediacommunications.com*

Allie Ellers, senior publicist, Allie@ChoiceMediaCommunications.com

Devon Brown, senior publicist, Devon@ChoiceMediaCommunications.com

Morgan Sampson, digital media consultant,
Morgan@ChoiceMediaCommunications.com

Parker Nayman, digital marketing and social media manager,
Parker@ChoiceMediaCommunications.com

Contact: website form

Services: media relations, branding and strategy, social media, events, podcast production

Books: nonfiction
Charges: flat fee, retainer-based partnership
Credentials/experience: "Choice Media & Communications is a
  boutique media and communications business dedicated to providing
  clients with quality public relations. Choice helps authors create
  a clear communications plan, gain media coverage, and receive
  guidance they won't get anywhere else. With more than two decades
  of high-level professional communications experience across varying
  industries and with many of today's tastemakers and thought leaders,
  Choice founder Heather Adams created a public relations business
  marked with warmth and enthusiasm, strategic development, clear
  communication, detailed execution, and thorough reporting."

CHRISTIAN INDIE PUBLISHING ASSOCIATION | SUSAN NEAL

PO Box 481022, Charlotte, NC 28269 | 704-277-7194
cipa@christianpublishers.net | *www.christianpublishers.net*

   Contact: email, website form
   Services: resources and tools for publishing and marketing for
     independent authors
   Specialty: marketing services
   Books: all genres
   Credentials/experience: "Our mission is to support, strengthen, and
     promote independent authors and small publishers in the Christian
     marketplace. We have been doing this since 2004."

CREATIVE CORNERSTONES | CAYLAH COFFEEN

Huntsville, AL
creativecornerstones@gmail.com | *creativecornerstones.com*

   Contact: phone, website form
   Services: digital marketing—social media, Facebook and Amazon
     advertising—media kits, brand advising
   Books: fiction
   Charges: custom, flat fee, hourly rate
   Credentials/experience: "Currently I work as the marketing manager
     for Monster Ivy Publishing and have also helped multiple indie
     authors to reach nearly 10K followers and bring in reviews. Using
     Amazon ad campaigns and keyword metrics, in just a couple months I
     made one author's novel rise from rank #1,484 to #283 in Religious
     Science Fiction and Fantasy. The Kindle deal I ran brought it to #2 in
     free Christian Futuristic Fiction. In the past, I've also worked as the
     marketing manager for The Philips Museum of Art."

EABOOKS PUBLISHING | CHERI COWELL

5840 Red Bug Lake Rd., Winter Springs, FL 32708 | 407-712-3431
yourpartner@eabookspublishing.com | *www.eabookspublishing.com*
Monica Miller, director of marketing, monica@eabookspublishing.com

Contact: website form

Services: social-media and email campaigns, book launch, blog tour, electronic media kit, radio and YouTube interviews

Books: fiction, nonfiction, devotional, memoir, children's, Bible study

Charges: flat fee

Credentials/experience: "Serving Christian authors with integrity since 2010."

EPIC—A RESULTS AGENCY | JENNIFER WILLINGHAM

117 Saundersville Rd., Henderson, TN 37075 | 615-829-6441
hello@epic.inc | *epic.inc*

Contact: email, phone, website form

Services: social-media management, email marketing, publicity campaigns, press materials, media training, platform development

Credentials/experience: Group of PR and marketing specialists with years of experience.

JONES LITERARY | JASON JONES

2233 Surrey Dr., Murfreesboro, TN 37129-1043 | 512-720-2996
jonesliterary.com
Jason Jones, jason@jonesliterary.com
Mark Breta, mark@jonesliterary.com
Marianna Gibson, marianna@jonesliterary.com

Contact: website form

Services: publicity, PR campaigns, website buildouts, social-media management, speaking engagements, podcast production

Specialty: publicity for books at the intersection of faith and culture, full-service PR campaigns for traditionally published authors, DIY PR tools for self-published authors

Books: nonfiction, fiction, traditionally published, self-published

Charges: custom

Credentials/experience: "Jason led campaigns for HarperCollins Christian/Thomas Nelson's top nonfiction books, brands, and authors between 2007 and 2013. For many years since he has run one of the nation's most successful literary publicity agencies, having directed PR campaigns for over 400 books and 12 *New York Times* bestsellers. He is also host of *The Book Publicist Podcast* and an author."

MC WRITING SERVICES | SHARON CARTER JENKINS
2162 Spring Stuebner Rd., Ste. 140-1018, Spring, TX 77389 | 832-930-0604
sharon@mcwritingservices.com | www.mcwritingservices.com
 Contact: email, phone, website form
 Services: digital marketing services, public relations support
 Specialty: helping aspiring authors develop a marketing plan and
 strategy that fits their specific Kingdom calling
 Books: fiction, nonfiction, children's, inspirational
 Charges: custom
 Credentials/experience: "Sharon C. Jenkins is the inspirational
 principal for The Master Communicator's Writing Services. Her
 business provides writing and coaching services to small businesses,
 nonprofits, and authors. Her professional experience ranges from
 working as an editor for a major minority communications and
 marketing company to being an author's virtual coach. She is also a
 certified authors assistant and life coach. She's hosted events, such
 as the Authors Networking Summit, America's Favorite Author, and
 Write Your Book in 90 Days at Alpine Resort, and is the founder of
 the Authorpreneur Coach Certification Program."

MEDIA CONNECT | SHARON FARNELL
301 E. 57th St., New York, NY 10022 | 212-715-1600
sharon.farnell@finnpartners.com | www.media-connect.com
 Contact: email
 Services: full-service book publicity firm with custom campaigns for
 each title/author, offering satellite TV tours, radio tours, media tours,
 as well as outreach to national and local media
 Books: all types
 Charges: custom, package rates
 Credentials/experience: "We are a full-service book publicity agency;
 and for over 50 years, we've worked with publishers, authors, artists,
 organizations, and more."

SIDE DOOR COMMUNICATIONS | DEBBIE LYKINS
224-234-6699
deb@sidedoorcom.net | www.sidedoorcom.net
 Contact: website form

Services: media relations, press-kit creation, consulting, publicity-plan development

Books: primarily nonfiction, also children's and fiction but highly selective, no self-published novels, few self-published nonfiction

Charges: custom

Credentials/experience: "Side Door Communications is a national publicity agency that connects faith-based publishers and personalities with national and local media outlets as well as bloggers, with the goal of obtaining coverage in newspapers and magazines and on radio, television, and the Internet. Based in the Milwaukee, Wisconsin, area, founder Debbie Lykins has more than two decades of experience in marketing, publicity, and communications."

VERITAS COMMUNICATIONS | DON OTIS
318 Huppert Ln., Sandpoint, ID 83864 | 719-275-7775
don@veritasincorporated.com | *www.veritasincorporated.com*

Contact: email

Services: publicity, training, writing

Specialty: Christian, conservative, biblically relevant

Books: nonfiction

Charges: flat fee

Credentials/experience: "Publicist, author, radio host, and producer with more than 30 years of experience scheduling authors on radio, TV, and podcast interviews."

WILDFIRE MARKETING | ROB EAGAR
3625 Chartwell Dr., Suwanee, GA 30024 | 770-887-1462
Rob@StartaWildfire.com | *www.StartaWildfire.com*

Contact: phone, website form

Services: all facets of book marketing, including book launches, author websites, email marketing, social media, public speaking, and author-revenue growth

Specialty: book marketing

Books: all genres

Charges: flat fee

Credentials/experience: "Rob Eagar is the founder of Wildfire Marketing, a consulting practice that has coached more than 1,000 authors and helped books hit *The New York Times* best-seller list in three different categories: new fiction, new nonfiction, and backlist nonfiction. His company has attracted numerous bestselling authors, including Dr. Gary Chapman, Lysa TerKeurst, DeVon Franklin, Wanda Brunstetter, and Dr. John Townsend."

22

LEGAL AND ACCOUNTING SERVICES

CHRIS MORRIS, CPA, LLC

11209 N. 161st Ln., Surprise, AZ 85379 | 623-451-8182

cmorris@chrismorriscpa.com | *chrismorriscpa.com*

> **Contact:** email, website form
> **Services:** accounting, taxes
> **Charges:** flat fee, hourly rate
> **Credentials/experience:** "I have been working with creative entrepreneurs as a certified public accountant for the last decade, with about 65% of my business in the author space. Clients include publishers, agents, authors, editors, and various others related to this space. I know the tax and accounting codes related to this space because I've dedicated the last decade to it. I'm also a published author myself, so I have even more motivation to learn everything well."

TOM UMSTATTD, CPA

13276 Research Blvd., Austin, TX 78750 | 512-250-1090

tom@taxmantom.com | *www.taxmantom.com*

> **Contact:** phone, website form
> **Services:** accounting, consultations, tax review, taxes
> **Charges:** hourly rate
> **Credentials/experience:** More than forty years of experience in accounting and taxes.

WINTERS & KING

2448 E. 81st St., Ste. 5900, Tulsa, OK 74137 | 918-494-6868

wintersking.com/attorneys/thomas-j-winters

Contact: phone, website form

Services: contract negotiation

Credentials/experience: "We understand that negotiating with major publishers can feel like a lopsided process, and we work hard to level the playing field. Our experience in the publishing industry allows us to negotiate comprehensive and ironclad publishing contracts based on the realities of the industry. Our goal is to help our clients tell their stories on their own terms and receive the rightful benefits of their hard work through royalties and advances."

23

SPEAKING SERVICES

ADVANCED WRITERS AND SPEAKERS ASSOCIATION (AWSA)
PO Box 6421, Longmont, CO 80501
ReachOut2Linda@gmail.com | *awsa.com*
  Director: Linda Evans Shepherd
  Contact method: email
  Services: website directory, coaching, online training and community, speaking and publishing courses, annual conference prior to the opening of Christian Product Expo, Golden Scroll and Christian Market Book Awards, daily devotion, and *Leading Hearts* magazine
  Fee: women only, $50/year
  Qualifications: main membership: published author, speaker, publisher, screenwriter, or have some other major form of communication; protégé membership: beginning to intermediate communicators

CHRISTIAN COMMUNICATORS CONFERENCE
contact@christiancommunicators.com | *www.ChristianCommunicators.com*
  Director: Pam Mitchael
  Contact method: email
  Services: annual conference to educate, validate, and launch speakers to the next level for beginning or seasoned speakers; maximum 50 attendees

CHRISTIAN SPEAKER NETWORK
christianspeaker.net
  Contact method: website form
  Service: web page that is listed in the online database
  Fee: $39.95 per year

CHRISTIAN SPEAKERS BOOT CAMP
PO Box 150473, Grand Rapids, MI 49505 | 616-363-4608
robyn@robyndykstra.com | *christianspeakersbootcamp.com/csbc/bootcamp*

Director: Robyn Dykstra
Contact method: phone
Services: a personalized program to catapult your speaking skills and opportunities, teaching you to craft a full-length signature talk that promotes your book, book engagements, negotiate fees, and handle contracts
Fee: custom

CHRISTIAN WOMEN SPEAKERS

4001 Marlin Dr. SE, St. Petersburg, FL 33705 | 877-774-6986
viamarnie@gmail.com | *womenspeakers.com*

Director: Marnie Swedberg
Contact method: website form
Services: list speakers on the website, free and paid training available
Fees: free; $49.99/month or $499/year for higher ranking, extra features and benefits; $1598/one time for highest level of promotion
Qualifications: Christian woman older than 18, at least one public link (a homepage or social media presence), recommendations for your life in Christ and/or speaking ministry, actively involved in a local church
Representation: nonexclusive

DECLARE

info@wearedeclare.com | *wearedeclare.com*

Directors: Eryn Hall, Megan Fish
Contact method: email, website form
Services: annual retreat, blog, podcasts, coaching, and local workgroups

NEXT STEP COACHING SERVICES

amy@amycarroll.org | *amycarroll.org/coaching*

Director: Amy Carroll
Contact method: website form
Services: coaching for women speakers, quarterly newsletter

NORTHWEST CHRISTIAN SPEAKERS

Bellingham, WA 360-966-0203
Christie@freshlookthinking.com | *www.christianspeakersnw.com*

Director: Christie Miller

Contact method: website form

Services: speakers bureau, not limited to the Northwest; speaker training

Requirements: attend training workshops/evaluation session

SPEAK UP SPEAKER SERVICES

3141 Winged Foot Dr., Lakeland, FL 33803 | 586-481-7661

gene4speakup@aol.com | speakupspeakerservices.com

Director: Carol Kent

Contact method: mail

Services: speakers bureau, fee negotiation, contracts for services, speech and TV-interview coaching, SpeakUp Conference (see listing in "Writers Conferences and Seminars")

Qualifications: at least two books or CDs currently available in the Christian market and regularly speaking nationally; see list of application details to mail

Representation: exclusive, nonexclusive

24

WRITING EDUCATION RESOURCES

ANN KROEKER, WRITING COACH
annkroeker.com/podcasts

> **Type:** podcast
> **Host:** Ann Kroeker
> **Description:** "These writing podcast episodes offer practical tips and motivation for writers at all stages. . . . Tune in for solutions addressing anything from self-editing and goal-setting . . . to administrative and scheduling challenges."

AUTHOR CONSERVATORY
www.authorconservatory.com

> **Type:** organization, courses
> **Directors:** Brett Harris, Kara Swanson Matsumoto, Jaquelle Ferris
> **Description:** "An online, college alternative focused on writing craft and entrepreneurship. Learn the writing and business skills you need to pursue publication and avoid becoming a starving artist. Download our syllabus and apply for a free consultation on our website."

AUTHOR SCHOOL
authorschool.com/courses

> **Type:** courses
> **Director:** Rachelle Gardner
> **Description:** "Giving you the tools you need while pursuing publishing and blogging. Courses are jam-packed with information and resources to help you take the next step toward publishing or building and growing an author blog."

BOOK MARKETING MANIA
kimstewartmarketing.com/podcast

Type: podcast

Host: Kim Stewart

Description: "God never intended for it to feel frustrating or yucky when getting your book out there. He simply wants you to serve those He called you to, and share how you can help them. Books change lives. Wouldn't you rather spend your time writing than marketing? . . . Learn how to use the power of podcasting to build your audience, market your book, and steward your message in a way that honors God and your time."

THE BOOK PUBLICIST PODCAST
podcasts.apple.com/us/podcast/the-book-publicist-podcast/id1503562889

Type: podcast

Host: Jason Jones

Description: "Helping authors become their own publicist. Join long-time literary agent/publicist/host Jason Jones as he asks authors, publicists, and media the key questions." No new episodes.

CHRISTIAN BOOK ACADEMY
christianbookacademy.com

Type: organization

Directors: CJ and Shelley Hitz

Description: "Save time, money and the frustration of figuring it all out alone with our clear and confident self-publishing roadmap. Establish yourself as an expert, opening doors for speaking engagements and more! Develop effective marketing strategies to reach and engage readers. Connect with new writing friends in our supportive community that get you. Get tools and mentoring to help you overcome self-doubt, grow as a writer, and leave a legacy with your writing. See results in just 15-minutes a day with our monthly challenges. Make significant progress on your book in our Monthly Virtual Retreats. Reach your goals with Take Action Weeks and our Unlock Your Writing Program."

CHRISTIAN EDITORS ASSOCIATION
www.ChristianEditorsAssociation.com

Type: organization

Director: Kathy Ide, *KathyIde@ChristianEditorsAssociation.com*

Description: "Our goal is to equip, empower, and encourage editors in the Christian market through our four divisions. Join a community of like-minded professionals at The Christian PEN. Advance your knowledge and skills through The PEN Institute. Attend the PENCON editors conference. Once you're established, apply to join Christian Editor Connection to get more job leads. Christian Editors Association also sponsors the Editors' Choice Award, honoring superbly written and well-edited recently published books."

CHRISTIAN INDIE WRITERS' PODCAST

christianindiewriters.net/category/podcast

Type: podcast

Hosts: Jenifer Carll-Tong, Christina Cattane, Rhonda Hagerman, Jamie Hershberger

Description: "We inform, encourage and support Christian indie writers on the journey toward publication."

CHRISTIAN PUBLISHING SHOW

christianpublishingshow.com

Type: podcast

Host: Thomas Umstattd, Jr.

Description: "The *Christian Publishing Show* is a podcast to help Christian authors change the world. We talk about how to improve in the craft of writing, how to get published, and how to market effectively. Get expert advice from industry insiders."

CHRISTIAN WRITERS INSTITUTE

christianwritersinstitute.com

Type: organization, courses

Directors: Becky Antkowiak, president and owner; Megan Brown, executive director; Dan Balow, conference director; Steve Laube, president emeritus

Description: "The Christian Writers Institute was created to help Christians become proficient in the skills, craft, and business of writing. To build the Kingdom of God word-by-word. It does so by providing audio and video courses taught by some of the industry's best teachers. Originally founded in 1945, it is estimated that over 30,000 students have been trained by the Christian Writers Institute. It also runs the Write-to-Publish Conference held in Wheaton, IL."

CREATE IF WRITING

createifwriting.com/podcast-and-show-notes

Type: podcast

Host: Kirsten Oliphant

Description: "*Create If Writing* is a podcast for writers and bloggers dealing with authentic platform building online. You will hear from experts on list-building, connecting through Twitter, and how to utilize Facebook. But tools for building an audience would feel empty without a little inspiration, so these training episodes are balanced with inspirational interviews with writers who share their creative process, ups and downs, and how they have dealt with success or failure." No new episodes.

THE DAILY WRITER

www.kentsanders.net/podcast

Type: podcast

Host: Kent Sanders

Description: "*The Daily Writer* podcast helps you cultivate the mindset and habits for creative success. Each weekday, author and ghostwriter Kent Sanders brings you a short lesson on writing inspired by some of history's greatest artists, authors, and thinkers, both past and present. The weekend edition features listener Q&A, conversations with notable writers and creatives, and teaching to help you take a deeper dive as a writer."

DECLARE PODCAST

declareconference.com/declare-podcast

Type: podcast

Host: Anne Watson

Description: "The mission of Declare is to equip women to walk in their callings as Christian communicators." No new episodes.

FIGHTWRITE PODCAST

www.fightwrite.net/podcast

Type: podcast

Host: Carla Hoch

Description: "A writer's resource for writing believable action and fight scenes." No new episodes.

THE GATECRASHERS PODCAST

gatecrasherspodcast.libsyn.com

Type: podcast

Hosts: Amanda Luedeke, Charis Crowe

Description: "Teaming up to talk about both sides of publishing (self-publishing and traditional), Amanda and Charis share their combined twenty years of experience in the industry from both sides of the desk. They offer a glimpse behind the 'gates' as they share the realities, opportunities, and difficulties of the publishing world." No new episodes.

GRACEWRITERS PODCAST

gracewriters.libsyn.com

Type: podcast

Hosts: Belinda Pollard, Donita Bundy, Alison Joy

Description: "Discussions and interviews that encourage and equip Christian writers who are called to influence popular culture through books, blogs, songwriting, poetry, scriptwriting, copywriting and other forms—whether writing for Christian or mainstream audiences."

THE HABIT

thehabit.co/the-habit-podcast

Type: podcast

Host: Jonathan Rogers

Description: "Conversations with writers about writing."

HOME ROW: JUST KEEP WRITING

homerowpod.com

Type: podcast

Host: J. A. Medders

Description: "Get inspired to write from some of today's best writers. Listen. Learn. Just keep writing. You might learn how to get a book deal, write a best-seller, or quit your day job. Maybe you'll get that nudge you need to . . . write the blog, article, or book you've been thinking on for far too long. As Christians, our aim is to write in such a way that Jesus is made much of and the Church is encouraged to follow our risen Lord." No new episodes.

INK AND IMPACT PODCAST

dalenebickel.com/ink-and-impact

> **Type:** podcast
>
> **Host:** Dalene Bickel
>
> **Description:** "If you're a writer who desires to create books that counteract the worldly titles featured prominently on bookstore shelves today, takes their craft seriously, and understands that God should be glorified in all they do, then this podcast is for you. *Ink and Impact* addresses not only tips and best practices to help you improve your craft and magnify your message, but also guide you through the ENTIRE writing journey."

JERRY JENKINS

jerryjenkins.com/online-creative-writing-courses

> **Type:** courses
>
> **Director:** Jerry Jenkins
>
> **Description:** Jerry Jenkins, the author of more than 200 books with sales of more than 73 million copies, including the bestselling Left Behind series and The Chosen novels, offers online courses to help you "become the best writer you can be." Most courses are recordings of live workshops, and all come with lifetime access. Plus he gives away a number of free writing guides by email.

THE JERRY JENKINS WRITERS GUILD

jerrysguild.com

> **Type:** organization, courses
>
> **Director:** Jerry Jenkins
>
> **Description:** "The Writers Guild is like a writing conference you can access from anywhere 24/7. Instant access to video training on any writing topic. Additionally, several times each month Jerry answers your questions live, hosts new writing workshops, interviews industry experts, and so much more." Membership is open only periodically; email *wecare@jerryjenkins.com* for the next open period.

THE KEEP WRITING PODCAST

podcasts.apple.com/us/podcast/the-keep-writing-podcast/id1071732977?mt=2

> **Type:** podcast
>
> **Host:** Nika Maples
>
> **Description:** "Nika Maples is a writer, speaker, and lupus and stroke survivor who loves to help Christian writers conquer what's holding them back so they can finish, publish, and market their amazing books."

KINGDOM WRITERS
authors.libsyn.com/podcast

> **Type:** podcast
> **Hosts:** CJ and Shelley Hitz
> **Description:** "CJ and Shelley Hitz are passionate about equipping and empowering Christian writers of all genres to share their unique gifts with the world. This podcast is filled with spiritual encouragement as well as prayers to help you overcome the resistance you face as a writer. Your story matters! We believe that you have a specific role to play in the kingdom of heaven to impact lives for eternity. And because of this, we will pour out our lives encouraging writers like you to not only tell your stories but to take the courageous step of self-publishing your stories in books that will outlive you and leave behind a powerful legacy."

NOVEL MARKETING PODCAST
authormedia.com/novel-marketing

> **Type:** podcast
> **Host:** Thomas Umstattd Jr.
> **Description:** "This is the show for writers who want to build their platform, sell more books, and change the world with writing worth talking about. Whether you self-publish or are with a traditional house, this podcast will make book promotion fun and easy. Thomas Umstattd Jr. interviews publishers, indie authors and bestselling traditional authors about how to get published and sell more books."

ON PUBLISHING
www.thebinderyagency.com/podcast

> **Type:** podcast
> **Hosts:** Alex Field, Ingrid Beck
> **Description:** "*On Publishing* is a podcast about books and publishing.... Each episode features an interview with a publishing professional, including book editors and publishers, marketers and publicists, book designers and sales executives, as well as writers and authors from all categories and genres of publishing. In each episode, we'll seek to draw out relevant stories and experiences from our guests, as well as the key lessons or truths they've discovered, providing an inside look at the industry for aspiring writers, book lovers, and anyone seeking a career in book publishing."

PASTOR WRITER
pastorwriter.com/episodes

> **Type:** podcast
> **Host:** Chase Replogle
> **Description:** "Join me as I interview pastors, authors, and writing experts in my journey to better understand the calling and the craft of writing, reading, and living the Christian life."

THE PEN INSTITUTE
PENInstitute.com

> **Type:** courses
> **Director:** Susan K. Stewart
> **Description:** "Whether you are just beginning your editing career or are looking for an advanced class to update your skills, The PEN Institute has training opportunities for you. We offer group courses, one-on-one instruction, webinars, videos, lesson packs, and individual mentoring for aspiring and established freelance and in-house editors. Instructors are all experienced industry professionals."

THE PORTFOLIO LIFE WITH JEFF GOINS
podcasts.apple.com/us/podcast/the-portfolio-life-with-jeff-goins/id844091351

> **Type:** podcast
> **Host:** Jeff Goins
> **Description:** "Jeff Goins shares thoughts & ideas that will help you to pursue work that matters, make a difference with your art & discover your true voice!" No new episodes.

THE PROFITABLE WRITER
www.theprofitablewriter.com

> **Type:** organization
> **Director:** Kent Sanders
> **Description:** "The Profitable Writer Community is the perfect place to grow and learn alongside other writers who want to build more impact and income with their gifts. When you join the community, you'll gain access to practical teaching by Kent Sanders and other experts, as well as a vibrant group of like-minded writers who understand and support you."

THE PROFITABLE WRITER PODCAST

www.theprofitablewriter.com/podcasts/the-profitable-writer

> **Type:** podcast
> **Host:** Kent Sanders
> **Description:** *"The Profitable Writer Podcast* helps you create more impact and income with a writing business. Episodes feature interviews with guest experts as well as content to help you grow your business, become more productive, and make a bigger difference in the world."

THE PROLIFIC CREATOR

www.audacy.com/podcasts/the-prolific-writer-23495

> **Type:** podcast
> **Host:** Ryan Pelton
> **Description:** *"The Prolific Creator* is about life, art, and doing the generous thing. Follow writer, artist, and publisher Ryan J. Pelton as he discusses processes and strategies for writing lots of words, creating lots of art, and the motivation driving the whole thing. TPC podcast also interviews fellow prolific creators, writers, artists, and entrepreneurs as they discuss tips, tricks, and motivation for making art, and doing the generous thing in the world." No new episodes.

THE PURPOSEFUL PEN

www.amylynnsimon.com/purposeful-pen-podcast

> **Type:** podcast
> **Host:** Amy Lynn Simon
> **Description:** *"The Purposeful Pen* podcast is for you if you struggle to understand how to use your writing to glorify God and serve others. We talk about all those thoughts that bounce around in your head telling you that you aren't good enough; what the Bible has to say about earning money for your work; why it's important to know who your ideal reader is and what exactly you have to offer him or her; how to think outside the box and figure out what you really want to accomplish through your writing; how to create a writing life that brings joy to you, glory to God, and benefit to others."

REDEMPTION PRESS UNIVERSITY

redemptionpressuniversity.com

> **Type:** organization, courses
> **Director:** Carol Tetzlaff

Description: "Available to all Christian communicators, membership includes: tailored courses for intermediate, freshman, sophomore, junior, and senior levels, so you can start right where you are and grow at your own pace; thriving community, our private Facebook group to collaborate, seek feedback, and build valuable relationships that will push you toward success; personalized coaching through bimonthly Zoom sessions, providing guidance, insights, and help to overcome any obstacles you may face along the way; exclusive, live, industry-expert interviews, where you'll learn from the best in the business; office hours Q&A sessions to get personalized answers to your queries directly from our team of experienced instructors; help-desk support to assist you every step of the way; monthly email newsletter to stay up-to-date with the latest industry trends, tips, and resources; community coffee chat to engage in casual conversations, share insights, and foster connections with fellow communicators in a relaxed setting; access to all Redemption Press 3-day challenges and other online training at no charge."

REFINED PEN NETWORK

refined-pen.mn.co

Type: organization
Director: Jessica Boudreaux
Description: "This community provides writers access to ask questions on the craft of writing, get feedback on portions of their work, and build relationships with other writers. Benefits include professional critiques, editing advice, live Q&A sessions, word-sprint events, and a book club for reading and discussing books on the craft of writing. Members also get discounts on professional editing services through Refined Pen Edits."

ROB EAGAR MARKETING CONSULTANT

www.startawildfire.com

Type: courses
Director: Rob Eagar
Description: Offers a private Book Marketing Master Course anytime and two online video courses—Mastering Amazon for Authors and Sell Books on a Shoestring Budget—at various times during the year.

SERIOUS WRITER

seriouswriter.com

Type: organization, courses

Directors: Cyle Young, Bethany Jett

Description: "The mission of Serious Writer is to build community, create networking opportunities, share current industry information, and provide free and affordable instruction, training, and best practices for writing, marketing, and publishing."

SERIOUS WRITER PODCAST

seriouswriterpodcast.buzzsprout.com

Type: podcast

Hosts: Cyle Young, Bethany Jett

Description: "No matter where you are in your writing journey—just starting out, working on proposals, looking for an agent, or marketing your book—we're happy you're here and we're happy to help."

THE STORY BLENDER PODCAST

www.thestoryblender.com

Type: podcast

Host: Steven James

Description: "We are passionate about well-told, impactful stories. We love to listen to them. Watch them. Create them. So, we decided to talk with premier storytellers from around the country. Hear their stories and get their insights. From novelists to comedians to film makers to artists. Stories are told through a variety of people in a variety of ways. And here they are. The secrets of great storytelling from great storytellers."

THE STORYTELLER'S MISSION WITH ZENA DELL LOWE

www.buzzsprout.com/872170

Type: podcast

Host: Zena Dell Lowe

Description: "Zena Dell Lowe is a seasoned and engaging teacher with a passion for writers and storytellers. Her focused, concise, and practical episodes (all under 20 minutes) not only explore the nuts and bolts of the craft, but also dive deep into the inner life of the artist and the 'why' behind creativity. If you believe that story matters, you'll want to give this podcast a listen."

THE YOUNG WRITER

www.theyoungwriter.com/workshop

Type: organization, courses

Directors: Brett Harris, Jaquelle Ferris

Description: "A supportive online Christian community for young writers ages 12–25. Learn how to write more, hone your craft, and finish projects you're proud of—all while connecting with published authors and like-minded peers. Enrollment opens every January, May, and August."

WRITE FOR A REASON
writeforareason.buzzsprout.com

Type: podcast

Host: Janet Wilson

Description: "For Christians new to writing novels for kids and teens. Creative writing tips, encouragement and inspiration."

WRITE FROM THE DEEP
writefromthedeep.com/write-from-the-deep-podcast

Type: podcast

Hosts: Karen Ball, Erin Taylor Young

Description: "Encouragement, refreshment, and truth from writers, for writers. Every writer, at some point, faces the deep places of crushing trials and struggles. But the deep is also a place where we can learn to abide in God as never before. This podcast reminds writers they're not alone, and equips and helps them to embrace the deep, to discover their truest voice and message, and to share it with refined craft and renewed passion."

WRITER WEDNESDAYS WITH SARA R. TURNQUIST
podcasters.spotify.com/pod/show/sara-r-turnquist

Type: podcast

Host: Sara R. Turnquist

Description: "Sara is a coffee lovin', word slinging, historical romance author; and she desires to speak into that space in women's lives when they are struggling with momming, with faith, with life in general."

A WRITER'S DAY
podcasts.apple.com/us/podcast/a-writers-day/id1472104073

Type: podcast

Host: R. A. Douthitt

Description: "A podcast to help writers learn more about the craft, talk with published authors, and learn more about the publishing industry in order to have a competitive edge. Today, it takes more than just a good story to become a successful writer. You must know about marketing strategies, publishing options, and platforms that will help you stand out from the millions of writers out there. This podcast will help you."

THE WRITERLY LIFE

podcasts.apple.com/us/podcast/the-writerly-life/id914574328

Type: podcast

Hosts: hope*writers

Description: "Each episode of *The Writerly Life* offers you practical tips and interviews with publishing pros to help you skip the long learning curve and put you ahead of the game. *The Writerly Life* is all about balancing the art of writing with the business of publishing so that you can hustle without losing heart. Listen in and be inspired to keep putting your pen to the page. We'll help you find clarity to take the next step in your writing journey. You have words, and your words matter. Let's get them out into the world!" No new episodes.

WRITING AT THE RED HOUSE

www.writingattheredhouse.com/podcast-2

Type: podcast

Host: Kathi Lipp

Description: "The podcast is for those who love God and want to share His story through writing, speaking, social media—and yes—even marketing. . . . The refreshing and honest take on the 'industry' do's and don'ts, as well as insight on what makes you stand out from the rest, will not only entertain, but will serve in helping you propel your career to the next level."

WRITING FOR YOUR LIFE

writingforyourlife.com

Type: organization

Director: Kate Rademacher

Description: "Writing for Your Life is committed to offering a wide variety of useful resources and services to support spiritual writers. We offer online and in-person conferences featuring leading spiritual writers and publishing industry experts. We also provide a host of services and free resources to support your spiritual writing. We cannot guarantee that you will become a best-selling author, but we will help you take your best shot. Learn to tell your own story; write for your life!"

WRITING PURSUITS

www.writingpursuits.com/podcast

Type: podcast

Host: Kathrese McKee

Description: "*Writing Pursuits* is a weekly podcast for authors who drink too much coffee, endure judgmental looks from their furry writing companions, and struggle for words. If you are a writer seeking encouragement, information, and inspiration, this podcast is for you." No new episodes.

YOUR BEST WRITING LIFE

www.buzzsprout.com/1127762

Type: podcast

Host: Linda Goldfarb

Description: "Christian writing industry experts share weekly content for all levels of Christian writers. Whether you're a beginner or bestseller, you receive practical information and how-to application you can use to grow your writing career as a faith-based author. Each week, Linda Goldfarb and her guests cover various topics, including the craft of writing, fiction topics, nonfiction topics, self-care for writers, and the business of writing to name a few. If you're an aspiring Christian writer, we have content to help you grow. Published writers, we have current content to make your next book proposal, manuscript editing, speaking event, and writer's conference worth your time and energy."

25

CONTESTS AND AWARDS

A listing here does not guarantee endorsement of the contest. For guidelines on evaluating contests, go to *www.sfwa.org/ otherresources/for-authors/writer-beware/contests*.

Note: Dates may not be accurate since many sponsors had not posted their 2025 dates before press time.

CHILDREN AND TEENS

ABC AWARDS
inscriptionsbooks.com

Description: Sponsored by Inscriptions Books. The ABC (Awesome Books for Children) Awards were created to highlight the classic, moral stories for children, to bring back classic, fun books for kids and remove all the political agenda they face each day. Children's book authors who write fun, classic-style books for kids deserve to be awarded for their excellence in storytelling and their focus on the child's needs instead of societal agendas. Submissions are open to all members of the children's publishing industry, including authors and publishers worldwide who produce children's books written in English.

Deadline: September 1

Entry fee: $60

Prizes: One Gold winner and one runner-up per category. Each Gold-winning book will receive a packet containing an engraved gold medal, a personalized ABC Gold winner certificate and 20 embossed foil award book seals (more seals can be ordered), a front-page highlight on *inscriptionsbooks.com*, a free book review, social-media congratulations posts on all Inscriptions Books pages (Instagram, Twitter, LinkedIn, and Facebook), a winner seal for their website, and chosen as staff picks at *Inscriptionsbooks.com*. Runners up will receive a front-page highlight on *Inscriptionsbooks.com*, a free book review, social-media congratulations posts on all Inscriptions Books pages (Instagram, Twitter, LinkedIn, and Facebook), a winner seal for their website, and chosen as staff picks at *Inscriptionsbooks.com*.

CORETTA SCOTT KING BOOK AWARDS

www.ala.org/awards/books-media/coretta-scott-king-book-awards

> **Description:** Sponsored by American Library Association. Annual award for children's books published the previous year by African-American authors and/or illustrators. Books must promote an understanding and appreciation of the "American Dream of a pluralistic society" and fit one of these categories: preschool to grade 4, grades 5–8, grades 9–12.
> **Deadline:** December 1
> **Entry fee:** none
> **Prizes:** $1,000 and plaque

SOCIETY OF CHILDREN'S BOOK WRITERS AND ILLUSTRATORS

www.scbwi.org/awards-and-grants

> **Description:** Sponsors a variety of contests and grants.
> **Deadline:** varies
> **Entry fee:** none
> **Prizes:** vary

WORDS AND MUSIC PATTY FRIEDMANN WRITING COMPETITION

wordsandmusic.org/contest

> **Description:** Sponsored by *Peauxdunque Review*. Categories: poetry, fiction, creative nonfiction, and short story by a high-school student, plus multigenre "Beyond the Bars" for incarcerated juveniles. Previously unpublished work only. Length: prose, 7,500 words maximum; poetry, five pages maximum.
> **Deadline:** August 1
> **Entry fee:** varies by category
> **Prizes:** $500–750, depending on category, plus publication in *Peauxdunque Review*

FICTION

AMERICAN CHRISTIAN FICTION WRITERS CONTESTS
acfw.com/acfw-contests

Description: Genesis Contest for unpublished Christian fiction writers in a number of categories/genres. First Impressions Contest for unpublished writers. Carol Awards for best Christian fiction published the previous year.

Deadline: Genesis Contest and Carol Awards: submit between January 2 and March 1; First Impressions Contest: submit between September 2 and October 15

Entry fee: varies by category and membership

AWP PRIZE FOR THE NOVEL
www.awpwriter.org/contests/awp_award_series_overview

Description: Sponsored by Association of Writers and Writing Programs. Open to published and unpublished authors. Length: 60,000–110,000 words.

Deadline: submit between January 1 and February 28

Entry fee: $15 for members, $30 for nonmembers

Prizes: $5,500 and publication by the University of Nebraska Press

THE BARD FICTION PRIZE
www.bard.edu/bfp

Description: Sponsored by Bard College. Awarded to a promising, emerging young writer of fiction, 39 years or younger and an American citizen. Entries must be previously published.

Deadline: June 1

Entry fee: none

Prizes: $30,000 and appointment as writer-in-residence for one semester at Bard College, Annandale-on-Hudson, New York

BULWER-LYTTON FICTION CONTEST
www.bulwer-lytton.com

Description: Sponsored by San Jose State University English Department. For the worst opening line to a novel. Each submission must be a single sentence; multiple entries allowed. Entries will be judged by categories: children's & young adult, adventure, crime & detective, historical, fantasy & horror, romance, etc. Overall winners, as well as category winners. Length:

50–60 words maximum.
Deadline: June 30
Entry fee: none
Prizes: publication on the website

THE CROWN AWARD
acfwvirginia.com/acfw-virginia-the-crown

Description: Sponsored by ACFW Virginia. Gives unpublished writers the opportunity to have those all-important, first five pages of their Christian fiction manuscript evaluated by industry professionals. Requires a one-page synopsis, which is not scored. Categories: contemporary, contemporary romance, historical/historical romance/historical romantic suspense, mystery/thriller/suspense/ romantic suspense, speculative, young adult/middle grade.
Deadline: submit between July 1 and 29
Entry fee: chapter members, $20; nonmembers, $25
Prizes: badge, certificate, and crown lapel pin or tie clip for each category winner

FAITH, HOPE, & LOVE READER'S CHOICE AWARD
fhlchristianwriters.com/fhlcw-readers-choice-award

Description: Sponsored by Faith, Hope and Love Christian Writers (FHLCW). For Christian romances or Christian novels with romantic elements in print form. FHLCW defines Christian fiction as "stories written by writers whose worldview, influenced by their faith in the God of the Bible, is woven into the fabric of the book or manuscript." Entries should not include inappropriate or gratuitous demonstration of sin, whether in language (profanity), violence, or sexual situations. Length: varies with category.
Deadline: March 1
Entry fee: $25 for FHLCW members, $35 for nonmembers
Prizes: Winner in each category, engraved box; finalists in each category, certificate

FLANNERY O'CONNOR AWARD FOR SHORT FICTION
www.ugapress.org/index.php/series/FOC

Description: Sponsored by University of Georgia Press. For collections of short fiction. Length: 40,000–75,000 words. Contestants must be residents of North America.
Deadline: submit between April 1 and May 31
Prizes: $1,000 plus publication under a royalty book contract

GET PUBBED

scriveningspress.com/get-pubbed

> **Description:** Sponsored by Scrivenings Press. Unpublished entries are divided among four broad categories: speculative, historical, contemporary, and mystery/suspense. Submit the first ten pages.
> **Deadline:** August 15
> **Entry fee:** $25
> **Prizes:** grand prize: publishing contract, paid registration for annual author retreat, thorough critique of up to 25 pages of the manuscript, and $75 Amazon gift card; entry with the highest score in each genre: critique of up to 25 pages of the manuscript and $25 Amazon gift card

GRACE PALEY PRIZE FOR SHORT FICTION

www.awpwriter.org/contests/awp_award_series_overview

> **Description:** Sponsored by Association of Writers and Writing Programs. Short-story collections. May contain stories previously published in periodicals. Length: 150–300 pages.
> **Deadline:** submit between January 1 and February 28
> **Entry fee:** $25
> **Prizes:** $5,500 and publication

HAVOK

gohavok.com/submission-guidelines

> **Description:** Sponsored by Havok Publishing. For flash fiction 300–1,000 words. Havok operates as an ongoing publishing contest, with monthly themes and deadlines. Publishes stories in five major genres (mashups allowed): science fiction, fantasy, mystery, thriller, and comedy. Each month, 20 stories win the website publication round. Then each six-month season, 30 of those published stories win their way into print and ebook anthologies.
> **Deadline:** monthly
> **Entry fee:** free
> **Prizes:** minimum $50

JAMES JONES FIRST NOVEL FELLOWSHIP

www.wilkes.edu/academics/graduate-programs/creative-writing-ma-mfa/
james-jones-fellowship-contest.aspx

> **Description:** Sponsored by Wilkes University. For a first novel or novel-in-progress by a US writer who has not published a novel. Submit a

two-page outline and the first 50 pages of an unpublished novel.
Deadline: submit between October 1 and March 15
Entry fee: $30 plus $3 processing fee
Prizes: first place, $10,000; first runner-up, $3,000; second runner-up, $2,000

KATHERINE ANNE PORTER PRIZE IN SHORT FICTION

untpress.unt.edu/authors/porter-prize-submissions

Description: Sponsored by University of North Texas Press. Quality unpublished fiction by emerging writers of contemporary literature. Can be a combination of short-shorts, short stories, and novellas from 100 to 200 pages (27,500–50,000 words). Material should be previously unpublished in book form.
Deadline: submit between May 1 and June 30
Entry fee: $25
Prizes: $1,000 and publication by UNT Press

NOVEL STARTS

scriveningspress.com/novel-starts

Description: Sponsored by Scrivenings Press. For an unfinished novel in four genres: speculative, historical, contemporary, and mystery/suspense. Submit the first five pages.
Deadline: submit between June 21 and August 15
Entry fee: $25
Prizes: grand prize: author retreat, invitation to submit novel for consideration by Scrivenings Press once it is finished, thorough critique of up to 25 pages of the manuscript, and $75 Amazon gift card; entry with the highest score in each genre: critique of up to 25 pages of the manuscript and $25 Amazon gift card

REALM AWARDS

www.realmmakers.com/enter-the-awards

Description: Sponsored by The Faith and Fantasy Alliance. Genre awards in these categories: science fiction, fantasy, supernatural, paranormal, horror, young adult, middle grade, short fiction, audio, and specialty. Children's and graphic novels every other year. Length: novels, 60,000 words minimum; YA, 50,000 words minimum; middle grade, 20,000 words minimum; short stories, 10,000 words maximum; novellas, 10,000–50,000 words.
Deadline: submit between January 1 and 21
Entry fee: $20–50, depending on category

Prizes: commemorative award, award stickers, promotional opportunities, and the opportunity to be carried in the Realm Makers Mobile Bookstore and Bookish bookstore

REALM MAKER'S READERS' CHOICE AWARD

www.realmmakers.com/realm-award-readers-choice-alliance-award

Description: Sponsored by The Faith and Fantasy Alliance to give readers their say in what speculative fiction novels they enjoyed most in the preceding year. Only readers may nominate books in this contest. Books may be traditionally published or self-published.

Deadline: submit between May 1 and 15

Entry fee: none

Prizes: certificate of recognition

SERENA MCDONALD KENNEDY AWARD

www.snakenationpress.org/snakenation

Description: Sponsored by Snake Nation Press. Novellas up to 50,000 words or short-story collections up to 200 pages, published or unpublished.

Deadline: March 31

Entry fee: $30

Prizes: $1,000 and publication

TAKING FLIGHT

wingedpublications.com/about-us/taking-flight-contest-2020

Description: Sponsored by Winged Publications. For clean and inspirational romance in any subgenre except steamy or erotica. Submit synopsis and first three chapters.

Deadline: submit between February 1 and May 30

Entry fee: $25

Prizes: first, book contract; second, critique of synopsis and first three chapters; third, critique of synopsis

TOBIAS WOLFF AWARD FOR FICTION

www.bhreview.org/general-submissions-guidelines

Description: Sponsored by Western Washington University's *Bellingham Review*. Length: 5,000 words maximum.

Deadline: submit between December 1 and March 15

Entry fee: $20

Prizes: $1,000 plus publication

ZOETROPE: ALL-STORY SHORT FICTION COMPETITION

www.all-story.com/zoetrope-all-story-short-fiction-competition

> **Description:** Sponsored by *Zoetrope: All-Story* magazine to launch writing careers. Unpublished submissions only. Multiple entries accepted. Length: maximum 5,000 words.
>
> **Deadline:** October 1
>
> **Entry fee:** $30
>
> **Prizes:** first place, $1,000 and publication on the magazine's website; second place, $500; third place, $250; all three plus seven honorable mentions, representation by a talent agency

MULTIPLE GENRES

ANGEL BOOK AWARDS

ffbookfestival.com

> **Description:** Sponsored by Faith & Fellowship Book Festival to promote excellent books with a Christian worldview. The awards are open to all writers whose Christian fiction or nonfiction books were originally published between January 1 and June 30. Books entered must be written from a Christian worldview. There should be no profanity, gratuitous violence, graphic sex, or other objectionable material not accepted by Christian publishing standards.
>
> **Deadline:** June 30
>
> **Entry fee:** $50
>
> **Prizes:** certificate and logo that can be uploaded to blogs, used on memes, etc., for each winner; first place winners also receive a display award

BLUE RIDGE MOUNTAINS CHRISTIAN WRITERS CONFERENCE CONTESTS

www.blueridgeconference.com/contest-info

> **Description:** Sponsors three book contests for fiction or nonfiction: Foundation Awards and The Selah Awards. Look for details about guidelines, deadlines, and entry fees on the website after January 1.
>
> **Deadline:** varies by contest
>
> **Entry fee:** $35–45

THE BRAUN BOOK AWARDS

wordalivepress.ca/pages/the-braun-book-awards

> **Description:** Sponsored by Word Alive Press. For unpublished

Christian books written by Canadian citizens and permanent residents in Canada. Categories: nonfiction and fiction.

Deadline: March 15

Entry fee: none

Prizes: one fiction and one nonfiction manuscript will each receive a royalty-based book publishing contract; select number of secondary winners will also receive prizes, including credit toward publishing

CASCADE WRITING CONTEST

www.oregonchristianwriters.org/cascade-contest

Description: Sponsored by Cascade Christian Writers. Open to anyone, with emphasis on unpublished works. All contestants receive three score sheets from the judges reviewing their work, and finalists receive an additional two score sheets.

Deadline: submit between January 15 and February 15

Entry fee: $35 for members, $45 for nonmembers

Prizes: certificates to all finalists; in addition, pins to the winners

CHRISTIAN INDIE AWARDS

www.christianaward.com

Description: Sponsored by Christian Indie Publishing Association. This award is designed to promote and bring recognition to quality Christian books by small publishers and independently published authors. Books must be printed in English, for sale in the United States, and promote the Christian faith. Awards are offered in 18 categories. Publishers and authors may nominate titles.

Deadline: October 1

Entry fee: $89–109, depending on submission date

Prizes: trophy and promotion

EDITORS' CHOICE AWARD

christianeditorsassociation.com/eca

Description: Sponsored by Christian Editors Association. This award (which ran for seven years as Excellence in Editing Award) celebrates the authors, editors, and publishers behind books that are superbly written, well edited, and published by a Christian publisher or self-published by a Christian author. Each year's contest is open to books published the previous calendar year. Winners announced at PENCON. Judges' notes provided on request.

Deadline: December 31

Entry fee: $60 before November 16, $75 after; discounts for members of The Christian PEN and Christian Editor Connection

Prizes: promotion of finalist and winning books on websites and social media, digital emblems, printed stickers, certificates, blog and newsletter interviews; winning authors and editors receive select benefits from divisions of Christian Editors Association

ERIC HOFFER BOOK AWARD

www.hofferaward.com

Description: Twenty-four categories for books from small, academic, and independent presses, including self-published, ebooks, and older books.

Deadline: January 21

Entry fee: varies by category

Prizes: $5,000 grand prize, other prizes awarded in categories

HIGHER GOALS AWARDS

www.evangelicalpress.com/contest

Description: Sponsored by Evangelical Press Association. Awards are given in a variety of categories for periodical manuscripts published in the previous year. Although most submissions are made by publication staff members, associate EPA members may also submit their articles.

Deadline: submit between mid-November and January 19

Entry fee: $30

Prizes: certificate and critique sheet

ICBA AWARDS

inscriptionsbooks.com

Description: Sponsored by Inscriptions Books. ICBA (Inscriptions Christian Book Awards) Awards are for adult and young adult Christian fiction and nonfiction. Submissions are open to all members of the Christian publishing industry, including authors, editors, and publishers worldwide who produce books written in English.

Deadline: June 14

Entry fee: $60

Prizes: Three medalists per category: Gold, Silver, Bronze. Each medal-winning book will receive a packet containing a personalized award certificate; a custom gold, silver, or bronze medal; and 20 foil seals. (More seals may be ordered.) Related publicity includes a front-page highlight on *inscriptionsbooks.com*, a free book review, social-media congratulations posts on all Inscriptions Books pages (Instagram,

Twitter, LinkedIn, and Facebook), an HTML winners seal for their website, and chosen as staff picks at *inscriptionsbooks.com*.

NARRATIVE MAGAZINE CONTESTS

www.narrativemagazine.com/submit-your-work

Description: Biannual contests in a variety of categories, including short stories, essays, memoirs, poetry, and literary nonfiction. Entries must be previously unpublished. Length: varies by category.
Deadline: any time, June 15 for annual Narrative Prize
Entry fee: varies
Prizes: vary by category plus annual Narrative Prize of $5,000 for the best short story, novel excerpt, poem, or work of literary nonfiction published by a new or emerging writer in *Narrative*

NATIONAL WRITERS ASSOCIATION CONTESTS

www.nationalwriters.com/page/page/2734945.htm

Description: Sponsors five contests: novel, young writers, poetry, short, and David Raffelock Award for Publishing Excellence.
Deadline: varies by contest
Entry fee: varies by contest
Prizes: vary by contest

NEW LETTERS EDITOR'S CHOICE AWARD

www.newletters.org/editors-choice-award

Description: Sponsored by *New Letters*. For short narratives, whether they are stories, essays, poems, or hybrid forms. Length: maximum 1,000 words.
Deadline: submit between July 1 and November 13
Entry fee: $20
Prizes: $1,000 and publication in magazine

NEW MILLENNIUM WRITING AWARDS

newmillenniumwritings.submittable.com/submit

Description: Sponsored by New Millennium Writings. Fiction and nonfiction, 7,499 words maximum; flash fiction, 1,000 words maximum; poetry, three poems to five pages total. No restrictions as to style or subject matter.
Deadline: August 15
Entry fee: $20, $35 for two entries, $45 for three entries, $60 for four entries, $80 for five entries
Prizes: $1,000 plus publication for each category

TENNESSEE WILLIAMS/NEW ORLEANS LITERARY FESTIVAL
tennesseewilliams.net/contests

> **Description:** Tennessee Williams gained some early recognition by entering a writing contest. The festival that bears his name now sponsors writing contests in poetry, fiction, very short fiction, and one-act playwriting.
> **Deadline:** varies according to genre
> **Entry fee:** varies
> **Prizes:** vary by category

THE WORD GUILD CHRISTIAN WRITING AWARDS
thewordguild.com/contests

> **Description:** The Word Awards recognize the best work published in the previous year in a wide variety of categories and are open to all Canadian writers who are Christian. You do not need to be a member of The Word Guild to submit an entry, but members save money on their entry fees.
> **Deadline:** March 31
> **Entry fee:** varies according to award
> **Prizes:** vary according to award

WRITER'S DIGEST COMPETITIONS
www.writersdigest.com/writers-digest-competitions

> **Description:** Sponsored by *Writer's Digest*. Contests are available for a wide variety of genres, including inspirational, feature articles, short stories, poetry, personal essays, and self-published books.
> **Deadline:** varies according to contest
> **Entry fee:** varies
> **Prizes:** vary

THE WRITERS' UNION OF CANADA AWARDS & COMPETITIONS
www.writersunion.ca/awards

> **Description:** Short Prose Competition for Emerging Writers in nonfiction by an author who has not yet published a book. Length: 2,500 words maximum. Danuta Gleed Literary Award for the best first collection of short fiction.
> **Deadline:** varies
> **Entry fee:** varies
> **Prizes:** Short Prose, $2,500; Danuta, $10,000 plus two finalist awards of $1,000 each

NONFICTION

ANNIE DILLARD AWARD

bhreview.org/general-submissions-guidelines

Description: Sponsored by Western Washington University's *Bellingham Review*. Unpublished essays on any subject. Length: 5,000 words maximum.

Deadline: submit between December 1 and March 15

Entry fee: $20 for first submission, $10 each additional one

Prize: $1,000

BECHTEL PRIZE

teachersandwritersmagazine.org/bechtel-prize

Description: Sponsored by *Teachers & Writers Magazine*. For unpublished essays describing a creative writing teaching experience, project, or activity that demonstrates innovation in creative writing instruction. Length: 2,500 words maximum.

Deadline: submit between October 1 and January 10

Entry fee: $20

Prizes: $1,000 and publication

EVENT NON-FICTION CONTEST

www.eventmagazine.ca/contest-nf

Description: Sponsored by *EVENT* magazine. Unpublished creative nonfiction. Length: 5,000 words maximum.

Deadline: October 15

Entry fee: $34.95, includes a one-year subscription to *EVENT*

Prizes: first place, $1,500; second place, $1,000; third place, $500 plus publication

GUIDEPOSTS WRITERS WORKSHOP CONTEST

guideposts.org/writers-workshop-contest

Description: Contest is held in even years. Submit an original, unpublished, true, first-person story (your own or ghostwritten for another person) about an experience that changed your life. Show how faith made a difference. Length: 1,500 words maximum.

Deadline: mid-June

Entry fee: none

Prizes: all-expenses-paid, weeklong writers workshop in New York to learn about inspirational storytelling and writing for Guideposts publications for 12 winners

INTREPID TIMES TRAVEL WRITING COMPETITION
intrepidtimes.com/competitions

> **Description:** Sponsored by Exisle Publishing. *Intrepid Times* has a proud history of running narrative, travel-writing contests that focus on stories, places, and people.
> **Deadline:** varies
> **Entry fee:** free
> **Prizes:** first place, $150, publication on website, and possible publication in anthology; runners-up, $50

RICHARD J. MARGOLIS AWARD
www.margolisaward.org

> **Description:** Sponsored by Blue Mountain Center. Given annually to a promising young journalist or essayist whose work combines warmth, humor, wisdom, and concern with social justice. Submit at least two examples of published or unpublished work and a short biographical note, including a description of current and anticipated work. Length: 30 pages maximum.
> **Deadline:** July 1
> **Entry fee:** none
> **Prizes:** first place, $5,000 plus a one-month residency at the Blue Mountain Center in Blue Mountain Lake, New York; finalists, $1,000

SUE WILLIAM SILVERMAN PRIZE FOR CREATIVE NONFICTION
www.awpwriter.org/contests/awp_award_series_overview

> **Description:** Sponsored by Association of Writers and Writing Programs. Open to published and unpublished authors. Book collection of nonfiction manuscripts.
> **Deadline:** submit between January 1 and February 28
> **Entry fee:** $15 for members, $30 for nonmembers
> **Prizes:** $2,500 and publication with the University of Georgia Press

PLAYS/SCRIPTS/SCREENPLAYS

ACADEMY NICHOLL FELLOWSHIPS IN SCREENWRITING
www.oscars.org/nicholl/about

> **Description:** International contest open to any writer who has not

optioned or sold a treatment, teleplay, or screenplay for more than $35,000. May submit up to three scripts. Length: 70–160 pages.

Deadline: submit between March 1 and May 1

Entry fee: $50–120, depending on submission date

Prizes: up to five $35,000 fellowships; recipients will be expected to complete at least one original feature-film screenplay during the fellowship year

AMERICAN ZOETROPE SCREENPLAY COMPETITION

www.all-story.com/american-zoetrope-screenplay-competition

Description: Sponsored by *Zoetrope: All-Story* magazine. To find and promote new and innovative voices in cinema. For screenplays and television pilots. No entrant may have earned more than $50,000 as a screenwriter for theatrical films or television or for the sale of, or sale of an option to, any original story, treatment, screenplay, or teleplay. Prizes, fellowships, awards, and other contest winnings are not considered earnings and are excluded from this rule. Length: film scripts, 140 pages maximum; one-hour television pilot scripts, 70 pages maximum; half-hour television scripts, 40 pages maximum.

Deadline: September 4

Entry fee: $40–50, depending on submission date

Prizes: first place, $5,000 plus consideration for film option and development; nine finalists will also get this consideration

AUSTIN FILM FESTIVAL SCREENWRITERS COMPETITION

austinfilmfestival.com/submit

Description: Offers a number of contest categories, including feature film, short film, produced digital series, screenplay, teleplay, short screenplay, scripted digital series, fiction podcast, and play.

Deadline: varies by type

Entry fee: $35–70, varies by type and submission date

Prizes: $1,000–$5,000

KAIROS PRIZE FOR SPIRITUALLY UPLIFTING SCREENPLAYS

www.kairosprize.com

Description: Sponsored by Timothy Plan. For unpublished, unoptioned feature-length screenplays and TV pilot shows. Judges consider not only a script's entertainment value and craftsmanship, but also whether it is uplifting, inspirational, and spiritual and if it teaches lessons in ethics and morality. Length: 87–130 pages; will accept scripts up to 150 pages (not counting the title page) for an additional $20.

Deadline: submit between July 18 and October 31
Entry fee: varies, depending on submission date
Prizes: $15,000 each for first-time and professional screenwriters

MILDRED AND ALBERT PANOWSKI PLAYWRITING COMPETITION

www.nmu.edu/forestrobertstheatre/playwritingcompetition

Description: Sponsored by Forest Roberts Theatre, Northern Michigan University. Unpublished, unproduced, full-length plays. Biennual award to encourage and stimulate artistic growth among educational and professional playwrights. Provides students and faculty members the opportunity to mount and produce an original work on the university stage.
Deadline: submit between October 1 and November 1
Entry fee: none
Prizes: $2,000, a summer workshop, a fully mounted production, and transportation to Marquette, Michigan

MOONDANCE INTERNATIONAL FILM FESTIVAL COMPETITION

filmfreeway.com/MoondanceInternationalFilmFestival

Description: Offers a variety of awards for films, screenplays, librettos, and features that raise awareness about social issues.
Deadline: submit between February 1 and October 31
Entry fee: $25–50
Prizes: promotion to film companies for possible option

SCRIPTAPALOOZA SCREENPLAY COMPETITION

www.scriptapalooza.com/competition/how-to-enter

Description: Any screenplay from any genre considered; must be the original work of the author (multiple authorship acceptable). Shorts competition: screenplays fewer than 40 pages.
Deadline: submit between December 4 and March 4
Entry fee: $50–75, depending on category and deadline
Prizes: first place, $10,000; each genre winner, $500; plus access to 90 producers through Scriptapalooza's network

SCRIPTAPALOOZA TV COMPETITION

www.scriptapaloozatv.com/competition

Description: Scripts for television pilots, one-hour dramas, reality shows, and half-hour sitcoms. Length: pilots, 30–60 pages; one-hour drama, 50-60 pages; reality show, one- to five-page treatment; half-hour sitcom, 25-35 pages.

Deadline: submit between September 30 and October 14

Entry fee: $45-55, depending on deadline

Prizes: first place, $500; second place, $200; third place, $100 in each category; plus access to more than 50 producers, managers, and agents through Scriptapalooza's network

POETRY

49TH PARALLEL AWARD FOR POETRY

bhreview.org/general-submissions-guidelines

> **Description:** Sponsored by Western Washington University's *Bellingham Review*. Up to three poems in any style or on any subject.
>
> **Deadline:** submit between December 1 and March 15
>
> **Entry fee:** $20; international entries, $30
>
> **Prizes:** $1,000 and publication

ACADEMY OF AMERICAN POETS

poets.org/academy-american-poets/american-poets-prizes

> **Description:** See the website for a list of multiple contests and prizes.

BARBARA MANDIGO KELLY PEACE POETRY AWARDS

www.peacecontests.org/#poetry

> **Description:** Sponsored by Nuclear Age Peace Foundation. Awards to encourage poets to explore and illuminate positive visions of peace and the human spirit. Poems must be original, unpublished, and in English. May submit up to three poems for one entry fee.
>
> **Deadline:** July 15
>
> **Entry fee:** adults, $15; youth ages 13-18, $5; ages 12 and under, none
>
> **Prizes:** adult winner, $1,000; youth winner, $200; ages 12 and under, $200

CAVE CANEM NORTHWESTERN PRESS POETRY PRIZE

cavecanempoets.org/prizes/cave-canem-poetry-prize

> **Description:** Sponsored by Cave Canem Foundation. Supports the work of black poets of African descent with excellent manuscripts and who have published one book. Length: 48-75 pages.
>
> **Deadline:** submit between April 1 and June 12
>
> **Entry fee:** none

Prizes: $1,000 plus publication by Northwestern University Press, 15 copies of the book, and a feature reading in New York City

THE DONALD HALL PRIZE FOR POETRY
www.awpwriter.org/contests/awp_award_series_overview

Description: Sponsored by Association of Writers and Writing Programs. Open to published and unpublished authors. Length: 48 pages minimum.
Deadline: submit between January 1 and February 28
Entry fee: $15 for members, $30 for nonmembers
Prizes: $5,500 and publication by University of Pittsburgh Press

HOLLIS SUMMERS POETRY PRIZE
www.ohioswallow.com/poetry_prize

Description: Sponsored by Ohio University Press. For an unpublished collection of original poems, 60–95 pages. Open to both those who do not have a published book-length collection and to those who have.
Deadline: submit between April 1 and December 31
Entry fee: $30
Prizes: $1,000 plus publication in book form by Ohio University Press

JAMES LAUGHLIN AWARD
www.poets.org/academy-american-poets/james-laughlin-award-guidelines

Description: Sponsored by Academy of American Poets. To recognize a second full-length print book of original poetry. Author must have published one book of poetry in English in a standard edition (48 pages or more) in the United States or under contract and scheduled for publication during the current calendar year; publication of chapbooks (less than 48 pages) does not disqualify. Length: 48–100 pages.
Deadline: submit between July 1 and October 1
Entry fee: none
Prizes: $5,000 plus publication

JESSIE BRYCE NILES CHAPBOOK CONTEST
comstockreview.org

Description: Sponsored by *Comstock Review*. Submissions must be unpublished as a collection, but individual poems may have been published previously in journals. Length: 25–34 pages. Poems may run longer than one page.

Deadline: submit between August 1 and October 31
Entry fee: $30
Prizes: $1,000 plus publication and author copies

KATE TUFTS DISCOVERY AWARD

arts.cgu.edu/tufts-poetry-awards

Description: Sponsored by Claremont Graduate University. Award presented annually for a first poetry volume published in the preceding year by a poet of genuine promise. Length: at least 48 pages
Deadline: July 1
Entry fee: none
Prize: $10,000

KINGSLEY TUFTS POETRY AWARD

arts.cgu.edu/tufts-poetry-awards

Description: Sponsored by Claremont Graduate University. Presented annually for a published book of poetry by a midcareer poet to both honor the poet and provide the resources that allow artists to continue working toward the pinnacle of their craft.
Deadline: July 1
Entry fee: none
Prizes: $100,000 and one week residence at Claremont Graduate University

MURIEL CRAFT BAILEY MEMORIAL POETRY AWARD

comstockreview.org/annual-contest

Description: Sponsored by *Comstock Review*. Unpublished poems up to 60 lines/70 characters. No limit on number of submissions.
Deadline: submit between April 1 and July 15
Entry fee: $25 plus $2.50 online fee for five poems; mail: $5 per poem
Prizes: first place, $1,000; second place, $250; third place, $100

PATRICIA CLEARY MILLER AWARD FOR POETRY

www.newletters.org/patricia-cleary-miller-award-for-poetry

Description: Sponsored by *New Letters*. A single poetry entry may contain up to six poems/30 pages, and the poems need not be related.
Deadline: submit between November 1 and May 19
Entry fee: $24 each entry, includes a one-year subscription to *New Letters*
Prize: $2,500 for best group of three to six poems

PHILIP LEVINE PRIZE FOR POETRY

cah.fresnostate.edu/english/centers-projects/levineprize/index.html

> **Description:** Sponsored by the Creative Writing Department at California State University, Fresno. An annual book contest for original, previously unpublished, full-length poetry manuscripts. Length: 48–80 pages with no more than one poem per page.
>
> **Deadline:** submit between July 1 and September 30
>
> **Entry fee:** $25
>
> **Prizes:** $2,000, publication by Black Lawrence Press, 25 copies, public reading

POETRY SOCIETY OF VIRGINIA POETRY CONTESTS

www.poetrysocietyofvirginia.org/adult-contests

> **Description:** More than twenty-five categories for adults and students. Form and length limit of entries vary according to the contests. All entries must be unpublished, original, and not scheduled for publication before the winners of the competition are announced.
>
> **Deadline:** varies
>
> **Entry fee:** members, none; nonmembers, $6 per poem
>
> **Prizes:** vary by specific competition

SLIPSTREAM ANNUAL POETRY CHAPBOOK COMPETITION

www.slipstreampress.org/contest.html

> **Description:** Sponsored by Slipstream Press. Entries may be any style, format, or theme. Length: 40 pages maximum.
>
> **Deadline:** December 1
>
> **Entry fee:** $25
>
> **Prizes:** $1,000 plus 50 published copies of chapbook

TOM HOWARD/MARGARET REID POETRY CONTEST

winningwriters.com/our-contests/tom-howard-margaret-reid-poetry-contest

> **Description:** Sponsored by Winning Writers. Poetry in any style or genre. Published poetry accepted. Length: 250 lines maximum.
>
> **Deadline:** submit between April 15 and October 1
>
> **Entry fee:** $22 for up to three poems
>
> **Prizes:** Tom Howard Prize, $3,500 for poem in any style or genre; Margaret Reid Prize, $3,500 for poem that rhymes or has a traditional style; $300 each for ten honorable mentions in any style

VIOLET REED HAAS PRIZE FOR POETRY

www.snakenation.press/contests

> **Description:** Sponsored by Snake Nation Press. Length: 50–75 pages. Previously published eligible.
> **Deadline:** March 31
> **Entry fee:** $25
> **Prizes:** $1,000 plus publication

WERGLE FLOMP HUMOR POETRY CONTEST

winningwriters.com/our-contests/wergle-flomp-humor-poetry-contest-free

> **Description:** Sponsored by Winning Writers. Submit one published or unpublished humor poem up to 250 lines.
> **Deadline:** submit between August 15 and April 1
> **Entry fee:** none
> **Prizes:** first place, $2,000; second place, $500; third place, $250; ten honorable mentions, $100; plus the top 12 entries will be published online

RESOURCES FOR CONTESTS

These websites are sources for announcements about other contests.

DAILY WRITING TIPS

www.dailywritingtips.com/25-writing-competitions

FREELANCE WRITING

www.freelancewriting.com/writing-contests

FUNDS FOR WRITERS

fundsforwriters.com/contests

NEW PAGES

www.newpages.com/classifieds/big-list-of-writing-contests

POETS & WRITERS

www.pw.org/grants

THE WRITE LIFE

thewritelife.com/writing-contests

DENOMINATIONAL PUBLISHERS

Note: Not all of these houses and publications are owned by denominational publishing companies, and some publish for a broader audience than the denomination.

ANGLICAN
Anglican House Publishers
Anglican Journal

ASSEMBLIES OF GOD
Influence
LIVE
My Healthy Church
Take 5 Plus

BAPTIST
The Alabama Baptist
B&H Kids
B&H Publishing
The Baptist Bulletin
Baptist Standard
The Brink
D6 Family Ministry
HomeLife
Judson Press
Light
Mature Living

Open Windows
ParentLife
The Secret Place
Torchbearer Press

CATHOLIC
America
American Catholic Press
The Arlington Catholic Herald
Ave Maria Press
Catholic Book Publishing Corp.
Celebrate Life Magazine
Chrism Press
Columbia
Commonweal
Creative Communications for
    the Parish
Franciscan Media
LEAVES
Ligouri Publications
Liturgical Press
Living Faith

Living Faith Kids
Loyola Press
Our Sunday Visitor
Our Sunday Visitor, Inc.
Paraclete Press
Parish Liturgy
Pauline Books & Media
Paulist Press
Resurrection Press
Scepter Publishers
St. Anthony Messenger
Twenty-third Publications
U.S. Catholic

CHARISMATIC/ PENTECOSTAL

Charisma
Charisma House
Chosen
Emanate Books
testimony/Enrich
Whitaker House

CHRISTIAN CHURCH/ CHURCH OF CHRIST

Christian Standard
College Press Publishing
Leafwood Publishers
The Pilgrim Press

CHURCH OF GOD

Beginner's Friend
Bible Advocate
Explorers
Gems of Truth
Now What?
Warner Press
Youth Compass

DISCIPLES OF CHRIST

Chalice Press

EPISCOPAL

Church Publishing Incorporated
Forward Day by Day
Forward Movement

EVANGELICAL COVENANT

The Covenant Companion

LUTHERAN

Augsburg Fortress
Beaming Books
Broadleaf Books
Café
Canada Lutheran
The Canadian Lutheran
Christ in Our Home
Fortress Press
Gather
The Lutheran Witness
Northwestern Publishing House
The Word in Season

MENNONITE

Canadian Mennonite
Christian Leader
The Marketplace
The Messenger
Rejoice!

MESSIANIC

The Messianic Times

METHODIST

Abingdon Press
The Upper Room
Upper Room Books

NAZARENE

The Foundry Publishing
Holiness Today
Reflecting God
Standard

ORTHODOX

Ancient Faith Publishing
Chrism Press

PRESBYTERIAN

byFaith
Flyaway Books
*These Days: Daily Devotions for
    Living by Faith*
Westminster John Knox Press

QUAKER/FRIENDS

Friends Journal
Fruit of the Vine

REFORMED

Calla Press Publishing
Celebrate Lit Publishers

Christian Courier
P&R Publishing
Tulip Publishing

THE SALVATION ARMY

Caring Magazine
Faith & Friends
Just for Kids
Peer
The War Cry

SEVENTH-DAY ADVENTIST

Guide
The Journal of Adventist Education
Ministry
Our Little Friend
Pacific Press
Primary Treasure

WESLEYAN

The Foundry Publishing
Invite Resources
Light from the Word

PUBLISHING LINGO

My first week working in a bookstore I learned a valuable lesson. I had a stack of books in my arms that I had taken from a shipment in the back room. My boss walked by; said, "Steve, please put those in the dump"; and kept walking.

I paused and thought, *Why should I throw these away? They are brand new books!* To my chagrin, I discovered that, in bookstore lingo, a dump was a cardboard display in the front of the store.

The lesson I learned is that knowing the lingo can keep you from being confused or potentially misunderstanding some instructions. Like bookstores, writing and publishing have their own lingo. The following definitions will acquaint you with some of the more important terms.

ABA: American Booksellers Association. This acronym has come to mean the general market, as opposed to CBA, the Christian market.

Advance: Money a publisher pays to an author up front, against future royalties. The amount varies greatly from publisher to publisher and is often paid in two or three installments (on signing the contract, on delivery of the manuscript, and on publication).

AE: An abbreviation for Acquisitions Editor. Not all publishing houses use this abbreviation, but they all have people who acquire in their editorial departments.

All rights: An outright sale of a manuscript. The author has no further control over any subsidiary rights or reusing the piece. You must sign a contract for this agreement to be legal.

Anecdote: A short, poignant, real-life story, usually used to illustrate a single thought. It need not be humorous.

ARC: Advance Reader Copy. An early paperback (or ebook) version of a book sent out for reviews around four to six months prior to publication.

Assignment: When an editor asks a writer to create a specific manuscript for an agreed-on price.

As-told-to story: A true story you write as a first-person account about someone else.

Audience: The people who are expected to be reading your manuscript, in terms of age, life experience, knowledge of and interest level in the story or subject. Editors want to be sure writers understand their assumed audiences well.

Audiobooks: Spoken-word books available by streaming via the Internet, on compact disc, or MP3 file.

Backlist: A publisher's previously published books that are still in print a year or more after publication.

Bible versions:
AMP–Amplified Bible
ASV–American Standard Version
CB–Confraternity Bible (Catholic)
CEB–Common English Bible
CEV–Contemporary English Version
CJB–Complete Jewish Bible
CSB–Christian Standard Bible
ESV–English Standard Version
GNB–Good News Bible
GW–GOD'S WORD Translation
HCSB–Holman Christian Standard Bible (replaced by CSB)
ICB–International Children's Bible
KJV–King James Version
KJV21–21st Century King James Version
MEV–Modern English Version
MSG–The Message
NAB–New American Bible
NABRE–New American Bible Revised Edition
NASB–New American Standard Bible
NCV–New Century Version
NEB–New English Bible
NET–New English Translation
NIrV–New International Reader's Version

NIV–New International Version
NJB–New Jerusalem Bible
NKJV–New King James Version
NLT–New Living Translation
NRSV–New Revised Standard Version
NRSVue–New Revised Standard Version Updated Edition
PHILLIPS–J.B. Phillips New Testament
RSV–Revised Standard Version (replaced by NRSV)
TEV–Today's English Translation (aka Good News Bible)
TLB–The Living Bible
TNIV–Today's New International Version
VOICE–The Voice Bible Translation
WEB–World English Bible

Bio: Brief information about the author.

BIPOC: Black, Indigenous, and People of Color.

Bluelines: The last printer's proofs used to catch errors before a book or periodical is printed. May be physical pages or digital proofs in PDF.

BOB: Back-of-Book ad for the author's previous book(s) or a similar book released by the publisher. It uses the blank pages in the back of a book or extra pages at the end of an ebook.

Book proposal: Submission of a book idea to an agent or editor. It usually includes a hook, summary and purpose of the book, target market, uniqueness of the book compared to similar ones in the marketplace, chapter-by-chapter summaries or plot synopsis, marketing and promotion information, your credentials, and delivery date, plus one to three sample chapters, including the first one.

Byline: Author's name printed below the title of a book, article, etc.

Camera-ready copy: The text and artwork that are ready for the press.

Category romance: Novels of around 50,000–60,000 words that are published in categories and according to strict guidelines. For example, Love Inspired novels, the Christian division of Harlequin.

CBA: Christian Booksellers Association. The acronym has come to describe the Christian market as opposed to ABA, the general market. As an entity, CBA folded in 2019, but the acronym still applies when referring to the Christian publishing industry.

Chapbook: A small book or pamphlet containing poetry, etc.

Circulation: The number of copies sold or distributed of a periodical.

Clips: Copies of articles you have had published in periodicals.

Colophon: The publisher's emblem or imprint used on the title page or spine of a book or a statement at the end of a book with information about its production, such as the type of font used.

Column: A regularly appearing feature, section, or department in a periodical with the same heading. It's written by the same person or a different one each time.

Comp copies: Complimentary copies given to the author by the publisher on publication.

Comps: Shorthand for "comparable." The publisher may have comps on cover designs or titles to help position the book in the marketplace.

Concept statement: A 50- to 150-word summary of your proposed book.

Contributing editor: A freelance writer who has a regular column or writes regularly for the periodical.

Contributor's copy: Copy of an issue of a periodical sent to an author whose work appears in it.

Copyedit: The editor checks grammar, punctuation, and citations to make sure the work is accurate. More detailed than a developmental edit. Some publishers refer to this as the line edit.

Copyright: Legal protection of an author's work. A manuscript is automatically copyrighted in your name when you produce it. You don't need to register it with the Copyright Office unless you are self-publishing a book or other publication since a traditional publisher registers it for you.

Cover copy: Or "copy." The text on the back cover of a book, in the online description, or in marketing materials. For a hardcover, it can also include flap copy, the text on the inside dust-jacket flaps.

Cover letter: A letter that accompanies some article submissions. Usually it's needed only if you have to tell the editor something specific, to give your credentials for writing a manuscript of a technical nature, or to remind the editor that the manuscript was requested or expected. Often used as the introduction to a book proposal.

Credits, list of: A listing of your previously published works.

Critique: An evaluation of a manuscript.

Defamation: A written (libel) or spoken (slander) injury to the reputation of a living person or organization. If what is said is true, it cannot be defamatory; but that does not prevent the injured party from bringing a lawsuit.

Derivative work: A work derived from another work, such as a condensation or abridgment. Contact the copyright owner for permission before doing the abridgment, and be prepared to pay that owner a fee or royalty.

Developmental edit: Usually the first round of editing done on a manuscript. The editor helps "develop" the book by shaping its content and structure. Also called a substantive edit or line edit.

Devotion: A short manuscript based on a Scripture verse or passage that shares a personal spiritual discovery, inspires to worship, challenges to commitment or action, or encourages. A book or periodical of devotions is called a devotional.

Ed board: Editorial board meeting. The editors meet to discuss the new proposals they received to determine which ones should go to the pub board.

Editorial guidelines: See "Writers guidelines."

Em dash (—): Used to create a break or set off nonessential material or extra information in a sentence instead of using commas. *The Chicago Manual of Style* calls this punctuation mark "the most versatile of the dashes."

En dash (–): An en dash is longer than a hyphen but shorter than an em dash. Often used between numbers and dates to show a range. It was called the "en" dash because in the early days of typesetting it was the same width as the capital letter N.

Endorsements: Flattering comments about a book, usually printed on the back cover or in promotional material.

Epub: File format used for ebooks.

Essay: A short composition expressing the author's opinion on a specific subject.

Evangelical: A person who believes that one receives God's forgiveness for sins through Jesus Christ and believes the Bible is the authoritative Word of God. This is a broad definition for a label with broad application. Often mistakenly used as a synonym for "Christian."

Exegesis: Interpretation of a Scripture passage.

Feature article: In-depth coverage of a subject, usually focusing on a person, an event, a process, an organization, a movement, a trend, or an issue. It's written to explain, encourage, help, analyze, challenge, motivate, warn, or entertain, as well as to inform.

Filler: A short item used to "fill" a page of a periodical. It could be a joke, anecdote, light verse, short humor, puzzle, game, etc.

First rights: A periodical editor buys the right to publish a manuscript that has never been published and to do so only once.

Foreign rights: Selling or giving permission to translate or reprint published material in another country.

Foreword: Opening remarks in a book to introduce the book and its author. Often misspelled as *forward*.

Freelance: Supplied by freelance writers.

Freelancer or freelance writer: A writer who is not on salary but sells his or her material to a number of different periodicals and publishers.

Galley proof: A typeset copy of a book or magazine used to detect and correct errors before printing.

General editor: Usually, the person who oversees a large work that has multiple authors writing individual chapters for a book or a series of books. This person is not an employee within a publishing house.

General market: Non-Christian market, sometimes called secular market.

Genre: Refers to a type or classification, as in fiction or poetry. For instance, westerns, romances, and mysteries are fiction genres.

Glossy: A photo with a shiny, rather than matte, finish. Also, a publication printed on such paper.

Go-ahead: When an editor tells you to write or submit your article.

Hard copy: A printed manuscript, as opposed to one sent via email.

Independent book publisher: A book publisher who charges authors to publish their books or buy a certain number of copies, as opposed to a royalty house that pays authors. Some independent publishers also pay a royalty. Sometimes called a subsidy, vanity, self, hybrid, or custom publisher.

ISBN: International Standard Book Number, an identification code needed for every version of a book.

Journal: A periodical presenting information in a particular area, often for an academic or educated audience.

Kill fee: A fee paid for a completed article done on assignment that is subsequently not published. The amount is usually 25–50 percent of the original payment.

Libel: A published false statement that is damaging to another person's reputation, a written defamation.

Line edit: See "Developmental edit" and "Copyedit." Check to see how your editor defines each process.

Little/literary: Small-circulation periodicals whose focus is providing a forum for the literary writer, rather than on making money. Often they do not pay or pay in copies.

Mainstream fiction: Other than genre fiction (such as romance, mystery, or fantasy). Stories of people and their conflicts handled on a deeper level.

Mass market: Books intended for a wide, general market; produced in a smaller format, usually with smaller type; and sold at a lower price. The expectation is that their sales will be higher.

Matte finish: A nonglossy, nonreflective finish on a book cover. Has a textured feel.

Ms: Abbreviation for manuscript.

Mss: Abbreviation for more than one manuscript.

NASR: Abbreviation for North American Serial Rights. Permission for a periodical targeting readers in the US and Canada to publish a manuscript.

New-adult fiction: A developing fiction genre with protagonists ages 18–25. In the general market, these novels often explore sexual themes considered too "adult" for the YA or teen market. They tend to be marketed to older teen readers.

Novella: A short novel, usually 20,000–35,000 words. The length varies from publisher to publisher.

On acceptance: Editor pays a writer at the time the manuscript is accepted for publication.

On assignment: Writing a manuscript at the specific request of an editor.

On publication: Publisher pays a writer when his or her manuscript is published.

On speculation/spec: Writing something for a periodical editor with the agreement that the editor will buy it only if he or she likes it.

Onetime rights: Selling the right to publish a manuscript one time to more than one periodical, primarily to nonoverlapping audiences, such as different denominations.

Over the transom: Unsolicited manuscripts sent to a book editor. Comes from the old transom, which was a window above the door in office buildings. Manuscripts could be pushed "over the transom" into the locked office.

Overrun: The extra copies of a book printed during the initial print run.

Pen name/pseudonym: A name other than your legal name used on a manuscript to protect your identity or the identities of people included or when you wish to remain anonymous. Put the pen name in the byline under the title and your real name with your contact information.

Perfect binding: When pages of a paperback are glued together (bound) on the spine and the cover is then attached.

Periodical: A magazine, journal, newsletter, or newspaper.

Permissions: Asking permission to use text or art from a copyrighted source.

Personal experience: An account based on a real-life experience.

Personality profile: A feature article that highlights a specific person's life or accomplishments.

Plagiarism: Stealing and using the ideas or writing of someone else as your own, either as is or rewriting slightly to make it sound like your own.

POD/Print-on-demand: A printing process where books are printed one at a time or in small numbers instead of in quantity. The production cost per book is higher, but no warehousing is necessary.

POV: Point-of-view. A fiction term that describes the perspective of the one telling the story, such as first person or third person.

Press kit: A compilation of promotional materials for a book or author, used to publicize a book.

Pub board: A formal meeting where people from editorial, marketing, sales, finance, and management meet to discuss whether or not to publish a book.

Public domain: Work for which copyright protection has expired. Copyright laws vary from country to country; but in the US, works published more than 96 years ago have entered the public domain. Because the US copyright law has changed several times, check with the Copyright Office (*copyright.gov*) to determine if a work is in public domain or not. Generally, since 1978, copyright endures for the author's life plus 70 years.

Query letter: A letter sent to an editor about an article or book you propose to write and asking if he or she is interested in seeing it.

Recto: The right-hand page in printing.

Reprint rights: Selling the right to reprint an article that has already been published. You must have sold only first or onetime rights originally and wait until it has been published the first time.

Response time: The number of weeks or months it takes an editor or agent to get back to you about a query, proposal, or manuscript you sent.

Review copies: Books given to reviewers or buyers for bookstore chains and online sellers.

Royalty: The percentage an author is paid by a publisher on the sale of each copy of a book.

Running head: The text at the top of each page that can show the author's name, book title, chapter, or page number.

SASE: Self-addressed, stamped envelope. Always send it with a hard-copy manuscript or query letter.

SASP: Self-addressed, stamped postcard. May be sent with a hard-copy manuscript to be returned by the editor to indicate it arrived safely. Rarely used.

Satire: Ridicule that aims at reform.

Second serial rights: See "Reprint rights."

Secular market: An outdated term for the non-Christian publishing market.

Self-publisher: See "Independent book publisher."

Serial: Refers to publication in a periodical, such as first serial rights.

Sidebar: A short feature that accompanies an article and gives additional information about the topic, such as a recommended reading list. It is often set apart by appearing within a box or border.

Signature: All books are printed in 16-page increments or signatures (occasionally in 32-page increments for large books like Bibles). A large sheet of paper is printed, then folded multiple times. Three sides are cut (top, side, and bottom). The fourth side holds eight double-sided pages. The signatures are compiled and bound into the finished book.

Simultaneous submissions: Sending the same manuscript to more than one editor at the same time. Usually this action is done with nonoverlapping periodical markets, such as denominational publications or newspapers in different cities, or when you are writing on a timely subject. Most periodical editors don't accept simultaneous submissions, but they are the norm in the book market. Be sure to state in a cover letter or on the first page that it is a simultaneous submission.

Slander: The verbal act of defamation.

Slanting: Writing an article to meet the needs of a particular market.

Slush pile: The stack of unsolicited manuscripts that arrive at an editor's desk or email inbox.

Subsidiary rights: All the rights, other than book rights, included in a book contract, such as translations, audiobooks, book clubs, and movies.

Subsidy publisher: See "Independent book publisher."

Substantive edit: See "Developmental edit."

Synopsis: A brief summary of a work, ranging from one paragraph to several pages.

Tabloid: A newspaper-format publication about half the size of a regular newspaper.

Take-home paper: A small periodical given to Sunday-school students, children through adults. These minimagazines are published with the curriculum.

Think piece: A magazine article that has an intellectual, philosophical, or provocative approach to a subject.

Trade book: Describes a 5½" x 8½" paperback book (sometimes 6" x 9"). This is a typical trim size for a paperback. Mass-market books are smaller, around 4" x 6".

Trade magazine: A magazine whose audience is in a particular business.

Trim size: The size of a book after being trimmed in the printing process. (See "Signature" for more information.)

Unsolicited manuscript: A manuscript an editor did not specifically ask to see.

Vanity publisher: See "Independent book publisher."

Verso: The left-hand page in printing.

Vignette: A short, descriptive literary sketch of a brief scene or incident.

Vita: An outline of one's personal history and experience.

Work-for-hire: A manuscript you create for an agreed payment, and you give the publisher full ownership and control of it. You must sign a contract for this agreement to be legal.

Writers guidelines: Information provided by an editor that gives specific guidance for writing for the publication or publishing house. If the information is not offered online, email or send an SASE with your request for printed guidelines.

INDEX

NOTES

WTP

WRITE TO PUBLISH

A DIVISION OF THE CHRISTIAN WRITERS INSTITUT

JUNE 10-13, 2025

WHEATON COLLEGE, WHEATON, ILLINOIS

Not a function of Wheaton College.

REGISTER ONLINE
WRITETOPUBLISH.COM

Since 1971, Write to Publish has been training, inspiring, an
encouraging writers like you, connecting them with editors an
publishers who are looking for good books, articles, and other type
of manuscripts; with literary agents who can represent them; an
with well-published authors who can help them improve their cra

WritetoPublish.com

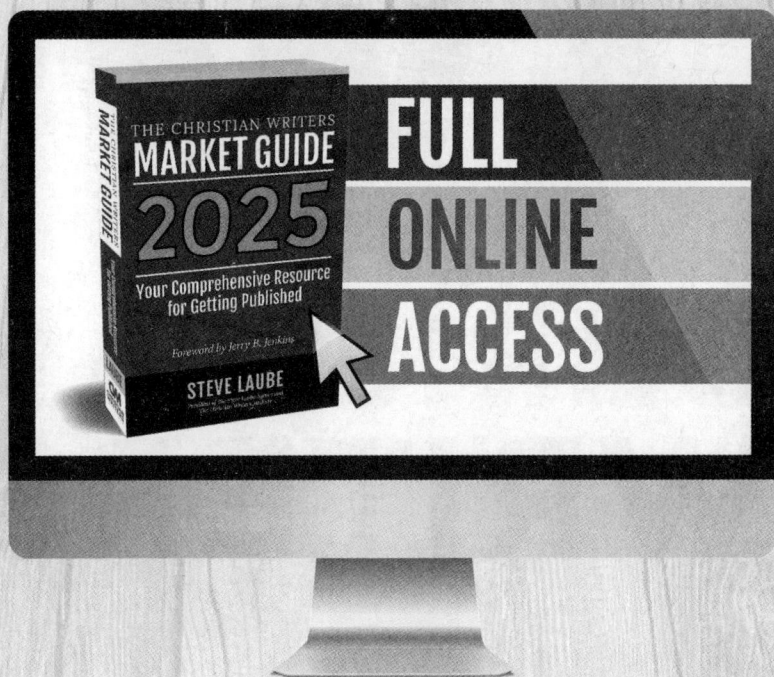